ARTIFICIAL
INTELLIGENCE
THROUGH PROLOG

ARTIFICIAL INTELLIGENCE THROUGH PROLOG

NEIL C. ROWE
U.S. Naval Postgraduate School

PRENTICE HALL, Englewood Cliffs, New Jersey 07632

Library of Congress Cataloging-in-Publication Data

Rowe, Neil C.
    Artificial intelligence through Prolog / Neil C. Rowe.
        p.   cm.
    Bibliography: p.
    Includes index.
    ISBN 0-13-048679-5
        1. Prolog (Computer program language)   2.   Artificial intelligence.
    I. Title.
    QA76.73.P76R69   1988
    005. 13'3—dc19   87-26219
                                                             CIP

Editorial/production supervision: **Claudia Citarella**
Cover design: Lundgren Graphics, Ltd.
Manufacturing buyer: S. Gordon Osbourne

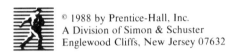 © 1988 by Prentice-Hall, Inc.
A Division of Simon & Schuster
Englewood Cliffs, New Jersey 07632

Printed in the United States of America
10   9   8   7   6   5   4   3   2   1

ISBN   0-13-048679-5   025

Prentice-Hall International (UK) Limited, *London*
Prentice-Hall of Australia Pty. Limited, *Sydney*
Prentice-Hall Canada Inc., *Toronto*
Prentice-Hall Hispanoamericana, S.A., *Mexico*
Prentice-Hall of India Private Limited, *New Delhi*
Prentice-Hall of Japan, Inc., *Tokyo*
Simon & Schuster Asia Pte. Ltd., *Singapore*
Editora Prentice-Hall do Brasil, Ltda., *Rio de Janeiro*

CONTENTS

PREFACE

Artificial intelligence is a hard subject to learn. I have written a book to make it easier. I explain difficult concepts in a simple, concrete way. I have organized the material in a new and (I feel) clearer way, a way in which the chapters are in a logical sequence and not just unrelated topics. I believe that with this book, readers can learn the key concepts of artificial intelligence faster and better than with other books. This book is intended for all first courses in artificial intelligence at the undergraduate or graduate level, requiring background of only a few computer science courses. It can also be used on one's own. No prior knowledge of the language Prolog is assumed.

Students often complain that while they understand the terminology of artifical intelligence, they don't have a gut feeling for what's going on or how you apply the concepts to a situation. One cause is the complexity of artificial intelligence. Another is the unnecessary baggage, like overly formal logical calculi, that some books and teachers saddle students with. But an equally important cause is the often poor connection made between abstract concepts and their use. So I considered it essential to integrate practical programming examples into this book, in the style of programming language and data structures books. (I stress *practical*, not missionaries and cannibals, definitions of "grandfather," or rules for identifying animals in zoos—at least rarely.) This book has about 500 chunks of code. Clear, concrete formalization of artificial-intelligence ideas by programs and program fragments is all the more critical today with commercialization and media discovery of the field, which has caused a good deal of throwing around of artificial-intelligence terms by people who don't understand them.

But artificial intelligence is a tool for complex problems, and its program examples can easily be forbiddingly complicated. Books attempting to explain artificial intelligence with examples from the programming language Lisp have repeatedly demonstrated this. But I have come to see that the fault lies more with Lisp than with artificial intelligence. Lisp has been the primary language of artificial intelligence for many years, but it is a low-level language, too low for most students. Designed in the early 1960s, Lisp reflects the then-primitive understanding of good programming, and requires the programmer to worry considerably about actual memory references (pointers). Furthermore, Lisp has a weird, hard-to-read syntax unlike that of any other programming language. To make matters worse, the widespread adoption of Common Lisp as a de facto standard has discouraged research on improved Lisps.

Fortunately there is an alternative: Prolog. Developed in Europe in the 1970s, the language Prolog has steadily gained enthusiastic converts, bolstered by its surprise choice as the initial language of the Japanese Fifth Generation Computer project. Prolog has three positive features that give it key advantages over Lisp. First, Prolog syntax and semantics are much closer to formal logic, the most common way of representing facts and reasoning methods used in the artificial-intelligence literature. Second, Prolog provides automatic backtracking, a feature making for considerably easier "search," the most central of all artificial-intelligence techniques. Third, Prolog supports multidirectional (or multiuse) reasoning, in which arguments to a procedure can freely be designated inputs and outputs in different ways in different procedure calls, so that the same procedure definition can be used for many different kinds of reasoning. Besides this, new implementation techniques have given current versions of Prolog close in speed to Lisp implementations, so efficiency is no longer a reason to prefer Lisp.

But Prolog also, I believe, makes teaching artificial intelligence easier. This book is a demonstration. This book is an organic whole, not a random collection of chapters on random topics. My chapters form a steady, logical progression, from knowledge representation to inferences on the representation, to rule-based systems codifying classes of inferences, to search as an abstraction of rule-based systems, to extensions of the methodology, and finally to evaluation of systems. Topics hard to understand like search, the cut predicate, relaxation, and resolution are introduced late and only with careful preparation. In each chapter, details of Prolog are integrated with major concepts of artificial intelligence. For instance, Chapter 2 discusses the kinds of facts about the world that one can put into computers as well as the syntax of Prolog's way; Chapter 3 discusses automatic backtracking as well as Prolog querying; Chapter 4 discusses inference and inheritance as well as the definition of procedures in Prolog; Chapter 5 discusses multidirectional reasoning as well as the syntax of Prolog arithmetic; and so on. This constant tying of theory to practice makes artificial intelligence a lot more concrete. Learning is better motivated since one doesn't need to master a lot of mumbo-jumbo to get to the good stuff. I can't take much of the credit myself: the very nature of Prolog, and particularly the advantages of the last paragraph, make it easy.

Despite my integrated approach to the material, I think I have covered nearly all the topics in ACM and IEEE guidelines for a first course in artificial intelligence. Basic concepts mentioned in those guidelines appear toward the beginning of chapters, and applications mentioned in the guidelines appear toward the ends. Beyond the guidelines however, I have had to make tough decisions about what to leave out—a coherent book is better than an incoherent book that covers everything. Since this is a first course, I concentrate on the hard core of artificial intelligence. So I don't discuss much how humans think (that's psychology), or how human language works (that's linguistics), or how sensor interpretation and low-level visual processing are done (that's pattern recognition), or whether computers will ever really think (that's philosophy). I have also cut corners on hard noncentral topics like computer learning and the full formal development of predicate calculus. On the other hand, I emphasize more than other books do the central computer science concepts of procedure calls, variable binding, list processing, tree traversal, analysis of processing efficiency, compilation, caching, and recursion. This is a computer science textbook.

A disadvantage of my integrated approach is that chapters can't so easily be skipped. To partially compensate, I mark some sections within chapters (usually sections toward the end) with asterisks to indicate that they are optional to the main flow of the book. In addition, all of Chapters 7, 10, and 14 can be omitted, and perhaps Chapters 12 and 13 too. (Chapters 7, 10, 13, and 14 provide a good basis for a second course in artificial intelligence, and I have used them that way myself.) Besides this, I cater to the different needs of different readers in the exercises. Exercises are essential to learning the material in a textbook. Unfortunately, there is little consensus about what kind of exercises to give for courses in artificial intelligence. So I have provided a wide variety: short-answer questions for checking basic understanding of material, programming exercises for people who like to program, "play computer" exercises that have the reader simulate techniques described, application questions that have the reader apply methods to new areas (my favorite kind of exercise because it tests real understanding of the material), essay questions, fallacies to analyze, complexity analysis questions, and a few extended projects suitable for teams of students. There are also some miscellaneous questions drawing on the entire book, at the end of Chapter 15. Answers to about one third of the exercises are provided in Appendix G, to offer readers immediate feedback on their understanding, something especially important to those tackling this book on their own.

To make learning the difficult material of this book even easier, I provide other learning aids. I apportion the book into short labeled sections, to make it easier for readers to chunk the material into mind-sized bites. I provide reinforcement of key concepts with some novel graphical and tabular displays. I provide "glass box" computer programs (that is, the opposite of "black box") for readers to study. I mark key terms in italics where they are defined in the text, and then group the most important of these terms into keyword lists at the end of every chapter. I give appendices summarizing the important background material needed for this book, concepts in logic, recursion, and data structures. In other appendices, I summarize the Prolog dialect of the book, make a few comments on Micro-Prolog, and provide a short bibliography (most of the artificial intelligence literature is now either too hard or too easy for readers of this book). The major programs of the book are available on tape or diskette from the publisher for a small fee. Also, I have prepared an instructor's manual.

It's not necessary to have a Prolog interpreter or compiler available to use this book, but it does make learning easier. This book uses a limited subset of the most common dialect of Prolog, the "standard Prolog" of *Programming in Prolog* by Clocksin and Mellish (second edition, Springer-Verlag, 1984). But most exercises do not require programming.

I've tried to doublecheck all examples, programs, and exercises, but some errors may have escaped me. If you find any, please write me in care of the publisher, or send computer mail to rowe@nps-cs.arpa.

ACKNOWLEDGMENTS

Many people contributed ideas to this book. Michael Genesereth first suggested to me the teaching of introductory artificial intelligence in a way based on logic. David H. Warren gradually eroded my skepticism about Prolog. Harold Abelson and Seymour Papert have steered my teaching style toward student activity rather than passivity.

Judy Quesenberry spent many long hours helping me with the typing and correction of this book, and deserves a great deal of thanks, even if she ate an awful lot of my cookies. Robert Richbourg has been helpful in many different ways, in suggesting corrections and improvements and in testing out some of the programs, despite his having to jump through all the hoops Ph.D. students must jump through. Richard Hamming provided valuable advice on book production. Other people who provided valuable comments include Chris Carlson, Daniel Chester, Ernest Davis, Eileen Entin, Robert Grant, Mike Goyden, Simon Hart, Greg Hoppenstand, Kirk Jennings, Grace Mason, Bruce MacLennan, Norman McNeal, Bob McGhee, James Milojkovic, Doug Owen, Jim Peak, Olen Porter, Brian Rodeck, Jean Sando, Derek Sleeman, Amnon Shefi, and Steve Weingart. Mycke Moore made the creative suggestion that I put a lot of sex into this book to boost sales.

Besides those named, I am grateful to all my students over the years at the Massachusetts Institute of Technology, Stanford University, and the Naval Postgraduate School for providing valuable feedback. They deserve a good deal of credit for the quality of this book—but sorry, people, I'm poor and unwilling to share royalties.

TO THE READER

Artificial intelligence draws on many different areas of computer science. It is hard to recommend prerequisites because what you need to know is bits and pieces scattered over many different courses. At least two quarters or semesters of computer programming in a higher-level language like Pascal is strongly recommended, since we will introduce here a programming language several degrees more difficult, Prolog. If you can get programming experience in Prolog, Lisp, or Logo, that's even better. It also helps to have a course in formal logic, though we won't use much of the fancy stuff they usually cover in those courses; see Appendix A for what you do need to know. Artificial intelligence uses sophisticated data structures, so a data structures course helps; see Appendix C for a summary. Finally, you should be familiar with recursion, because Prolog is well suited to this way of writing programs. Recursion is a difficult concept to understand at first, but once you get used to it you will find it easy and natural; Appendix B provides some hints.

Solving problems is the best way to learn artificial intelligence. So there are lots of exercises in this book, at the ends of chapters. Please take these exercises seriously; many of them are hard, but you can really learn from them, much more than by just passively reading the text. Artificial intelligence is difficult to learn, and feedback really helps, especially if your're working on your own. (But don't plan to do all the exercises: there are too many.) Exercises have code letters to indicate their special features:

- R means a particularly good problem recommended for all readers;
- A means a question that has an answer in Appendix G;
- H means a particularly hard problem;
- P means a problem requiring actual programming in Prolog;
- E means an essay question;
- G means a good group project.

In addition to exercises, each chapter has a list of key terms you should know. Think of this list, at the end of the text for each chapter, as a set of "review questions."

The symbol * on a section of a chapter means optional reading. These sections are either significantly harder than the rest of the text or significantly far from the core material.

ARTIFICIAL INTELLIGENCE THROUGH PROLOG

INTRODUCTION

1.1 WHAT ARTIFICIAL INTELLIGENCE IS ABOUT

Artificial intelligence is the getting of computers to do things that seem to be intelligent. The hope is that more intelligent computers can be more helpful to us—better able to respond to our needs and wants, and more clever about satisfying them.

But "intelligence" is a vague word. So artificial intelligence is not a well-defined field. One thing it often means is advanced software engineering, sophisticated software techniques for hard problems that can't be solved in any easy way. Another thing it often means is nonnumeric ways of solving problems, since people can't handle numbers well. Nonnumeric ways are often "common sense" ways, not necessarily the best ones. So artificial-intelligence programs—like people—are usually not perfect, and even make mistakes.

Artificial intelligence includes:

- Getting computers to communicate with us in human languages like English, either by printing on a computer terminal, understanding things we type on a computer terminal, generating speech, or understanding our speech (*natural language*);
- Getting computers to remember complicated interrelated facts, and draw conclusions from them (*inference*);

- Getting computers to plan sequences of actions to accomplish goals (*planning*);
- Getting computers to offer us advice based on complicated rules for various situations (*expert systems*);
- Getting computers to look through cameras and see what's there (*vision*);
- Getting computers to move themselves and objects around in the real world (*robotics*).

We'll emphasize inference, planning, and expert systems in this book because they're the "hard core" of artificial intelligence; the other three subareas are getting quite specialized, though we'll mention them too from time to time. All six subareas are hard; significant progress in any will require years of research. But we've already had enough progress to get some useful programs. These programs have created much interest, and have stimulated recent growth of the field.

Success is hard to measure, though. Perhaps the key issue in artificial intelligence is *reductionism*, the degree to which a program fails to reflect the full complexity of human beings. Reductionism includes how often program behavior duplicates human behavior and how much it differs when it does differ. Reductionism is partly a moral issue because it requires moral judgments. Reductionism is also a social issue because it relates to automation.

1.2 UNDERSTANDING ARTIFICIAL INTELLIGENCE_____

Artificial intelligence techniques and ideas seem to be harder to understand than most things in computer science, and we give you fair warning. For one thing, there are lots of details to worry about. Artificial intelligence shows best on complex problems for which general principles don't help much, though there are a few useful general principles that we'll explain in this book. This means many examples in this book are several pages long, unlike most of the examples in mathematics textbooks.

Complexity limits how much the programmer can understand about what is going on in an artificial-intelligence program. Often the programs are like simulations: the programmer sets conditions on the behavior of the program, but doesn't know what will happen once it starts. This means a different style of programming than with traditional higher-level languages like Fortran, Pascal, PL/1, and Ada,[1] where successive refinement of a specification can mean we know what the program is doing at every level of detail. But artificial-intelligence techniques, even when all their details are hard to follow, are often the only way to solve a difficult problem.

Artificial intelligence is also difficult to understand by its content, a funny mixture of the rigorous and the unrigorous. Certain topics are just questions of style (like much of Chapters 2, 6, and 12), while other topics have definite rights

---

[1] A trademark of the U.S. Department of Defense, Ada Joint Program Office.

and wrongs (like much of Chapters 3, 5, and 11). Artificial-intelligence researchers frequently argue about style, but publish more papers about the other topics. And when rigor is present, it's often different from that in the other sciences and engineering: it's not numeric but *logical*, in terms of truth and implication.

Clarke's law says that all unexplained advanced technology is like magic. So artificial intelligence may lose its magic as you come to understand it. Don't be discouraged. Remember, genius is 5% inspiration and 95% perspiration according to the best figures, though estimates vary.

1.3 PREVIEW

This book is organized around the important central ideas of artificial intelligence rather than around application areas. We start out (Chapters 2–5) by explaining ways of storing and using knowledge of the world inside computers: facts (Chapter 2), queries (Chapter 3), rules (Chapter 4), and numbers and lists (Chapter 5). We examine rule-based systems in Chapters 6–8, an extremely important subclass of artificial-intelligence programs. We examine search techniques in Chapters 9–11, another important subclass. We address other important topics in Chapters 12–14: Chapter 12 on frame representations extends Chapter 2, Chapter 13 on long queries extends Chapter 3, and Chapter 14 on general logical reasoning extends Chapter 4. We conclude in Chapter 15 with a look at evaluation and debugging of artificial-intelligence programs; that chapter is recommended for everyone, even those who haven't read all the other chapters. To help, Appendices A–C review material on logic, recursion, and data structures, respectively. Appendix D summarizes the Prolog language subset we use in this book, Appendix E summarizes the Micro-Prolog dialect, Appendix F gives a short bibliography, and Appendix G provides answers to those exercises marked with an "A."

KEYWORDS

artificial intelligence
natural language
inference
planning
expert systems
vision
robotics
reductionism

REPRESENTING FACTS

If we want computers to act intelligent, we must help them. We must tell them all the commonsense *knowledge* we have that they don't. This can be hard because this knowledge can be so obvious to us that we don't realize that a computer doesn't know it too, but we must try.

Now there are many different kinds of knowledge. Without getting deep into philosophy (or specifically *epistemology*, the theory of knowledge), there are two main kinds: facts and reasoning procedures. Facts are things true about the world, and reasoning procedures (or *inferences*) are ways to follow reasoning chains between facts. Since facts are easier to represent than procedures, we'll consider them first, and postpone procedures to Chapter 4.

2.1 PREDICATES AND PREDICATE EXPRESSIONS

To talk about facts we need a "language." Artificial intelligence uses many languages and sublanguages. But in this introductory book we don't want to confuse you. We'll use only one, simple (*first-order*) *predicate logic* (sometimes called *predicate calculus* and sometimes just *logic*). And we'll use a particular notation compatible with the computer programming language Prolog.[1] Prolog isn't predi-

---

[1] In this book we use a subset of the "standard Prolog" in Clocksin and Mellish, *Programming in Prolog*, second edition, Springer-Verlag, 1984. For a complete description of what we use, see Appendix D.

cate logic itself; computer languages try to accomplish things, whereas logic just says that certain things are true and certain things are false. But Prolog does appear close to the way logic is usually written. That is, its *grammar* or *syntax* or form is that of logic, but its *semantics* or meaning is different.

And what is that grammar? Formally, a *predicate expression* (or *atomic formula*, but that sounds like a nuclear weapons secret) is a name—a *predicate*—followed by zero or more arguments enclosed in parentheses and separated by commas (see Figure 2-1).[2] Predicate names and arguments can be composed of any mixture of letters and numbers, except that names for now must start with a lower-case letter. (Upper-case letters first in a word have a special meaning in Prolog, as we'll explain shortly.) The underscore symbol "_" also counts as a letter, and we will often use it to make names more readable. So these are all predicate expressions:

```
p(x)
q(y,3)
r(alpha,-2584,beta)
city(monterey,california)
tuvwxy(abc345)
noarguments
pi(3.1416)
long_predicate_name(long_argument_name,3)
```

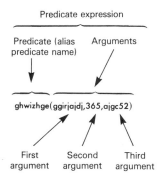

Figure 2-1. Terminology about predicates.

We can put predicate expressions like these into computers. They can represent facts true about the world. But what exactly do these expressions *mean* (their *semantics*)? Actually, anything you want—it's up to you to assign reasonable and consistent interpretations to the symbols and the way they're put together,

---

[2] Several terms closely related to "predicate expression" are used in the logic and artificial-intelligence literature. A *literal* is like a predicate expression only it can have a negation symbol in front of it (negations will be explained in Section 3.6). A *structure* or *compound term* is like a predicate expression only it isn't necessarily only true or false. A *logical formula* is a predicate expression or a set of predicate expressions put together with "and"s, "or"s, and "not"s.

though there are some conventions. The better job you do, the more reasonable the conclusions you'll reach from all these facts.

2.2 PREDICATES INDICATING TYPES

Predicates can mean many things. But they do fall into categories. We summarize the major categories in Figure 2-2.

	Type predicate	Property predicate	Relationship predicate	Database predicate	Function predicate	Probability predicate
Number of arguments	1	2	2	1 or more	2 or more	1 or more
Nature of arguments	a thing	a thing and a property	two things	a thing and properties	last is result of operation on others	last is probability of the fact truth
Description	gives a class that the thing belongs to	gives property of a thing	describes relationship of two things	like a data record	describes a function mapping	variant of previous kinds for partly certain facts
Examples	ship (kennedy) vehicle (ship)	color (kennedy, gray) location (kennedy, 14n35e)	part_of (kennedy, u_s_navy) a_kind_of (kennedy, ship)	ship (kennedy, gray, 14n35e, 16feb85)	sum (3, 4, 7)	color (kennedy, gray, 0.8)
Meaning of the examples	"The Kennedy is a ship" "A ship is a vehicle"	"The color of the Kennedy is gray" "The location of the Kennedy is 14n35e"	"The Kennedy is part of the U.S. Navy" "The Kennedy is a kind of ship"	"There is a ship record with entries Kennedy, gray, 14n35e, and 16feb85"	"The sum of 3 and 4 is 7"	"We believe with certainty 0.8 that the Kennedy is gray"

Figure 2-2. Summary of the kinds of predicates in Chapter 2.

One thing they can mean is something like data-type information in a language like Pascal or Ada. Except that in artificial intelligence there are generally a lot more types than there are in most programming, because there must be a type for every category in the world that we want the computer to know about.

For instance, suppose we want the computer to know about some U.S. Navy ships.[3] We could tell it

```
ship(enterprise).
```

to say that the Enterprise is a ship (remember we must use lower case). Or in other words, the Enterprise is an example of the "ship" type. A period will signal the end of a fact. We could also tell the computer

```
ship(kennedy).
ship(vinson).
```

to give it the names of two more ships—two more things of the "ship" type. Here ship is a *type predicate*. If we knew code numbers for planes we could tell the computer about them too, using the code numbers as names:

```
plane(p54862).
plane(p79313).
```

Similarly, we can label people with types:

```
commodore(r_h_shumaker).
president(r_reagan).
```

and label more abstract things like institutions:

```
university(naval_postgraduate_school).
university(stanford_university).
```

and label concepts:

```
day_of_week(monday).
day_of_week(tuesday).
day_of_week(wednesday).
```

A thing can have more than one type. For instance:

```
ship(enterprise).
american(enterprise).
```

And types can have subtypes:

```
carrier(vinson).
ship(carrier).
```

---

[3] The occasional use of military examples in this book is deliberate: to serve as a reminder that much artificial-intelligence work in the United States has been, and remains, supported by the military. We make no endorsements.

These are all *type predicates*, and they all have one argument. The argument is the name of some thing in the world, and the predicate name is the class or category it belongs to. So the predicate name is *more general* than the argument name; this is usual for predicate names in artificial intelligence. So it wouldn't be as good to say

```
enterprise(ship).
kennedy(ship).
```

2.3 ABOUT TYPES

We've said these predicates are like the types in computer languages, but there are some differences. The main one is that they need never be defined anywhere. If for instance we are using Pascal, we either use the built-in types (integer, real, character, array, and pointer) or define the type we want in terms of those built-in types. But for artificial intelligence, the type (predicate) names are just arbitrary codes used in lookup. This is because you can put integers and characters in a computer, but not a ship. You can't even put in a full representation of a ship, or a full representation of any other real object—real objects have too many complexities, while integers and characters are abstractions.

How then, if we expect the computer to be intelligent, will it ever know what a ship is? Much the way people know abstract concepts. Ships are defined in a dictionary using the concept of a vehicle, the concept of water, the concept of floating, and so on. A dictionary might say a ship is "an oceangoing vessel." But it might define "vessel" as a "craft for traveling on water" and "craft" as an "individual ship"—so the definitions are circular, as all dictionary definitions are sooner or later. But we can indirectly figure out what is being talked about by the secondary words like "oceangoing" and "traveling." So concepts must be defined in terms of one another.

So we won't expect each type predicate to be *implemented* (that is, understood by a computer) by a separate procedure or processing routine. The same holds for arguments. In fact, we could store all predicate names and arguments the same way in the computer, as characters. This is a bit wasteful of computer storage space—so some Prolog dialects do store numbers differently—but there's nothing wrong philosophically with it.

2.4 GOOD NAMING

So predicate and argument names can be arbitrary; we just have to remember what they represent. But one name can be better than another, if it is easier to remember what it means. Writing facts for an artificial-intelligence program to use is a kind of programming, and we should follow the usual rules of good programming style. In choosing names, we suggest these guidelines:

1. As much as possible, use English words for names. If you need more than one word, use the underscore character between them for clarity, like in day_of_week (though sometimes you can leave out the underscores like in dayofweek when the reading is reasonably clear).

2. Choose names that describe their function precisely. For instance, use day_of_week instead of day, which could describe both monday and october_19_1985.

3. Avoid names with multiple meanings. For instance, if there is a Commander Kennedy as well as a ship named Kennedy, include the first initial of the person; or if you call the Enterprise a "ship," don't also record that a unit "shipped" somewhere.

4. Avoid numbers in names, with two exceptions: arithmetic (see Chapter 5) and closely related variables and predicates (like X and X2 in Section 5.5 and iterate and iterate2 in Section 10.8).

5. Abbreviate only when absolutely necessary. Since artificial-intelligence programs often require many names, abbreviations can be confusing.

6. Predicate names should be more general than their argument names, but not so general that they don't really mean anything (for then facts can't be indexed well).

7. A few predicate names are built-in or "special" to Prolog, so you can't use them for your own needs.

8. Always use the same name for the same thing.

2.5 PROPERTY PREDICATES

We can tell the computer (or *assert*):

```
ship(enterprise).
gray(enterprise).
big(enterprise).
```

which could mean "The Enterprise is a ship, it is gray, and it is big." (Never mind that "big" is vague; we could define it as "more than 800 feet long," and "gray" and even "ship" are vague to a lesser extent (is a toy ship a ship? and is an imaginary ship a ship?), and much human knowledge is vague anyway.) Or this could mean the Enterprise is a member of the class of ships, a member of the class of gray things, and a member of the class of big things. But those last two phrases are awkward. "Gray" and "big" are adjectives, not nouns like "ship," and they should be treated differently.

So we'll represent properties of things as *property predicate expressions*, two-argument expressions in which the predicate name is the name of a property, the first argument is the name of a thing, and the second argument is the value of the property. The preceding example could be rewritten better as:

```
ship(enterprise).
color(enterprise,gray).
size(enterprise,big).
```

This has the advantage of using predicate names that are more general. It also shows the relation between **gray** and **enterprise**, and that between **big** and **enterprise**: **color** and **size** are the property names for which **gray** and **big** are the values. So we've made some implicit (unstated "commonsense") knowledge explicit (stated), a key goal in artificial intelligence.

Again, the computer won't actually know what **gray** and **big** mean if we type in the preceding three example lines; those are just codes that it uses for comparison. For instance, if the computer also knows

```
color(kennedy,gray).
```

then it knows the Enterprise and the Kennedy have the same color, though it doesn't know what a "color" is (but don't blame it, because most computers don't have eyes).

An important class of property predicates concerns space and time. For instance

```
location(enterprise,14n35e).
last_docking(enterprise,16feb85).
```

could mean that the Enterprise is currently at latitude 14N and longitude 35E, and its last docking was on February 16, 1985.

2.6 PREDICATES FOR RELATIONSHIPS _____

Perhaps the most important predicates of all relate two different things. Such *relationship predicates* are important because a lot of human reasoning seems to use them—people need to relate ideas. For instance, we can use a **part_of** predicate of two arguments which says that its first argument is a component within its second argument. We could give as facts:

```
part_of(enterprise,u_s_navy).
part_of(u_s_navy,u_s_government).
part_of(naval_postgraduate_school,u_s_government).
part_of(propulsion_system,ship).
```

In other words, the Enterprise is part of the U.S. Navy, the Navy is part of the U.S. government, the Naval Postgraduate School is part of the U.S. government, and the propulsion system is part of a ship. An **owns** relationship predicate can say that something is owned by someone:

```
owns(tom,fido).
owns(tom,toms_car).
```

These facts say that Tom owns two things: something called **fido**, and an unnamed car which we can just refer to as **toms_car**.

It's easy to get confused about argument order in relationship-predicate expressions. So we'll try to follow this convention: if the predicate name is inserted between the two arguments, the result will be close to an English sentence giving the correct meaning. So if we insert "owns" between "tom" and "fido" we get "Tom owns Fido," and if we insert "part of" between "enterprise" and "u. s. navy" we get "Enterprise part of U. S. Navy."

An important class of relationship predicates relates things in space and time. A real-world object can be north, south, east, west, etc., of another object. Viewed by a fixed observer, an object can also be right, left, above, below, in front, or behind another object. We can describe a picture with these predicates. Similarly, an event in time can be before, after, during, overlapping, or simultaneous with another event, so we can describe history with these predicates.

Relationship predicates can describe relationships between people. For instance, the **boss_of** relationship is important for describing bureaucracies, an important application of artificial intelligence. It says that a person (first argument) is the boss of another person (second argument), and this shows direction of responsibility. People can also be related by kinship relationship predicates (**father, mother, child, uncle, cousin, stepfather, half-brother, grandfather**, etc.). People can also be related with **friend** and **acquaintance** relationship predicates.

Besides all these, another special relationship predicate is frequently used in artificial intelligence. It's called **a_kind_of** or **is_a** (we prefer the first name, because "is" is vague), and it can replace all type predicates. Its first argument is a thing, and its second argument is the type of that thing (the predicate name in the one-argument form considered before). For instance:

```
a_kind_of(enterprise,ship).
a_kind_of(tanker,ship).
a_kind_of(tuesday,day_of_week).
```

which says that the Enterprise is a kind of ship, a tanker is a kind of ship, and

Tuesday is a kind of day of the week.[4] Some reasoning is easier with this two-argument form than the equivalent one-argument form.

There are other predicates, but as any psychotherapist will tell you, relationships are the key to a happy life.

2.7 SEMANTIC NETWORKS

Pictures can make a complicated set of facts a lot clearer. There's a simple pictorial way to show the predicate expressions we've been discussing: the *semantic network*. Unfortunately, there is a major restriction on it: semantic networks can only directly represent predicates of two arguments (so type predicates must be in the two-argument form).[5]

A semantic network is what computer scientists call a *labeled directed graph* (see Appendix C for a definition). We make every fact argument a small named circle (node) in the graph. For each two-argument fact, we draw an arrow (edge) from the circle for its first argument to the circle for its second argument, and label the arrow with the predicate name. So the fact p(a,b) is represented as an arrow from a circle labeled "a" to a circle labeled "b," with the arrow itself labeled "p." If for instance our facts are:

    a_kind_of(enterprise,ship).
    a_kind_of(kennedy,ship).
    part_of(enterprise,u_s_navy).
    part_of(kennedy,u_s_navy).
    part_of(u_s_navy,u_s_government).
    a_kind_of(u_s_government,government).
    color(ship,gray).
    location(enterprise,15n35e).
    has(u_s_government,civil_service_system).

then our semantic network looks like Figure 2-3. Note that these arrows should not be confused with the access pointers often used in data structures; these arrows just keep straight the order of arguments in facts.

---

[4] Some researchers don't agree with this use of a_kind_of. They think that the first two facts should have different predicate names since the Enterprise is an individual while tankers are a group of individuals; often they'll use the predicate name **element** for the "Enterprise" fact, and keep a_kind_of for the "tanker" fact. But a set whose size is 1 is still a set, and there doesn't seem to be anything fundamentally different between restricting the body type of a ship to be a tanker and restricting the name of a ship to be the word "Enterprise"—it just happens that people try, not always successfully, to make names unique. Researchers who argue against this may be getting this issue confused with the important "extensions versus intensions" problem which we'll discuss in Section 12.8.

[5] But we can represent predicate expressions with more than two arguments indirectly, as sets of two-argument predicate expressions.

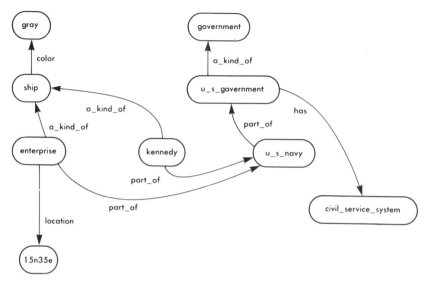

Figure 2-3. Example semantic network.

2.8 GETTING FACTS FROM ENGLISH DESCRIPTIONS_____

Usually programmers building artificial-intelligence programs don't think up facts themselves. Instead, they look up facts in documents and books, or ask people knowledgeable about the subject ("experts") to tell them what they need to know—the process of *knowledge acquisition*. But English and other "natural languages" are less precise than computer languages (though more flexible), and the programmer must be careful to get the meanings right.

The sorts of facts we've considered so far are usually often signaled by the verb "to be" in English ("is," "are," "was," "were," "will be," "being," and so on). For instance:

> The Enterprise is a ship.
> A ship is a vehicle.
> The Enterprise is part of the U.S. Navy.
> A ship is gray.

Here "to be" is used for type predicates (the first and second sentences), a part_of relationship predicate (the third sentence), and a property predicate (the fourth sentence). Plurals can also be used:

> Ships are gray.
> Ships are vehicles.

English verbs with narrower meanings can be used too:

> The Enterprise belongs to the U.S. Navy.
> The Enterprise has a hull.
> They color ships gray.
> The Enterprise resides at 15N35E.

The first two suggest **part_of** relationship predicates, and the last two suggest property predicates.

2.9 PREDICATES WITH THREE OR MORE ARGUMENTS

You can have as many arguments to a predicate as you want if you're not concerned about easily representing them in a semantic network. One idea is to include multiple property values and relationship information in a single fact, much like adjectives and adverbs modifying a noun or verb. So for instance we could put everything we know about a ship together:

> ship_info(enterprise,15n35e,1200,16feb85,gray,j_kirk).

which we could read as "The Enterprise is a ship that was at 15N35E at 12 noon on February 16, 1985, and its color is gray, and its captain is J. Kirk." To interpret such facts we need to keep a description somewhere of the arguments, their format, and their order.

These sort of predicates define a *relational database* of facts. Much research has studied efficient implementation and manipulation of such databases. The information about the format of such predicates is called a *database schema*.

Another important category of predicates with often many arguments (though they can also have just two) is that representing results of actions—in mathematical terminology, *functions*. Suppose we want a computer to know about arithmetic. We could use a predicate **sum** of three numerical arguments, which says that the sum of the first two arguments is the third. We could give as facts:

> sum(1,1,2).
> sum(1,3,4).
> sum(1,4,5).
> sum(1,5,6).
> sum(2,1,3).
> sum(2,2,4).
> sum(2,3,5).
> sum(2,4,6).

And we could do this for lots of different numbers and different arithmetic operations. Of course for this to be useful in general, we would need very many facts and this would be unwieldy (we will describe a better way in Chapter 5), but it will suffice to define operations on any finite set of numbers.

We will use function predicates frequently. To avoid confusion, we follow the convention that the last argument always represents the result of (value returned by) the function, with the exception noted in the next section.[6]

Functions can also be nonnumeric. An example is a function that gives, for two employees of a company, the name of the lowest-ranking boss over both of them. Since artificial intelligence emphasizes nonnumeric (*symbolic*) reasoning, you'll see more nonnumeric than numeric functions in this book.

2.10 PROBABILITIES

We have assumed so far that facts are always completely certain. In many situations (as when facts are based on reports by people), facts are only probably true. Then we will use the mathematical idea of *probability*, the expected fraction of the time something is true. We will put an approximate probability as a last argument to a predicate, after the previously discussed function result if any. So for instance

        color(enterprise,gray,0.8).

could say that we're 80% sure (or sure with probability 0.8) that the Enterprise is gray. We'll ignore this topic until Chapter 8.

2.11 HOW MANY FACTS DO WE NEED?

An infinity of facts are true about the world. How then do we decide which to tell a computer? This question has no easy answers. Generally, you must decide what you want the computer to do. Then make sure to tell the computer every fact that might be relevant to that behavior. "Libraries" of useful facts for particular subjects will help. But the smarter you want the computer to be, the more facts you must tell it. The next chapter will discuss the next question, how to get the computer to do things with facts.

---

[6] If you're familiar with Lisp, be careful to include the function result as an argument to Prolog predicates. In Lisp, a value is always associated with the whole expression, something you can't do in Prolog.

KEYWORDS

knowledge
facts
logic
predicate calculus
Prolog
predicate
predicate expression
arguments
semantics
type predicate
assertion
property predicate
relationship predicate
part_of
a_kind_of
semantic network
knowledge acquisition
relational-database predicate
function predicate
probability predicate

EXERCISES

(Note: Exercises marked with the code A have answers at the back of the book.)

2-1. (A,E)   Which of the following facts is better knowledge representation? Explain. ("Better" means less likely to confuse people.)

        color(enterprise,gray).
        size(enterprise,big).

2-2. (R,A,E) Suppose you want to store facts about when and where memos were sent in an organization. Which is the best Prolog format for such facts, and why?

        (i) <date>(<name>,<author>,<distribution>).
        (ii) memo(<name>,<date>,<author>,<distribution>).
        (iii) fact(memo,<name>,<date>,<author>,<distribution>).

2-3. Draw a semantic network representing the following facts:

       Ships are things.
       Carriers are ships.
       Ships have a position.
       Ships have a crew.
       Carriers have planes.
       Planes are things.
       A crew consists of people.
       People are things.

2-4. Represent the nonnumeric meaning of the picture in Figure 2-4 as a set of nonnumeric Prolog facts. (Hint: Describe the circles and their relationships.)

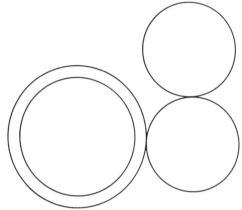

Figure 2-4. Picture for Exercise 2-4.

2-5. (A) One-argument and two-argument predicates are very common in Prolog knowledge representation. Most of the facts you want to put into computers can be represented with them. Someone might say that this shouldn't be surprising, because most operations in mathematics are either unary (applied to a single thing like the square root operation or the sine operation) or binary (applied to two things, like addition and exponentiation). What's wrong with this comment?

2-6. (R,A) Consider the six-argument ship_info facts in Section 2.9. To represent them in a semantic network, we need to convert each to a set of two-argument facts. Explain how. Assume that six-argument facts only record the most recent position of a ship.

2-7. (A,E) Why might it be a good idea to put falsehoods (statements false in the world) into a computer?

2-8. Suppose you want to write a program that reasons like Sherlock Holmes did, about the facts of some crime to decide who is responsible. You want to represent in Prolog style the facts you find about the crime and the reports of witnesses. The argument types used for facts will vary. But certain arguments must be included in every fact about the crime—what are they? And certain arguments must be included in every fact giving a report from a witness—what are they?

2-9. (E) Why must the representation in Prolog of these two facts be fundamentally different?

> Clint is mayor.
> Someone is mayor.

2-10. (E) Consider the use of the word "boss" in the following facts. Suppose you wanted to represent these facts in Prolog. Would it be a good idea for any two of these to use the same word "boss" as either a predicate name or an argument name?

> Mary is the boss of Dick.
> Dick and Mary boss their children around.
> "Boss" has four letters.
> A boss has managerial responsibilities.

2-11. (E) Another way to put facts inside computers is with a restricted subset of English. For instance:

> The Enterprise is a ship.
> The Enterprise is part of the U.S. Navy.
> The color of the Enterprise is gray.
> The Enterprise is at 15N25E.

(a) Discuss the advantages of storing facts this way instead of with predicate expressions as we have done in the chapter.

(b) Give a disadvantage for efficient use of the facts.

(c) Give a disadvantage for programming errors.

3

VARIABLES
AND QUERIES

We can put facts into a computer. So what can we do with them? Well, we want to *reason* about facts and conclude new facts—what's called *inference*. For this we'll need the concepts of queries, variables, and backtracking.

3.1 QUERYING THE FACTS

One thing we can do with facts in a computer is to look them up. This is the usual mode of *Prolog interpreters*, software that interprets and executes code written in the Prolog language:[1] they wait for us to give them things they can try to look up. You're in this *query mode* when the Prolog interpreter types ?- at the front of every line. Query mode is the way database query languages work, like SQL and QUEL.

To make this clearer, assume these facts (the semantic network example from Section 2.7) have been entered into a computer running a Prolog interpreter:

---

[1] Most Prolog-understanding software are interpreters and not *compilers*. A Prolog interpreter is not an "artificial-intelligence program" but a tool to execute artificial-intelligence programs written in the Prolog language.

```
a_kind_of(enterprise,ship).
a_kind_of(kennedy,ship).
part_of(enterprise,u_s_navy).
part_of(kennedy,u_s_navy).
part_of(u_s_navy,u_s_government).
a_kind_of(u_s_government,government).
color(ship,gray).
location(enterprise,15n35e).
has(u_s_government,civil_service_system).
```

We call such a set of facts known to a Prolog interpreter a *Prolog database* or just *database*. As we'll explain shortly, databases can be loaded from files. The block diagram in Figure 3-1 summarizes these basics.

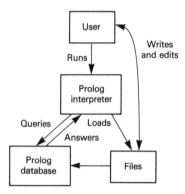

Figure 3-1. Block diagram of the usual use of Prolog.

Now in query mode with the preceding database we can type

part_of(kennedy,u_s_navy).

so that what actually shows on the computer terminal will be

?- part_of(kennedy,u_s_navy).

Note the period indicating the end of the query; the interpreter will wait (forever if necessary) until we type it (and usually a carriage return too). Then the interpreter will type in reply the single word **yes** to acknowledge that the fact is in its database. If we ask instead

?- part_of(pequod,u_s_navy).

(again the **?-** is typed by the interpreter and not us), the computer will type the single word **no**. So **yes** means "I found it" and **no** means "I couldn't find it." We call a **yes** a query *success* and **no** a query *failure*. So to make the computer say **no** when a query is *false*, the database must include every truth about its subject, for otherwise **no** could mean incomplete data.

3.2 QUERIES WITH ONE VARIABLE_____

But this isn't too interesting. These queries must give the precise fact we want to look up, including every argument. We might instead want to ask if a part_of fact has **enterprise** as its first argument and anything at all as its second argument. We can do this by querying

>   ?- part_of(enterprise,X).

Read this as "Find me an X such that part_of(enterprise,X) is true," or simply as "What is the Enterprise part of?" The Prolog interpreter will go through its two-argument facts in order, trying to match each to the query. When it finds one that matches in predicate name and first argument, it will type "X = " followed by the fact's second argument, instead of typing **yes**. Or in technical jargon, it *binds* or *matches* X to a value and prints it. So for this query with the previous database, we will get

>   X = u_s_navy

or X is bound to u_s_navy.

   X here is a *variable*. Prolog variables have similarities to variables in other programming languages, but also important differences we'll encounter as we proceed. Prolog variables are designated by a capitalized first letter in a word (followed by other letters and numbers, either capitalized or uncapitalized), and this is why in the last chapter we used lower case for other words in Prolog.
   Variables can only be arguments in Prolog; they can't appear as predicate names (though we'll give a way around this limitation in Chapter 12). This means Prolog represents only *first-order logic*. First-order logic is sufficient for nearly all artificial-intelligence applications, so that's no big deal. First-order logic is a reason we recommended in Chapter 2 that predicate names be more general than their nonvariable argument names: variables pay off when they stand for lots of concrete possibilities. (*Variable names* can be more general than their predicate names.)

3.3 MULTIDIRECTIONAL QUERIES_____

A variable can appear anywhere among the arguments to a predicate expression in a query, with some exceptions to be discussed later. So we could also query with the previous database

>   ?- part_of(X,u_s_navy).

and the Prolog interpreter will type back

    X = enterprise

In other words, we can be flexible about which arguments are *inputs* (constants) and which are *outputs* (variables) in a query. This means Prolog can answer quite different questions depending on where we put variables in the query. This flexibility extends to calls of Prolog procedures (subroutines and functions) too, as you will see in Chapter 4, a big difference from most programming languages.

3.4 MATCHING ALTERNATIVES

More than one thing (value) can match (bind) a query variable. The Prolog interpreter will find the first, print it out, and stop and wait. If just one answer is sufficient, type a carriage return. But to see the next answer (if any), type a semicolon (";") and a carriage return. We can keep typing semicolons, and it will keep finding new matches, until it can't find any more and it must answer **no**. So for our example database if we query

    ?- a_kind_of(X,ship).

which means "Find me an X that's a kind of ship," the interpreter will first type

    X = enterprise

and then if we type a semicolon and a carriage return it will type

    X = kennedy

and then if we type a semicolon and a carriage return it will type **no**. The semicolon prints at the end of the line, so what this will all look like on the computer terminal will be

    ?- a_kind_of(X,ship).
    X = enterprise;
    X = kennedy;
    no

where we typed the two semicolons and the first line except for the ?- , and the interpreter typed the rest.

We can have more than one variable in a query. If we were to query for our example database

    ?- part_of(X,Y).

("What things are part of other things?") and we kept typing semicolons, we would eventually see on the computer terminal something like this (some Prolog dialects format this output differently):

```
X = enterprise, Y = u_s_navy;
X = kennedy, Y = u_s_navy;
X = u_s_navy, Y = u_s_government;
no
```

So semicolons typed after a query answer find us every combination of bindings of the variables that satisfies a query. Since the Prolog interpreter works top to bottom through the database, the bindings will reflect database order.

3.5 MULTICONDITION QUERIES_____

A Prolog interpreter also lets us specify that several different conditions must succeed together in a query. This lets us specify "chains of reasoning," like those so important to detectives in mystery fiction.

Suppose we want to know the color of the Enterprise. If we type

```
?- color(enterprise,C).
```

we get no with our example database, because the color fact is about ships in general and not the Enterprise. This problem of information in the "wrong place" happens often in artificial-intelligence systems. Instead we can ask if there is some category or type T that the Enterprise belongs to, such that everything of type T has color C:

```
?- a_kind_of(enterprise,T), color(T,C).
```

This represents an "and" (*conjunction*) of two predicate expressions, both of which must succeed for the whole match to succeed. It works this way: we first try to answer the query

```
?- a_kind_of(enterprise,T).
```

Then for that particular T, we answer the query

```
?- color(T,C).
```

Using our example database, we first match T to ship in the first-listed fact. We then look for a color fact in which this T is the first argument, and the seventh-listed fact qualifies; we can then match **C** to **gray**. The Prolog interpreter now types out

   T = ship, C = gray

So commas between predicate expressions in a query line mean to query the predicate expressions in order, reusing the same values for any same-named variables. Commas are much like a logical "and" since all the subqueries (predicate expressions) must succeed for the whole query to succeed. But Prolog commas, unlike the logical "and," imply an order of processing. To make commas easier to spot, we'll often put spaces after them in queries; these spaces are ignored by the interpreter. (Don't put spaces in predicate expressions.)

   As another example, suppose we want to know what the Enterprise is part of. We could say

   ?- part_of(enterprise,X).

and get X = u_s_navy, but that's not the only reasonable answer since the U.S. Navy is part of something else. So we could say

   ?- part_of(enterprise,Y), part_of(Y,X).

and get back Y = u_s_navy, X = u_s_government.

   Logical "or" (*disjunction*) is represented by a semicolon instead of a comma. For instance

   ?- color(enterprise,C); color(ship,C).

asks for the color of the Enterprise if any is recorded, otherwise the color of ships in general. As with "and"s, the expressions of the "or" are tried in order. Parentheses can group subexpressions of "and"s and "or"s. So for instance the two conditions under which something is part of something else could be compressed into one with

   ?- part_of(enterprise,X); (part_of(enterprise,Y), part_of(Y,X)).

This reads: "Find me an X such that either the Enterprise is part of it, or the Enterprise is part of some Y that is part of it." We won't use these "or" semicolons much, because (1) "and"s occur more often in applications, (2) they often require parentheses and so are hard to read, and (3) there is a better way to get the effect of an "or," to be discussed in the next chapter.

   Figure 3-2 should help you keep straight the special symbols we've used so far, plus previewing a few to come.

Symbol	Description	Meaning
?-	Question mark, minus sign	Query prompt (typed by Prolog)
.	Period	(1) Query terminator (typed by user) (2) Database fact and rule terminator
,	Comma	(1) "And" of predicate expressions in a query (2) Separator of arguments (3) Separator of list items (see Chapter 5)
;	Semicolon	(1) "Or" of predicate expressions in a query (2) Forces new alternative after a query answer
( )	Parentheses	(1) For grouping arguments (2) For grouping query expressions
_	Underscore	No special meaning, but we often use as a character to make long names legible
:-	Colon, minus sign	Rule definition symbol (see Chapter 4); read as "if"
[ ]	Square brackets	Indicators of a list (see chapter 5)
< >	Angular brackets	Not a Prolog symbol, but we use it to enclose descriptions of things (like Backus–Naur Form)

Figure 3-2. Special symbols used with Prolog in this book.

3.6 NEGATIVE PREDICATE EXPRESSIONS

So we have "and"s and "or"s. All we need to complete a Boolean algebra is a negation or "not." This is accomplished by the built-in predicate **not** whose one argument is a predicate expression. (A *built-in* predicate is one with special meaning to the interpreter, a meaning not given by facts.) A **not** succeeds whenever querying its argument fails, and fails whenever querying its argument succeeds. So the query

?- not(color(enterprise,green)).

will succeed whenever there's no fact that the color of the Enterprise is green, and fail when there is such a fact. We'll extend the term "predicate expression" to include such **not** expressions too. They can be included in "and"s and "or"s just like other predicate expressions.

How will the Prolog interpreter ever be sure something is *not* true? Strictly speaking, it can't, since facts that directly say something is false are not permitted in Prolog (Chapter 14 discusses this further). So **not** is defined to mean the interpreter couldn't find a fact in its database—*negation-by-failure* or the *closed-world assumption*. Yet this is a curious and awkward interpretation of "not," not what we usually mean by the word in English. So we must be careful with **not** in Prolog.

One big problem is that we can't ever bind variables within a **not** if the whole thing is to succeed. So this query won't work:

?- not(color(X,gray)), a_kind_of(X,ship).

(This attempts to ask for a ship X that isn't gray.) Instead we must reverse the order of the two things:

?- a_kind_of(X,ship), not(color(X,gray)).

3.7 SOME QUERY EXAMPLES_____

Questions in English about a database often map directly into Prolog queries. Words like "is," "are," "does," and "did" at the beginning of a question suggest queries without variables (yes/no queries). Words like "what," "which," "who," "where," "when," and "how" suggest variables.

Here are some examples. We assume the meanings of the **part_of, color, a_kind_of**, etc. predicates we've been assuming all along. (These queries print out additional variable values than those desired; Chapter 4 will explain how to prevent this.)

1. What things are part of gray things?

    ?- part_of(X,Y), color(Y,gray).

2. What things are part of parts of other things?

    ?- part_of(A,B), part_of(B,C).

3. What things are gray or blue?

    ?- color(T,gray); color(T,blue).

4. What is an example of something that isn't gray? ("Example" suggests the reverse of the a_kind_of relationship.)

    ?- a_kind_of(E,T), not(color(T,gray)).

5. What is the Enterprise, either directly or through one level of indirection?

    ?- a_kind_of(enterprise,J); (a_kind_of(enterprise,K), a_kind_of(K,J)).

6. What things of which the Enterprise is part, are themselves part of something that has a civil service system?

    ?- part_of(enterprise,U), part_of(U,V), has(V,civil_service_system).

3.8 LOADING A DATABASE_____

How do we load a database of facts into a Prolog interpreter in the first place? This varies between implementations of Prolog interpreters, but usually we must first enter the facts we want into a text file, using an editor program. We exit the editor and start up the Prolog interpreter. We then query a special *built-in* loading predicate, called consult in this book. This consult is not something we must give facts for, but an internal Prolog name like not; it takes one argument, the name of a file, and loads it (as a sort of side effect of querying it) into the Prolog interpreter's internal memory (database). From then on, the facts in that file will be used to answer queries.

For instance, suppose we use the editor to create a file called "test" containing

```
boss(harry).
employee(tom).
employee(dick).
```

We can start the Prolog interpreter, type the query

```
?- consult(test).
```

and then type the query

```
?- employee(X).
```

and get

```
X = tom
```

from the first fact in the file that matches.

We can load more than one file into the Prolog interpreter, if several files contain useful facts. Just query consult again. New facts are put after the old facts, so you can get answers in a different order if you load the same files in a different order.

3.9 BACKTRACKING_____

Let's consider in more detail how the Prolog interpreter answers complicated queries. To make this easier, consider for now queries with only commas ("and"s), no semicolons ("or"s) or nots.

Predicate expressions "and"ed in a query are first taken left to right. That is, the leftmost expression is tried first, then the second expression from the left (using whatever variable matches were found for the first) and so on. So predicate expressions in a query are initially done in order, like lines of a program in a conventional language like Pascal.

But suppose that a predicate expression fails—that is, no fact matching it can be found. If the expression has variables that were bound earlier in the query line, the fault may just be in the bindings. So the interpreter automatically *backtracks* (goes back to the immediately previous expression in the query) and tries to find a different fact match. If it cannot, then *that* predicate expression fails and the interpreter backtracks to the previous one, and so on.

Anytime the interpreter cannot find another matching for the leftmost expression in a query, then there's no way the query could be satisfied; it types the word no and stops. Anytime on backtracking it can find a new matching for some predicate expression, it resumes moving right from there as it did originally, restarting match searches at the database top for query expressions to the right.

The purpose of backtracking is to give "second chances" to a query, by undoing earlier decisions. Backtracking is very important in artificial intelligence, because many artificial-intelligence programs use intelligent guessing and following of hunches. Guesses may be wrong, and backtracking is a way to recover.

Here's an example:

```
?- part_of(X,Y), has(Y,civil_service_system).
```

which asks for an X that is part of some Y that has a civil service system. Assume the standard database example of this chapter. Then the only facts that will help with this query (the only facts with predicate names part_of and has) are

```
part_of(enterprise,u_s_navy).
part_of(kennedy,u_s_navy).
part_of(u_s_navy,u_s_government).
has(u_s_government,civil_service_system).
```

Here in detail is what the Prolog interpreter does to answer this query:

1. It takes the first predicate expression in the query as a subquery, and matches X to enterprise, and Y to u_s_navy. It stores the information that it has chosen the first fact to match the first expression.

2. It then moves to the second predicate expression, and tries to answer the subquery

```
?- has(u_s_navy,civil_service_system).
```

That is, it substitutes in the value bound to variable Y. But the subquery fails since there's no such fact.

3. So it must backtrack, or return to the first predicate expression in the query. From its stored information, it knows it chose the first part_of fact last time, so now it tries the second, binding X to kennedy and Y to u_s_navy. It stores the information about what it chose.

4. It then tries to answer the subquery

    ?- has(u_s_navy,civil_service_system).

This is the same query it did in step 2, but the interpreter is stupid and doesn't remember (Chapter 6 will explain how to force it to remember), so it checks the facts and fails to find anything again. The subquery fails.

5. So it backtracks again, to the first predicate expression in the query. It chose the second fact last time, so it now chooses the third (and last) part_of fact. So X is bound to u_s_navy and Y is bound to u_s_government.

6. The second expression is considered with the new binding for Y, and the interpreter tries to answer the subquery

    ?- has(u_s_government,civil_service_system).

And this succeeds because it's the fourth fact.

7. So both predicate expressions in the query succeed, and the whole query succeeds. The interpreter prints out the bindings that it found:

    X = u_s_navy, Y = u_s_government

Notice that the interpreter wouldn't have had to backtrack if we just reversed the order of the query (an "and" without "not"s is commutative or rearrangeable in Prolog):

    ?- has(Y,civil_service_system), part_of(X,Y).

because only one fact can match the has predicate expression. But such insights require analyzing the facts in advance, and the rearrangement isn't better with some other databases.

The automatic backtracking of the Prolog interpreter has both advantages and disadvantages. A big advantage is that combinatorial problems are easier to specify than with most computer languages, because the interpreter does more work for you. It also means that Prolog is a more flexible language than most: if you refer to an unbound variable in Pascal, Ada, PL/1, or Fortran, you get an error message and the program stops. The disadvantages are that Prolog programs run slower than those of other languages, and they're sometimes harder to understand and debug, because the language tries to do more.

3.10 A HARDER BACKTRACKING EXAMPLE: SUPERBOSSES

Here is another backtracking example. It's trickier than the last because two predicate expressions both have alternatives. Furthermore, the same predicate name is used twice, and we have to distinguish the alternatives for each use.

Suppose we have facts about employees in an organization, represented with a two-argument predicate **boss**. Its first argument is a boss, and its second argument is an employee of that boss. Take the following example database:

```
boss(dick,harry).
boss(tom,dick).
boss(ann,mary).
boss(mary,harry).
```

Suppose we want to find "superbosses," people who are bosses of bosses. That is, those X that are a boss of some Y while at the same time Y is a boss of some Z. We can issue the query

```
?- boss(X,Y), boss(Y,Z).
```

and every match the interpreter finds for variable X will be a superboss. (Matches for Y and Z will also be found, but X is all that we want, according to the way we stated the problem.)

Let's trace query execution (summarized in Figure 3-3). As usual, assume facts are placed in the Prolog database in the order listed.

1. The first predicate expression in the query will match the first fact in the database, with X = dick and Y = harry.

2. Moving to the second predicate expression in the query, the interpreter searches for a **boss** fact with **harry** as its first argument. But there's no such fact in the database, so the second expression in the query fails.

3. So the interpreter backtracks, returning to the first expression to make another choice. Last time it used the first fact in the database, so this time it uses the second fact and sets X = tom and Y = dick.

4. Things proceed just as if these matchings happened originally. The interpreter goes to the second predicate expression, and searches from the start of the database for a **boss** fact where **dick** is the first argument. And yes, there is such a fact, the first fact in the database.

5. So Z = harry, and since we're at the end of the query, the query succeeds.

Therefore Tom is a superboss. The interpreter types out X = tom, Y = dick, Z = harry.

Query:

?-boss(X,Y), boss(Y,Z).

Database:

boss(dick,harry).
boss(tom,dick).
boss(ann,mary).
boss(mary,harry).

Processing:

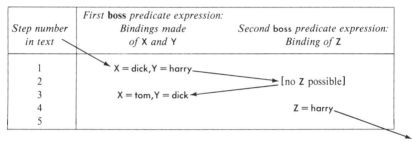

Step number in text	First **boss** predicate expression: Bindings made of X and Y	Second **boss** predicate expression: Binding of Z
1	X = dick, Y = harry	
2		[no Z possible]
3	X = tom, Y = dick	
4		Z = harry
5		

Figure 3-3. Processing state at generation of first answer to superboss query: X = tom, Y = dick, Z = harry.

Now we can explain better what typing a semicolon does after the Prolog interpreter types out a positive query answer (not to be confused with a semicolon in a *query*): it forces failure and backtracking. For instance, suppose after that last answer we type a semicolon instead of a carriage return. What happens now is summarized in Figure 3-4, together with the previous events.

6. The interpreter will go back to what it just finished, the second expression of the query, and try to find a different match.

7. The old match for the second query expression was from the first fact, so now it examines the second, third, and fourth facts in order. Unfortunately, none have dick as their first argument, so the expression fails.

8. So the interpreter must return to the first predicate expression yet again. The first and second facts have been tried, so it uses the third fact and sets X = ann and Y = mary.

9. It resumes normal left-to-right processing and tries to find a match for the second query expression, starting at the top of the list of facts. (Each time it reaches a query predicate expression from the left, it starts searching for a match at the top of the database.) This means finding a fact where mary is the first argument, and indeed the fourth fact qualifies.

10. So Z = harry, and the entire query succeeds when X = ann, meaning that Ann is a superboss. The interpreter types out X = ann, Y = mary, Z = harry.

Query:

   ?-boss(X,Y), boss(Y,Z).

Database:

   boss(dick,harry).
   boss(tom,dick).
   boss(ann,mary).
   boss(mary,harry).

Processing:

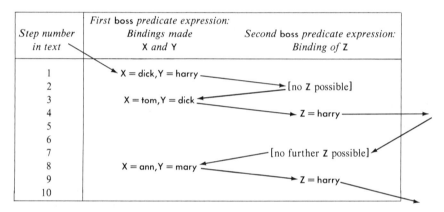

Figure 3-4. Processing state at generation of second answer to superboss query: X = ann, Y = mary, Z = harry.

3.11 BACKTRACKING WITH "NOT"S

Negated predicate expressions (expressions with a not) are easy with backtracking. Since they can't bind variables to succeed, they can be skipped in backtracking. For instance, we could add another expression to our superboss query to insist that the superboss not be the boss of Dick:

   ?- boss(X,Y), not(boss(X,dick)), boss(Y,Z).

Then when the interpreter executes the new query (see Figure 3-5):

1. The first predicate expression matches the first fact in the database as before, setting X = dick and Y = harry.

2. This binding of X satisfies the second condition, the not (Dick isn't his own boss).

3. For the third expression, there's no fact with **harry** as its first argument, so it fails. The interpreter backtracks to the immediately previous (second) expression.
4. But the second expression is a **not**, and **not**s always fail on backtracking, so the interpreter returns to the first expression and matches X = **tom** and Y = **dick**.
5. But this X now makes the second expression fail—there is a fact that Tom is the boss of Dick.
6. The interpreter returns to the first predicate expression and takes the next matching from the database, X = **ann** and Y = **mary**.
7. This X succeeds with the second expression since Ann isn't the boss of Dick.
8. The Y match succeeds with the third expression if Z = **harry**. So the interpreter reports that X = **ann**, Y = **mary**, Z = **harry**.

Query:

        ?-boss(X,Y), not(boss(X,dick)), boss(Y,Z).

Database:

        boss(dick,harry).
        boss(tom,dick).
        boss(ann,mary).
        boss(mary,harry).

Processing:

Step number in text	First predicate expression: Bindings made of X and Y	Second predicate expression: What happens?	Third predicate expression: Binding of Z
1	X = dick, Y = harry		
2		succeeds	
3			[no possible Z]
4		fails	
4	X = tom, Y = dick		
5		fails	
6	X = ann, Y = mary		
7		succeeds	
8			Z = harry

Figure 3-5. Processing order for the extended superboss example: answer X = ann, Y = mary, Z = harry.

Notice the backtracking works differently if we rearrange the query into this equivalent form:

?- boss(X,Y), boss(Y,Z), not(boss(X,dick)).

This is processed very much like the original two-expression superboss query, except that the **not** expression forces failure instead of success for X = tom; we got the same effect by typing a semicolon after the first answer to the query in the last section. But the query won't work right if we reorder it as

?- not(boss(X,dick)), boss(X,Y), boss(Y,Z).

because now a **not** with an unbound variable is first, violating the guideline of Section 3.6.

3.12 THE GENERATE-AND-TEST SCHEME

When a variable occurs more than once in a Prolog query, the Prolog interpreter chooses a value (binding) at the first occurrence, and then uses that value in all other occurrences of the variable. So processing of the predicate expression containing the first occurrence "generates" a value, which is "tested" by the predicate expressions containing later occurrences. This idea is often used in artificial intelligence, and it's called the *generate-and-test* scheme or paradigm. Often the generating predicate expressions define the types of the variables, so their predicates are type predicates (Section 2.2).

Generate-and-test is a good way to attack problems for which we don't know any particularly good way to proceed. We generate potential solutions, and apply a series of tests to check for a true solution. This works well when it's hard to reason backward about a problem (from a statement of the problem to a solution), but it's easy to reason forward from a guess to a solution (or verify a proposed solution). An example is cryptography (decoding ciphers): an approach is to guess possible coding (encryption) methods, and see if any of them gives coded text resembling a coded message. Many other interesting problems work well for generate-and-test. But problems with well-defined solution methods, like many mathematical problems, aren't suitable for it.

3.13 BACKTRACKING WITH "OR"S*

Semicolons in queries ("or"s) are tricky for backtracking. We'll mostly ignore them in this book because, as we say, there's a better way to get their effect; but for the record, here's what happens. When a predicate expression before a semicolon succeeds, all the other expressions to the right that are "or"ed with it can be skipped. When such an expression fails, the next term to the right within the "or" should be tried. If there aren't any more, the whole "or" should fail, which means backtracking to the left. So while backtracking with "and"s always goes left, backtracking with "or"s sometimes goes left and sometimes goes right.

3.14 IMPLEMENTATION OF BACKTRACKING

Implementing backtracking requires allocation of a pointer (Appendix C defines pointers) for every predicate expression in a query, a pointer to where in the database the interpreter last found a match for the predicate expression. So Prolog is more complicated to implement than conventional higher-level languages like Pascal that only need extra storage in the form of a stack for procedure calls (Appendix C defines stacks too). Prolog needs a stack for this purpose too, as you'll see in Chapter 4.

Queries don't necessarily require inspection of facts in the database in sequence (*sequential search*). All Prolog interpreters *index* facts in some way, usually at least by predicate name. This means keeping lists of addresses of facts with the same predicate name. So when the interpreter sees an a_kind_of predicate in a query, it need only search through the a_kind_of facts pointed to in the a_kind_of index list for a match. Figure 3-6 gives an example of a database and its index. More selective indexing (not standard in most Prolog dialects, though) can examine the arguments too.

Database:

Memory location	Contents
10000	a_kind_of(enterprise,ship).
10026	a_kind_of(kennedy,ship).
10052	part_of(enterprise,u_s_navy).
10070	part_of(kennedy,u_s_navy).
10088	part_of(u_s_navy,u_s_government).

Index:

Predicate name	Locations of facts using it
a_kind_of	10000,10026
part_of	10052,10070,10088

Figure 3-6. Example of predicate indexing.

Indexing by predicate name means that Prolog facts can go in many different orders and still provide exactly the same behavior. For instance, the facts in Figure 3-6

a_kind_of(enterprise,ship).
a_kind_of(kennedy,ship).
part_of(enterprise,u_s_navy).
part_of(kennedy,u_s_navy).
part_of(u_s_navy,u_s_government).

can be rearranged as

```
part_of(enterprise,u_s_navy).
a_kind_of(enterprise,ship).
part_of(kennedy,u_s_navy).
a_kind_of(kennedy,ship).
part_of(u_s_navy,u_s_government).
```

and all queries will give the same answers in the same order, as they will for

```
part_of(enterprise,u_s_navy).
part_of(kennedy,u_s_navy).
part_of(u_s_navy,u_s_government).
a_kind_of(enterprise,ship).
a_kind_of(kennedy,ship).
```

But this is only because the three part_of facts maintain their order and the two a_kind_of facts maintain their order. The following database will give answers in a different order than the preceding, though it gives the same answers eventually:

```
a_kind_of(kennedy,ship).
part_of(u_s_navy,u_s_government).
part_of(enterprise,u_s_navy).
a_kind_of(enterprise,ship).
part_of(kennedy,u_s_navy).
```

The speed of query answering depends on how many facts are indexed for each predicate in a query; the more facts, the slower the queries. Queries will also be slower when variables appear multiple times in the query. This situation, called a *join* in database systems, often requires embedded iterative loops, and loops can take a lot of time. With joins, possibilities literally multiply. For our previous example

```
?- a_kind_of(S,X), color(X,C).
```

if there are 100 a_kind_of facts and 50 color facts, 5,000 combinations must be tried to find all answers, as when we type a semicolon repeatedly or when there are no such X and C.

3.15 ABOUT LONG EXAMPLES

We've studied several long examples in this chapter. Are all the examples of artificial intelligence like this? Yes, unfortunately. Artificial intelligence is a set of techniques for managing complexity, and you can only see its advantages in at least moderately complex problems.

This disturbs some students. They feel that since they can't get all of a long example into their heads at once, they can't really understand what's going on. One reply is to think of programming languages. There's a lot of activity behind the scenes that the programmer isn't usually aware of—parsing, storage management, symbol tables, stacks, type checking, register allocation, and optimization. But you don't need to know this to program. The complexity of artificial-intelligence examples comes from the need to explain, at least initially, similar behind-the-scenes details. Once you understand what details are necessary, you can ignore them as you program.

Most artificial-intelligence programs and systems do provide additional help for understanding complex program activities in the form of *explanation* facilities that summarize and answer questions about reasoning activity. These facilities provide program tracing, and answer questions like "Why did you conclude boss(tom,dick)?" and "Why didn't you conclude boss(dick,tom)?" More on this in Section 15.8.

KEYWORDS

inference
Prolog database
Prolog interpreter
query
success
failure
variable
binding variables
first-order logic
inputs
outputs
match
matching alternatives
database order
conjunction

disjunction
negation
not
built-in predicates
closed-world assumption
consult
backtracking
indexing
generate-and-test

EXERCISES

3-1. (A) Good programming style in Prolog doesn't allow the argument to a **not** to
be more than one predicate expression, and doesn't allow composite queries
(queries not just a single predicate expression) "or"d together.

    (a) Using good programming style, write a Prolog query that is true if the
"nor" of predicate expressions a and b (both of no arguments) is true.
("Nor" means the opposite of an "or").

    (b) Using good programming style, write a Prolog query that is true if the
"exclusive or" of predicate expressions a and b is true. ("Exclusive or"
means either is true but not both.)

3-2. (R,A) Suppose you have the following Prolog database:

```
incumbent(csprofessor,davis).
incumbent(csprofessor,rowe).
incumbent(csprofessor,wu).
incumbent(csprofessor,zyda).
incumbent(cschairman,lum).
incumbent(dean_ips,marshall).
incumbent(provost,shrady).
incumbent(superintendent,shumaker).
incumbent(director_milops,bley).
bossed_by(csprofessor,cschairman).
bossed_by(cschairman,dean_ips).
bossed_by(orchairman,dean_ips).
bossed_by(dean_ips,provost).
bossed_by(provost,superintendent).
bossed_by(director_milops,superintendent).
```

    (a) The **incumbent** predicate means that the person that is its second argu-
ment has the job description that is its first argument; the **bossed_by**
predicate means that the boss of the first argument is the second argument. Paraphrase each of the following Prolog queries in English.

```
?- bossed_by(csprofessor,X), bossed_by(X,Y).
?- bossed_by(X,Y), incumbent(X,rowe), incumbent(Y,Z).
?- incumbent(dean_ip,X); incumbent(dean_ips,X).
?- incumbent(J,P), (bossed_by(J,provost); bossed_by(J,dean_ips)).
?- bossed_by(P,superintendent), not(incumbent(P,shrady)).
```

    (b) Without using a computer, what will be the first answer found by a Pro-
log interpreter with the preceding database and with each query given?

3-3. Suppose two queries each represent an "and" of a number of predicate
expressions. Suppose the expressions of query 1 are a subset of the expres-

sions in query 2. How do the answers to query 1 relate to the answers to query 2?

3-4. The words "the" and "a" mean different things in English. What analogous important feature of Prolog querying does the difference between them demonstrate in the following sentences?

> Find a memo we sent headquarters last week. The memo reported on a board meeting last October 10. The board meeting was noisy, and this is mentioned in the memo.

3-5. (A) Suppose in your Prolog database you have N one-argument facts for the predicate name p and M one-argument facts for the predicate name q.

(a) What is the maximum number of answers, not counting no, that you will get to the query

    ?- p(X), q(Y).

(b) How many total times will the Prolog interpreter backtrack from q to p for the situation in part (a) before it types no?

(c) What is the minimum number of answers to the query in part (a)?

(d) What is the maximum number of answers, not counting no, you will get to the query

    ?- p(X), q(X).

(e) How many total times will the Prolog interpreter backtrack from q to p for the situation in part (d) before it types no?

(f) What is the minimum number of answers to the query in part (d)?

3-6. (R,A) Suppose we keep in a Prolog database information about grades on two tests in a course.

(a) Suppose we ask if Joe got an A on test 1 and the Prolog interpreter says yes. Suppose we then ask if Joe got an A on test 2 and it says yes. It seems fair to summarize this by saying Joe got A's on both tests 1 and 2. Now suppose we ask if someone got an A on test 1 and the interpreter gives a name. We ask if someone got an A on test 2 and it gives another name. It is unfair now to conclude that someone got an A on both test 1 and test 2. How is this situation different? How does this illustrate an important feature of Prolog querying?

(b) Suppose the database consists of facts of the form

    grade(<person>,<test-number>,<grade>).

Write a query that establishes if everyone in the class got an A on test 1, without using an "or" (semicolon). (Hint: Use the exact opposite.)

(c) Suppose you ask if everyone in the class got an A on test 1 and the Prolog interpreter agrees. Suppose you then ask if everyone in the class got an A on test 2 and it agrees. Can you conclude that everyone in the class got both an A on test 1 and an A on test 2? Why? Assume this is a real class at a real college or university.

3-7. Here's a summary of the current situation on the fictitious television soap opera *Edge of Boredom:*

> Jason and Phoebe are married, but Phoebe is in love with Perry. Perry doesn't love her because he is still married to Stacey, but Zack is romantically inclined toward Phoebe. He's in competition with Lane, who also loves Phoebe despite being married to Eulalie, whom Jason is feeling romantic about.

(a) Represent the basic meaning of these statements by facts using only two different predicate names. Notice that if X is married to Y, Y is married to X.

(b) A marriage is on the rocks if both its participants are in love with other people and not with each other. Which people are in marriages that are on the rocks? Show the necessary Prolog query and its result.

(c) A person is jealous when a person they love is loved by a third person, or a person is jealous when married to someone loved by a third person. Which people are jealous? Show the necessary Prolog query and its result.

3-8. Consider the query

    ?- a(X,Y), b(X,Y).

with the database

    a(1,1).
    a(2,1).
    a(3,2).
    a(4,4).
    b(1,2).
    b(1,3).
    b(2,3).
    b(3,2).
    b(4,4).

(a) Without using a computer, what are all the answers that you will get to the query, in order (as you keep typing semicolons)?

(b) Without using a computer, what does this query print out (as you keep typing semicolons)?

    ?- a(X,Y), b(X,Y), a(Y,Y).

3-9. (A) Consider this Prolog query:

>   ?- r(X,Y), s(Y,Z), not(r(Y,X)), not(s(Y,Y)).

with this database:

>   r(a,b).
>   r(a,c).
>   r(b,a).
>   r(a,d).
>   s(b,c).
>   s(b,d).
>   s(c,d).
>   s(c,c).
>   s(d,e).

>   **(a)** Without using a computer, what is the first answer found to the query? (Hint: You don't have to do it Prolog's way.)
>   **(b)** Without using a computer, how many times does a Prolog interpreter backtrack from the third to the second predicate expression to get this first answer?

3-10. Consider this Prolog database:

>   u(a,b).
>   u(b,b).
>   u(c,d).
>   u(c,a).
>   u(d,a).
>   u(d,c).

Now consider this Prolog query, without actually using a computer:

>   ?- u(X,Y), u(Y,Z), not(u(X,Z)).

>   **(a)** How many times will a Prolog interpreter backtrack to the first query predicate expression u(X,Y) to find the first answer to this query?
>   **(b)** How many times will a Prolog interpreter backtrack to the second query predicate expression u(Y,Z) to find the first answer to this query?
>   **(c)** How many times will a Prolog interpreter backtrack to the third query predicate expression not(u(X,Z)) to find the first answer to this query?
>   **(d)** How many further times will a Prolog interpreter backtrack to the first query predicate expression u(X,Y) to find the second answer to this query?

(e) How many further times will a Prolog interpreter backtrack to the second query predicate expression u(Y,Z) to find the second answer to this query?

3-11. (H) Design a good set of predicates for the following data about an organization and its employees. Assume you have to do this in Prolog. Try to be efficient: avoid duplicate data, empty data, and too many linking arguments, while keeping data access reasonably fast.

Assume we have an organization with departments, subdepartments, and projects. A subdepartment can belong to only one department, but a project can belong to more than one subdepartment or department (but most of the time only one). Employees belong to one subdepartment and one or more projects. Employees have a name, social security number, date of birth, address, and a list of successfully completed projects that they participated in since they joined the organization. Employees also are characterized by Personnel by "job skills" they have from a rough list (e.g., "can type," "has truck license," "experience in writing"). Projects have a name, code, starting date, projected or actual completion date, and the room number for the office of each employee on the project. Employees have only one office, but there may be more than one employee in the same office.

Design these predicates to answer these questions easily:
- Give the name, department, and office number for each employee on project 93521.
- Give the name, department, and office number for each employee on projects started last year.
- Give the people in department 43 who have typing skills.

3-12. Questions in English have subtleties that are sometimes hard to translate into Prolog queries. This became obvious in building the first *natural language front ends* to databases, computer programs that tried to answer, in English, questions about the database contents. Here are illustrations of two bugs discovered in those early programs. Try to explain what a program like a Prolog interpreter is missing when it makes such errors. (Brackets give our explanatory comments.)

(a) Person: Can you tell me the commander of the Enterprise and his rank?
Computer: Yes. [That's all it types in response.]

(b) Person: Who commands the Pequod?
Computer: Nobody. [That's strange, because every ship must have a commander.]
Person: Where is the Pequod currently?
Computer: Nowhere. [Strange ship this Pequod.]
Person: Does the Pequod exist?
Computer: No. [So that's the reason.]

DEFINITIONS AND INFERENCES

Much human intelligence consists of conclusions or *inferences* drawn from facts, instead of facts themselves. We'll now show how inference methods can be represented, including a famous one called *inheritance*. That is, we'll formalize chains of reasoning.

4.1 RULES FOR DEFINITIONS

If we ask a lot of queries of a database, especially queries about related things, we may be typing the same expressions over and over again. Nearly all programming languages have subroutines or procedures to modularize knowledge, group it into its natural pieces. Prolog has them too, and they're called *rules* or *definitions*. Rules are a way to create the ability to query new predicates without specifying new facts, by defining the new predicate names in terms of old predicate names.

Prolog rules have a *left side* and a *right side*, and the symbol :- in between (it is supposed to look like a backward arrow, but you need a good imagination). Read the symbol as "if." To its left side is a single predicate expression, usually with variables as arguments. To its right side is a query, with possibly multiple predicate expressions combined with the comma ("and"), semicolon ("or"), and not symbols. For instance

```
gray_enterprise :- part_of(enterprise,X), color(X,gray).
```

This says that predicate expression (*conclusion*) gray_enterprise succeeds if the query (*premise*)

?- part_of(enterprise,X), color(X,gray).

succeeds. In other words, gray_enterprise is true if the Enterprise is part of something that is gray in color. So gray_enterprise is a code representing a query.
     More formally, the gray_enterprise rule defines a new predicate of no arguments called gray_enterprise. When queried

?- gray_enterprise.

the interpreter succeeds (answers **yes**) if it can succeed in querying the right side of the gray_enterprise rule. Otherwise the interpreter fails (answers **no**). It's like the right side of the rule is substituted for the left side whenever it occurs in a query. The variable X is a *local variable* in the rule, a variable whose value will be "thrown away" when the rule is done, and will not be printed out in any query answer. Any Prolog variable that appears only on the right side of a rule is local to that rule.
     But gray_enterprise isn't too useful because it only covers one color. What we really want is a rule that will *tell us* what color something is. We can do this with a variable on the left side of the rule, a variable representing the color:

color_enterprise(C) :- part_of(enterprise,X), color(X,C).

C is a *parameter variable* of the rule, and a value for it will be "returned" as a result of executing the rule. So if we query

?- color_enterprise(C).

when our database is that of Section 3.1 and the interpreter uses the color_enterprise rule, it will type

C = gray

in reply. Rules can have any number of such parameter variables, as well as constants (ordinary words and numbers), as arguments on their left sides. So if we wanted an even more general color rule, one that would tell us the color for many objects, we could say:

color_object(X,C) :- part_of(X,Y), color(Y,C).

Here X and C are parameter variables, and Y is a local variable. So values for X and C only will be returned.

Figure 4-1 summarizes our terminology about rules. You can think of local variables as being existentially quantified ("there exists some X such that something is true"), and parameter variables as universally quantified ("for every X something is true") — see Appendix A for more about quantification, an important concept in logic. The distinction of "local" from "parameter" variables can be misleading, because the opposite of "local" is "global," and there aren't any true "global" variables in Prolog. Rules just give a shorthand for queries, and a variable X in one query is always different from a variable X in another query. The only way to get anything like a global variable in Prolog is by a fact.

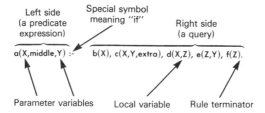

Read a rule as meaning: the left side is true if querying the right side succeeds.

Figure 4-1. Terminology about rules.

Here are more rule examples. This defines X to be the son of Y if X is the child of Y and X is male:

son(X,Y) :- child(X,Y), male(X).

This defines X to be the "superboss" of Y if X is the boss of the boss of Y:

superboss(X,Y) :- boss(X,Z), boss(Z,Y).

This defines something X you own to be stolen if it isn't present and you haven't given it to someone:

stolen(X) :- owns(you,X), not(present(X)), not(given(you,X,Y)).

This defines the previous example predicate color_object in a different way, using a_kind_of instead of part_of. It says that the color of X is C if X is a type of Y and the color of Y is C:

color_object(X,C) :- a_kind_of(X,Y), color(Y,C).

Usually predicates defined by rules can be used in queries just like fact predicates. This means that we can usually put variables for any of the arguments to defined-predicate expressions in queries, a powerful feature. (A few exceptions to this will be discussed in later chapters: some rules with **nots**, the arithmetic and **is** constructs of Chapter 5, and the "cut" ("!") of Chapter 10.) That is, we can designate arbitrary inputs and outputs. This means that Prolog is fundamentally more powerful than conventional programming languages, which usually require all but one thing (the output) associated with a procedure to be known at the time of any call of that procedure.

4.2 RULE AND FACT ORDER

Rules can go into a Prolog database just like facts. And the interpreter then uses both those rules and facts to answer queries. But we must worry a little about rule and fact order.

To see why, consider combining several reasoning methods in the same rule, as for instance three ways of establishing the color of something:

```
color_object(X,C) :- color(X,C); (part_of(X,Y), color(Y,C));
   (part_of(X,Y), part_of(Y,Z), color(Z,C)).
```

(Queries and rules can take more than one line; the period at the end indicates where they stop.) But that's poor rule-writing style, since it's hard to read the right side. Instead, we can write three separate rules with the same left side:

```
color_object(X,C) :- color(X,C).
color_object(X,C) :- part_of(X,Y), color(Y,C).
color_object(X,C) :- part_of(X,Y), part_of(Y,Z), color(Z,C).
```

Now each rule's right side gives *sufficient* conditions for the left-side predicate expression to be true, but not *necessary* conditions. That is, each describes some but not all the situations for which **color_object** succeeds. When each rule is very specific, we have *definition by examples*.

The order of those three rules matters. Whenever a query on predicate **color_object** with two arguments is issued, the rules will be tried to answer the query in database order, just as if they were facts. The order shown is probably the best, because the simplest rule will be tried first, then the next simplest, then the most complex (where we measure "complexity" by the number of expressions).

Facts and rules can be freely intermingled in a Prolog database; the overall order is all that matters. Facts should generally come first, though, if there are both facts and rule left sides for a predicate name. That's because facts require less symbol matching than rules—and a lot less than some of the recursive rules we'll discuss later in this chapter. Putting facts before recursive rules of the same predicate is also the standard way to write recursive programs (as we discussed in Appendix B).

4.3 RULES AS PROGRAMS_____

So this is how we'll write a Prolog program: by giving a list of facts and rules (definitions) that explain about some area of human knowledge. To match a query predicate expression, rules and facts will be considered in order, somewhat like sequential execution of the lines of a program in a conventional computer language, but stopping when a match is found. "And"s on the right sides of queries will initially be done in left-to-right order, like multiple procedure calls in a line of a conventional language. And like those languages, we can have "procedure" (rule) hierarchies; that is, a rule right side can use predicate names defined in rules, including its own left-side predicate name (*recursion*).

This mapping of predicate expressions to actions means that we can model *procedures* in Prolog, not just facts. For instance, here's a way to describe a daily agenda for a student:

```
day_agenda :- wakeup, classes, lunch, classes, dinner, study, sleep.
wakeup :- late, dress, travel(home,campus).
wakeup :- not(late), shower, dress, breakfast, travel(home,campus).
classes :- class, class, class.
class :- check_schedule, go_room, take_notes.
```

This notation is useful for describing processes, even if we never define what the basic actions (like take_notes) are. A computer doesn't need to know *everything* to be intelligent, just the important things. (However, we'll introduce a better way to describe sequences of actions in Chapter 9.)

4.4 RULES IN NATURAL LANGUAGE_____

As we said in Section 2.8, an artificial-intelligence system is often built from natural-language (e.g., English) specifications, either oral or written. Rules can be specified several ways in English. The easiest to spot is the "if...then" statement:

If a vehicle floats on water, then it's a ship.

which could become the Prolog rule (note the reversed order):

ship(X) :- vehicle(X), floats(X,water).

But the "then" is often omitted:

If a vehicle floats on water, it's a ship.

"Define" or "assume" often signals a rule, taking the things in the opposite (Prolog) order:

Define a ship as anything that floats on water.
Assume as a ship anything that floats on water.

"Anything," "anyone," "any," "something," "some," and "a" in such definitions often map to Prolog variables.

Besides expressing facts, the verb "to be" can be used to express rules:

A ship is any vehicle that floats on water.

Ships are water-floating vehicles.

The borderline between facts and rules can be fuzzy, but generally speaking, use a rule when variable bindings seem possible. The "a" and "any" in the first sentence suggest a variable, and hence a rule.

When an "and" occurs in the "if" part of a definition, we can just put commas into the right side of the rule. For instance

Something that is a vehicle and floats on water is a ship.

takes the form of the preceding ship(X) rule. If an "and" occurs in the "then" part of a definition, multiple conclusions hold for some situation. Prolog doesn't allow "and"s in rule left sides, but we can instead write multiple rules with the same right side and different left sides. So

If a vehicle floats on water and is gray, then it is a ship and of military origin.

becomes

```
ship(X) :- vehicle(X), floats(X,water), gray(X).
origin(X,military) :- vehicle(X), floats(X,water), gray(X).
```

4.5 RULES WITHOUT RIGHT SIDES

The right side of a rule represents sufficient conditions for the left-side predicate expression to be true. What if a rule doesn't have anything on its right side? Then we'd be saying that nothing is necessary to make the left side true, that the left side is always true. In other words, a fact. So facts are just a special case of rules. That's why Prolog facts and rules are put together in one big database: they're the same thing.

But rules can have variables. What would it mean for a fact to have a variable? Consider:

```
part_of(X,universe).
```

If you think of that as a rule with no right side, it says that for any X, nothing is necessary to say that X is part of the universe. In other words, every X is part of the universe. So using the term from logic (see Appendix A), facts with variables are *universally quantified*.

4.6 POSTPONED BINDING

An interesting consequence of the Prolog interpreter's handling of rules is "postponed" binding of variables. This is interesting because most other programming languages can't do anything like this. Suppose we query:

> ?- color_object(enterprise,C).

Here the first argument is bound (that is, it's an input) and the second argument is unbound (that is, it's an output). If there's a fact in the database

> color_object(enterprise,gray).

then the query can immediately bind C to gray. But if there are no color_object facts, only rules with color_object expressions on their left sides, or if such a rule is first in the database, the binding may be delayed. For instance, suppose the interpreter picks the rule

> color_object(X,C) :- part_of(X,Y), color_object(Y,C).

The variable C won't be bound when the rule is invoked, and it won't be bound in the part_of (which doesn't mention C), so if it's ever bound it won't be until the recursive query of color_object. But this query may require other recursive calls. It may take a long time for an appropriate color_object fact to be found, and hence a long time for variable C to get bound.

In fact, some query variables may *never* get bound to values in successful queries. Consider

> recommended(X,J) :- not(bad_report(X)).

a rule that recommends person X for job J if they haven't had a bad report recently. Here J is never bound if the query's second argument isn't initially bound. Most Prolog dialects will invent a name like "_14" for such unbound variables, to print out if they must.

Postponing of binding in Prolog interpreters has the advantage that binding is only done when truly necessary to answer a query. This saves on the computer's overhead cost of binding, for one thing. Furthermore, *multiway* reasoning becomes easier, reasoning for which we don't know in advance which arguments to a predicate expression (procedure) will be bound (or be inputs). Multiway reasoning means the same rule can be used many ways. We'll look more into this in the next chapter.

4.7 BACKTRACKING WITH RULES

As we discussed in Chapter 3, backtracking is the "backing up" the interpreter does when it can't find a match for a predicate expression in a query. When predicates in a query have rule definitions, the interpreter acts somewhat as if the right side of the definition were typed as part of a query instead of the single predicate expression that is the left side. (We say "somewhat" because variable names in a rule are local in meaning, and parameter variables in a rule may get bound on entering the rule.) So backtracking into a predicate expression for a rule-defined predicate means returning to the last expression in the rule. Tracing backtracking with rules is hard because we move both left and right (through backtracking) and up and down (through procedure calls and returns). This is a common problem with powerful computer languages such as Prolog: simply because they're powerful, it's hard to follow everything they're doing.

Here's an example that isn't too hard. Suppose we have two kinds of facts about an organization: the department each employee works for and the manager of each department. Suppose we define a **boss** predicate of two parameter arguments **B** and **E**, a predicate that says that **B** is the boss of **E** if **B** manages a department **D** in which **E** is an employee; **D** will be a local variable. Assume that Tom works in the sales department, Harry works in the production department, Dick manages the sales department, and Mary manages the production department. Then the Prolog database is

```
department(tom,sales).
department(harry,production).
manager(dick,sales).
manager(mary,production).
boss(B,E) :- department(E,D), manager(B,D).
```

Now suppose we want to find a boss different from Tom's. It will be **X** in the query

```
?- boss(X,Y), not(boss(X,tom)).
```

Notice that the **not** must come second in the query because **X** must be bound by the other expression.

Let us trace execution (see Figure 4-2).

1. The first predicate expression in the query matches only a rule in the database, no facts, so the first job to do is searching for a match for the first expression on the right side of the rule, **department(E,D)**. This can be matched to the first fact, with **E** = tom and **D** = sales.

2. Moving on to the second predicate expression in the rule, **manager(B,D)**, the interpreter finds a match in the third fact with **B** = dick, so the rule succeeds and the first expression in the original query succeeds. So **X** = dick and **Y** = tom.

3. Moving to the second and last expression in the query, **not(boss(X,tom))**, the interpreter tries to find if Dick is the boss of Tom. It has no memory of what it just proved, so it goes back to the rule.

Query:

   ?-boss(X,Y), not(boss(X,tom)).

Database:

   department(tom,sales).
   department(harry,production).
   manager(dick,sales).
   manager(mary,production).
   boss(B,E) :- department(E,D), manager(B,D).

Processing:

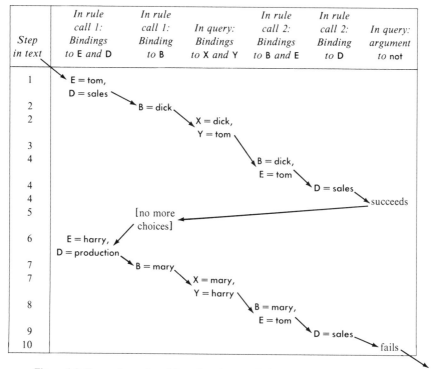

Step in text	In rule call 1: Bindings to E and D	In rule call 1: Binding to B	In query: Bindings to X and Y	In rule call 2: Bindings to B and E	In rule call 2: Binding to D	In query: argument to not
1	E = tom, D = sales					
2		B = dick				
2			X = dick, Y = tom			
3						
4				B = dick, E = tom		
4					D = sales	
4						succeeds
5		[no more choices]				
6	E = harry, D = production					
7		B = mary				
7			X = mary, Y = harry			
8				B = mary, E = tom		
9					D = sales	
10						fails

Figure 4-2. Processing order of the other-than-tom's-boss query: answer X = mary,
Y = harry.

4. Again, both predicate expressions on the right side of the rule can match the same facts, so the rule succeeds. But the condition in the original query is the opposite ("not" or negation) of this, so the second half of the original query fails and the interpreter backtracks to the first expression. (There's never a new way to satisfy a **not** when it fails.)

5. Backtracking into a predicate expression satisfied previously by a rule means that the interpreter must go to the last (rightmost) expression on the right

side of the rule and see if it can find another match there. But there is no other boss of the sales department so it must now backtrack to the first expression of the rule, **department(E,D)**, with unbound **B** and **E**.

6. Fortunately for this there is another choice: **E** = **harry** and **D** = **production**.

7. With this success, the interpreter can start moving right again. It considers the second predicate expression in the rule. And it can find a match of **B** = **mary** (remember, **D** = **production** now). So the rule succeeds, and thus the first expression of the query succeeds with **X** = **mary** and **Y** = **harry**.

8. Now in the second query expression, it must check that it is not true that Mary is the boss of Tom. To do this, it tries to prove the **boss** rule fails with first argument **mary** and second argument **tom**.

9. In the first expression on the right side of the rule, it can match **D** to **sales**, but there is no fact that Mary manages the sales department. So the rule fails, and since there is no other rule or fact for the **boss** predicate, the second **boss** expression in the query fails.

10. But since there's a **not** in front of this expression, the whole query succeeds. So **X** = **mary** is the answer we needed.

To help in debugging, most Prolog interpreters will automatically print out abbreviated trace information if you ask. To ask in most Prolog dialects, query the built-in predicate **trace** of no arguments. To stop the tracing, query the built-in predicate **notrace** of no arguments. Some other debugging facilities of most Prolog dialects are described in Appendix D.

4.8 TRANSITIVITY INFERENCES

Certain rule forms occur frequently in artificial intelligence. A very important form states *transitivity* of a two-argument predicate. For instance, consider bosses in an organization. If your boss has a boss in turn, that big boss is your boss too. If that big boss has a boss in turn, that even bigger boss is your boss too. So bossing relationships form chains, and that's transitivity.

Formally, a relationship predicate **r** is transitive if this rule is correct:

r(X,Y) :- r(X,Z), r(Z,Y).

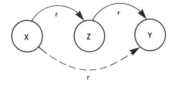

Figure 4-3. General form of transitivity.

(See Figure 4-3.) This says that if predicate r holds from some X to some Z, and also from Z to some Y, the predicate should also hold from X to Y. This rule can be used recursively too; that is, it can refer to itself on its right side, not just to r facts. So the rule can follow indefinitely relationship long chains. For instance, suppose these facts are placed in front of the rule in the Prolog database:

    r(a,b).
    r(b,c).
    r(c,d).

Then if we query

    ?- r(a,d).

no facts match, so the interpreter will use the rule, and will first query

    ?- r(a,Z).

For this, Z can match b in the first fact. The interpreter will then query

    ?- r(b,d).

There's no fact stating this either, so it must use the rule again recursively. For this new call of the rule, X = b and Y = d, so the next query is

    ?- r(b,Z).

This new Z is different from the previous Z, since each recursive call has its own variables (see Appendix B), in the same way that X's in different rules represent different X's. For this new query, the interpreter can bind Z to c since there is a r(b,c) fact, and then the second part of the rule becomes the query

    ?- r(c,d).

That predicate expression is a fact. So the rule succeeds in proving r(b,d). And thus it succeeds in proving r(a,d), the original query.

Many of the relationship predicates in Section 2.6 are transitive: a_kind_of, part_of, right_of, during, and ancestor, for instance. Some example applications:

- If the Vinson is a kind of carrier, and the carrier is a kind of ship, then the Vinson is a kind of ship.
- If the electrical system is part of the car, and the battery is part of the electrical system, then the battery is part of the car.

- If the Vinson is north of the Enterprise, and the Enterprise is north of the Kennedy, then the Vinson is north of the Kennedy.
- If during the day Monday you had a meeting with your boss, and during the meeting you found out you got promoted, then during the day Monday you found out you got promoted.
- If a number X is greater than a number Y, and Y is greater than a number Z, then X is greater than Z.

And a graphical example is shown in Figure 4-4. Here we are representing facts about a pile of blocks on a table. Block b is above block a, block c is above block b, and block d is above block c. Hence, by transitivity, block d is above block a.

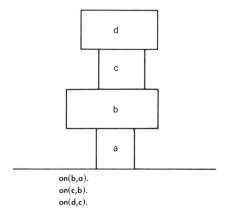

on(b,a).
on(c,b).
on(d,c).

Figure 4-4. Transitivity example.

Why is transitivity important? Because it can save fact space, by figuring out "indirect" facts from a few direct ones. So it reduces redundancy. Transitivity will work best when we store facts relating only the "closest" things—like for part_of, the very smallest thing B that still contains thing A. That's because transitivity explains relationships between things farther apart from relationships between things closer together, not the other way around.

4.9 INHERITANCE INFERENCES

An even more important rule form for artificial intelligence is the *inheritance* form. Consider a bureaucratic organization. If it has only one business address, then that is the business address of all the employees. It wouldn't make sense for a computer to keep a separate business address fact for each employee; that would mean a lot of unnecessary facts. Instead it should store a single address fact with the name of the organization, and reason from that. This reasoning is called inheritance; we say the address *inherits* from organization to employee.

Inheritance always involves two predicates, generally a property predicate and a relationship predicate. Formally, we say property predicate p inherits with respect to relationship predicate r if either of these rules is correct:

p(X,Value) :- r(X,Y), p(Y,Value).
p(X,Value) :- r(Y,X), p(Y,Value).

(See Figure 4-5.) That is, we can prove that property p of X has value Value if we can prove that Y is related to X by predicate r, and Y does have value Value for property p. (This generalizes the rule for predicate color_object in Section 4.1.) Sometimes we use the term "inheritance" when p is a relationship predicate too. Like the transitivity rule, the inheritance rule can be used recursively—that is, the p on the right side can use the rule itself to achieve its ends—but this isn't too common because the r predicate can recurse too.

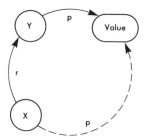

Figure 4-5. General form of inheritance.

Inheritance frequently occurs when the relationship predicate (r in the preceding) is a_kind_of. That is, if you want to know some property p of some X, find some Y that X is an example of, and Y's value is X's value too. Some examples:

- If people are animals, and animals eat food, then people eat food.
- If the Enterprise is a kind of ship, and ships float on water, then the Enterprise floats on water.

But inheritance can occur with relationship predicates besides a_kind_of:

- If the hood is part of my car's body, and my car's body is gray, then the hood is gray too.
- If the U.S. Navy is part of the U.S. Government, and the U.S. Government is everywhere mired in bureaucratic inefficiency, then the U.S. Navy is everywhere mired in bureaucratic inefficiency.
- If the Enterprise is at Norfolk, and Captain Kirk is on the Enterprise, then Captain Kirk is at Norfolk.

And a semantic network example is shown in Figure 4-6. Here we have facts about a particular truck called truck_4359 and its battery. The truck has a loca-

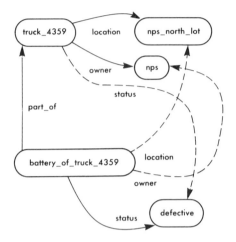

Figure 4-6. Inheritance example.

tion (nps_north_lot) and an owner (nps). These properties inherit *downward* to the battery via the **part_of** relationship to the battery, and that's what those two dotted lines from the battery node mean. ("Downward" means from a larger or more general thing to a smaller or more specific thing.) In other words, the location of the battery of a truck comes from the location of the whole truck, and the owner of the battery comes from the owner of the whole truck. Inheritance can also proceed upward from the battery. The status property of the battery (**defective**) inherits upward, because we can say that the truck is defective when its battery is defective. (Note that the inheritance direction need not be the direction of the arrows in the semantic network.)

Generally, properties that represent universal or "for every X" quantification (see Appendix A) inherit downward, while properties that represent existential or "there exists an X" quantification inherit upward. For instance, the "animals eat food" example is downward: this says that for every X an animal, it eats food, and so since people are animals, they eat food too. But consider the property of people that some of them live in North America, i.e. that there exist some people that live in North America. Then since people are animals, some animals live in North America, so that existential property inherits upward.

Inheritance of a property need not be absolute—there can always be exceptions. For instance, the battery may be removed from the truck for repair, so even though the truck location is the NPS north lot, the battery location isn't. For such an exception, the location of the battery can be put into the database in front of the inheritance rule, so a query on the truck's battery location will find the fact first. So an inheritance rule is a *default*, general-purpose advice that can be overridden.

Inheritance is often associated with transitivity, because the interpreter actually follows a transitivity chain to follow an inheritance chain. For instance (see

Figure 4-7), suppose in our Prolog database we have the facts

    a_kind_of(vinson,carrier).
    a_kind_of(carrier,ship).
    a_kind_of(ship,vehicle).
    purpose(vehicle,transportation).

and, after them, a rule for inheritance of **purpose** with respect to **a_kind_of**:

    purpose(X,V) :- a_kind_of(X,Y), purpose(Y,V).

Suppose we query:

    ?- purpose(vinson,P).

The facts don't match, so the rule will be used, and the interpreter will query itself:

    ?- a_kind_of(vinson,Y).

and Y = carrier is a solution. So now the interpreter handles the second half of the rule, and queries itself with:

    ?- purpose(carrier,V).

But there's no fact matching this, so the rule must be used recursively. So the interpreter asks itself:

    ?- a_kind_of(carrier,Y).

(note this is a different Y variable than before—every recursive call has its own local variables), gets Y = ship, and then asks:

    ?- purpose(ship,V).

This requires the rule again, so it asks recursively

    ?- a_kind_of(ship,Y).

giving Y = vehicle, and then finally

    ?- purpose(vehicle,V).

which can match the given fact with V = transportation. So that's the purpose of
ships, carriers, and the Vinson, too. So we seem to have proved an implicit
a_kind_of relationship here (the left dotted line in Figure 4-7) as well as a purpose
property (the right dotted line).

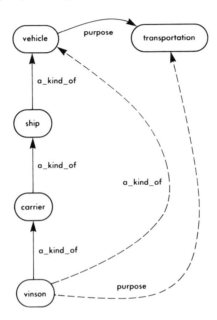

Figure 4-7. Example of both transitivity
and inheritance.

Thus inheritance is useful for the same reason as transitivity: it can extrapo-
late an explicit set of facts to a much larger implicit set of facts, by inferences with
rules. It usually makes sense, then, to only store nonredundant property facts that
can't be inherited (though it won't give wrong answers to store redundant information, just increase the size of the database and slow other queries a little). So we
typically should store property facts about properties for the *most general* things
having those properties. This is because inheritance usually goes downward from
more general things to more specific things.

4.10 SOME IMPLEMENTATION PROBLEMS FOR TRANSITIVITY AND INHERITANCE

Unfortunately, peculiarities of Prolog interpreters can prevent transitivity and
inheritance rules from working properly. The problem is a possible *infinite loop*, a
frequent danger in Prolog programming. An infinite loop is when the same thing is
done over and over forever when trying to answer a query. Typically, a rule calls
itself forever or a set of rules call one another in cycle forever. (A good clue is the

error message "Out of stack space" when running a simple program.) You can get into infinite loops in other programming languages too, but it's easier with Prolog because of its emphasis on recursion and complicated backtracking.

To avoid infinite loops for inheritance, we must pay careful attention to database order. We must put any rules about inheriting values for some property after facts about values of that property. We should also use

p(X,Value) :- r(X,Y), p(Y,Value).

instead of

p(X,Value) :- p(Y,Value), r(X,Y).

The second rule can cause an infinite loop in which p continually calls itself with the same arguments. This won't happen at first, if facts that can match the p query come before this rule in the Prolog database; but whenever the proper answer is no (either when the only possible answer to the query is no, or when we type enough semicolons after other answers), the interpreter will recurse forever instead of saying no. This is because Prolog executes *top-down* like other programming languages: the left side of a rule is matched to some query, and then the right side provides new things to match. So be careful with inheritance rules. In fact, as much British detective fiction demonstrates, inheritances can lead to murder.

But it's tougher to eliminate the infinite loop with the transitivity rule:

r(X,Y) :- r(X,Z), r(Z,Y).

This works fine when the queried r relationship is provable from the facts, but will never say no when r is unprovable. For instance, query

?- r(a,b).

won't say no when there are no facts in the database involving either a or b: the first predicate expression on the right side of the rule has no choice but to call on this rule itself. Here reordering the expressions on the right side of the rule won't change anything, because both have predicate r. Instead we must rewrite the rule as two, and use another predicate name, one for queries only. For instance, consider transitivity for the boss relationship, where boss(X,Y) means that person X is the boss of person Y. To describe indirect bosses, we'll use a new predicate superior of two arguments:

superior(X,Y) :- boss(X,Y).
superior(X,Y) :- boss(X,Z), superior(Z,Y).

This will avoid the infinite loop because the only recursion is in the second rule, and the form of the second rule is the same as the first (better) form for inheritance rules given previously.

A similar trick can be used to state symmetry or *commutativity* of a two-argument predicate. Examples of commutative predicates are the **equals** predicate for numbers, the "distance-between" predicate for places, and the "is-friends-with" predicate for people. The obvious rule can easily cause infinite loops:

    p(X,Y) :- p(Y,X).

Querying a **p2** instead avoids this problem:

    p2(X,Y) :- p(X,Y).
    p2(X,Y) :- p(Y,X).

provided we don't use **p2** in a recursive rule itself.

4.11 A LONGER EXAMPLE: SOME TRAFFIC LAWS_____

Rules can do many things. As we have seen, rules can define new predicates and extend the power of old predicates. Rules can also state policies, prescriptions of what to do in particular situations. Here is an example of the representation of California traffic laws. These are the laws about signal lights, for both vehicles and pedestrians, from the *California Driver's Handbook*, 1985. The letters in brackets are paragraph codes for later reference.

> [A] New Signals-Note: California is adopting red arrows and yellow arrows in addition to green arrows, as signals for vehicle traffic. This is what the colors of traffic lights mean: A red light or arrow means "STOP" until the green appears. A flashing RED traffic light or arrow means exactly the same as a stop sign, namely STOP! But after stopping, proceed when safe, observing the right-of-way rules.
>
> [B] A GREEN light or arrow means "GO," but you must let any vehicles or pedestrians remaining in the intersection when the signal changes to green, get through before you move ahead. Look to be sure that all cross traffic has stopped before you enter the intersection.
>
> [C] A YELLOW light or arrow warns you that the red signal is about to appear. When you see the yellow light or arrow, you should stop if you can do so safely. If you can't stop, look out for vehicles that may enter the intersection when the light changes. A flashing YELLOW light or arrow is a warning of a hazard. Slow down and be especially alert.
>
> [D] A lighted GREEN ARROW, by itself or with a RED, GREEN or YELLOW light, means you may make the turn indicated by the green arrow. But give the right-of-way to pedestrians and vehicles which are moving as permit-

ted by the lights. The green arrow pointing left allows you to make a "protected" left turn; oncoming traffic is stopped by a red light as long as the green arrow is lighted.

[E] If the green arrow is replaced by a flashing yellow light or arrow, slow down and use caution; make the move which the green arrow would permit, only when safe for you and others.

[F] If the green arrow is replaced by a flashing red light or arrow, stop for either signal; then go ahead when it's safe to do so.

[G] NEW SIGNALS—Note: California is adopting international symbols to guide pedestrians at street crossings. An upraised hand (orange) means the same as the "WAIT" or "DON'T WALK" sign. A walking person symbol (white) means the same as the "WALK" sign.

[H] Special signs for walkers: The "DON'T WALK" or "WAIT" or upraised hand sign, if flashing, warns the walker that it is safe to cross, first yielding to any vehicles which were still in the crossing when the light changed.

[I] At a crossing where there are no special pedestrian signals, walkers must obey the red, yellow, or green lights or arrows. But walkers facing a green arrow must not cross the street.

We can represent the preceding text as a set of Prolog rules in four groups: rules about arrows, rules about regular lights, rules about pedestrians, and *default* rules (the last three action rules). As we said, defaults are weak prescriptions for general cases, only used if more specific advice cannot be found; for instance, the last default rule says that if nothing prevents you from going forward, go forward.

In listing these rules, we follow a standard Prolog convention of putting blank lines between groups of rules with the same left-side predicate name; this makes reading long programs easier. We also use comments; anything between the symbols /* and */ is treated as a comment and ignored by the Prolog interpreter. The codes at the beginning of lines reference the relevant paragraph(s) of the *Driver's Handbook* text. Note that the text and rules do not correspond exactly; in fact, some "obvious" rules included are nowhere in the text. What's "obvious" to people isn't always so obvious to computers.

```
/* ————— Rules for arrow lights ————— */
/* A */ action(car,stop) :- light(yellow_arrow,Direction),
  safe_stop_possible.
/* D,E */ action(car,yield_and_leftturn) :-
  light(yellow_arrow,left), not(safe_stop_possible).
/* D,E */ action(car,yield_and_rightturn) :-
  light(yellow_arrow,right), not(safe_stop_possible).
/* D */ action(car,yield_and_leftturn) :- light(green_arrow,left).
/* D */ action(car,yield_and_rightturn) :- light(green_arrow,right).
```

```
/* ————— Rules for regular lights ————— */
/* A */ action(car,stop) :- light(red,steady).
/* A */ action(car,stop_and_go) :- light(red,flashing).
/* C */ action(car,stop) :- light(yellow,steady),
  safe_stop_possible.
/* C */ action(car,yield_and_go) :- light(yellow,steady),
  not(safe_stop_possible).
/* B */ action(car,yield_and_go) :- light(green,steady).
/* C */ action(car,slow) :- light(yellow,flashing).
/* A */ action(car,stop) :- light(red_arrow,Direction).
/* ————— Rules for pedestrian lights ————— */
action(pedestrian,stop) :- pedhalt(steady).
/* I */ action(pedestrian,stop) :- not(pedsignals), greenfacing.
action(pedestrian,stop) :- pedhalt(flashing), safe_stop_possible.
/* H */ action(pedestrian,yield_and_go) :- pedhalt(flashing),
  not(safe_stop_possible).
/* ————— Default rules ————— */
/* I */ action(pedestrian,A) :- not(pedsignals), not(greenfacing),
  action(car,A).
action(car,go) :- not (caution_needed(car)).
action(pedestrian,go) :- not(caution_needed(pedestrian)).
/* ————— Rules defining the special terms ————— */
/* G */ pedhalt(State) :- light(wait,State).
/* G */ pedhalt(State) :- light(dont_walk,State).
/* G */ pedhalt(State) :- light(hand,State).

/* G */ pedgo(State) :- light(walk,State).
/* G */ pedgo(State) :- light(walking_person,State).

pedsignals :- pedhalt(State).
pedsignals :- pedgo(State).

greenfacing :- light(green_arrow,right), not(clockwise_cross).
greenfacing :- light(green_arrow,left), clockwise_cross.

caution_needed(X) :- action(X,stop); action(X,stop_and_go);
  action(X,yield_and_go); action(X,yield_and_rightturn);
  action(X,yield_and_leftturn).
```

To understand programs like this, it's often a good idea to draw a *predicate hierarchy* (actually, a lattice) showing which predicates refer to which other predicates within their definitions. This helps distinguish *high-level* predicates about abstract things from *low-level* predicates about details. Figure 4-8 shows the predicate hierarchy for this program.

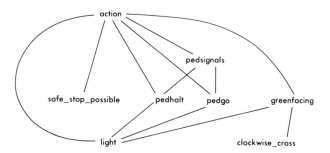

Figure 4-8. Predicate hierarchy for the traffic lights program.

The rules of this program define legal actions in particular traffic situations. To use them, we query the predicate **action** with unbound variables (outputs) for one or both of its arguments. The first argument to **action** represents whether you are a pedestrian or in a car, and the second argument represents a legal action in the situation. So for instance, **action(car,stop)** means that it is legal for the car to stop. The most useful way to query **action** is to make the first argument an input and the second argument an output. So to know what is legal for a car, query

?- action(car,X).

and the variable **X** will be bound to a description of some action legal with the current facts; to know what is legal for a pedestrian, query

?- action(pedestrian,X).

To check if some particular action is legal, fill in both arguments. If a sequence of actions is legal, instead of just one, the program has the characters "_and_" between the actions to form one long word.

To describe a situation, three kinds of facts are needed:

- **light(<kind-of-light>,<light-status>)**: this is the main kind of fact. The first argument is either:

    red (a circular red light)
    yellow (a circular yellow light)
    green (a circular green light)
    red_arrow
    yellow_arrow
    green_arrow
    wait (the word "wait" lit up)
    dont_walk (the words "don't walk" lit up)
    hand (a picture of a human palm)
    walk (the word "walk" lit up)
    walking_person (a picture of a walking person)

The second argument describes the condition of the light; this is either **left** or **right** for the arrow lights, and either **steady** or **flashing** for all the other lights.

- **safe_stop_possible**: this predicate of no arguments asserts that you can stop quickly and safely.
- **clockwise_cross**: if you are a pedestrian, this predicate of no arguments asserts that the path by which you will cross a street is clockwise with respect to the center of that street.

For example, here are the facts for when you are in a car approaching an intersection with plenty of room to stop, and you see a steady yellow light and a green arrow light pointing to the left:

```
safe_stop_possible.
light(yellow,steady).
light(green_arrow,left).
```

Rule order matters, since it establishes priorities among actions. Rules for arrows should go before rules for other kinds of lights, because arrows override other lights showing. Within each of the three main groups of rules—arrows, regular lights, and pedestrian lights—the rules for stopping should go first to handle malfunctions of the lights in which more than one light is lit. Finally, defaults should go last, like the last two **action** rules.

4.12 RUNNING THE TRAFFIC LIGHTS PROGRAM

Here are some examples of the program working. Suppose our database is the example facts just given. Suppose we ask what a car can do:

```
?- action(car,X).
```

The first three rules fail because there are no facts about yellow arrows. But a green arrow to the left is visible, so the fourth rule succeeds, and we get

```
X = yield_and_leftturn
```

In other words, in this situation it is legal to yield and then make a left turn. Now if we type a semicolon, the interpreter will try to find an alternative action. It starts from where it left off in the rules, so it next examines the fifth rule. Neither the fifth, sixth, or seventh rules are satisfied by the three facts, but the eighth rule does succeed. So we get

```
X = stop
```

In other words it is legal to stop your car. If we type a semicolon once more, the query will fail (the last action rule fails because it is legal to stop the car, as we just showed). So there are only two alternatives.

For another example, suppose a pedestrian walking along a sidewalk comes to an intersection where they wish to cross the street in a clockwise direction with respect to the center of the intersection. Suppose that in the direction the pedestrian wants to go there is a steady green light and a flashing white picture of a walking person. The representation is:

```
clockwise_cross.
light(green,steady).
light(wait,flashing).
```

To discover what we can do, the query is

```
?- action(pedestrian,X)
```

None of the first twelve rules succeed because the query specifies a pedestrian. The interpreter then considers the four pedestrian rules. For the first of them to succeed, the "wait" light must be steady, but it's flashing. The second fails because the "wait" light is a kind of pedestrian signal, causing the pedsignals predicate to succeed. The third fails because there's no safe_stop_possible fact. But the fourth pedestrian rule succeeds, and we get typed out:

```
X = yield_and_go
```

which recommends to the pedestrian to first yield the right-of-way, then go ahead.

This program should be invoked repeatedly, say every second to decide what to do for that second. And each second something must delete old facts and write new facts into the Prolog database. This general approach is followed by most real-time artificial-intelligence programs. For speed, each updating can be done by a separate concurrent processor, to avoid interfering with inference. Notice that we have ignored the biggest obstacle to making this program practical, the recognizing of lights in the real world. This is addressed in the "vision" subarea of artificial intelligence.

4.13 DECLARATIVE PROGRAMMING

The traffic lights program may not seem much like programs in other programming languages. Programming in Prolog (and much artificial-intelligence programming, whatever the language) is different in style from most programming. The style is programs in lots of small modular pieces, pieces smaller than the usual subroutines and procedures of other languages. The emphasis is on writing correct pieces, and not on putting the pieces together. In writing and debugging each piece, the emphasis is on whether it makes sense by itself and whether it is logically correct, not how it is used—the "what" instead of the "how." This is called *declarative* programming.[1]

This bothers some students. They feel they don't really understand artificial-intelligence programs because there's often no clear, easily understandable sequence in which programs do things. Prolog interpreters for instance work from top to bottom through facts and rules with the same predicate name, but for each new predicate in a query, they jump to the first occurrence of that predicate name, and jump around in quite complicated ways when they backtrack. And Prolog's operation represents one of the simpler ways to do artificial-intelligence programs, as we'll see in Chapter 6. A programmer accustomed to flowcharts may find this bewildering.

In reply, one can say that artificial intelligence solves hard problems, problems on which conventional software-engineering techniques (including numerical ones) struggle, and for which artificial-intelligence methods seem to be the only ones that work. And there are no clear criteria for "intelligent behavior," so in designing intelligent programs it would seem more important to ensure that the individual pieces of the program make sense rather than imposing some grand (necessarily controversial) organizing scheme. Usually, researchers don't want artificial-intelligence programs to be brilliant, just not dumb, and concentrating on the pieces helps avoid being dumb. Also, the well-known software technique of recursion (see Appendix B and Chapter 5) is best understood in a declarative way, and artificial intelligence often uses recursion.

This still may not sound too reassuring, but remember there are lots of ways to program. As we say in California, stay mellow.

KEYWORDS

> *rule*
> *left side of a rule*
> *right side of a rule*
> *local variable in a rule*
> *parameter variable of a rule*
> *hierarchies of rules*
> *postponed binding*
> *transitivity of a predicate*
> *inheritance of a predicate*
> *commutativity of a predicate*
> *infinite loop*
> *database order*
> *default*
> *declarative programming*

[1] It's also close to what is called *nondeterminism* or *nondeterministic programming*.

EXERCISES

4-1. (E) What's the difference between :- and logical implication? In other words, what's the difference between a :- b. and the logical statement "If b is true, then a is true."

4-2. (A)

  (a) Suppose in a database you had a rule whose right side was guaranteed to be always true. How could you get the effect of such a rule in a simpler way?

  (b) Suppose in a database you had a rule whose right side was always guaranteed to be false for any assignment of bindings. How could you get the effect of such a rule in a simpler way?

4-3. Write rules for reasoning about genealogies (or "family trees"). Assume the genealogy is represented by facts of the single four-argument form

child(<name_of_father>,<name_of_mother>,<name_of_child>,<sex>).

Assume all married people have children. Define the following new predicates based on the child facts:

  father(X,Y), meaning X is the father of Y
  mother(X,Y), meaning X is the mother of Y
  son(X,Y), meaning X is the son of Y
  grandfather(X,Y), meaning X is the grandfather of Y
  sister(X,Y), meaning X is the sister of Y
  uncle(X,Y), meaning X is the uncle of Y
  ancestor(X,Y), meaning X is the ancestor of Y
  half_sister(X,Y), meaning X is the half-sister of Y

4-4. (P) Figure 4-9 is a picture of three stacks of blocks on a table.

  (a) Represent in Prolog the facts describing the relationships between the blocks. Use two predicates, one that says a block is on another, and one that says a block is immediately to the left of another. Only give facts of the second type for blocks at the bottom of piles.

  (b) Type your facts into a file.

  (c) Now ask the Prolog interpreter:

    • what blocks are on block B;
    • what blocks block A is on;
    • what blocks are on other blocks;
    • what blocks are on blocks that are immediately to the left of other blocks?

  (d) Define a new predicate **above** which is true when a block is anywhere in the stack above another block. Define a new predicate **stackleft** when a block is in a stack that is immediately to the left of the stack of another block. Put these into your file, and load the whole thing.

(e) Now ask the Prolog interpreter:

- what blocks are above other blocks;
- what blocks are either above block F or in a stack immediately to the left of its stack;
- what blocks are above other blocks but are not in a stack immediately to the left of any block?

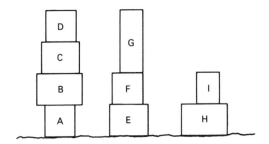

Figure 4-9. Some blocks on a table.

4-5. (A) Consider the rules:

a(X) :- not(b(X)).

b(X) :- not(c(X)).

Assuming predicate b is never referenced except in the preceding, and is never queried directly, and there are no facts with predicate b, would it be equivalent to define a single rule

a(X) :- c(X).

Why?

4-6. (A)

(a) Consider the following to be true:

Clint is the mayor.
The mayor is respected.

From this we can conclude that:

Clint is respected.

But now suppose:

Clint is the mayor.
The mayor is an elected office.

From this we would seem to be able to conclude:

Clint is an elected office.

What is the fallacy in reasoning?

(b) Consider the following to be true:

Clint is a movie star.
Clint is mayor.

From this it makes sense to conclude:

A movie star is mayor.

But now suppose as true:

John is a little stupid.
John is mayor.

It is fallacious then to conclude:

A little stupid is mayor.

What is the fallacy?

4-7. (A,E) Explain using Prolog concepts the different meanings of the word "and" in the following.

(a) A food crop is anything that is a plant and provides substantial human nutrition.

(b) A department chairman is a professor and is responsible to the provost.

(c) To put out a fire, your options are to apply flame retardants and to let it burn itself out.

(d) Tom and Sue are managers.

(e) Tom and Sue are friends.

4-8. Consider this query:

?- a(X,Y), b(X,Y).

used with this database:

a(1,2).
a(3,5).
a(R,S) :- b(R,S), b(S,R).

b(1,3).
b(2,3).
b(3,T) :- b(2,T), b(1,T).

Without using the computer, what is the first answer found to the query?

4-9. Inheritance involves a thing and a property. Suppose the thing is a computer program. Give two different examples of relationship predicates that are involved in inheritance, and the corresponding properties.

4-10. (A) Consider the type predicate **some** of two arguments <set> and <property> which is true whenever some members of <set> have <property>.

So for instance some(people,american) means that some people are American. Consider inheritance involving the "set containment" relationship predicate.

(a) Does some inherit upward (to an including set), downward (to an included set), both, or neither? (Note: Inheritance is only "yes" or "no," never "maybe.")

(b) Write the inheritance for part (a) as a Prolog rule.

(c) Consider the similar predicate all which is true whenever all members of <set> have <property>. So for instance all(employees,american) means that all employees are American. Does it inherit upward, downward, both, or neither?

(d) Consider the similar predicate most which is true whenever most members of <set> have <property>. Does it inherit upward, downward, both, or neither?

4-11. (R,A) Suppose we have facts about the components of a car. Suppose:

- front_of(X,Y) means part X of the car is in front of part Y (toward the headlights);

- inside_of(X,Y) means part X of the car is inside (contained in) part Y.

(a) Is inside_of transitive?

(b) Does front_of inherit with respect to inside_of? If so, in which direction?

(c) Why could it be more useful for a program to have a description of where things are under the hood of a car in terms of front_of, right_of, and above facts instead of in terms of Cartesian (x, y, and z) coordinates?

4-12. Consider the accounting department of some organization you know. For each of the following properties, say whether it inherits (1) upward, to some entity including the accounting department, (2) downward, to some entity included in the accounting department, (3) both directions, or (4) neither direction.

(a) There are crooks in it.

(b) Half the employees in it are crooks.

(c) Regulations controlling crookedness are enforced.

(d) All crooks in it have been caught and punished.

4-13. (R,A,P)

(a) Represent the following facts in Prolog (binary-relationship predicates are recommended). Represent what the words mean, not what they say; each different word shouldn't necessarily be a different predicate name or argument. Type your Prolog facts into a computer file.

> An Acme hotplate has a cord and a body.
> Part of the body of an Acme hotplate is the heating element.
> The heating element is metal.
> Another part of the body of an Acme hotplate is the cover.
> The cover has a knob.

Plastic is always used for knobs.
One of the things a cord consists of is a wire.
Metal comprises the wire.
Part of the cord is an insulater.
The insulater is fiber.

(b) Start up the Prolog interpreter, load the file, and ask

- what things are stated to contain metal;
- what things are stated to be parts of the body of a hot plate?

(c) Define rules for transitivity of **part_of** and upward inheritance of material with respect to **part_of**, rules that can be applied to your answer to part (a). Put these in the file.

(d) Now ask:

- what things contain plastic;
- what things do not contain fiber;
- what things containing metal also contain fiber?

4-14. Suppose we have **a_kind_of** facts about 31 objects. Suppose by transitivity on these facts we can show that object **a** is a kind of object **b**. Suppose the facts have no redundancy (two different routes between the same two objects by following arrows) and no cycles (ways to leave an object and return by following arrows).

(a) What is the minimum number of times that you could successfully use the recursive transitivity rule (the rule, not any fact) proving this? Use the two-rule form in Section 4.10.

(b) What is the maximum number?

(c) Suppose 30 of the 31 objects appear once and only once each as the first argument to the **a_kind_of** facts. Suppose 16 of the 31 objects never appear as a second argument and suppose the rest appear exactly twice, each as a second argument. Of the remaining 15 that do appear as a second argument, 8 of them appear in facts with the 16; of the remaining 7, 4 appear in facts with the 8; of the remaining 3, 2 appear in facts with the 4; and the remaining 1 appears in facts with the 2. What data structure does the semantic network resemble?

(d) For the situation in part (c), what is the maximum number of times the recursive transitivity rule could be successfully used to prove that object **a** is a kind of object **b**?

(e) Suppose **b** has property **v**, and suppose that **a** inherits this value because **a** is a kind of **b**. Assume as before there are 31 objects total. What is the maximum number of times the inheritance rule (of the form of the first one in Section 4.9) could be successfully used proving this?

4-15. (a) Represent the following as Prolog facts and rules (definitions). (Hint: Represent what these mean, not what they literally say.) Be as general as you can.

A VW Rabbit is a VW.
Tom's car is a VW Rabbit.
Dick's car is a VW Rabbit.
A VW has an electrical system.
Part of the electrical system is the alternator.
The alternator is defective on every VW.

(b) Write Prolog inference rules that will allow conclusion that Tom's car or
Dick's car is defective. Hint: You need to define transitivity and inheritance for concepts in part (a).

(c) Prove that Dick's car is defective, given the facts and rules of parts (a)
and (b). (Don't prove it the way a Prolog interpreter would—omit dead
ends.)

4-16. (P) Write Prolog definitions for the California speed laws that follow, as
extracted from the *California Driver's Handbook*. Your top-level predicate
should be called limit, with one argument, an output variable. The program
should set that variable to the legal maximum speed under the current conditions. The current conditions should be specified as Prolog facts.

Don't worry too much about the predicates you use here; there's much room
for personal taste. Instead, worry about the *order* of Prolog definitions and
facts. Note you must handle the situation in which you may have seen
several road signs recently, some perhaps contradictory, and you must decide
which ones apply. Assume though that any other facts (like the presence of
children) apply to the immediate vicinity. Warning: you'll find the laws
unclear about certain situations; just pick something reasonable in those cases.

"The maximum speed limit in California is 55 miles per hour. Other
speed limit signs tell you the highest speed at which you can expect to
drive with safety in the places where the signs are set up...."

"In business or residence districts, 25 miles per hour is the speed limit
unless signs show other limits. When you see a "SCHOOL" sign, the
speed limit is 25 miles per hour while children are outside or are crossing the street during school hours. The 25 mph limit applies at all
times when a school ground is unfenced and children are outside, even
though the road is posted for a higher speed. Lower speed must be
obeyed if posted...."

"When you come within 100 feet of a railroad crossing and you cannot
see the tracks for 400 feet in both directions, the limit is 15 mph. This
limit does not apply if the crossing is controlled by gates, a warning signal or a flagman."

"The 15 mph limit also applies at blind intersections where you cannot
see for 100 feet both ways during the last 100 feet before crossing,
unless yield or stop signs on the side streets give you the right of way—
also in any alley."

As tests, run the program to find the limit at each point in the following scenario:

(a) You enter a residential district. A sign says 55 mph.

(b) You are still in the residential district. You come to a SCHOOL sign, and students are on the sidewalks. The time is within school hours.

(c) A speed limit sign says 35 mph. You enter an alley.

4-17. (E) Explain in what ways legal definitions are different from Prolog definitions. Is this a weakness of legal definitions, a weakness of Prolog, both, or neither? Should the two evolve closer together?

4-18. (E) Definitions of terms in politics don't seem to be very much like Prolog terms. For instance, what one nation calls an unprovoked military attack may be considered by the attacking nation as "claiming what is rightfully theirs" or "preventing terrorism." These excuses are not arbitrary but are supported by dictionary definitions. What makes political definitions so much more slippery than the Prolog definitions of this chapter?

4-19. There are several part-whole relationships, even for the same object. Consider a piece of rock consisting of 10^{24} molecules of silicon dioxide, whose chemical formula is SiO_2.

(a) Give an interpretation of **part_of** for which the **color** property inherits to any part of this rock.

(b) Give an interpretation of **part_of** for which the **number_of_molecules** property inherits to any subpart.

4-20. Consider the following proof that God does not exist. Take the following statement as true from the definition of God:

God saves those who can't save themselves.

(a) Write this as a Prolog rule whose left side and right side both refer to a **saves** predicate of two arguments.

(b) Suppose the person saved is God. Show the bindings in the rule, and explain what the rule becomes in this case.

(c) As you can see, there's a serious logical problem here. Does this prove God doesn't exist? Why?

5

ARITHMETIC
AND LISTS IN PROLOG

Before going any further, we need to introduce two additional features of Prolog that will come in handy in writing future programs, arithmetic and lists. These give rules new capabilities. As we've seen already, rules can:

1. Define new predicates in terms of existing predicates
2. Extend the power of existing predicates (as with inheritance rules)
3. Recommend what to do in a situation (as with the traffic lights program)

To these, we'll now add:

4. Quantify and rank things
5. Store, retrieve, and manipulate sets and sequences of data items

5.1 ARITHMETIC COMPARISONS

Prolog has built-in arithmetic comparison predicates. But their predicate expressions are written differently from those shown so far: they're written in the *infix* notation of mathematics. The predicate name is a symbol that comes between the arguments, like this:

3 > 4 means 3 is greater than 4

15 = 15 means 15 equals 15

X < Y means X is less than Y

Z > = 4 means Z is greater than or equal to 4

PPPP = < 3 means PPPP is less than or equal to 3

We'll usually put spaces around infix symbols to make them easier to see, but it's not required. As an example, here's the definition of a predicate that checks if a number is positive:

positive(X) :- X > 0.

With this definition in our database, it could be used like this:

?- positive(3).
yes
?- positive(-6).
no

Here's the definition of a predicate that checks if its first argument is a number lying in the range from its second to its third argument, assuming all arguments are bound:

in_range(X,Y,Z) :- X > = Y, X = < Z.

Using this definition, the query

?- in_range(3,0,10).

gives the response yes.

5.2 ARITHMETIC ASSIGNMENT _____

Like any computer language, Prolog has arithmetic computations and assignment statements. Arithmetic assignment is done by expressions with the infix **is** predicate. Querying these peculiar expressions has the side effect of binding some variable to the result of some arithmetic computation. For instance

X is (2 * 3) + 7

binds (assigns) X to the value 13 (2 times 3 plus 7). The thing to the left of the **is** must be a variable name, and the stuff to the right must be an algebraic formula of variables and numeric constants, something that evaluates to a number. The algebraic formula is written in standard infix form, with operations + (addition), -

(subtraction), * (multiplication), and / (division). We'll often put spaces around these symbols to make them more readable, but spaces aren't required. The algebraic formula can have variables only if they're bound to values, as in

    Y is 2, X is Y * Y.

where Y is first bound to 2, and then X is bound to 4. A practical example is this definition of the square of a number, intended to be a function predicate:

    square(X,Y) :- Y is X * X.

If this rule is in the Prolog database, then if we query

    ?- square(3,Y).

(that is, if we ask what the square of 3 is), the Prolog interpreter will type

    Y = 9

Notice that since predicate expressions aren't functions in Prolog, we can't write anything like

    f(X,Y) + g(X,Z)

even if f and g are function predicates, because expressions only succeed or fail; expressions don't have "values." Instead, to add the two function values we must say something like

    f(X,Y), g(X,Z), T is Y + Z

Another warning: don't confuse = with is. The = is a purely logical comparison of whether two things are equal. (Originally intended for numbers, it usually also works for words.) The **is** works like an operation, an arithmetic assignment statement, that figures out a value and binds a variable to it.

5.3 REVERSING THE "IS"

A serious weakness of arithmetic, which makes it different from everything else in Prolog we've talked about so far, is that it isn't multiway or reversible. For instance, if we have the preceding definition of square in our database, and we query

    ?- square(X,9).

wondering what number squared is 9, the interpreter will refuse to do anything because the right side of the is statement refers to an unbound variable. This is different from having a bunch of arithmetic facts in prefix form like

```
square(0,1).
square(1,1).
square(2,4).
square(3,9).
```

for which we could query square(3,Y) or square(X,9) or even square(X,Y) and get an answer. Similarly, for the preceding definition of positive, the query

```
?- positive(X).
```

won't work: the interpreter can only do a > comparison for things that are numbers or variables bound to numbers. So it will complain and refuse to do anything.

The Prolog interpreter's excuse for its behavior is that function inversion and other such *multiway reasoning* are hard to do in general, and sometimes impossible. A square of a number is easy to compute, but a square root requires iterative approximation and a lot more code. And there are an infinity of positive numbers; where should an interpreter start when asked to give one? Artificial intelligence requires flexible reasoning capable of going in many different directions—people seem to do it. So it's desirable to get around the interpreter's limitations.

One way is to provide additional rules for a predicate definition. Helpful in this is the built-in Prolog predicate var of one argument, which succeeds if that argument is an unbound variable, and fails otherwise. As an example of its use, consider a better_add predicate of three arguments which says the sum of the first two arguments is the third argument. If all three arguments are bound (inputs), then it checks the addition. If the first two arguments are bound, it binds the third to their sum. If the first and third arguments are bound, it binds the second to the difference of the third and the first. Similarly if the second and third arguments are bound, it binds the first to the difference of the third and second. Here's the code (Z is a temporary-storage variable):

```
better_add(X,Y,S) :- not(var(X)), not(var(Y)), not(var(S)),
    Z is X + Y, Z = S.
better_add(X,Y,S) :- not(var(X)), not(var(Y)), var(S),
    S is X + Y.
better_add(X,Y,S) :- not(var(X)), var(Y), not(var(S)),
    Y is S - X.
better_add(X,Y,S) :- var(X), not(var(Y)), not(var(S)),
    X is S - Y.
```

We can't handle the situation in which two arguments are unbound; then there's an infinite number of possibilities for the bindings. But at least the preceding handles three more cases than the Prolog is can handle by itself.

The in_range predicate of Section 5.1 can provide another example of a predicate enhancement. That predicate checked whether its first argument (an input number) was between the second and third arguments (input numbers too). We can improve in_range so that an unbound first argument will make it *generate* a number between other two arguments, and generate further numbers on backtracking. To make things easier, we'll assume all numbers will be integers. Here's the definition of this integer_in_range:

```
integer_in_range(X,Y,Z) :- not(var(X)), not(var(Y)), not(var(Z)),
    X > = Y, X = < Z.
integer_in_range(X,Y,Z) :- var(X), not(var(Y)), not(var(Z)),
    Y = < Z, X is Y.
integer_in_range(X,Y,Z) :- Y = < Z, Y2 is Y + 1,
    integer_in_range(X,Y2,Z).
```

This is a *tail-recursive* program of a form we'll use many times in this chapter. (Again, see Appendix B to review recursion.) The first rule handles the case handled before. The second rule says if X is unbound and Y and Z are bound, and we want to generate an integer on the range Y to Z, we can always pick Y. Otherwise (if a semicolon is typed), the third rule is used. It "crosses out" Y from the range by increasing the lower limit of the range by 1, and generates an integer from this new, narrower range. If the range ever decreases so much that it disappears, all the rules fail. So if we query

```
?- integer_in_range(X,1,10).
```

the interpreter first replies X = 1; then if we type a semicolon, X = 2; then if we type a semicolon, X = 3; and so on up to 10.

5.4 LISTS IN PROLOG

Another important feature of Prolog is linked-lists. Every argument in a predicate expression in a query must be anticipated and planned for. To handle sets and sequences of varying or unknown length, we need something else: linked-lists, which we'll henceforth call just *lists*.

Lists have always been important in artificial intelligence. Lisp, the other major artificial-intelligence programming language, is almost entirely implemented with lists—even programs are lists in Lisp. The extra space that lists need compared to arrays (see Appendix C) is more than compensated for in artificial-intelligence applications by the flexibility possible.

Square brackets indicate a Prolog list, with commas separating items. For example:

```
[monday,tuesday,wednesday,thursday,friday,saturday,sunday]
```

(Don't confuse square brackets, "[]," with parentheses, "()"; they're completely different in Prolog. Brackets group lists and parentheses group arguments.) Lists can be values of variables just like words and numbers. Suppose we have the following facts:

```
weekdays([monday,tuesday,wednesday,thursday,friday]).
weekends([saturday,sunday]).
```

Then to ask what days are weekdays, we type the query

> ?- weekdays(Days).

and the answer is

> Days = [monday,tuesday,wednesday,thursday,friday]

We can also bind variables to items of lists. For instance, if we query

> ?- weekends([X,Y]).

with the preceding facts in the database, we get

> X = saturday, Y = sunday

But that last query requires that the weekends list have exactly two items; if we query

> ?- weekends([X,Y,Z]).

we get no because the query list can't be made to match the data list by some set of bindings.

We can work with lists of arbitrary length by the standard methods for linked-pointer list manipulation. We can refer to any list of one or more items as [X|Y], where X is the first or front item and Y is the rest of the list (that is, the list of everything but the first item in the same order).[1] We'll call | the *bar* symbol. Note that [X|Y] is quite different from [X,Y]; the first can have any nonzero number of items, whereas the second must have exactly two items. Note also that X and Y are different data types in [X|Y]; X is a single item, but Y is a list of items. So [X|Y] represents an uneven division of a list.

Here are some examples with the previous weekdays and weekends facts.

> ?- weekdays([A|L]).
> A = monday, L = [tuesday,wednesday,thursday,friday]
>
> ?- weekdays([A,B,C|L]).
> A = monday, B = tuesday, C = wednesday, L = [thursday,friday]
>
> ?- weekends([A,B|L]).
> A = saturday, B = sunday, L = []

The [] is the list of zero items, the *empty list*.[2]

---

[1] In the language Lisp, X is called the *car* and Y is called *cdr* of the list.
[2] Called *nil* in the language Lisp.

5.5 DEFINING SOME LIST-PROCESSING PREDICATES _____

Let's write some famous list-processing programs (summarized in Figure 5-1). Programs requiring many lines of code in conventional programming languages can
often be quite short in Prolog because of its declarative nature. We'll define mostly
function predicates. Following the convention of Section 2.9, the function result is
the last argument of their predicate expressions.

Predicate	Arguments	What it means
first(L,I)	a list, an item	I is the first item of the list L
last(L,I)	a list, an item	I is the last item of the list L
member(I,L)	an item, a list	I is an item somewhere inside the list L
length(L,N)	a list, a number	N is the length of the list L
max(L,N)	a list, a number	N is the largest number in the list of numbers L
delete(I,L1,L2)	an item, a list, a list	L2 is L1 with all occurrences of the I removed from it
append(L1,L2,L3)	a list, a list, a list	L3 is the glueing together of the lists L1 and L2
subset(L1,L2)	a list, a list,	all items in L1 are in L2
sort(L1,L2)	a list, a list	L2 is the sorting of list of numbers L1

Figure 5-1. Classic list-processing predicates defined in this chapter (to be used
in the rest of this book).

First, here's a definition of a predicate that computes the first item of an
indefinitely long list:

first([X|L],X).

This definition is a fact, not a rule—but remember, facts are just rules with no
right side. So X stands for any item, and L stands for any list.
    Here's a definition for the last item of a list:

last([X],X).
last([X|L],X2) :- last(L,X2).

The first line says that the last item of a list of one item is that item. The second
line says the last item of any other nonempty list is the last item of the list formed
by removing the first item. This is a tail-recursive program with the first line the

basis step (simple nonrecursive case) and the second line the *induction step* (recursive case). Tail recursion is the standard way to define list-processing predicates in Prolog, with each recursion chopping one item off a list.

We can use first and last just like the predicate definitions in Chapter 4, to work on data we type in. For instance

```
?- last([monday,tuesday,wednesday,thursday,friday],X).
X = friday
```

We can also use it on lists in the database by doing a database retrieval first. Suppose we have a database fact

```
weekdays([monday,tuesday,wednesday,thursday,friday]).
```

Then we could find out the last weekday by

```
?- weekdays(L), last(L,X).
L = [monday,tuesday,wednesday,thursday,friday], X = friday
```

As another example of a list-processing definition, consider member(X,L) which we want to be true if item X is a member of list L. We can give a complete definition by the following fact and rule (note the order: the recursive part of a definition should usually come after the nonrecursive, to avoid an infinite loop):[3]

```
member(X,[X|L]).
member(X,[Y|L]) :- member(X,L).
```

The fact says that X is a member of any list where it is the first item; there's no need to check the rest of the list then. Otherwise, figure out if X is a member of the rest of the list, and that's the answer. Notice there's no need to give conditions under which member fails, like

```
member(X,[]) :- 1 = 2.
```

Since 1 can never equal 2, this rule never succeeds. But in Prolog, failure when we use a rule means the same thing as no rule at all. So the immediately preceding rule is completely useless.

We just gave a declarative explanation of the member predicate. For a *procedural* explanation (though we emphasize that this is not the best way to under-

---

[3] Recursive list-processing predicate definitions, and many other recursive definitions too, can be made considerably more efficient by Prolog's built-in "cut" predicate (symbolized by !), to be explained in Section 10.7. For instance, a better version of member for most purposes is

```
member(X,[X|L]) :- !.
member(X,[Y|L]) :- member(X,L).
```

stand recursive programs), consider the query

   ?- member(dick,[tom,dick,harry]).

The first line of the member definition fails because dick is not tom. So the second line is used, creating a recursive call

   ?- member(dick,[dick,harry]).

for which the first line succeeds. So the original query gives yes.
   The member definition will also work when the first argument is unbound (an output). Then the program *generates* members of a list in succession under backtracking, something quite useful for artificial-intelligence programs. Consider the query

   ?- member(X,[tom,dick,harry]).

When the interpreter executes this, the first line of the program can match X = tom, and this binding is printed out. If we now type a semicolon, we request a different binding, forcing the interpreter to use the second rule. So this recursive call is executed:

   ?- member(X,[dick,harry]).

And for this new query the first line can succeed, giving the result X = dick. If we type another semicolon, we'll be querying

   ?- member(X,[harry]).

and we'll get X = harry; and if we type yet another semicolon, we'll be querying

   ?- member(X,[]).

and we'll get no.
   Here's a predicate length(L,N) that computes length N of a list L:

length([],0).
length([X|L],N) :- length(L,N2), N is N2 + 1.

Remember, [] represents the *empty list*, the list with no members. The first line says the empty list has length zero. The second line says that the length of any other list is just one more than the length of the list created by removing the first item. For instance

   ?- length([a,b,c,d],N).
   N = 4

Here's a predicate max(L,M) that computes the maximum of a list L of numbers:

```
max([X],X).
max([X|L],X) :- max(L,M), X > M.
max([X|L],M) :- max(L,M), X = < M.
```

The first line says the maximum of a list of one item is that item. The second line says that the first number in a list is the maximum of the list if it's greater than the maximum for the rest of the list. The third line says the maximum of a list is the maximum for all but the first item of the list if neither of the first two rules applies. For instance

```
?- max([3,7,2,6,1],N).
N = 7
```

5.6 LIST-CREATING PREDICATES _____

Suppose we want to delete every occurrence of some item from a list, creating a new list. We can do this with a predicate delete of three arguments: (1) the item X we want to get rid of (an input), (2) the initial list L (an input), and (3) the final list M (an output). And we'll assume that's the only pattern of inputs and outputs we'll ever use. For instance

```
?- delete(b,[b,a,b,b,c],M).
M = [a,c]
```

To define this, we could write (though this use of arithmetic assignment isn't legal in some dialects)

```
delete(X,[],[]).
delete(X,[X|L],M) :- delete(X,L,M).
delete(X,[Y|L],Mnew) :- not(X = Y), delete(X,L,M), Mnew is [Y|M].
```

But there's a better way to write the last rule: we can move the [Y|M] list to the left side. This is good because (1) the is is unnecessary because left sides can also bind variables, and (2) is isn't completely reversible, and we'd like a more multiway program. So we could use instead

```
delete(X,[],[]).
delete(X,[X|L],M) :- delete(X,L,M).
delete(X,[Y|L],[Y|M]) :- not(X = Y), delete(X,L,M).
```

This works the same, even with the third argument unbound, because nothing can be done with the [Y|M] on the left side of the third rule until the right side is exe-

cuted and **M** is bound. So the construction of [Y|M] remains the last thing done by
the third rule.

  You may be puzzled why the not($X = Y$) in the third line is necessary. We
could write

  delete(X,[ ],[ ]).
  delete(X,[X|L],M) :- delete(X,L,M).
  delete(X,[Y|L],[Y|M]) :- delete(X,L,M).

The delete predicate never fails for its first two arguments bound; one of those
three rules must always succeed. So if the second line fails, its left side must be at
fault, and X and Y must be different, right? Yes, but only the *first* time through.
If we ever backtrack into this delete, we'll be in trouble because backtracking
would use the third rule for some situation in which it used the second rule previously. For instance

  ?- delete(b,[a,b,a,b,c],L).
  L = [a,a,c] ;
  L = [a,a,b,c] ;
  L = [a,b,a,b,c] ;
  no

So be careful in Prolog programming: just because something works OK for its first
answer doesn't mean it will work OK on backtracking to get new answers.

  Next, here's a useful predicate that "appends" (concatenates) one list to
another. It has three arguments: the first list, the second list, and the combined
list.

  append([ ],L,L).
  append([X|L1],L2,Lnew) :- append(L1,L2,L3), Lnew is [X|L3].

As with delete, we can rewrite the last rule to eliminate the awkward and undesir-
able (and in some dialects, illegal) is, moving the [X|L3] to the left side:

  append([ ],L,L).
  append([X|L1],L2,[X|L3]) :- append(L1,L2,L3).

This says first that anything appended on the empty list is that thing itself. Otherwise, to append some nonempty list (having first item X) to a second list L2, append
the *rest* of that first list (without X) to L2, and then put X in front of that. Study
this revised definition carefully; it's a good example of how the style of Prolog programming differs from the style of most other programming.

  Figure 5-2 shows an example using append with the first two arguments
bound (inputs) and the third argument unbound (an output), for the query

  ?- append([gas,oil],[tires,battery,radiator],Things_to_check_before_trip).

Given the definition of append:

```
append([],L,L).
append([X|L],L2,[X|L3]) :- append(L,L2,L3).
```

Given the query:

```
?- append([gas,oil],[tires,battery,radiator],Things_to_check_before_trip).
```

Nested environments created:

Query: ?- append([gas,oil],[tires,battery,radiator],Things_to_check_before_trip).
In definition line 2: [X|L] = [gas,oil], L2 = [tires,battery,radiator], [X|L3] = ???
So X = gas, L = [oil], [X|L3] = [gas|???]

Query: ?- append([oil],[tires,battery,radiator],L3).
In definition line 2: [X|L] = [oil], L2 = [tires,battery,radiator], [X|L3] = ???
So X = oil, L = [], [X|L3] = [oil|L3]

Query: ?- append([],[tires,battery,radiator],L3).
In definition line 1: L = [tires,battery,radiator]

Note: ??? means unknown

Figure 5-2. Example of using append with first two arguments bound (inputs) and last argument unbound (an output); the processing state is just after the innermost recursion succeeds.

The nested boxes represent the rule invocation environments created with each recursion. The outer one with its parameter and local variables represents the initial invocation of **append**. This invocation recursively calls itself, creating the middle box, with its own distinct variables. This invocation of **append** in turn recursively calls itself, resulting in the inner environment (box) with yet more distinct variables. The processing state at this point is depicted in the figure. Now:

1. For the inner box, the first line of **append** says to bind its third argument to its value of L, [tires,battery,radiator], and the inner box succeeds.
2. Returning next to the middle box, [tires,battery,radiator] is the value of L3, and its X is oil, so [X|L3] is [oil,tires,battery,radiator]. So the invocation of the middle box succeeds.
3. Returning to the outer box, [oil,tires,battery,radiator] is the value of *its* L3, so its [X|L3] is [gas,oil,tires,battery,radiator]. The outer box succeeds.
4. So the original third argument Things_to_check_before_trip is bound to [gas,oil,tires,battery,radiator].

Like the **member** predicate and many other predicates defined without arithmetic, **append** will work several ways. In fact, it will work seven ways (see Figure 5-3).

Given the definition of append:

```
append([],L,L).
append([X|L1],L2,[X|L3]) :- append(L1,L2,L3).
```

First arg.	Second arg.	Third arg.	What happens?	Example
bound	bound	bound	Answers yes if third argument is the first two arguments glued together (in order), else no	?- append([a,b],[c],[a,b,c]). yes
bound	bound	unbound	Glues the second argument on the end of the first argument, binds result to the third argument	?- append([a,b],[c,d],L). L = [a,b,c,d]
bound	unbound	bound	Checks if the first argument is on the front of the third, binding the second to the rest of the third	?- append([a,b],L,[a,b,c]). L = [c]
unbound	bound	bound	Checks if the second argument is on the back of the third, binding the first to the rest of the third	?- append(L,[c,d],[a,b,c,d]). L = [a,b]
unbound	unbound	bound	Generates all divisions of the third argument into two pieces (preserving term order)	?- append(L1,L2,[a,b,c]). L1 = [], L2 = [a,b,c]; L1 = [a], L2 = [b,c]; L1 = [a,b], L2 = [c]; L1 = [a,b,c], L2 = []
unbound	bound	unbound	Generates in abstract form all results of glueing something on the front of the second argument	?- append(L1,[a,b],L2). L1 = [], L2 = [a,b]; L1 = [_1], L2 = [_1,a,b]; L1 = [_1,_2], L2 = [_1,_2,a,b] (The _1 and _2 are Prolog-invented variable names.)
bound	unbound	unbound	Generates in abstract form all results of glueing something on the back of the first argument	?- append([a,b],L1,L2). L1 = _1, L2 = [a,b|_1] (The _1 is a Prolog-invented variable name.)

Note: Any bound arguments to append must be lists for the above program to work.

Figure 5-3. Different possible uses of the append predicate.

For instance, it will handle the case in which the third argument is bound (an input) but the first and second arguments are unbound (outputs). Then the first two arguments are bound to binary partitions (breakings-in-half) of the third argument. So

> ?- append(L1,L2,[tom,dick,harry]).

gives the following if you keep typing a semicolon:

> L1 = [], L2 = [tom,dick,harry];
> L1 = [tom], L2 = [dick,harry];
> L1 = [tom,dick], L2 = [harry];
> L1 = [tom,dick,harry], L2 = [];
> no

The other rows in Figure 5-3 show other ways **append** can be used. Basically, we've got seven quite different programs in one. This comes about from the declarative interpretation of the definition: it describes conditions that hold when its third argument is the result of appending the first two arguments, not how to do it. Again, it describes "what" instead of "how."

5.7 COMBINING LIST PREDICATES_____

List predicate definitions can refer to other list predicates. For instance, we can use **member** to define a **subset** predicate that determines whether all the members of some list **L1** are members of some list **L2**. Here it is, and we print **member** as well to refresh your memory.

> subset([],L).
> subset([X|L1],L2) :- member(X,L2), subset(L1,L2).
>
> member(X,[X|L]).
> member(X,[Y|L]) :- member(X,L).

We leave a blank line between the rule groups with the same predicate name, following the convention (also followed in the traffic lights program of Section 4.11). Here's an example use of the program:

> ?- subset([b,c],[a,c,e,d,b]).
> yes

Here's a program for sorting lists of numbers into increasing order, *insertion sort* in particular:

```
sort([],[]).
sort([X|L1],L2) :- sort(L1,L3), insert_item(X,L3,L2).

insert_item(X,[],[X]).
insert_item(X,[Y|L],[X,Y|L]) :- X < Y.
insert_item(X,[Y|L1],[Y|L2]) :- X > = Y, insert_item(X,L1,L2).
```

The first argument to sort is an unsorted input list, and the second argument is the output sorted list. The first argument to insert_item is an input item, the second argument an input list, and the third argument is the result of inserting that item into that list, an output. Here's one example of the overall behavior:

```
?- sort([3,2,7,4],L).
L = [2,3,4,7]
```

5.8 REDUNDANCY IN DEFINITIONS

Basis conditions in a recursive definition are simple cases that don't require recursion. We always need at least one basis condition in a recursion, but we can have more than one. For instance, we could define length of a list this way:

```
length([],0).
length([X],1).
length([X,Y],2).
length([X,Y,Z|L],N) :- length(L,N2), N is N2 + 3.
```

instead of equivalently

```
length([],0).
length([X|L],N) :- length(L,N2), N is N2 + 1.
```

But the extra lines can speed calculation when our lists are very short on the average: we're able to answer many queries without recursion. Here's a similar alternative to the member definition of Section 5.5:

```
member(X,[X|L]).
member(X,[Y,X|L]).
member(X,[Z,Y|L]) :- member(X,L).
```

Here the second line is redundant, since its case can be covered by a slightly modified third line. But if lists are often short, or the things we're looking for are usually toward the front of the lists, the preceding definition may be faster than the original definition.

Such modifications are a kind of *caching*, a concept that occurs in many disguises in artificial intelligence, and which will reappear in a quite different form in Chapter 6. Caching means asserting unnecessary or redundant facts to improve efficiency. The idea is to waste a little space (the extra facts) in the hope of improving calculation speed. Caching doesn't always improve speed significantly, so to justify it you first need to do experiments, or do some mathematical analysis like that we'll do in Sections 9.14 and 13.3.

5.9 AN EXAMPLE: DEJARGONIZING BUREAUCRATESE*_____

Natural language (human language) is a major subarea of artificial-intelligence research. Lists and list processing routines are the obvious way to represent and use sentences and languages in Prolog. As an example, consider a critical technical problem facing the United States today: the translation of bureaucratic jargon into real English. Bureaucratic organizations typically use their own terminology to make their accomplishments look a little less pathetic than they really are. It would be useful to take a sentence of such bureaucratic jargon, expressed as a Prolog list, and convert it to understandable everyday English. Such a translation program might be used routinely on government documents.

For instance, "impact" is often misused as a verb, as in "The study will impact the department." When so used, it can be replaced by the simpler and more standard English word "affect." Similarly, "adversely impact" and "negatively impact" can be replaced by "hurt." "Transition" is also misused as a verb, as in "The project will transition to phase 3," and can be replaced by "change." "Evaluate options" and "consider options" can be changed to "study" and "under advisement" and "under consideration" to "being studied." You can probably recall many more examples. These substitutions usually but not always have the same meanings, so the sentence created by applying them should always be carefully double-checked.

It's easy to write a Prolog program for this, once English sentences are represented in Prolog list format. First we represent the substitution pairs as facts. For example

```
substitution([adversely,impact],[hurt]).
substitution([negatively,impact],[hurt]).
substitution([impact],[affect]),
substitution([will,transition],[will,change]).
substitution([must,transition],[must,change]).
substitution([to,transition],[to,change]).
substitution([consider,options],[study]).
substitution([evaluate,options],[study]).
substitution([under,advisement],[being,studied].
substitution([under,consideration],[being,studied].
substitution([expedite],[do]).
substitution([expeditiously],[fast]).
substitution([will,secure],[will,close]).
substitution([must,secure],[must,close]).
substitution([prioritize],[rank]).
```

The first argument contains the original words, and the second argument the words to be substituted. Note that extra words in the first argument narrow the applicability of the substitution, but reduce the possibility of making mistakes.

Next we define a predicate that recurses through the sentence list, like **member** and **delete** defined in Sections 5.5 and 5.6 respectively:

```
dejargonize([],[]).
dejargonize(L,NL) :- substitution(S,NS), append(S,L2,L),
   append(NS,L2,L3), dejargonize(L3,NL).
dejargonize([X|L],[X|L2]) :- dejargonize(L,L2).
```

The first line sets the basis condition as the empty list, and the last line recurses through the list without changing any words. The middle two lines do the work of substitution. They check through the substitution facts for one whose first argument matches the front of the list (using the **append** predicate according to the third line of Figure 5-3, for second argument unbound), and substitute (using **append** according to the second line of Figure 5-3, for the third argument unbound), and recurse on the new list. Here's an example:

```
?- dejargonize
([we,must,consider,options,to,transition,expeditiously],L).
L = [we,must,study,to,change,fast]
```

Despite the somewhat frivolous nature of this program, the idea of substituting into strings of words is important in much natural language work, and we'll look some more into it at the end of the next chapter.

KEYWORDS

infix
arithmetic assignment
is
prefix
multiway reasoning
recursion
tail recursion
basis of a recursion
induction step of a recursion
lists
Lisp
linked-pointer list representation
the bar symbol
the member *predicate*
the delete *predicate*
the append *predicate*
caching

E X E R C I S E S

5-1. (A,P) Define a Prolog predicate max(X,Y,Z,M) that says that M is the maximum of the three input numbers X, Y, and Z. Use only ">" to compare numbers.

5-2. (R,A) A student familiar with Pascal was writing a compiler in Prolog. This required translating an error code number into an English description, so they wrote rules like this:

> translate(Code,Meaning) :- Code = 1, Meaning is integer_overflow.
> translate(Code,Meaning) :- Code = 2, Meaning is division_by_zero.
> translate(Code,Meaning) :- Code = 3, Meaning is unknown_identifier.

This is poor Prolog programming style. How can it be improved?

5-3. (P) Write a **better_divide** like **better_add** that handles similar cases for division. Have the program prevent division by zero.

5-4. To figure out a tax amount, you subtract the deductions from the gross and multiply by the tax rate (expressed as a decimal number less than 1). Using the **better_add** predicate defined in Section 5.3 and an analogous predicate **better_multiply** that you define yourself, write two Prolog rules that can be used to answer all the following questions by a single query each:

- If my gross is 1,000, my deductions 270, and my tax rate 0.15, what is my tax?
- If my tax was 170 at a tax rate of 0.17, with no deductions, what was my gross?
- If my tax was 170 at a tax rate 0.17 and a gross of 1500, what amount of deductions did I take?
- What tax rate would result in a tax of 80 on a gross of 1200 with 400 in deductions?

If your Prolog dialect can handle decimal numbers, show your program works correctly for the preceding questions.

5-5. (P) (This requires a Prolog dialect with floating-point numbers.) Define a predicate square(X,Y) that says that its second argument is the square of its first argument (the result of multiplying the first argument by itself). Using the built-in var predicate, have it handle each of the four cases of binding of its arguments:

- if both arguments are bound, it checks that the second argument is the square of the first;
- if the first argument is bound and the second argument unbound, it computes the square of the first argument;
- if the first argument is unbound and the second argument is bound, it computes an approximation of the first argument within 0.001 by bisection search or some other iterative method from numerical analysis;

- if both arguments are unbound, it generates all possible pairs of positive integers and their squares starting with 1.

5-6. (P)

(a) Define a new predicate integer_better_add, like better_add, but able to handle the case in which its first two arguments are unbound (outputs), finding all pairs of integers that sum to a bound (input) integer third argument.

(b) Use part (a) to write a program to generate three-by-three duplicate-allowing magic squares that have a given number as characteristic sum. (A *magic square* is a two-dimensional array of integers such that the eight sums—the three columns, the three rows, and the two diagonals—are the same.)

5-7. Consider this query:

a(X,Y), not(c(X)), d(X,Y).

Suppose our Prolog database contains this, in order:

d(X,Y) :- X > 1, Y > 1.
a(0,1).
a(0,2).
a(2,1).
a(M,N) :- b(P,Q), b(Q,P), M is P + 1, N is Q + 1.

c(0).

b(3,1).
b(2,1).
b(1,2).

(a) Without using the computer, what is the first answer found to the query by a Prolog interpreter?

(b) Without using the computer, what is the second answer found to the query (when you type a semicolon after the first answer)?

5-8. (R,A) Suppose we have Prolog facts about named events in terms of the following three predicates:

start(<event>,<time>), an event started at a particular time
end(<event>,<time>), an event ended at a particular time
duration(<event>,<length>), an event lasted for a particular length of time

We may have one, two, or all three of these facts about some event, and we can't know in advance which we will have if we have one or two.

(a) Write Prolog rules to infer an end time for some event when there is no end(Event,Time) fact for it, and to infer a start time when there is no start(Event,Time) fact for it.

(b) Define a new Prolog predicate after(Event1,Event2) which is true when its first argument Event1 definitely happened after its second argument Event2.

(c) Define a new Prolog predicate during(Event1,Event2) which is true when its first argument Event1 definitely happened while its second argument Event2 was happening.

(d) Explain where in a Prolog database of facts these rules should go for things to work right.

5-9. (R,A) The transmission of a car contains gears that transmit power to the car's wheels. You can infer the speed and direction of the wheels, given facts about what gears are connected to what other gears and what is driving them. Assume gears are labeled g1, g2, g3, and so on. Assume the number of teeth on each gear is specified by facts of the form

teeth(<gear_name>,<number_of_teeth>).

Assume all rigid connections between gears on the same rigid shaft are specified by facts of the form

same_shaft(<gear_name_1>,<gear_name_2>).

Assume that all meshed (teeth-to-teeth) connections between gears are specified by facts of the form

meshed(<gear_name_1>,<gear_name_2>).

(a) We want to reason about the rotational speed and direction of gears. Give a good format for such facts for each gear.

(b) Anytime two gears are rigidly attached to the same rigid shaft, their rotational speeds are the same. Write a Prolog rule that can infer the rotational speed of one such gear on a shaft from the known rotational speed of another such gear. Use the fact format from part (a).

(c) Anytime two gears are connected or "meshed" the product of the number of teeth and the rotational speed for each gear is the same, except that one gear rotates in the opposite direction from the other. Write a Prolog rule that can infer the rotational speed of a gear from the rotational speed of a gear meshed with it, assuming the number of teeth on both gears is known. Use the fact format from part (a).

(d) Suppose gear g1 has a rotational speed of 5000 rpm in a clockwise direction. Suppose it is on the same shaft as g2, g2 is meshed to g3, and g2 is meshed to g4. Suppose g1 has 100 teeth, g2 has 30 teeth, g3 has 60 teeth, and g4 has 90 teeth. Give a Prolog query that will figure out the rotational speed and direction of gear g4 from a database of these facts.

Then show the steps that the Prolog interpreter will take to answer that query. Note: You must write the facts with the correct order of arguments in order for your inference rules to apply properly to them.

(e) Explain how infinite loops could happen when reasoning about gears, if you weren't careful in specifying the facts.

(f) Suppose for some arrangement of gears and specified gear speeds you find gear g8 has a speed of 1200 rpm by one chain of reasoning and 800 rpm by another chain of reasoning. What does this mean for the gears?

5-10. (P) Define a predicate **convert** that does units conversion for length measurement; for instance, it converts a measurement in feet to meters. The **convert** predicate should take four arguments: a number (an input), the units for that number (an input), the units to which you want to convert (an input), and the result number (an output). Handle the following units: meters, decimeters, centimeters, millimeters, decameters, kilometers, inches, feet, yards, and miles. Hint: Don't write a separate rule for every pair of possible units, but chain inferences.

5-11. Consider representing maps of highway routes in Prolog. Suppose you don't have much memory space, so representing squares of the map as a two-dimensional array is out of the question. Instead, you want to store just information about what towns are connected by which highways segments (assume segments have names and numbers, not unique, like "California 62") and distances. Suppose highway segments are in different counties, states, and countries, and we want to remember which. Suppose we also store the different maximum speed limits for different states and countries. Assume each route is in a single county (you can create imaginary towns on county lines to ensure this). Assume highway segments meet only at towns.

(a) Give formats for the fact predicates you need.

(b) Give a rule or rules for inferring the maximum speed limit on a road.

(c) Give a rule or rules for inferring a distance (not necessarily the shortest, that's hard) between two towns. Don't worry about getting into an infinite loop; assume the Prolog interpreter is smart enough not to visit the same town twice in a route (we'll explain how to do this in Chapter 10).

(d) Suppose there are R routes (connecting two towns each), C counties, S states, and K countries. How many facts do you save with the inference in part (b)? Make reasonable assumptions if necessary.

(e) Suppose there are R routes (connecting two towns each) and T towns. Approximately how many facts do you save with the inference in part (c)? Perhaps consider different arrangements of towns. Make reasonable assumptions if necessary.

5-12. (P) Define a completely multidirectional **inference_distance** of three arguments. Its first argument is a kind of the second argument. Its third argument is the number of linking **a_kind_of** facts that must be followed to get from the first argument to the second. By "completely multidirectional" we mean able to handle any pattern of bindings of the arguments. Assume there are only a_kind_of facts, no rules, and the facts don't have any cycles, and there is only one route between any two things. (The inference distance concept is important in psychology, because some psychologists believe that humans have semantic networks in their heads and that the speed of human reasoning is proportional to the inference distance.)

5-13. (E) Consider a Prolog definition written to implement a function, in other words written to be used when all arguments but the last are bound (inputs), which binds its last argument to some unique value. In abstract mathematical terms, what characteristics must the function have to be easily used multidirectionally, that is, with last argument bound and other arguments unbound?

5-14. (A,P)

    (a) Using a single call to append and no other predicates, implement the member predicate. (Hint: The fifth row of Figure 5-3 is closest to what you need.)

    (b) Using a single call to append and no other predicates, implement the last predicate.

    (c) Using just two calls to append and no other predicates, implement a deleteone predicate that removes a single occurrence of some item from a list.

    (d) Using just two calls to append and no other predicates, implement a before predicate of three arguments that succeeds if its first two arguments are both members of its list third argument, and where the first argument item occurs before the second argument item.

5-15. (E) Figure 5-3 is missing a row for the case in which all variables are unbound. Explain why for this case the predicate definition will not work properly.

5-16. Consider the delete predicate defined in the chapter:

```
delete(X,[],[]).
delete(X,[X|L],M) :- delete(X,L,M).
delete(X,[Y|L],[Y|M]) :- not(X = Y), delete(X,L,M).
```

    (a) Suppose you rewrite it as

```
delete(X,[],[]).
delete(X,[X|L],M) :- delete(X,L,M).
delete(X,[Y|L],[Y|M]) :- delete(X,L,M).
```

    What happens when you query this predicate with second and third arguments bound and first argument unbound?

    (b) What happens if you change the second line to

```
delete(X,[X|L],L).
```

and query this predicate with first and second arguments bound and third argument unbound?

5-17. (A)

(a) Suppose that Prolog predicate mystery is queried with its first argument a bound (input) list and its second argument unbound (an output). Describe what the predicate mystery does, in a sentence of 20 or less English words. (Hint: Try it on sample lists.)

```
mystery([],[]).
mystery([X],[X]).
mystery([X,Y|L],[X,censored|M]) :- mystery(L,M).
```

(b) Most recursive list-processing definitions have only one basis condition. Why does the preceding definition need two?

5-18. In the language Logo and other languages with *turtle geometry* primitives, there are special commands to control a plotting pen. The pen has a position (measured in millimeters in a coordinate system) and a direction it is pointing in the plane of the paper (measured in degrees). Two built-in predicates manipulate the pen: forward(X) which moves the pen forward a distance X in the direction it is pointing, and right(X), which turns the pen around X degrees (without moving its location) so it points in a new direction. This program draws spirals, increasing the length it moves forward each step:

```
spiral(Side,Angle,Increment) :- forward(Side), right(Angle),
   Side2 is Side + Increment, spiral(Side2,Angle,Increment).
```

(a) Draw what the query

```
?- unknown(4).
```

causes to be drawn. Assume the pen is pointing north at the start. Indicate the lengths of lines in your drawing. Here is the definition:

```
unknown(1) :- right(90).
unknown(N) :- Nm1 is N-1, unknown(Nm1), N2 is 5-N,
   forward(N2), unknown(Nm1).
```

(b) Draw what the query

```
?- flake(3).
```

causes to be drawn. Again assume the pen is pointing north at the start. Here is the definition:

flake(1) :- forward(1).
flake(N) :- Nm1 is N-1, flake(Nm1), right(-60), flake(Nm1),
right(120), flake(Nm1), right(-60), flake(Nm1).

Hint: This one is too complicated to figure out procedurally—reason about the declarative meaning of the rules.

5-19. (A) Consider use of the member predicate with both arguments bound, and with the second (list) argument N items long.

(a) How many times is the rule invoked when the answer to the query is no?

(b) Suppose the answer to the query is yes and suppose the item being searched for is equally likely to appear at any position in the list. How many times on the average will the rule be invoked now?

5-20. Consider our "dejargonizing" program. Each substitution of one set of words for another takes one line to define. Explain how to compress this set of substitutions so one line can handle many substitutions. (Hint: Variables can be items in lists.)

5-21. (E) What is wrong with the following "proof" that all horses are the same color? "One horse is obviously the same color as itself. Suppose for some N, every set of N horses is the same color. Then consider some horse Snowy, a white horse, for purposes of argument. Consider the set of N+1 items formed by including Snowy in an arbitrary set of N horses. Now if we take out some other horse than Snowy from this set (call him Blacky), we have a set of N horses. By the induction assumption, these horses are all the same color. But Snowy is white. Therefore all the other horses in the original set must have been white. So put Blacky back in and take out some other horse (besides Snowy, call him Alabaster) to create a new set of N horses. This new set must also be all of the same color, so since it includes Snowy, the color must be white. But Blacky is in the set too, and so must be white too. Hence every set of N+1 horses must be white. Hence if any set of N horses is all the same color, any set of N+1 horses is of the same color. Hence by recursive argument, all horses are the same color."

5-22. (A,P) Write a modified transitivity rule (for let's say transitivity of a(X,Y)) that can't ever get into infinite loops when answering a query of the form

?- a(r,s).

Show your program working on some sample data that contains cycles with respect to the a predicate. (A "cycle" means a closed loop in the semantic network.) Hint: Use an extra list argument.

5-23. (P) Create a Prolog database and query it appropriately to create poems of the following form:

A A B C C B D D D E E B

Here each capital letter stands for a class of nonsense words that must rhyme together. B represents one-syllable words, and the other letters represent two-syllable words. In addition, the poem cannot have duplicate words. Here is an example poem:

uga buga ru batta hatta nu fitty pitty witty ditty garra farra tu

It will help to define a predicate **different** of two arguments that says whether two words are identical. Present your resulting poem as the value of a single variable, a list of lists for which each list is a line of the poem. Type semicolons to see what similar poems you get.

6

CONTROL STRUCTURES FOR RULE-BASED SYSTEMS

Rule-based systems for artificial intelligence (also called *production systems*, but that sounds like an assembly line) can work quite differently from the usual (built-in) way that Prolog interpreters work. We'll now discuss some of these ways. The differences are in the *control structure* or *conflict resolution* or *inference engine*, the way and order in which facts, rules, and parts of rules are used. That is, changes in the procedural interpretation of rules. The choice of a control structure can enormously affect the success and efficiency of a rule-based system—Prolog interpreters aren't always best.

Control structures are somewhat like the algorithms in other parts of computer science. However, they are more general and less precise in their effects. As we said in Section 4.13, artificial-intelligence programs tend to consist of many small pieces of code, and the control structure usually serves as a coordinator or manager for all these pieces instead of trying to impose a sequence on them all.

The control structure is critical for an important and practical class of rule-based systems. Called *rule-based expert systems*, these rule-based systems try to mimic the performance of human experts on specialized tasks. Their rules are usually more like recommendations than definitions, often like the traffic lights example of Section 4.11. Rule-based expert systems typically need large numbers of rules about a problem area or *domain* in order to approach skilled human performance. Because of their size, efficiency is important, and choice of control structure strongly affects efficiency. We'll frequently have expert systems in mind in this and the next two chapters, if not explicitly.

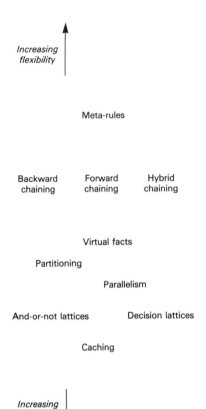

Figure 6-1. Spectrum of control-structure concepts for rule-based systems.

Just like everything else in computer science, there's a tradeoff of generality and flexibility against speed with control-structure ideas. The ideas we'll discuss in this chapter can be placed on an flexibility/efficiency spectrum (see Figure 6-1). Those that are flexible, "high-level," and slow appear at the top, while those that are inflexible, "low-level," and fast (*compiled control structures*) appear at the bottom.

6.1 BACKWARD-CHAINING CONTROL STRUCTURES

Many control structures impose a single sequential ordering on everything that happens. But sequential control structures differ in the relative importance they assign to rule order, fact order, and query (*goal*) order. The usual Prolog-interpreter control structure described in Chapter 4 gives goal (query) order top priority, and then treats rule and fact order of equal importance after that, using the database order as a way of assigning priorities to individual rules and facts. This is *backward chaining* or *goal-directed reasoning*. It is told something to prove, and it tries to find a way, binding variables as necessary. If alternative conclusions are possible (as in the traffic lights example in which several actions are considered until one is found), backward chaining can try to prove the first, then try the second if the first fails, and so on like an "or." Backward chaining is often a good control structure when there are many more facts than final conclusions (goals).

As an example, consider these rules, labeled with codes for easy reference:

```
/* R1 */ goal1 :- fact1.
/* R2 */ goal1 :- a, b.
/* R3 */ goal2(X) :- c(X).
/* R4 */ a :- not(d).
/* R5 */ b :- d.
/* R6 */ b :- e.
/* R7 */ c(2) :- not(e).
/* R8 */ d :- fact2, fact3.
/* R9 */ e :- fact2, fact4.
```

Suppose the goals in this rule-based system are goal1 and goal2(X), and suppose we consider them in that order. In other words, it's like a query was

```
?- goal1; goal2(Z).
```

Suppose further that only facts fact2 and fact3 are true. R1 is tried first, but fact1 isn't true so it fails. Next R2 is tried, invoking R4 and then R8. R8 succeeds because fact2 and fact3 are both true. So the subgoal d succeeds, and therefore R4 (and a) fails because of the meaning of not. R2 and goal1 fail. So finally goal2 is tried, which invokes R3. This invokes R7, then R9. The latter fails because fact4 isn't true. So R7 succeeds, hence R3 succeeds with X=2, and hence goal2(2) succeeds.

There are several useful enhancements of backward chaining. A simple trick that can often greatly improve efficiency is to *cache* or enter as facts some or all of the conclusions reached. For instance, once we prove conclusion b with the preceding rules, we could add a b fact to the database. We should put a fact b in front of rules that can prove it, so a subsequent query will find it before the rules. The more times b is queried later, the more effort this caching can save. The disadvantage is more facts to search through to answer other queries.

Conclusion caching is simple with Prolog: just use the asserta built-in (that is, you don't have to define it) predicate of one argument, a fact to be asserted. This predicate asserta is like not in that the argument must be a predicate expression; querying it always succeeds, but has the side effect of adding that expression as a new fact to the database, in front of the facts with that same predicate name and rules with that name on their left side. Like most of Prolog's built-in predicates, asserta always fails on backtracking: there's no second way you can assert a fact. Prolog also has two related built-in predicates: assertz which caches a fact *after* the last fact or rule in the database having the same predicate name, and retract which removes (or "un-caches") a fact from the database.

Another trick to improve efficiency of backward chaining is not to require a complete starting database, but ask for facts as needed—that is, designate *virtual facts.* For instance, if there's something wrong with a car's electrical system, you could check for loose wiring. But that's a lot of work, and some wires are hard to find. We shouldn't require checking wires before running a car diagnosis program, only if more obvious problems like a dead battery have been ruled out. Backward chaining works well with virtual facts because it only queries facts immediately relevant to its conclusions. The control structure we discuss next, forward chaining, does not have this advantage, but it has some others.

6.2 FORWARD CHAINING

Often rule-based systems work from just a few facts but are capable of reaching many possible conclusions. Examples are "sensory" and "diagnosis" expert systems, like those that identify an object from a description of what you see at a distance, or those that tell you what to do when your car breaks down from a description of what isn't working. For these, it often makes more sense to start with the facts and reason to goals (conclusions), what is known as *forward chaining* or *data-directed computation* or *modus ponens* reasoning.

As an example, take the rule

    a :- b, c.

and suppose b and c are facts. Then we can conclude a is a fact, and add it to the facts we have. This is called *modus ponens* inference in logic. There's no query, no goals; we just use the facts we know to infer some new fact. (The built-in predicate asserta can help implement this too; see the next chapter.)

To use modus ponens as the basis of a control structure, take the facts in order. For each fact, find all rules whose right sides contain a predicate expression that can be matched to it. (We can index predicate names mentioned on right sides to speed this up.) Now "cross out" the predicate expressions matched in the rules; that is, create new rules like the old rules except without these expressions. But wherever a fact matched the last expression on the right side of some rule, the left side of the rule has been proved a new fact, after substituting in any bindings made on the right side; so cache that new fact in the database. The last paragraph gave an example. For another, consider:

    a(X,3) :- b(X).

Then if b(20) is a fact, modus ponens would conclude a(20,3) is a fact.

It matters where we put a new fact among the others, since the facts are pursued in order. Usually it's good to put the new fact in front of those not yet considered, a *most-recent-fact* or *focus-of-attention* idea. So the fact just proved will be the next fact examined; the fact list then is much like a stack (last thing "in" is the first thing "out"). This might be good if we want to reach some particular conclusion as fast as possible. But, on the other hand, if we want to systematically find every conclusion possible from the facts, we should put new conclusions at the end of the set of facts; the fact list is then like a queue (last thing "in" is the last thing "out").

Any nots in rules require special handling. Since we want to follow the closed-world assumption for forward chaining too (it's simplest), we want not to mean "it can't be proved." So forward chaining must first assume all nots to be false, prove all possible facts, and only then consider as true those nots whose arguments are not now facts. Those nots may then prove new facts with new consequences. (To avoid such awkwardness, some artificial-intelligence systems let you state certain facts to be false, and we'll discuss how to handle such "unfacts" in Chapter 14, but this creates its own complications, so it isn't allowed in Prolog.)

Here's the formal algorithm for (pure) forward chaining:

1. Mark all facts as unused and get a fresh copy of the rules.
2. Until no more unused facts remain, pick the first-listed one; call it F. "Pursue" it:
   (a) For each rule R in order that can match F with a predicate expression on its right side, ignoring appearances of F in nots:
       (i) Create a new rule just like R except with the expression matching F removed. If variables had to be bound to make the match, substitute these bindings for the variables in the rule.
       (ii) If you've now removed the entire right side of rule R, you've proved a fact: the current left side. Enter that left side into the list of facts, and mark it "unused." (The focus-of-attention approach here puts the new fact in front of other unused facts.) Eliminate from further consideration all rules whose left sides are equivalent to (not just matchable to) the fact proved.
       (iii) Otherwise, if there's still some right side remaining, put the new simplified rule in front of the old rule, with one exception: If the fact can match other expressions in the same rule, put the new rule *after* the old rule. Cross out the old rule if it is now redundant. It is redundant if the old rule always succeeds whenever the new rule succeeds, which is true, for instance, when no variables were bound to make the match.
   (b) Mark F as "used."
3. For each not expression in rules whose argument does not match any used fact, add it to the fact list, mark it as "unused," and redo step 2. Consider the expressions in rule order.

6.3 A FORWARD CHAINING EXAMPLE

Let's take an example of forward chaining with focus-of-attention handling of new facts. Consider the same rules used for backward chaining:

```
/* R1 */ goal1 :- fact1.
/* R2 */ goal1 :- a, b.
/* R3 */ goal2(X) :- c(X).
/* R4 */ a :- not(d).
/* R5 */ b :- d.
/* R6 */ b :- e.
/* R7 */ c(2) :- not(e).
/* R8 */ d :- fact2, fact3.
/* R9 */ e :- fact2, fact4.
```

Suppose the rules are taken in the given order; and that as before, only fact2 and fact3 are true, in that order (see Figure 6-2).

1. We start with fact2, and find matching predicate expressions in R8 and R9. This gives the new rules (placed together before R8)

   ```
   /* R10 */ d :- fact3.
   /* R11 */ e :- fact4.
   ```

   Rules R8 and R9 are now redundant since no variables were bound in the match, and R8 and R9 can be eliminated.

2. No new facts were discovered, so we pursue next fact3. This matches an expression in R10. So now R10 succeeds, and the new fact d is put in front of any remaining unused facts (though there aren't any now). R10 can be eliminated.

3. We pursue fact d, and find that rule R5 mentions it in its right side. (R4 mentions it too, but as not(d), and we're saving nots for last.) Matching R5 gives the new fact b. Rules R5 and R6 can now be eliminated.

4. Fact b matches something in R2, giving

   ```
   /* R12 */ goal1 :- a.
   ```

   and rule R2 can be eliminated. The current set of rules is

   ```
   /* R1 */ goal1 :- fact1.
   /* R12 */ goal1 :- a.
   /* R3 */ goal2(X) :- c(X).
   /* R4 */ a :- not(d).
   /* R7 */ c(2) :- not(e).
   /* R11 */ e :- fact4.
   ```

5. We have no more facts to pursue. But we're not done yet, since R4 and R7 have nots.

6. Fact d is true, so rule R4 can't ever succeed. But fact e has not been proved. Hence add not(e) to the list of facts.

7. This matches the right side of R7. Hence c(2) is a fact too. Eliminate R7.

8. This matches the only expression on the right side of R3, when X = 2, and hence goal2(2) is a fact. We can't eliminate R3 now because we had to bind a variable to make the match.

9. That's everything we can conclude.

Step number	Which fact being pursued?	Which rule matched?	What happens?
1	fact2	R8	Define R10: d :- fact3.
	fact2	R9	Define R11: e :- fact4.
2	fact3	R10	New fact found: d.
3	d	R4	Nothing
	d	R5	New fact found: b.
4	b	R2	Define R12: goal1 :- a.
5	—	—	
6	not(d)	R4	Nothing, since d a fact
7	not(e)	R7	New fact found: c.
8	c(2)	R3	New fact found: goal2(2).

Figure 6-2. Summary of the example of pure forward chaining.

Though Prolog interpreters don't *automatically* forward chain, it's not hard to teach them—see Section 7.10.

This "pure" forward chaining is rarer in applications than backward chaining. There's a story about a huge metal robot that came clanking into a bar one day. "I'm a pure-forward-chaining robot, and I can do a complete analysis of the quality of any liquor-dispensing establishment with a single sample. Please mix a martini for me, and pour it down the analysis chute in my chest." The bartender did so, and said, "That'll be eleven dollars. Say, we don't get too many forward-chaining robots in here." "At your prices I'm not surprised," replied the robot.

6.4 HYBRID CONTROL STRUCTURES

Different control structure ideas can be combined in *hybrid* control structures. Hybrids of forward and backward chaining, compromising on the advantages and disadvantages of both, are often used. The most common is the *rule-cycle hybrid*[1] because it is easy to implement (see Section 7.9).

With the rule-cycle hybrid, rules are tried in order as with backward chaining, but each rule is used in a forward chaining (modus ponens) way to assert new facts. The rule list is cycled through repeatedly, first ignoring any rules with nots. If the conditions on the right side of some rule all match facts (that's *facts*, not just something provable), then the rule succeeds and its left side (with appropriate bindings) is added to the database as a new fact. When no new rules succeed on a cycle through all of them, rules with nots are now considered; cycling resumes at the top

---

[1] The rule-cycle hybrid is often confused with pure forward chaining.

of the rules, with the **not** expressions now succeeding if their arguments aren't now facts. Again we continue until no new rules succeed on a cycle. So with the rule-cycle hybrid, rule order takes precedence over fact order, but it's different than with backward chaining. Figure 6-3 summarizes the differences between forward chaining, backward chaining, and the rule-cycle hybrid. The chief disadvantage of the rule-cycle hybrid is an unnecessary repeated reexamination of the rules.

Pure backward chaining:	*Pure forward chaining:*	*Rule-cycle hybrid:*
Query order	Fact order	Rule order
has priority over	*has priority over*	*has priority over*
rule order	rule order	rule-right-side order
which has priority over	*which has priority over*	*which has priority over*
rule-right-side order	rule-right-side order	fact order
which has priority over		
fact order		

Figure 6-3. Ordering priorities for three kinds of chaining.

Here's a more formal algorithm. Warning: it will only work with the restriction that no **not**(p) occurs in the right side of a rule before a rule having **p** as its left side, for any **p**, but that's usually easy to satisfy.

> Cycle through the rules repeatedly until no new facts are found on a cycle, ignoring rules with **nots**.
>> For each cycle, consider the rules in order.
>>> For each rule R, treat its right side as a query about the facts (without using any other rules via backward chaining). If R succeeds, add its left side (with substitution of bindings made) as a fact at the front of the list of facts. And then eliminate from further consideration all rules whose left sides are equivalent to this new fact. If the rule left side has variables, do this for every possible way of binding those variables.
> Now repeat the previous step with *all* the original rules, taking also as true the **nots** whose arguments are not facts.

Take our standard example:

```
/* R1 */ goal1 :- fact1.
/* R2 */ goal1 :- a, b.
/* R3 */ goal2(X) :- c(X).
/* R4 */ a :- not(d).
/* R5 */ b :- d.
/* R6 */ b :- e.
/* R7 */ c(2) :- not(e).
/* R8 */ d :- fact2, fact3.
/* R9 */ e :- fact2, fact4.
```

With the rule-cycle hybrid when **fact2** and **fact3** are true (see Figure 6-4):

1. R1, R2, R3, R5 and R6 are tried (we skip R4 and R7 because they have **not**s). None succeed because nothing on any right side matches a fact that is stated to be true.

2. R8 is tried, and it succeeds. Fact **d** is asserted. Eliminate R8.

3. R9 fails.

4. We return to the top of the rule list and start a new cycle. Rules R1 through R3 fail as before, and R4 is ignored.

5. But R5 now succeeds since **d** is a fact. Fact **b** is asserted. Eliminate R5 and R6.

   Now the rules are

```
/* R1 */ goal1 :- fact1.
/* R2 */ goal1 :- a, b.
/* R3 */ goal2(X) :- c(X).
/* R4 */ a :- not(d).
/* R7 */ c(2) :- not(e).
/* R9 */ e :- fact2, fact4.
```

6. R9 fails (R7 is ignored). And all the remaining rules fail on the next cycle.

7. Possibilities are exhausted, so we must now include rules with **not**s. Now on cycle 4, R1, R2, and R3 fail as before, and R4 fails because **d** is a fact.

8. The **not** in R7 succeeds because **e** is not a fact. So **c(2)** is a fact. Eliminate R7.

9. None of R9, R1, and R2 succeed. But R3 succeeds, with **X = 2**, and **goal2(2)** must be a fact. We can't eliminate R3 because **goal2(2)** is more specific than the left side of R3. But we're done now if we only want to reach one goal.

Cycle No.	R1	R2	R3	R4	R5	R6	R7	R8	R9
1	fails	fails	fails	—	fails	fails	—	succeeds	fails
2	fails	fails	fails	—	succeeds	fails	—	—	fails
3	fails	fails	fails	—	—	fails	—	—	fails
4	fails	fails	fails	fails	—	fails	succeeds	—	fails
5	fails	fails	succeeds	—	—	—	—	—	—

Figure 6-4. Summary of the example of rule-cycle hybrid chaining (the — means not necessary to test).

A different hybrid of forward and backward chaining alternates (*time-shares*) between forward and backward chaining steps. It picks a fact, and finds what rule right sides mention it; it does backward chaining in those right sides to try to establish the left side as a fact. Then it picks another fact and does the same thing over again. This hybrid sometimes pays off when neither forward, backward, nor rule-cycle hybrid chaining works well.

6.5 ORDER VARIANTS

Query, fact, and rule ordering is important in backward, forward, and rule-cycle hybrid chaining, and control structures can apply many criteria to it.

With backward chaining, predicate expressions in the query can be sorted by priority. In an "and," the expressions easiest to process or least likely to succeed can be done first. Sections 13.2 through 13.7 discuss these ideas at length.

With forward chaining, facts can be sorted by priority. The facts most useful (matchable in the right sides of the most rules) can go first, to help reach interesting conclusions faster. Or the facts most powerful in reaching conclusions can go first (statistics on queries can be kept for this).

Rule order is important to both forward and backward chaining. One common ordering is by *specificity*. Specificity doesn't mean how "concrete" the rules are, but whether conditions on the right side of rule 1 are a subset of conditions on the right side of rule 2; or in other words, whether the success of rule 2 means success of rule 1. The specificity ordering puts rules for the most narrowly described situations (or *exceptions*) first, then those for less narrow situations, then those still less narrow, and so on up to very broad *default* rules. (If the broadest rules came first, the others would never get a chance to work.) Since catching subset relationships between rule right sides requires some analysis, a variant is to put the *longest* rules first, but this doesn't work quite as well.

Here's an example for rule-cycle-hybrid chaining in which all the rule left sides are goals:

```
/* R1 */ u :- b.
/* R2 */ v :- c.
/* R3 */ w :- b, c, d.
/* R4 */ x :- d, e.
/* R5 */ y :- b.
/* R6 */ z :- b, d.
```

A rule-specificity ordering would insist that R3 be in front of R1, R2, R5, and R6, and insist that R6 be in front of R1 and R5.

There are two problems with specificity ordering. The first is that there are often few such subset relationships among rules, leaving undecided how to complete the ordering. The second is that the narrowest rules apply rarely, meaning wasted work if they're first. Chapter 13 will study these issues. But usually a quick fix is available in the adding of extra **not** expressions to the broader rules, and putting those rules first. For instance, for our last example it may be possible to rewrite R1 as

```
/* R1 */ u :- b, not(c), not(d).
```

and then it doesn't matter where it goes. Something like this is often what the original rules really meant, since we often forget the minor exceptions to rules—there are just too many. For example, with the rule "if a car won't start and the radio won't play and the lights don't light, then the battery is dead," we don't rule out the chance that aliens from outer space have nullified all electric fields.

6.6 PARTITIONED CONTROL STRUCTURES

When there are a thousand or more rules as in major current expert systems, the rules can interrelate in many ways, and a bug can be hard to trace. So just as with large computer programs, it's a good idea to divide rules into groups, modules, or partitions for which members of each group have minimal interactions with members of other groups. You can think of each group as a separate rule-based system that may occasionally decide to call on another for a separate analysis. An advantage is that the rule groups can be written and debugged mostly separately. This idea is called a *partitioning* or *context-limiting* control structure.

Diagnosis expert systems provide good examples. For instance in diagnosis of a malfunctioning car, there are major systems of the car that don't interact much with one another. If electrical devices aren't working, you can be pretty sure that the problem is in the electrical system; or if the car goes forward but not backward, you can be pretty sure the problem is in the transmission. So you can put rules for electrical problems in one partition, and rules for transmission problems in another, rules for the engine and fuel system in another, rules for the car body in another, and so on. You'll need one other partition of rules, a "startup" partition, to look at key evidence and decide which partition appears most relevant to a problem. And partitions can choose to transfer control to other partitions, if say none of their own rules succeed.

6.7 META-RULES

A general approach can encompass all the control structure ideas so far: specification of control by a rule-based system itself. *Meta-rules* are just rules whose domain of knowledge is the operation of another rule-based system; they're a kind of *heuristics*, a topic we'll investigate more thoroughly in Chapter 9. Rules deciding to load partitions (Section 6.6) are one simple example of meta-rules, but they can do many other things. Remember that one goal for putting knowledge into computers was to make explicit the complicated "commonsense" knowledge people have but don't realize they have. How to order rules and use them is another kind of commonsense knowledge, also formalizable. Here are some example meta-rules for a backward-chaining-like rule-based system, to control selection of the next rule to try to satisfy instead of following the database order of rules:

- Prefer the rule that handles the most serious issue.
- Prefer the rule that was written by the most knowledgeable human.
- Prefer the rule that is fastest to execute.
- Prefer the rule that has been used successfully the most times.
- Prefer the rule with the most things in common with the last rule successfully applied.

The big advantage of meta-rules is their flexibility and modifiability, which allows precise control of a rule-based system.

Meta-rules can express things besides rule orderings and partition referrals. Prolog interpreters make the *closed-world assumption* or *lack-of-knowledge inference*: if you can't prove something true, assume it false. This may be unfair for some predicates; a meta-rule could then override normal reasoning. For instance, a meta-rule could say to use the closed-world assumption only when querying predicates from a certain list, and to assume a failure means **yes** otherwise.

Meta-rules seem to be important in human reasoning. People aren't generally systematic enough to use any of the chaining methods successfully, but instead they rely on problem-specific meta-rules for deciding what to do next. So to reason more naturally, meta-rules are critical. But figuring out just what meta-rules people do use is hard.

6.8 DECISION LATTICES

We'll now consider some lower-level control structure ideas: decision lattices, concurrency, and and-or-not lattices. In the terminology of computer science, these are *compiled* structures. But they're compiled in a different sense than what programming-language "compilers" produce: they represent a simplifying first step before the traditional compiler operates. Some people don't consider these compiled structures true artificial intelligence, but they're so closely linked to artificial intelligence that we'd better explain them.

Choosing a good sequence for rules can be important and hard, as we discussed in Section 6.5. But computers can use storage structures besides sequences (see Appendix C). They can organize rules in a hierarchy, what is called a *decision lattice* or *discrimination net*. Decision lattices do a restricted but very efficient kind of reasoning, a kind of classification. The idea is to always specify where to go next in the computer based on question answers. In other words, a kind of *finite-state machine* without cycles. (Sometimes they're called *decision trees*, but technically they're lattices since branches that diverge can converge or "grow back together" later. Any graph without cycles in which this convergence can happen is a lattice and not a tree; cycles wouldn't make much sense for a decision lattice because you'd be asking the same question twice.)

For instance, consider an expert system to diagnose malfunctions of small household appliances (see Figure 6-5). It is important first to distinguish problems within the appliance from problems outside the appliance. A good way is to ask if the appliance works at all. If it doesn't, ask if it is plugged in. If it isn't, that is the problem. If it is, ask if other electric devices nearby (lights, clocks, etc.) work. If they don't, the problem sounds like a blown fuse. If other appliances definitely work, the problem must be internal to the faulty appliance. If no such observations can be made (as when there are no electrical appliances nearby), try plugging the faulty appliance into another outlet to see if the problem reappears.

On the other hand, if the appliance partially works, then it matters what kind of appliance it is. That's because interpretation of partial-failure clues is quite appliance-dependent, like smoke when the device has a heating element. As another example, strange noises are more serious in a device with no moving parts than in a blender. So the next question for a partially working appliance should classify it.

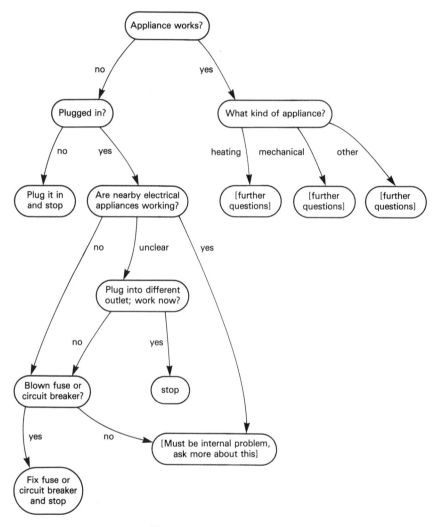

Figure 6-5. Decision lattice.

So decision lattices impose a classification hierarchy on the universe based on observations. They are useful for simple expert systems, with several advantages:

1. Implementation is easy: just use pointers (memory references) to indicate where in the computer to go next. They can even be implemented without a computer, as printed text with cross references.

2. They can easily support partitioning of an expert system.

3. They need not explicitly question a human being: they can examine buffer

contents or sensor readings. Then they can be fast, faster than the chaining methods, because no matching, binding, or backtracking is needed.

4. They can be designed to ask the absolutely minimal number of questions necessary to establish conclusions, unlike chaining methods for which such optimization can be difficult.

But decision lattices have major disadvantages as a compiled or "low-level" control structure:

1. They can't reason properly or efficiently for many applications because they don't easily permit variables or backtracking.
2. They are difficult to modify and debug, since later questions must assume certain results to earlier questions.
3. They can't easily reuse query answers since they don't explicitly cache.
4. They may be hard to build, because at each point you try to determine the best question to always ask, something not so easy to judge.

Decision lattices were around long before computers. Expert-system technology only made significant progress when decision-lattice control structures were mostly abandoned, due to the limitations mentioned.

6.9 CONCURRENCY IN CONTROL STRUCTURES

If speed of a rule-based system is important (as in a real-time application), and multiple processors are available, a control structure can use concurrency as another form of "compilation." Usually the processors must share and access the same database of facts and rules for this to work well. For a Prolog-style rule-based system, four types of parallelism for concurrency are identified (see Figure 6-6): (1) *partition parallelism*, (2) *or parallelism*, (3) *and parallelism*, and (4) *variable-matching parallelism*. These parallelisms are useful with all three kinds of chaining.

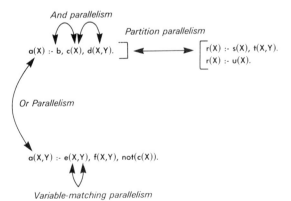

Figure 6-6. Types of parallelism.

Partition parallelism means running different partitions of the rules simultaneously. Each partition can reason separately, though they can explicitly pass conclusions to one another, or cache into a global database. This is good if we've got groups of rules that don't interact much, each group relevant to a problem.

"And" parallelism is parallelism among expressions "and"ed on the right side of a rule or a query. Usually it is only done for the predicate expressions that do not bind variables, the "tests" in the generate-and-test concept (see Section 3.12), or expressions that bind *different* variables. These tests can be done concurrently on separate processors; if any test fails, the whole "and" should fail, and the other processors should be sent a message to stop work. Otherwise, the "and" should succeed. "And" parallelism is probably not a good idea when some tests are much harder to satisfy than others; then the hard tests should be done first (see Chapter 13).

"Or" parallelism usually means parallelism between rules with the same left-side predicate name. It is good when there are many such rule groups. Or-parallel rules are sometimes called *demons* because they're like little people each waiting for their own particular set of conditions to be satisfied. "Or" parallelism can also mean parallel pursuit of facts in forward chaining.

Variable-matching parallelism is parallelism in the argument matching done when matching two predicate expressions to one another. It makes each match attempt faster, but it doesn't change the usual sequential examining of the database. It only pays off when you have a significant number of predicates with two or more arguments.

Concurrency can be simulated on a sequential machine. This gives a new class of control structures, the sequential reductions of concurrent process descriptions. This idea is often associated with the "agenda" search methods in Chapter 10.

Parallelism is not just an efficiency trick, however. Parallelism is necessary to model many real-world phenomena. These phenomena are often addressed in *object-oriented programming*, for which the world is divided into clusters of facts representing *objects*, each with its own partitioned module of rules governing its behavior. Object-oriented programming is especially useful for simulations. For instance, objects (and their facts) can represent organisms in an ecosystem, and a rule module for the particular organism can govern the behavior of each object. Another application is to modeling components of a car, where each object represents a part of a car. We'll talk more about object-oriented programming in Chapter 12. While it emphasizes rule-partition parallelism, it can also involve the other three kinds. For instance in modeling organisms in an ecosystem, "and" and "or" parallelism can reflect the ability of organisms to do and think several things simultaneously.

6.10 AND-OR-NOT LATTICES

The extreme case of parallelism in rule-based systems is the *and-or-not lattice* representation of rules, in which each rule can be thought (or maybe actually is) a hardware logic gate incessantly computing a certain logical combination of input logic signals representing facts and intermediate conclusions. (It's sometimes incorrectly called an *and-or tree*, but like in the decision lattice, the paths can recombine after splitting, so it isn't a tree necessarily.) "And"s in a rule become "and" gates, "or"s become "or" gates, and "not"s becomes inverter gates.

For instance, for the rules used previously:

```
/* R1 */ goal1 :- fact1.
/* R2 */ goal1 :- a, b.
/* R3 */ goal2(X) :- c(X).
/* R4 */ a :- not(d).
/* R5 */ b :- d.
/* R6 */ b :- e.
/* R7 */ c(2) :- not(e).
/* R8 */ d :- fact2, fact3.
/* R9 */ e :- fact2, fact4.
```

the and-or-not lattice is shown in Figure 6-7. Here we follow the usual conventions for gate shapes (see Appendix A); facts are the far-left-side "inputs" and goals are the far-right-side "outputs" of this logic network. Truth of a fact or conclusion is represented by a high or "on" voltage along a line, falsity by a low or "off" voltage. The output (right-side) voltage of a gate is determined by the logic function of the voltages representing input(s) on the left side; "and" gates determine a logical "and," "or" gates logical "or," and inverter gates logical "not." A given set of facts sets the input voltages for a group of initial gates, which determine voltages of others, and so on, with everything proceeding in parallel. The and-or-not lattice is a useful visual interpretation of rules and facts for the many applications in which order within "and"s and "or"s doesn't mean anything. It also provides a specification for an integrated-circuit chip that could do this very fast.

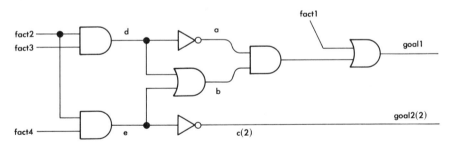

Figure 6-7. And-or-not lattice.

This unordered interpretation of rules takes us to the opposite extreme of the classical Eckert–Mauchly[2] model of the computer as a sequential processor. The main advantage of the and-or-not lattice is processing speed. Another advantage is

---

[2] Sometimes called the von Neumann model, but evidence now suggests that von Neumann had little to do with it.

the partitionability into modules: we can identify subnetworks and their inputs and outputs, and then build them easily into large networks. We don't need to worry much about *redundancies*, gates whose effect is also accomplished by other gates; they can't slow computation. But it is true we can't have contradictory gates or results will be meaningless.

Like decision lattices, and-or-not lattices do have the disadvantage that they can't handle variables well (you'll notice the example has none). Gates can't directly "bind" variables, though we could indirectly represent alternative bindings by having multiposition switches on each input to the logic network, switches that could connect the inputs to one of several lines representing the truths of different facts with the same predicate name. Then binding means selecting a switch position, and trying possible bindings means turning the switch and watching the conclusions reached. But this is awkward, and—especially when there is more than one variable—can greatly increase the time to get an answer, a main reason for using and-or-not lattices in the first place.

6.11 RANDOMNESS IN CONTROL STRUCTURES

A control structure need not be deterministic (that is, always work the same way on the same rules and facts). Human beings seem to have some randomness in their actions. So a control structure can make some random choices, especially when alternatives seem of equal worth. For instance, maybe in backward chaining when there are more than ten rules applicable to a situation, choose one at random. Randomness is most appropriate for rule-based systems trying to model skilled real-time performance by people. Randomness can prevent infinite loops, because when you choose randomly you can't get stuck in a rut.

6.12 GRAMMARS FOR INTERPRETING LANGUAGES*

Human and computer languages can be handled and processed with *grammars*. Grammars are rule-based systems different from those considered so far. For one thing, grammar rules don't deal with facts, but with strings of words or symbols in a particular order. All grammar rules are of a particular narrow form: a statement that one string of words can be substituted for another string of words. Though we didn't say so, we saw an example of a grammar in Section 5.9: those substitution pairs, though disguised as facts. But grammars can also have *nonterminal* words, words that symbolize grammatical categories and are not part of the language itself. For instance, the nonterminal "noun" can be substituted for the word "man" or the word "computer." Nonterminals can also describe sequences of words, like identifying a "noun phrase" as a determiner followed by an adjective followed by a noun. Linguists have lots of these categories.

Grammars are essential for getting computers to understand sentences in a language, because they make it possible to determine the structure of a sentence. Used this way, grammars are analogous to the rule-based systems in this chapter.

The "facts" are the words of a sentence, and the goal is to change that sentence, by substitutions, into the sentence consisting of the single nonterminal called "sentence." Such a process is analogous to forward chaining, and is called *bottom-up parsing*. It usually involves substituting shorter sequences of words for longer sequences of words. But you can also work in the opposite direction from "sentence" to a list of actual language words, analogously to backward chaining, and this is called *top-down parsing*. It usually involves substituting longer sequences of words for shorter sequences of words, and so is likely to require more backtracking than bottom-up parsing, but less work per backtrack since shorter sequences are searched for. Figure 6-8 shows an example; upward arrows represent bottom-up parsing, downward arrows top-down.

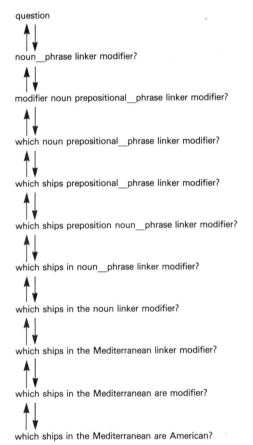

question

noun__phrase linker modifier?

modifier noun prepositional__phrase linker modifier?

which noun prepositional__phrase linker modifier?

which ships prepositional__phrase linker modifier?

which ships preposition noun__phrase linker modifier?

which ships in noun__phrase linker modifier?

which ships in the noun linker modifier?

which ships in the Mediterranean linker modifier?

which ships in the Mediterranean are modifier?

which ships in the Mediterranean are American?

Figure 6-8. Parsing example (downward arrows represent top-down parsing, upward arrows represent bottom-up).

Hybrids that compromise on the advantages and disadvantages of both bottom-up and top-down parsing are possible. Grammar rule order is important for efficiency: the most likely rules should be tried first. Parts of the sentence can be processed concurrently. Partitioning can be used to group information about related words and related parsing rules into modules. Meta-rules can be used for sophisticated control more like what people do.

Today most artificial-intelligence work in understanding sentences from human languages (or *natural languages*) uses a variation on top-down parsing called *augmented transition networks* (ATNs). These are a "smarter" kind of top-down parsing that attaches additional conditions to the parsing rules, so that only the most "reasonable" rules that apply will be tried. They also use recursion in a complicated way similar to the one in Chapter 11.

KEYWORDS

> *rule-based systems*
> *control structure*
> *conflict resolution*
> *expert systems*
> *compiled control structures*
> *backward chaining*
> *goal*
> *virtual facts*
> *the* asserta *predicate*
> *the* retract *predicate*
> *forward chaining*
> *focus-of-attention feature*
> *rule-cycle hybrid control structure*
> *rule and fact priorities*
> *rule specificity*
> *partitioned control structures*
> *meta-rules*
> *decision lattice*
> *partition parallelism*
> *"or" parallelism*
> *demons*
> *"and" parallelism*
> *variable-matching parallelism*
> *object-oriented programming*
> *and-or-not lattice*
> *grammar*
> *top-down parsing*
> *bottom-up parsing*
> *augmented transition networks (ATNs)*

EXERCISES

6-1. (A) Here's a rule-based system:

```
/* R1 */ k(X) :- j(X), b(X).
/* R2 */ f(X) :- a(X), not(g(X)).
/* R3 */ a(X) :- b(X), i.
/* R4 */ d :- i.
/* R5 */ d :- e(X), c.
/* R6 */ g(X) :- h, a(X).
/* R7 */ g(X) :- l.
/* R8 */ b(X) :- c.
```

Assume the goals are f(X), d, and k(X), in that order, and the facts are c, l, e(a), and j(b), in that order. Assume no extra caching. Assume we stop when a goal is proved.

(a) Suppose we use pure forward chaining. List the rule invocations, successes, and failures in order as they occur. Use the rule numbers to indicate rules.

(b) Now list the rule invocations, successes, and failures for backward chaining, in order.

(c) Does fact order affect which goal is proved first with forward chaining? Why?

(d) Does fact order affect which goal is proved first with backward chaining here? Why?

6-2. Consider this database:

```
top(X,Y,Z) :- bottom(Z,W,Y,X).
bottom(A,B,7,D) :- data(A,0,B), data(A,D,1).
data(3,0,1).
data(3,2,1).
```

List in order the facts that are proved by pure forward chaining using focus-of-attention placement of new facts. Don't stop until everything provable is proved.

6-3. Suppose we are doing pure forward chaining on a set of R rules, rules without semicolons ("or"s), nots, arithmetic, and variables. Suppose these rules have L distinct predicate expressions on the left sides, and S distinct predicate expressions, each occurring no more than M times, on the right sides. Suppose there are T total predicate expressions on right sides. Suppose there are F facts, $F > 0$.

(a) What is the maximum number of locations immediately matchable to facts (that is, without having to prove new facts) on rule right sides?

(b) What is the maximum number of new facts that can be eventually found by forward chaining?

(c) What would be the effect on your answer to part (a) of allowing one-argument variables in rules and facts?

(d) What would be the effect on your answer to part (b) of allowing one-argument variables in rules and facts? (A conclusion with an unbound variable still counts as one new fact.)

6-4. Consider the following Prolog database:

```
a(X) :- b(X).
b(X) :- c(X), d(X).
d(X) :- e, f(X).
c(X) :- g(X).
g(2).
f(5).
g(5).
e.
```

(a) What new facts are proved in order by the rule-cycle hybrid of forward and backward chaining? Continue until all possible facts are found.

(b) What new facts are proved in order by the pure form of forward chaining with focus-of-attention conflict resolution for facts? Continue until all possible facts are found.

6-5. (R,A) Consider the following rules and facts:

```
a :- v, t.
a :- b, u, not(t).
m(X) :- n(X), b.
b :- c.
t :- r, s.
u :- v, r.
r.
v.
c.
n(12).
```

(a) Suppose we do pure forward chaining with focus-of-attention placement of new facts. Suppose we want all possible conclusions. List in order the new facts derived from the preceding. Remember we must save nots for last.

(b) Suppose we do rule-cycle hybrid chaining with focus-of-attention placement of new facts, saving nots for last, and we want all possible conclusions. List in order the new facts derived.

(c) One problem with rule-cycle hybrid chaining is that it repeatedly checks the same rules again on each cycle. Describe a way to know when not to check a rule because of what happened on the last cycle, besides the idea of deleting a rule without variables when it succeeds. (Hint: Using this

idea you only need check nine rules total for the preceding rules and
facts.)

6-6. (E) Consider a variant of the rule-cycle hybrid that only cycles through the
rules once. How is this like an assembly line in a factory?

6-7. (A) Suppose we are doing rule-cycle hybrid chaining on R rules, rules
without variables and nots. Suppose there are L distinct predicate names on
rule left sides, and S distinct predicate names on rule right sides out of T
total predicate names on right sides. Suppose there are F facts, F > 0. What
is the maximum number of cycles needed to prove everything that can be
proved?

6-8. (A,H) Reasoning about rules and facts written in English instead of Prolog
can be tricky, and you must be careful. Consider the following rule-based
system for actions of a small reconnaissance robot. Suppose the following
facts are true, in this order:

> F1: There is an object with branches to the right of you.
> F2: This object is 2 feet tall.
> F3: This object occupies 20 cubic feet.
> F4: This object is stationary.
> F5: Another object is moving toward you.
> F6: You hear speech from that object. (Assume speech is not a loud noise.)

Assume all other facts mentioned in rules are false. Assume any new facts,
when added, will be put at the front of the list of facts. Assume the rule-
based system can result in the following actions, in this order:

> A1: Turn around.
> A2: Stop and wait.
> A3: Turn toward something.
> A4: Move a short distance forward.
> A5: Turn 20 degrees right.
> A6: Move a long distance forward.

Here are the rules:

> R1: If you hear a loud noise in front of you, then turn around and move a
> long distance.

> R2: If you want to hide, and there is a bush nearby, then turn toward the
> bush, and move a short distance.

> R3: If you want to hide, and are beneath a bush, then stop and wait.

> R4: If an object is moving toward you, and it is a person or vehicle, then
> hide.

> R5: If an object is moving, and it is an animal, then stop and wait.

> R6: If an object is an obstacle and you are moving, and the object is block-
> ing your path, then turn right 20 degrees, and move a short distance.

> R7: Move forward a long distance. [notice no "if" part here]

> R8: If an object has long branches, and the branches are moving, and it
> does not have wheels, then it is an animal.

> R9: If an object makes irregular noises, then it is an animal.

R10: If an object makes regular noises, and it is moving, it is a vehicle.

R11: If an object has wheels, then it is a vehicle.

R12: If an object is stationary, and occupies more than 1 cubic foot, it is an obstacle.

R13: If an obstacle has branches, and is less than 3 feet tall, it is a bush.

R14: If an obstacle has branches, and is more than 3 feet tall, it is a tree.

R15: If an obstacle has no branches, it is a rock.

R16: If an animal has four branches in two pairs, and one pair supports the animal, it is a person.

R17: If an animal speaks, it is a person.

(a) List in order the rule invocations, successes, and failures with backward chaining. Assume conflict resolution based on the rule order given. Assume caching of proved facts, so once something is concluded it need never be figured out again.

(b) List in order the rules invoked with forward chaining, ignoring rule R7. Again, take rules in the order given.

(c) Give a different kind of conflict resolution that would work well for this rule-based system.

6-9. (A) A rule-based system is monotonic if anything that can be concluded at one time can be concluded at any later time. Consider a consistent (that is, non-self-contradictory) "pure" backward-chaining rule-based system, one that doesn't use **asserta** or **retract** or any built-in predicates besides **not**. Such a system is necessarily monotonic.

(a) Suppose the system is partitioned into modules whose rules cannot "see" the rules of other modules until those modules are specifically loaded. Must the new scheme be monotonic?

(b) Suppose we cache intermediate and final conclusions reached by the system, using **asserta**. Must the new scheme be monotonic?

(c) Suppose we add to right sides of rules in the system **asserta** predicate expressions with arbitrary arguments. Must the new scheme be monotonic?

6-10. (E)

(a) Despite their similar names, decision lattices and and-or-not lattices are quite different things. List their major differences.

(b) List their major similarities.

6-11. Consider the following rule-based system for self-diagnosis and treatment of colds and flu:

    A. To sleep, go to bedroom.
    B. To drink fluids, go to kitchen.
    C. To drink fluids, go to bathroom.
    D. To take temperature, go to bathroom.
    E. To take aspirin, go to bathroom.
    F. To telephone, go to living room.
    G. To telephone, go to kitchen.

H. If feel headache or nasal congestion, then feel sick.

I . If feel sick, then take temperature.

J . If have fever, then take aspirin.

K. If have fever, then call boss.

L. If have fever, then go to bed.

M. If have nasal congestion or fever, then drink fluids.

(a) Order the rules in a good way. Show how backward chaining would work applied to the circumstance when you wake up with a headache, nasal congestion, and a fever. (Use the letter in front of each rule to identify it.)

(b) Suggest a fundamentally different control structure than the preceding, one good for this problem. (Find a general control structure that could work in many daily-living rule-based systems, not just this problem.) Show how it would work on the first eight rules applied to the same situation.

6-12. (R,A) Consider using a rule-based system as the brains of a "smart house," a house that automatically does a lot of things that people do for themselves in other houses. Assume the smart house can control power to all the electrical sockets, so it can turn lights, heat, and appliances on and off at programmed times. The smart house can also monitor many different kinds of sensors—for instance, light sensors to turn off outside lights during the daytime, infrared sensors to detect when people are in a room, audio sensors to detect unusual noises, and contact sensors to detect window openings (as by a burglar). Sensors permit flexible, unprogrammed action, like sounding a burglar alarm in the master bedroom only if someone is there, or turning off appliances when they seem to have been left on accidentally and no one is in the room anymore. Priorities could be established, so routine activities won't be allowed when sensors say a fire is in progress. Assume the rule-based system is invoked repeatedly to check for new conditions.

(a) Which is better for this problem, backward chaining or forward chaining? Why?

(b) Is caching a good idea? Why? If so, how would it work?

(c) Are virtual facts a good idea? Why? If so, how would they work?

(d) Is rule partitioning a good idea? Why? If so, how would it work?

(e) Are decision lattices a good idea? Why? If so, how would they work?

(f) Are and-or-not lattices implemented on integrated circuits a good idea? Why? If so, how would they work?

6-13. On the popular fictitious television show *The Citizenry's Courtroom*, Judge Wimpner hears small-claims cases and makes monetary awards of varying amounts to the plaintiff. But the award is misleading because the plaintiff and defendant are also paid for their appearance on the program, as one will discover on reading the small print of a disclaimer flashed on the screen for a second during the closing credits. The plaintiff is given 25 dollars plus the amount of the award plus half of a pool. The defendant is given 25 dollars plus the other half of the pool. The pool is zero if the amount of the award is

500 dollars or more, otherwise the difference between 500 dollars and the amount of the award.

(a) Suppose the award amount is represented in Prolog as a fact with predicate name **award** and one argument representing the amount of the award in dollars. Write four Prolog rules representing the above-stated calculations necessary for the plaintiff's amount, the defendant's amount, and the pool amount. Don't simplify; represent exactly what was stated.

(b) Now "compile" the above rules into four rules, two for the plaintiff amount and two for the defendant amount. Refer to the **award** predicate only once in each of those rules, and do not refer to pool amount. Also, the plaintiff rules should not refer to the defendant amount, nor the defendant rules to the plaintiff amount. Make all valid simplifications, both logical and arithmetic, of the rules that you can.

(c) Discuss what is needed to do this compilation for any set of rules involving arithmetic. Will a few simple tricks do it, or is a large rule-based expert system of its own necessary?

(d) What are the disadvantages of this form of compilation?

(e) Compare and contrast this kind of compilation with and-or-not lattices.

6-14. (E) *Occam's Razor* is the principle that when several alternative explanations are possible for something, you should pick the simplest one. Suppose we try to apply Occam's Razor to a rule-based system in which the left sides of rules represent explanations of phenomena.

(a) Which of the terms in Figure 6-1 best describes Occam's Razor?

(b) Why would it be very difficult to apply Occam's Razor to a practical problem?

6-15. (E) Compare and contrast the control structures discussed in this chapter with control of activities (by directive) in bureaucracies.

6-16. (P) Write a Prolog program to drive a car. Assume the following sensor facts are known to you, as "data":

S1: you are traveling below the speed limit
S2: you are traveling at the speed limit
S3: you are traveling above the speed limit
S4: you are on a two-lane road
S5: you are on a four-lane road
S6: you see an intersection coming up
S7: a car is less than 100 meters in front of you
S8: the road changes from two-lane to four-lane shortly
S9: the road will change from four-lane to two-lane shortly
S10: the brake lights of the car in front of you are on
S11: you are getting closer to the car in front of you
S12: you are passing another car going in the same direction

Assume the only actions are

A1: speed up
A2: slow down
A3: maintain speed
A4: pass a car in front of you (or keep passing one you're passing)

Here are examples of what you want the program to do. (These would not make good rules—they're too specific.)

    S2,S4,S6: slow down (A2)
    S2,S5,S8,S10: slow down (A2)
    S1,S5,S11: pass (A4)
    S1,S5: speed up (A1)
    S3,S4,S7: slow down (A2)

Write a Prolog program that decides what to do for every possible combination of the sensor facts. (Since there are 12 kinds, you must handle 2^{12} or 4096 different situations.) Assume your program is called every second to decide what to do that second. Choose a good control structure, and discuss (justify) your ordering of rules. Try to drive safely.

6-17. (E) Sometimes the ideas of science fiction writers seem pretty wild, but sometimes the ideas that seem wild really aren't when you think about them a bit.

(a) In *Camp Concentration* by Thomas Disch (1968), it's suggested that a disease that rearranges nerve patterns in the human brain could cause people to become a lot smarter, more able to reason and make inferences. Why is this not reasonable based on the assumption that people reason using the methods of this chapter? Suggest a small change to ideas from this chapter that would permit this phenomenon.

(b) In *Brain Wave* by Poul Anderson (1954), it's suggested that a small increase in speed of the nerve impulses in the human brain could lead to a much larger increase in the speed at which humans reason and make inferences. Why is this not reasonable based on the assumption that people reason using the methods of this chapter? Give a small change to ideas from this chapter that permit this phenomenon.

7

Let's examine how different control structures for rule-based systems can be implemented in Prolog. We'll cover backward chaining, rule-cycle hybrid chaining, forward chaining, input and output routines, meta-rules, and decision lattices. This will mean a lot of details; the last section of this chapter brings together the key Prolog code. Code similar to that discussed here provides the core of commercial software products called *expert systems shells*.

7.1 IMPLEMENTING BACKWARD CHAINING

Though Prolog is designed for backward chaining, there are many details for an implementer of a backward-chaining rule-based system to worry about when using Prolog, especially when the rule-based system is large. The traffic lights program in Section 4.11 was simple because traffic laws are *supposed* to be simple, so even people unenlightened enough never to have taken an artificial-intelligence course can understand them. Many rule-based systems can't be so nice, like those that diagnose and fix hard problems. Such rule-based systems are often called *expert systems*, because they automate the role of human experts. We'll introduce some general-purpose programming aids for expert systems in this chapter.

The goal of most expert systems is to reach a diagnosis, which we'll assume is obtained in Prolog-style backward chaining by typing the query

    ?- diagnosis(X).

125

So what is X? It should describe a diagnosis. We could connect words with under-scores as before, but there's an alternative: we can put single quotation marks (apostrophes) around a string of words to force treatment of it as a unit. That is, a *character string*. An advantage of character strings is that they can start with capi-tal letters and contain periods and commas, while ordinary words can't.

Here are some example diagnosis rules for an appliance-malfunction expert system for common household appliances:

```
diagnosis('Fuse blown') :- doesnt_work, all_lights_out.
diagnosis('Fuse blown') :- noise(pop).
diagnosis('Break in cord') :- doesnt_work, cord_frayed.
```

Of course we must define those right-side predicates.

7.2 IMPLEMENTING VIRTUAL FACTS AND CACHING_____

One problem is those rules require advance entry of facts (often, many facts) so that rule right sides can work properly. As we mentioned in the last chapter, vir-tual facts (facts demanded when needed) are a simple improvement. A good way to get them is to define a function predicate ask of two bound arguments. The first argument can be an input, a string containing question text to be typed out on the terminal, and the second argument can be an output, a variable to be bound to the question's answer that the user types.

```
ask(Q,A) :- write(Q), write('?'), read(A), nl.
```

Here write, read, and nl are Prolog predicates built-in in most implementations (see Appendix D); write prints its argument on the terminal, read reads something typed by the user and binds that something to the variable that is the read's argument, and nl sends a carriage return to the terminal. All always succeed.

Now we never want to ask a user the same question twice; we should cache answers so we can reuse them. It's easy to add this feature to the ask predicate. We just use the asserta built-in predicate introduced in Section 6.1, which takes a fact as argument and adds it to the Prolog database. Using it, conclusions can be added to the database as they are discovered. We can stick the asserta at the end of the definition of the ask predicate:

```
ask(Q,A) :- write(Q), write('?'), read(A), nl, asserta(ask(Q,A)).
```

Then if the same question is asked again, the fact will be used to answer it instead of this rule. This works because facts put in the database with asserta are put in front of all other facts and rules with the same first predicate name. Here's an example of the use of ask:

```
diagnosis('Fuse blown') :- ask('Does the device work at all',no),
    ask('Are the lights in the house off',yes).
```

This says to diagnose that the fuse is blown if (1) the user answers **no** when asked whether the device works at all, and (2) the user answers **yes** when asked whether all the lights in the house are off.

    You should carefully phrase the questions to be issued by a rule-based system. In particular, avoid pronouns and other indirect references to things, since rules and questions may be invoked in hard-to-predict orders. Generally, though there are exceptions, phrase questions so a **yes** answer means unusual things are going on, while a **no** means things are normal. For instance, after "Are the lights in the house off?," don't ask "Is the fuse OK?" but "Is the fuse blown?." And be consistent in phrasing questions. After that question "Are the lights in the house off?," ask "Does the fuse look blown?" in preference to "The fuse looks blown doesn't it?," to maintain the same verb-noun-adjective order.

7.3 INPUT CODING

We could implement a big expert system this way, with diagnosis rules having **ask** predicates on their right sides. But this can require much repetition. So two important coding tricks are used in large rule-based systems: coding of input (answers) and coding of output (questions and diagnoses).

    Input coding groups user answers into categories. An important case is questions with only **yes** or **no** answers; expert systems often to rely on them for simplicity. We can define two new predicates **affirmative** and **negative**, which say whether a word the user typed is a positive or a negative answer respectively:

```
affirmative(yes).
affirmative(y).
affirmative(ye).
affirmative(right).
affirmative(ok).
affirmative(uhhuh).
negative(no).
negative(n).
negative(not).
negative(never).
negative(impossible).
negative(haha).
```

Then we can define a predicate **askif** of one input argument. It will be just like **ask** except it will have only one argument, the question, and it will succeed if that question is answered affirmatively and fail if the question is answered negatively.

We can also fix it so that if an answer is neither positive nor negative (in other words, it is unclear), we will complain and ask for another answer.

```
askif(Q) :- ask(Q,A), positive_answer(Q,A).
positive_answer(Q,A) :- affirmative(A).
positive_answer(Qcode,A) :- not(negative(A)), not(affirmative(A)),
  write('Please answer yes or no.'), read(A2),
  retract(asked(Qcode,A)), asserta(asked(Qcode,A2)),
  affirmative(A2).
```

We can also define:

```
askifnot(Q) :- not(askif(Q)).
```

which saves some parentheses.

Users may not always understand a question. We can let them type a ? instead of an answer, give them some explanatory text, and provide them another chance to answer:

```
ask(Q,A) :- asked(Q,A).
ask(Q,A) :- not(asked(Q,A)), write(Q), write('? '), read(A2),
  ask2(Q,A2,A).
ask2(Q,'?',A) :- explain(Q), ask(Q,A).
ask2(Q,A,A) :- not(A = '?'), asserta(asked(Q,A)).
```

where **explain** facts store explanatory text. Minor humanizing touches such as these can be immensely important to user satisfaction, while imposing little on the programmer.

7.4 OUTPUT CODING

Another useful trick is to code questions, so we need not repeat their text at each mention in the rules. Codes for questions also make rules easier to read, and help prevent mistakes because it's easy to err in typing a long string of text (and with caching, every slightly different question is asked and cached separately). For this we can use a predicate **questioncode** of two arguments, a code word and a text string for the corresponding question. Here's an example from appliance diagnosis:

```
diagnosis('Fuse blown') :- askif(device_dead), askif(lights_out).
diagnosis('Fuse blown') :- askif(hear_pop).
diagnosis('Break in cord') :- askif(device_dead),
  askif(cord_frayed).
questioncode(device_dead,'Does the device refuse to do anything').
questioncode(lights_out,
  'Do all the lights in the house seem to be off').
questioncode(hear_pop,'Did you hear a sound like a pop').
questioncode(cord_frayed,
  'Does the outer covering of the cord appear to be coming apart').
```

To handle this, we must redefine ask:

```
ask(Qcode,A) :- asked(Qcode,A).
ask(Qcode,A) :- not(asked(Qcode,A)), questioncode(Qcode,Q),
  write(Q), write('? '), read(A2), ask2(Q,Qcode,A2,A).
ask2(Q,Qcode,'?',A) :- explain(Qcode), ask(Qcode,A).
ask2(Q,Qcode,A,A) :- not(A = '?'), asserta(asked(Qcode,A)).
```

A further refinement is to handle a class of related questions together. We can do this by giving arguments to output codes, as for instance using hear(X) to represent a question about hearing a sound X. Then to make the query we need string concatenation, something unfortunately not available in many Prolog dialects. But there is a simple shortcut to concatenation by writing a **questioncode** rule instead of a fact, that types extra words before succeeding:

```
questioncode(hear(X),X) :- write('Did you hear a sound like a ').
```

So to ask if the user heard a pop sound you use

```
askif(hear(pop)).
```

which prints on the terminal as

Did you hear a sound like a pop?

Yet another coding trick is to code diagnoses. This isn't as useful as question coding, but helps when diagnoses are provable in many different ways. Diagnosis coding requires a new top-level predicate that users must query instead of diagnosis, as

```
coded_diagnosis(D) :- diagnosis(X), diagnosis_code(X,D).
```

For instance, we could use

```
diagnosis(fuse) :- ask('Does the device work at all',no),
  ask(Are the lights in the house off',yes).
diagnosis_code(fuse,'Fuse blown').
```

Then we could get this behavior:

```
?- coded_diagnosis(X).
Does the device work at all? no.
Are the lights in the house off? yes.
X = Fuse blown
```

7.5 INTERMEDIATE PREDICATES_____

Building expert systems is straightforward when there are less than a hundred rules averaging less than three expressions on the right side. But it can get confusing when, as in a typical expert system today, there are thousands of rules averaging ten expressions per right side. It just gets too difficult to keep track of all the symbols used and to determine everything necessary for each rule. The solution is to frequently use intermediate predicates, predicates that occur on both the left and right sides of rules. Intermediate predicates can represent important simplifying generalizations about groups of facts. Viewing expert-system predicates as a hierarchy with diagnoses or final conclusions at the top and asked questions at the bottom, intermediate predicates are everything in between. Much of the intelligence and sophistication of expert systems can come from a good choice of intermediate predicates to reduce redundancy and simplify rules.

A useful intermediate predicate with appliance diagnosis is **power_problem**, a predicate that is true if the appliance is not getting any electricity for its innards. It's useful because appropriate diagnoses when it is true are quite different from those when it is false: a nonpower problem must be in the device itself and can't be in the cord or external fuse. So **power_problem** can go into many rules, typically early in the right side of the rule to prevent inappropriate rule use. But **power_problem** clearly is an intermediate predicate, not a fact we can establish from a single question, because it has many different symptoms. And some symptoms are very strong, as when all the lights in the house went off when you tried to turn on the device, or when the device stopped working when you moved its frayed cord slightly.

Generally speaking, intermediate predicates are needed for any important phenomena that aren't diagnoses. Here are some more ideas for intermediate predicates in appliance diagnosis:

- whether the problem is mechanical;
- whether the problem is in a heating element;
- whether the appliance has had similar problems before;
- whether you can improve things by adjusting the controls or buttons;
- whether danger of electrocution is present;
- whether anything unusual was done to the appliance lately (like being dropped or having liquids spilled on it);
- how much troubleshooting expertise the user has (note that intermediate predicates can have arguments).

Intermediate-predicate expressions won't be arguments to **askifs**, since they don't directly query a user. Caching is a good idea with intermediate predicates, even more so than caching of query answers (as we did with the **ask** predicate); a single intermediate-predicate fact can summarize many questions, and caching it saves having to ask all those questions over again. Nevertheless, caching of intermediate-predicate conclusions should not necessarily be automatic, as it only makes sense when a result might be reused.

7.6 AN EXAMPLE PROGRAM_____

Let's put together the ideas we've introduced in this chapter into a larger rule-based system for the diagnosis of malfunctions in small household appliances. Figure 7-1 shows some of the terminology, and Figure 7-2 gives the predicate hierarchy. We list rules in three groups: diagnosis (top-level) rules, intermediate predicate rules, and question-decoding rules.

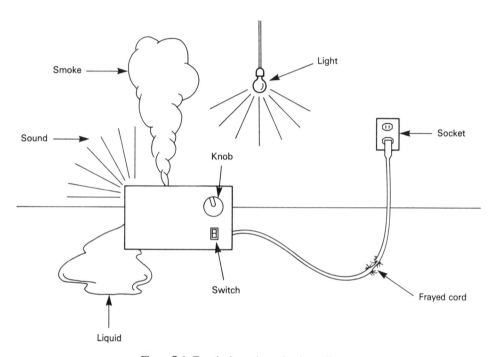

Figure 7-1. Terminology about simple appliances.

To get a diagnosis from this program, query diagnosis(X). Typing a semicolon will then give you an alternative diagnosis, if any; and so on. So if several things are wrong with the appliance, the program will eventually find them all.

```
/* Top-level diagnosis rules */
diagnosis('Fuse blown') :- power_problem, askif(lights_out).
diagnosis('Fuse blown') :- power_problem, askif(hear(pop)).
diagnosis('Break in cord') :- power_problem, askif(cord_frayed).
diagnosis('Short in cord') :- diagnosis('Fuse blown'),
  askif(cord_frayed).
diagnosis('Device not turned on') :- power_problem,
  klutz_user, askif(has('an on-off switch or control')),
  askifnot(device_on).
diagnosis('Cord not in socket properly') :- power_problem,
  klutz_user, askif(just_plugged), askifnot(in_socket).
```

```
diagnosis('Foreign matter caught on heating element') :-
  heating_element, not(power_problem), askif(smell_smoke).
diagnosis('Appliance wet(emdry it out and try again') :-
  power_problem, klutz_user, askif(liquids).
diagnosis('Controls adjusted improperly') :- klutz_user,
  askif(has('knobs or switches')).
diagnosis('Kick it, then try it again') :- mechanical_problem.
diagnosis('Throw it out and get a new one').


/* Definitions of intermediate predicates */
power_problem :- askif(device_dead).
power_problem :- askif(has('knobs or switches')), askifnot(knobs_do_something).
power_problem :- askif(smell_smoke), not(heating_element).
klutz_user :- askifnot(handyperson).
klutz_user :- askifnot(familiar_appliance).
mechanical_problem :- askif(hear('weird noise')),
  askif(has('moving parts')).
heating_element :- askif(heats).
heating_element :- askif(powerful).

/* Question decoding */
questioncode(device_dead,'Does the device refuse to do anything').
questioncode(knobs_do_something,
  'Does changing the switch positions or turning
  the knobs change anything').
questioncode(lights_out,
  'Do all the lights in the house seem to be off').
questioncode(cord_frayed,
  'Does the outer covering of the cord appear to be coming apart').
questioncode(handyperson,'Are you good at fixing things').
questioncode(familiar_appliance,
  'Are you familiar with how this appliance works').
questioncode(device_on,'Is the ON/OFF switch set to ON').
questioncode(just_plugged,'Did you just plug the appliance in').
questioncode(in_socket,'Is the cord firmly plugged into the socket').
questioncode(smell_smoke,'Do you smell smoke').
questioncode(liquids,
  'Have any liquids spilled on the appliance just now').
questioncode(heats,'Does the appliance heat things').
questioncode(powerful,'Does the appliance require a lot of power').
questioncode(has(X),X) :- write('Does the appliance have').
questioncode(hear(X),X) :- write('Did you hear a ').
```

Here we use variables inside question codes for questions about components and sounds heard. We also use a *subdiagnosis* ('Fuse blown') as input to another diagnosis, a useful trick.

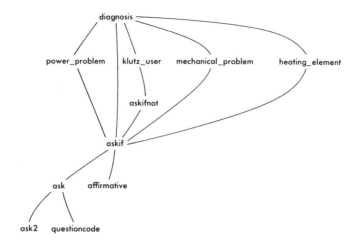

Figure 7-2. Predicate hierarchy for the appliance diagnosis expert system, including the problem-independent predicates.

7.7 RUNNING THE EXAMPLE PROGRAM_____

Here's an actual run of this program (which requires definitions of **askif** and other predicates given earlier in this chapter). Note the same diagnosis is repeated when there are different ways to prove it.

```
?- diagnosis(X).
Does the device refuse to do anything? yes.
Do all the lights in the house seem to be off? no
Does the appliance have knobs or switches? yes.
Does changing the switch positions or turning
the knobs change anything? no.
Do you smell smoke? yes.
Does the appliance heat things? no.
Does the appliance require a lot of power? no.
Did you hear a pop? yes.
X = Fuse blown;
X = Fuse blown;
X = Fuse blown;
Does the outer covering of the cord appear to be
coming apart? no.
Are you good at fixing things? no.
Does the appliance have an on-off switch or control? yes.
Is the ON/OFF switch set to ON? no.
X = Device not turned on;

Are you familiar with how this appliance works? no.
X = Device not turned on;
```

X = Device not turned on;
X = Device not turned on;
X = Device not turned on;
X = Device not turned on;

Did you just plug the appliance in? yes.
Is the cord firmly plugged into the socket? no.
X = Cord not in socket properly;
X = Cord not in socket properly;
X = Cord not in socket properly;
X = Cord not in socket properly;
X = Cord not in socket properly;
X = Cord not in socket properly;

Have any liquids spilled on the appliance just now? maybe.
Please type yes or no. no.
X = Controls adjusted improperly;
X = Controls adjusted improperly;
Did you hear a weird noise? no.
X = Throw it out and get a new one;
no

7.8 PARTITIONED RULE-BASED SYSTEMS_____

Intermediate predicates group related rules together, but they are only a conceptual grouping, more a help to understanding and debugging programs. A stronger way of grouping is putting rules into partitions that can't "see" one another. This is easy to do with Prolog by putting rules in separate files and only loading the files you need into the database. Loading is done with the **consult** built-in predicate in Prolog, a predicate of one argument which is the name of the file to load. So if the rule

    a :- b, c.

is used for backward chaining, and we want whenever it succeeds for the file "more" to be loaded, we should rewrite it as

    a :- b, c, consult(more).

Like most built-in predicates, **consult** always fails on backtracking since there's only one way to load a file.

Often one partition is designated the "starting" partition, loaded automatically when the rule-based system begins. It then decides which other partitions to load and invoke. If a loaded partition later decides it's not relevant (as when none of its rules fire), it can itself load another partition and start that one running.

7.9 IMPLEMENTING THE RULE-CYCLE HYBRID_____

Prolog's features make backward chaining easy. But it's also a general-purpose programming language, and can implement quite different control structures.

First consider the rule-cycle hybrid of backward and forward chaining, easier to implement than pure forward chaining and hence used in many simple expert systems. It can be approximated by writing each rule in a new form, a transformation of each backward chaining rule:

1. "and" a new **asserta** on the right end of the right side of the rule, whose argument is the left side of the rule;
2. "and" a new **not** on the left end of the right side of the rule, with the same argument;
3. then replace the left side of the rule by r (first renaming any r predicates already in the rules).

So these backward chaining rules

```
a :- b.
c :- d, e, f.
```

become

```
r :- not(a), b, asserta(a).
r :- not(c), d, e, f, asserta(c).
```

And two sample rules from the appliance diagnosis program

```
diagnosis('Fuse blown') :- power_problem, askif(lights_out).
power_problem :- askif(device_dead), askif(has(knobs)),
  askif(knobs_do_something).
```

become

```
r :- not(diagnosis('Fuse blown')), power_problem, askif(lights_out),
  asserta(diagnosis('Fuse blown')).
r :- not(power_problem), askif(device_dead), askif(has(knobs)),
  askif(knobs_do_something), asserta(power_problem).
```

(We'll discuss later how to convert automatically.) So we replace our old rules with new rules whose only effect is caching of particular conclusions. Note that these new rules never call on one another, even if there are intermediate predicates, because r is the only left side. We'll assume for now that no predicate expressions in the original rules contain **not**s, since they introduce complications. If we really need negatives, we can define fact predicates that stand for the opposite of other fact predicates.

Now we must cycle through the rules; that is, consider each rule in order, and go back to the first when we finish the last. Within each pass, we can force the Prolog interpreter to repeatedly backtrack to a query of r. A simple way is

```
?- r, 1 = 2.
```

Since the = can never be true, the interpreter will keep trying r rules, regardless of whether they succeed or fail. Eventually it will run out of all r rules and fail. Actually, there's a built-in Prolog predicate called fail that has exactly the same effect as $1 = 2$, so we can say equivalently

```
?- r, fail.
```

To give us a handle on this code, let's give it a name:

```
one_cycle :- r, fail.
```

To get the Prolog interpreter to repeat indefinitely a cycle through the rules, we might think that we could do the same fail trick, like

```
hybrid :- one_cycle, fail.
```

But this won't work because one_cycle won't ever return to the *top* of the list of rules. And one_cycle itself never succeeds, so the fail is useless. We could try

```
hybrid :- not(one_cycle), fail.
```

which answers the second objection but not the first: we need each call to one_cycle to be a fresh call. That suggests recursion:

```
hybrid :- done.
hybrid :- not(one_cycle), hybrid.
```

The done is a stopping condition that must be defined by the builder of the rule-based system. For diagnosis expert systems, it could be defined as

```
done :- diagnosis(X).
```

which says to stop whenever some diagnosis is proved.

The preceding definition of hybrid only checks once per cycle whether it is done. To stop sooner, we could put the check inside one_cycle like this:

```
hybrid :- done.
hybrid :- not(one_cycle), hybrid.
one_cycle :- r, done.
```

But this requires more calls to **done**, not a good idea if **done** is a complicated calculation.

Note: This approach can handle **nots** in rules, though differently from the algorithm in Section 6.4 since **nots** will be evaluated on every cycle. But as with the algorithm, any **not** must occur before any rule with the argument to the **not** as its left side, or we'll get wrong answers.

7.10 IMPLEMENTING PURE FORWARD CHAINING*_____

Pure forward chaining requires yet another rule form. (See Section 7.14 for how to rewrite rules automatically in this form.) Since pure forward chaining repeatedly finds and "crosses out" expressions on the right sides of rules, it would help to express rule right sides as lists, for then we can use our **member** and **delete** list-processing predicates from Chapter 5. We can do this by making rules a kind of fact, say using a **rule** predicate name. We require rules without "or"s. The first argument to **rule** can be the left side of the original rule, and the second argument the list of predicate expressions "and"ed on the right side. So these rules

```
a :- b.
c :- d, e, f.
g(X) :- h(X,Y), not(f(Y)).
```

become

```
rule(a,[b]).
rule(c,[d,e,f]).
rule(g(X),[h(X,Y),not(f(Y))]).
```

and the two sample rules from the appliance diagnosis program

```
diagnosis('Fuse blown') :- power_problem, askif(lights_out).
power_problem :- askif(device_dead), askif(has(knobs)),
   askif(knobs_do_something).
```

become

```
rule(diagnosis('Fuse blown'),[power_problem,askif(lights_out)]).
rule(power_problem,
   [askif(device_dead),askif(has(knobs)),askif(knobs_do_something)]).
```

For now, we'll assume that the rules don't contain **nots**.

We also must represent facts. Pure forward chaining requires that we identify all facts, distinguishing them from rules. We can do this by making each fact an argument to a predicate named **fact**, of one argument. Then to bind F to every fact in turn, we query

> ?- fact(F), done.

which will backtrack repeatedly into **fact**. For every fact **F**, we must find the rules whose right sides can match it, to derive new rules and possibly new facts. This suggests

> forward :- fact(F), not(pursuit(F)), done.

To implement "focus-of-attention" forward chaining, we can't insert new facts just after the last fact we selected, only at the beginning (with **asserta**) and end (with **assertz**) of the database. To prevent fact reuse, we can delete facts once pursued. But deleted facts are still important to us (obtaining facts is the whole point of forward chaining) so we'll copy them into **usedfact** facts before we delete them. The revised code:

> forward :- done.
> forward :- fact(F), not(pursuit(F)), assertz(usedfact(F)),
>   retract(fact(F)), forward.

(Remember from Section 6.1 that **retract** removes a fact from the database.) Then when we're done, all the things we learned plus all the starting facts are in the database as arguments to the **fact** and **usedfact** predicates.

The **pursuit** predicate can cycle through the rules with a **fail** like **one_cycle** did in the hybrid implementation:

> pursuit(F) :- rule(L,R), rule_pursuit(F,L,R), fail.

For **rule_pursuit** we must search through the right side of a rule, deleting anything that matches the fact **F**; we can use the **member** and **delete** predicates of Sections 5.5 and 5.6, respectively. As you may dimly recall, **member** checks whether an item is a member of a list, and **delete** removes all occurrences of an item from a list. We need them both because **delete** always succeeds, and we'd like to fail when a match doesn't occur in the list. So (Figure 7-3)

> forward :- done.
> forward :- fact(F), not(pursuit(F)), assertz(usedfact(F)),
>   retract(fact(F)), forward.
> pursuit(F) :- rule(L,R), rule_pursuit(F,L,R), fail.
> rule_pursuit(F,L,R) :- member(F,R), delete(F,R,Rnew),
>   new_rule(L,Rnew).
> new_rule(L,[]) :- not(fact(L)), asserta(fact(L)).
> new_rule(L,R) :- not(R = []), asserta(rule(L,R)).

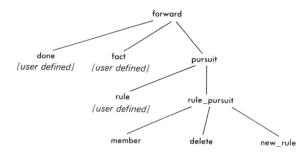

Figure 7-3. Predicate hierarchy for the forward-chaining program.

The two **new_rule** lines say that when you've deleted everything on the right side of a rule, the left side is a new fact; otherwise just write a new, shorter, and simpler rule. And here again are **member** and **delete**:

    member(X,[X|L]).
    member(X,[Y|L]) :- member(X,L).
    delete(X,[],[]).
    delete(X,[X|L],M) :- delete(X,L,M).
    delete(X,[Y|L],[Y|M]) :- not(X = Y), delete(X,L,M).

As with the rule-cycle hybrid, you must define **done** appropriately. If you want to make sure that all possible conclusions are reached, use

    done :- not(fact(X)).

which forces forward chaining to continue until there are no more **fact** facts, in which case everything learned (as well as the initial facts) is a **usedfact**. (Note this rule violates our advice in Section 3.6 to avoid **not**s whose variables aren't bound. Here we want to continue if there's any unexamined fact **X** remaining, a kind of existential quantification, so it makes sense. A universally quantified negation is equivalent to the negative of an existentially quantified unnegation; see Appendix A.) Alternatively, **done** can be defined to mean that one of a set of diagnosis facts have been proved.

The **asserta** in the first **new_rule** rule is important because it forces focus-of-attention handling of new facts. That is, the last fact found will be the next fact pursued, like a stack data structure, because of the recursion. As we pointed out in the last chapter, the focus-of-attention approach often reaches interesting conclusions fast. If we change that **asserta** to **assertz**, we get a queue instead of a stack, with new facts pursued only after old facts.

Amazingly, the program works just fine when rules contain variables.[1] This is because the basis step (first line) in the **member** predicate definition can bind vari-

---

[1] This won't work in Turbo Prolog. The programs in Sections 7.12 and 7.14 won't work in Turbo Prolog either.

ables to succeed, and when it does those variables keep the same bindings through the rest of the rule. If there is more than one matching of a fact to a rule, the program will find each by backtracking to **member**. For instance, the rule

rule(a(X,Y),[b(X,Y),b(Y,X),b(X,X)]).

can match the fact b(tom,dick) to either the first or second predicate expression on its right side, giving two new rules:

rule(a(tom,dick),[b(dick,tom),b(tom,tom)]).
rule(a(dick,tom),[b(dick,tom),b(dick,dick)]).

When forward chaining with the preceding program is slow, a simple change can often speed things up. That is to delete the old rule when a new rule is formed. To do this, we need only add a single expression to the **rule_pursuit** rule:

rule_pursuit(F,L,R) :- member(F,R), delete(F,R,Rnew),
    retract(rule(L,R)), new_rule(L,Rnew).

We can only do this safely for rule-based systems representable as and-or-not lattices, where there are either no variables or only variables that can take a single binding. Otherwise deletion will throw away still possibly useful rules, but this may not bother us if the odds are small they're still useful.

7.11 FORWARD CHAINING WITH "NOT"S* _____

As with hybrid chaining, we can avoid rules containing **nots** by substituting "unfact" predicate names representing the opposite of other predicate names. Or we can require that arguments to **nots** never be matchable to anything appearing on the left side of a rule (DeMorgan's laws can get the rules into this form; see Appendix A). Then we rewrite the top level of the program to handle **nots** after it's done everything else:

full_forward :- succeeding_forward, not(handle_nots),
    succeeding_forward.
succeeding_forward :- forward.
succeeding_forward.
handle_nots :- rule(L,R), remove_matched_nots(L,R,Rnew),
    retract(rule(L,R)), not(member(not(X),Rnew)), new_rule(L,Rnew),
    fail.
remove_matched_nots(L,[],[]).
remove_matched_nots(L,[not(X)|R],Rnew) :- not(usedfact(X)),
    not(fact(X)), remove_matched_nots(L,R,Rnew).
remove_matched_nots(L,[I|R],[I|Rnew]) :-
    remove_matched_nots(L,R,Rnew).

(Some dialects require that you use **not** X instead of not(X) for the above to work, even when the language itself usually accepts not(X).) This is not quite the algorithm in Section 6.2, but it's close.

7.12 GENERAL ITERATION
WITH ''FORALL'' AND ''DOALL''* _____

The iteration method of the rule-cycle hybrid and forward chaining programs can be generalized. First, suppose we want to check whether some predicate expression **Q** succeeds for all possible variable values that satisfy some other predicate expression **P**; that is, we want to check *universal quantification* of **Q** with respect to **P**. We can do this by requiring that there be no way for **Q** to fail when **P** has succeeded previously, taking into account any bindings. We can use the built-in **call** predicate of most Prolog dialects, which queries a predicate expression given as argument:

```
forall(P,Q) :- not(somefailure(P,Q)).
somefailure(P,Q) :- call(P), not(call(Q)).
```

As an example, assume this database:

```
a(1).
a(2).
b(1).
b(2).
c(1).
c(2).
c(3).
d(1,5).
d(5,1).
```

Here are some example queries and their results:

```
?- forall(a(X),b(X)).
yes
?- forall(b(X),c(X)).
yes
?- forall(c(X),b(X)).
no
?- forall(c(X),d(X,Y)).
no
?- forall(d(X,Y),d(Y,X)).
yes
```

Similarly, we can define a predicate that repeatedly backtracks into predicate expression P until P fails:

```
doall(P) :- not(alltried(P)).
alltried(P) :- call(P), fail.
```

Assume this database:

```
a(1).
a(2).
a(3).
u(X) :- a(X), write(X).
v(X) :- a(X), Y is X*X, write(Y), nl.
```

Then here are two examples:

```
?- doall(u(X)).
123
yes
?- doall(v(X)).
1
4
9
yes
```

(Remember, write prints its argument on the terminal, and nl prints a carriage return.) This doall is just what the forward chaining program accomplishes in the pursuit predicate. So we can rewrite the first four lines of the forward chaining program as

```
forward :- done.
forward :- fact(F), doall(pursuit(F)), assertz(usedfact(F)),
   retract(fact(F)), forward.
pursuit(F) :- rule(L,R), rule_pursuit(F,L,R).
```

instead of

```
forward :- done.
forward :- fact(F), not(pursuit(F)), assertz(usedfact(F)),
   retract(fact(F)), forward.
pursuit(F) :- rule(L,R), rule_pursuit(F,L,R), fail.
```

And in the rule-cycle hybrid

```
hybrid :- done.
hybrid :- doall(r), hybrid.
```

can be used instead of

```
hybrid :- done.
hybrid :- not(one_cycle), hybrid.
one_cycle :- r, fail.
```

And the code for handling nots in forward chaining given in Section 7.11 can be improved to

```
full_forward :- succeeding_forward, doall(handle_nots),
  succeeding_forward.
handle_nots :- rule(L,R), remove_matched_nots(L,R,Rnew),
  retract(rule(L,R)), not(member(not(X),Rnew)), new_rule(L,Rnew).
```

instead of

```
full_forward :- succeeding_forward, not(handle_nots),
  succeeding_forward.
handle_nots :- rule(L,R), remove_matched_nots(L,R,Rnew),
  retract(rule(L,R)), not(member(not(X),Rnew)), new_rule(L,Rnew).
  fail.
```

The changes improve program readability.

7.13 INPUT AND OUTPUT OF FORWARD CHAINING*_____

Fact pursuit is only part of what we need for forward chaining. We must also handle input and output differently than with backward chaining. Backward chaining asked the user a question whenever an answer was relevant to some conclusion under study. This can mean that many irrelevant questions are asked before backward chaining hits on the right conclusions to try to prove. Forward chaining, on the other hand, focuses on a set of facts. The facts must get into the database somehow to start things off.

Two approaches are possible. First, give a *questionnaire*, a fixed set of questions to a user presented one at a time, and code answers into facts. Fixed questionnaires are common in the early part of medical diagnosis, when a doctor tries to get a broad picture of the health of a patient before moving on to specifics. Second (especially if most possible facts don't have arguments), give a *menu*, a set of questions presented simultaneously to the user, and ask which questions should be answered yes. For diagnosis applications, the menu can contain common symptoms. Menus are good when there are lots of possible facts, few of which are simultaneously relevant to a case.

Both are straightforward to implement in Prolog. Questionnaires can be done by a fixed sequence of calls to the askif predicate defined in Section 7.3. The answer to each question will cause the assertion of asked and fact facts. Menus can be implemented by an ask_which predicate:[2]

```
ask_which([A,B,C,D,E,F,G,H|L]) :-
  screen_ask_which([A,B,C,D,E,F,G,H],[A,B,C,D,E,F,G,H]),
  ask_which(L).
ask_which([]).
ask_which(L) :- length(L,N), N<9, N>0, screen_ask_which(L,L).
screen_ask_which([X|L],L2) :- length(L,N), length(L2,N2),
  N3 is N2 - N, write(N3), write(': '), questioncode(X,Q),
  write(Q), write('?'), nl, asserta(asked(X,no)),
  screen_ask_which(L,L2).
screen_ask_which([],L2) :-
  write('Give numbers of questions whose answer is yes.'),
  read(AL), create_facts(AL,L2), nl.
create_facts([N|L],L2) :- item(N,L2,I), assertz(fact(I)),
  retract(asked(I,no)), asserta(asked(I,yes)), create_facts(L,L2).
create_facts([N|L],L2) :- not(item(N,L2,I)), create_facts(L,L2).
create_facts([],L2).
item(1,[X|L],X).
item(N,[X|L],I) :- N > 1, N2 is N-1, item(N2,L,I).
member(X,[X|L]).
member(X,[Y|L]) :- member(X,L).
length([],1).
length([X|L],N) :- length(L,N2), N is N2 + 1.
```

Here's an example use, assuming the questioncode definitions for appliance diagnosis given earlier (Section 7.6):

```
?- ask_which
([device_dead,knobs_do_something,lights_out,cord_frayed,
handyperson,familiar_appliance,device_on,just_plugged,in_socket,
smell_smoke,liquids,heats,powerful,has(knobs),has('moving parts'),
has('knobs, switches, or other controls'),
hear(pop),hear('weird noise')]).
1: Does the device refuse to do anything?
2: Does changing the switch positions or turning
the knobs change anything?
3: Do all the lights in the house seem to be off?
4: Does the outer covering of the cord appear to be
coming apart?
5: Are you good at fixing things?
6: Are you familiar with how this appliance works?
7: Is the ON/OFF switch set to ON?
```

---

[2] It's interesting to compare this program to the forward-chaining program in Section 7.10: this represents more a Lisp style of programming, with recursion through lists and no expectation of backtracking. The forward-chaining program represents more a Prolog style of programming, with frequent backtracking and no lists.

8: Did you just plug the appliance in?
Give numbers of questions whose answer is yes.[3,4,5,7].

1: Is the cord firmly plugged into the socket?
2: Do you smell smoke?
3: Have any liquids spilled on the appliance just now?
4: Does the appliance heat things?
5: Does the appliance require a lot of power?
6: Does the appliance have knobs?
7: Does the appliance have moving parts?
8: Does the appliance have knobs, switches, or other controls?
Give numbers of questions whose answer is yes.[6,8].

1: Did you hear a pop?
2: Did you hear a weird noise?
Give numbers of questions whose answer is yes.[].
yes

To verify that the correct facts were asserted, we can use Prolog's built-in listing predicate that takes one argument, a predicate name, and prints out every fact and rule with that name:

```
?- listing(fact).
fact(device_dead).
fact(lights_out).
fact(cord_frayed).
fact(handyperson).
fact(device_on).
fact(has(knobs)).
fact(has('knobs, switches, or other controls')).
yes
```

Fact order is very important to the operation and hence the efficiency of forward chaining (see Figure 6-3). Furthermore, if your definition of the **done** predicate is anything besides not(fact(X)), an incorrect fact order may prevent all correct conclusions. So it is a good idea to order presentation from most important question to least important question, since facts are entered with **assertz**. To allow some user control, the preceding program asserts choices for each individual menu in user-supplied order. We set the menu size to eight questions in the program, but you can easily increase it if you want to improve user control and your terminal screen is tall enough.

For most applications, you shouldn't put every possible fact into menus. You should put the things most common in rules in a first set of menus, and then run forward chaining and see what conclusions you reach. If no "interesting" conclusions are reached (interestingness could mean membership in a particular set), then present further menus to the user (perhaps about things mentioned on the right sides of the shortest remaining rules), assert new facts, and run forward chaining again. You can repeat the cycle as many times as you like. This is a *fact partitioning* trick for rule-based systems, as opposed to the *rule partitioning* trick in Section 7.8. For appliance repair for instance, the first menu could list key classificatory information, such as whether it has a heating element, whether it has mechanical parts, whether it gets electricity from an outlet or from batteries, and what part of the appliance is faulty. After forward chaining on these facts, further menus could obtain a detailed description of the malfunction.

Both menus and questionnaires should not "jump around" too much between topics as backward chaining often does. People are easily confused by rapid shifts in subject, and asking related questions, even irrelevant ones, makes them feel more comfortable. Doctors know this.

Ordering of output (conclusions) presentation is important too for forward chaining. Backward chaining just establishes one conclusion at a time, but forward chaining may establish a whole lot of interesting conclusions about some problem. In fact this is one of its advantages, that it can determine not one but multiple simultaneous problems are causing observed symptoms. If these conclusions are numerous, it's good to sort them by a fixed priority ordering.

7.14 RULE FORM CONVERSIONS* _____

The rule forms needed for backward chaining, hybrid chaining, and forward chaining are all different. So it would be nice to automatically convert rules from one form to another. That means treating rules as data, something important in many different areas of artificial intelligence, and supported by most dialects of Prolog and Lisp.

Prolog does this with the **clause** predicate in most dialects. This has two arguments representing a left and a right side of a rule. A query on **clause** succeeds if its arguments can match the left and right sides of a database rule. (Remember, facts are rules without left sides.) So for instance

　　　?- clause(a,R).

binds the variable **R** to the right side of the first rule it can find that has **a** as its left side. The arguments to **clause** can also be predicate expressions containing arguments themselves. So

　　　?- clause(p(X),R).

will try to find a rule with a **p** predicate of one argument on its left side, and will bind that one argument (if any) to the value of **X**, and **R** to the query representing the right side of that rule. [3]

---

[3] Many Prolog dialects require that the predicate name in the first argument be bound, though arguments to that predicate name may have variables. If you have a list of all predicate names, you can iterate over them to get the effect of an unbound predicate name.

Facts are just rules with no left sides. And **clause** recognizes this, also matching facts in the database as well as rules. Then its first argument is bound to the fact, and the right side is bound to the word **true**. For example, if for the preceding query we have a fact **p(a)** in our database, one answer will be **X = a** and **R = true**.

To automatically convert a rule to forward chaining form, we can access it with **clause**, then convert the right side of the rule to a list. The second argument of the clause predicate is bound to a query, not a list, so we need a list conversion operation. This is called "univ" and is symbolized in most Prolog dialects by the infix predicate " =.." for which the stuff on the left side is a predicate expression and the stuff on the right side is an equivalent list. So we can say

```
?- clause(L,R), R  =.. Rlist.
```

and **Rlist** is a list, as we need for forward chaining. Here's some code for converting all rules in a Prolog database to forward-chaining form, assuming no semicolons in the rules:

```
forward_convert :- clause(L,R), not(overhead_predicate(L)),
   R  =.. Rlist, new_rule(L,Rlist), fail.
overhead_predicate(new_rule(X,Y)).
overhead_predicate(rule(X,Y)).
overhead_predicate(fact(X)).
new_rule(L,[]) :- not(fact(L)), asserta(fact(L)).
new_rule(L,R) :- not(R =[]), asserta(rule(L,R)).
overhead_predicate(forward_convert).
overhead_predicate(overhead_predicate(X)).
```

If your Prolog dialect doesn't allow **L** to be unbound, you can use

```
forward_convert(All_predicates) :- member(L,All_predicates),
   forward_convert2(L).
forward_convert2(L) :- clause(L,R), R  =.. Rlist, new_rule(L,Rlist), fail.
new_rule(L,[]) :- not(fact(L)), asserta(fact(L)).
new_rule(L,R) :- not(R =[]), asserta(rule(L,R)).
```

and you must query **forward_convert** with a list of all the predicates you want to convert.

But all this won't work in some Prolog dialects that treat commas like infix operators. If the preceding doesn't work for you, try (again, only on rules without semicolons):

```
forward_convert(Preds) :- member(Pred,Preds), forward_convert2(Pred).
forward_convert2(Pred) :- clause(Pred,R), remove_commas(R,R2),
  new_rule(Pred,R2), fail.
remove_commas(true,[]).
remove_commas(S,[Y|L]) :- S = ..[Comma,Y,Z], remove_commas(Z,L).
remove_commas(X,[X]) :- not(X = true), not(X = ..[Comma,Y,Z]).
member(X,[X|L]).
member(X,[Y|L]) :- member(X,L).
new_rule(L,[]) :- not(fact(L)), asserta(fact(L)).
new_rule(L,R) :- not(R = []), asserta(rule(L,R)).
```

We can apply the same approach to the hybrid control structure. We convert the right side of each backward-chaining rule to a list, insert a **not** expression at the front of this list, insert an **asserta** expression at the end of the list, and replace the original left side with the single symbol **r**. We then can use the =.. operation in reverse (the left side unbound and the right side bound), converting the list of right-side expressions to a query. We enter this new rule into the Prolog database using **asserta** with this new rule as argument, though this only works in some dialects. Here's the full code:

```
hybrid_convert :- clause(L,R), R =.. Rlist,
  add_last(asserta(L),Rlist,Rlist2),
  R2 =.. [not(L)|Rlist2], asserta(r :- R2), fail.
add_last(X,[],[X]).
add_last(X,[Y|L],[Y|L2]) :- add_last(X,L,L2).
```

If your Prolog dialect doesn't allow L to be unbound, you can try

```
hybrid_convert(All_predicates) :- member(L,All_predicates),
  hybrid_convert2(L).
hybrid_convert2(L) :- clause(L,R), R =.. Rlist,
  add_last(asserta(L),Rlist,Rlist2),
  R2 =.. [not(L)|Rlist2], asserta(r :- R2), fail.
add_last(X,[],[X]).
add_last(X,[Y|L],[Y|L2]) :- add_last(X,L,L2).
```

7.15 INDEXING OF PREDICATE EXPRESSIONS*_____

Prolog interpreters automatically index predicate names appearing on the left sides of rules to help in backward chaining; that is, they keep lists of pointers to all rules with a particular left-side predicate name to speed finding them. But this won't help our rule-cycle hybrid and forward-chaining implementations, for which we must do our own indexing if we want efficiency.

Let's take pure forward chaining as an example. Indexing could mean storing for each predicate name a list of which rule *right* sides it appears in. One way is to generalize the **rule** predicate of Section 7.10 to a **rules** predicate whose first argument is a predicate expression **P** and whose second argument is a list of pairs representing rules containing **P** on their right side. The first item of each pair is a rule left side, and the second item is a rule right side containing the specified predicate name. So the rules

    a :- b, c.
    d :- c, e, f.

are written as

    rules(b,[[a,[b,c]]]).
    rules(c,[[a,[b,c]],[d,[c,e,f]]]).
    rules(e,[[d,[c,e,f]]]).
    rules(f,[[d,[c,e,f]]]).

and just changing **pursuit**, the forward chaining program becomes

    forward :- done.
    forward :- fact(F), doall(pursuit(F)), assertz(usedfact(F)),
      retract(fact(F)), forward.
    pursuit(F) :- rules(F,Rlist), member([L,R],Rlist), rule_pursuit(F,L,R).
    rule_pursuit(F,L,R) :- member(F,R), delete(F,R,Rnew), new_rule(L,Rnew).
    new_rule(L,[]) :- not(fact(L)), asserta(fact(L)).
    new_rule(L,R) :- not(R =[]), asserta(rule(L,R)).

A rule with K expressions on its right side is repeated K times this way, so this indexing buys speed at the expense of space. The speed advantage comes from eliminating the **member** predicate in the earlier implementation; we have cached in advance the results of running **member**.

Clever indexing techniques have been developed in both artificial-intelligence and database research, and much further can be done along these lines.

7.16 IMPLEMENTING META-RULES*_____

Meta-rules are rules that treat other rules as data, usually by choosing the one to use next (*conflict resolution*). So meta-rule implementation needs special rule formats like those for hybrid and pure-forward chaining, and can exploit **clause** and =.. for rule-form conversion. We can represent meta-rules as rules with a special **prefer** predicate name on their left sides. The **prefer** will take four arguments: the left side of a rule 1, the right side of rule 1 (as a list), the left side of a rule 2, and the right side of rule 2 (as a list). It should succeed when rule 1 is preferable (to execute next) to rule 2. (Of course, none of your regular rules can have a **prefer** predicate name for this to work.) Here's an example:

    prefer(L1,R1,L2,R2) :- length(R1,Len1), length(R2,Len2),
      Len1 < Len2.

This says a rule with shorter right side should be preferred. Predicate **length** was defined in Section 5.5, and computes the number of items in a list:

    length([],0).
    length([X|L],N) :- length(L,N2), N is N2 + 1.

Another example:

    prefer(a(X),R1,a(Y),R2) :- member(b(Z),R1), not(member(b(W),R2)).

This says that if two rules both conclude something about one-argument predicate **a**, one is preferred if it mentions a one-argument predicate **b** that the other does not.

Meta-rules are most useful when they refer, unlike these two examples, to the current state of reasoning rather than the unvarying text of rules. As an example, consider this meta-rule to be used with pure forward chaining:

    prefer(L1,R1,L2,R2) :- member(b,R1), not(member(b,R2)), fact(b).

This says to prefer a rule that mentions predicate expression **b** to one that doesn't, whenever **b** was proved a fact. A more useful meta-rule says to prefer the rule used most recently:

    prefer(L1,R1,L2,R2) :- used(L1,R1,T1), used(L2,R2,T2), T1 > T2.

Here we assume **used** is a fact asserted after each successful rule application, stating the time a rule was used (times can be increasing integers). Such meta-rules permit flexible control adjustable to the processing context, something general-purpose control structures can't do by themselves.

Programmers can write these meta-rules at the same time they write the rules for an application. The set of meta-rules can express a lattice of orderings (or *partial ordering*) of rule preferences, but not necessarily a complete ordering or sorting. So it's possible for neither of two rules to be preferred to the other, in which case we can pick one arbitrarily.

Meta-rules enhance general-purpose control structures, and aren't a control structure by themselves. This means that meta-rule implementation is different for backward, hybrid, and forward chaining. With backward chaining, meta-rules pick a rule or fact (not necessarily the first in database order) to try to match to a predicate expression in a query or rule right side. With hybrid chaining, meta-rules pick a rule to run next. With pure forward chaining, meta-rules can both pick a fact to try next and pick a rule to try to match the fact to. As an example, here's an implementation of meta-rules with hybrid chaining.

```
metahybrid :- done.
metahybrid :- pick_rule(R), call(R), metahybrid.
pick_rule(R) :- clause(r,R), not(better_rule(R)).
better_rule(R) :- clause(r,R2), remove_commas(R,NR),
   remove_commas(R2,NR2), prefer(r,NR2,r,NR).
remove_commas(true,[]).
remove_commas(S,[Y|L]) :- S = ..[Comma,Y,Z], remove_commas(Z,L).
remove_commas(X,[X]) :- not(X = true), not(X = ..[Comma,Y,Z]).
```

This assumes rules are written in the standard hybrid form with **r** on the left side and the two extra things on the right side. Rules are repeatedly executed (using the **call** predicate, which executes a query as if it were typed in) until the **done** condition is satisfied. A rule is chosen to execute only if no other rules are preferred to it according to the meta-rules.

7.17 IMPLEMENTING CONCURRENCY*

Several Prolog dialects provide for concurrency of rules and expressions in rules. The emphasis is on programmer's tools to indicate good places to do concurrency rather than automatic choice. For instance, a special "and" symbol, used in place of a comma, can specify "and"-parallelism on the right side of a rule. These approaches to concurrency are complicated and incompatible with each other, and we won't discuss them here.

7.18 DECISION LATTICES: A COMPILATION OF A RULE-BASED SYSTEM*

Compilers and compilation are important concepts in computer science. Compilers take a program in an easy-to-read but slow-to-execute form and convert it to a more efficient, easier-to-interpret form. Compilation is often rule-based itself, especially often-complicated *code optimization*. But compilation techniques can also make artificial-intelligence programs themselves more efficient. Since rule-based systems are further steps in power beyond traditional higher-level languages like Pascal, Ada, PL/1, and Fortran, secondary compilations are usually done before the primary compilation to machine language. These secondary compilations convert rules to the format of those languages: formats without references to backward, forward, or hybrid chaining, and with no backtracking, no postponing of variable bindings, and no multiway designation of inputs and outputs to predicate expressions. The decision lattice representation of rules introduced in Section 6.8 is one such secondarily compiled format. It starts at some node in a lattice, and depending on how a user answers a question, it goes to some next node in the lattice. Each question represents another branch point. When it gets to a node that is a *leaf* (a node from which it cannot go any further), it retrieves the conclusion associated with that node.

A decision lattice for a set of rules can be created systematically (albeit not algorithmically, since it involves some subjective judgment) from rules without "or"s on their right sides, by the following (similar to "automatic indexing" methods):

1. For every top-level or **diagnosis** rule, repeatedly substitute in the definitions for (right sides of) all intermediate predicates on its right side, until no more remain. If there is more than one rule proving an intermediate predicate, make multiple versions of the diagnosis rule, one for each possibility. (This is a useful compilation method even if you don't want a decision lattice; it's called *rule collapsing*.)

2. Examine the right sides of the new rules. Pick a predicate expression that appears unnegated in some rules and negated in an approximately equal number (the more rules it appears in, the better, and the more even the split, the better). Call this the partitioning predicate expression, and have the first question to the user ask about it. Create branches from the starting node to new nodes, one corresponding to each possible answer to this question. Partition the rules into groups corresponding to the answers, and associate each group with one new node (copies of rules not mentioning the predicate expression should be put into every group). Then remove all occurrences of the expression and its negation from the rules. Now within each rule group, separately apply this step recursively, choosing a predicate that partitions the remaining rules in the group best, and taking its questioning next.

An example will make this clearer. Suppose we have facts, a, b, c, d, and e, and possible diagnoses (final conclusions) r, s, t, u, and v. Suppose these are the rules:

```
r :- a, d, not(e).
s :- not(a), not(c), q.
t :- not(a), p.
u :- a, d, e.
u :- a, q.
v :- not(a), not(b), c.
p :- b, c.
p :- not(c), d.
q :- not(d).
```

For the first step (preprocessing), we substitute in the intermediate predicates p and q. (Intermediate predicates are anything that occurs on both a left and a right side.)

```
r :- a, d, not(e).
s :- not(a), not(c), not(d).
t :- not(a), b, c.
t :- not(a), not(c), d.
u :- a, d, e.
u :- a, not(d).
v :- not(a), not(b), c.
```

For the second step we first examine right sides of rules to find something mentioned in a lot of rules that partitions them evenly as possible. Expression a is the obvious choice, because it is the only expression occurring in every rule. So we partition on a, deleting it from the rules, getting two rule sets:

```
r :- d, not(e).  /* Subdatabase for "a" true */
u :- d, e.
u :- not(d).

s :- not(c), not(d).  /* Subdatabase for "not(a)" true */
t :- b, c.
t :- not(c), d.
v :- not(b), c.
```

The first set will be used whenever the fact a is true, and the second set will be used whenever the fact a is false. In the first group d appears in all rules, so it can be the partitioning expression. Likewise, c can partition the second group. This gives four rule groups or *subdatabases*:

```
r :- not(e).            /* The "a, d" rule subdatabase */
u :- e.



u.                      /* The "a, not(d)" subdatabase */



t :- b.                 /* The "not(a), c" subdatabase */
v :- not(b).



s :- not(d).            /* The "not(a), not(c)" subdatabase */
t :- d.
```

Three of the four groups are two-rule, for which one more partitioning gives a unique answer. The final decision lattice created by this analysis is shown in Figure 7-4.

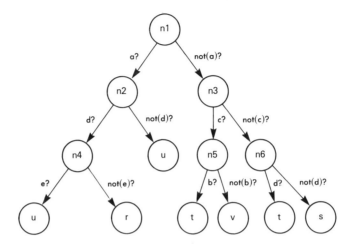

Figure 7-4. Derived decision tree.

Decision lattice compilations of rule-based systems can be easily written in any computer language, including Prolog. Give code names to every node in the decision lattice, including the starting and ending nodes. Then define a *successor* predicate of two arguments that gives conditions for one node to be followed by another node. For instance, for our previous example:

```
successor(n1,n2) :- askif(a).
successor(n1,n3) :- askifnot(a).
successor(n2,n4) :- askif(d).
successor(n4,u) :- askif(e).
successor(n4,r) :- askifnot(e).
successor(n2,u) :- askifnot(d).
successor(n3,n5) :- askif(c).
successor(n5,t) :- askif(b).
successor(n5,v) :- askifnot(b).
successor(n3,n6) :- askifnot(c).
successor(n6,t) :- askif(d).
successor(n6,s) :- askifnot(d).
```

Then we query a new *diagnosis* predicate defined by

```
diagnosis(Node,Node) :- not(successor(Node,X)).
diagnosis(D,Start) :- successor(Start,X), diagnosis(D,X).
```

For the preceding example we also need a way to query the facts:

```
questioncode(X,X) :- member(X,[a,b,c,d]), write('Is this correct: ').
member(X,[X|L]).
member(X,[Y|L]) :- member(X,L).
```

And here's what happens:

```
?- diagnosis(X,n1).
Is this correct: a? no.
Is this correct: c? yes.
Is this correct: b? no.
X = v;
no
```

This program is a simple example of "search" programs, which we'll study in much more detail in Chapters 9, 10, and 11.

7.19 SUMMARY OF THE CODE DESCRIBED IN THE CHAPTER*_____

Warning: In using the following, make sure your own code does not redefine or even duplicate the definitions of any predicates used, or you can be in serious trouble.

The following rules assist question-asking for backward, forward, and hybrid chaining. The ask predicate asks the user a question, providing extra explanation if the user types a question mark, and returns the answer (after caching it). The questioncode and explain predicates must be provided by the programmer; the first decodes questions, and the second provides additional explanation for particular questions when the user has trouble understanding. The askif predicate handles yes/no questions; it succeeds if the user answers positively, fails if the user answers negatively, and requests another answer if the user answers anything else. Warning: Do abolish(asked,2)) to erase memory before a new situation (problem), if you want to solve more than one situation.

```
/* Tools for questioning the user */
askif(Qcode) :- ask(Qcode,A), positive_answer(Qcode,A).
askifnot(Qcode) :- not(askif(Qcode)).

positive_answer(Qcode,A) :- affirmative(A).
positive_answer(Qcode,A) :- not(negative(A)),
  not(affirmative(A)), write('Please answer yes or no.'),
  read(A2), retract(asked(Qcode,A)),
  asserta(asked(Qcode,A2)), affirmative(A2).

ask(Qcode,A) :- asked(Qcode,A).
ask(Qcode,A) :- not(asked(Qcode,A)), questioncode(Qcode,Q),
  write(Q), write('? '), read(A2), ask2(Q,Qcode,A2,A).

ask2(Q,Qcode,'?',A) :- explain(Qcode), ask(Qcode,A).
ask2(Q,Qcode,A,A) :- not(A = '?'), asserta(asked(Qcode,A)).
```

affirmative(yes).
affirmative(y).
affirmative(ye).
affirmative(right).
affirmative(ok).
affirmative(uhhuh).

negative(no).
negative(n).
negative(not).
negative(never).
negative(impossible).
negative(haha).

To do rule-cycle hybrid chaining with rules without nots, write the rules with r on their left sides, and an asserta of the original left side on the right end of the right side. Then query hybrid, using this program:

```
/* Problem-independent rule-cycle hybrid chaining */
hybrid :- done.
hybrid :- doall(r), hybrid.

doall(P) :- not(alltried(P)).

alltried(P) :- call(P), fail.
```

To do pure forward chaining with rules without nots, write the rules as facts with predicate name rule, for which the first argument is a left side and the second argument is the corresponding right side. Then query forward, defined this way:

```
/* Problem-independent forward chaining */
forward :- done.
forward :- fact(F), doall(pursuit(F)), assertz(usedfact(F)),
  retract(fact(F)), forward.

pursuit(F) :- rule(L,R), rule_pursuit(F,L,R).

rule_pursuit(F,L,R) :- member(F,R), delete(F,R,Rnew),
  new_rule(L,Rnew).

new_rule(L,[]) :- not(fact(L)), asserta(fact(L)).
new_rule(L,R) :- not(R=[]), asserta(rule(L,R)).

doall(P) :- not(alltried(P)).

alltried(P) :- call(P), fail.
```

```
member(X,[X|L]).
member(X,[Y|L]) :- member(X,L).

delete(X,[],[]).
delete(X,[X|L],M) :- delete(X,L,M).
delete(X,[Y|L],[Y|M]) :- not(X = Y), delete(X,L,M).
```

When this program stops, the learned facts are left as assertions of fact and usedfact predicates. If you want to make sure that all possible conclusions are reached, use this definition of done:

```
done :- not(fact(X)).
```

If you want to speed up forward chaining, and your rule-based system can be represented as an and-or-not lattice, you can rewrite the preceding rule_pursuit rule as:

```
rule_pursuit(F,L,R) :- member(F,R), delete(F,R,Rnew), retract(rule(L,R)),
   new_rule(L,Rnew).
```

If you want to do forward chaining with predicate expressions having nots, first make sure the nots all refer to fact predicates. Then execute full_forward:

```
full_forward :- succeeding_forward, doall(handle_nots),
   succeeding_forward.
succeeding_forward :- forward.
   succeeding_forward.
handle_nots :- rule(L,R), remove_matched_nots(L,R,Rnew),
   retract(rule(L,R)), not(member(not(X),Rnew)), new_rule(L,Rnew).
remove_matched_nots(L,[],[]).
remove_matched_nots(L,[not(X)|R],Rnew) :- not(usedfact(X)),
   not(fact(X)), remove_matched_nots(L,R,Rnew).
remove_matched_nots(L,[I|R],[I|Rnew]) :-
   remove_matched_nots(L,R,Rnew).
```

Meta-rules can enhance other control structures. They can be written as rules with predicate name prefer, of four arguments (the left and right sides of two rules, respectively) that give conditions under which the first rule should be executed before the second rule. For meta-rules with hybrid chaining, execute the query metahybrid with this alternative code:

```
/* Problem-independent rule-cycle hybrid chaining using meta-rules */
metahybrid :- done.
metahybrid :- pick_rule(R), call(R), metahybrid.

pick_rule(R) :- clause(r,R), not(better_rule(R)).
```

```
better_rule(R) :- clause(r,R2), remove_commas(R,NR),
  remove_commas(R2,NR2), prefer(r,NR2,r,NR).


remove_commas(true,[]).
remove_commas(S,[Y|L]) :- S = ..[Comma,Y,Z], remove_commas(Z,L).
remove_commas(X,[X]) :- not(X = true), not(X = ..[Comma,Y,Z]).
```

To implement menus as a way of getting facts to do forward chaining, execute ask_which with argument the list of question codes for the facts you want to check.

```
/* Menu generation for forward chaining */
ask_which([A,B,C,D,E,F,G,H|L]) :-
  screen_ask_which([A,B,C,D,E,F,G,H],[A,B,C,D,E,F,G,H]),
  ask_which(L).
ask_which([]).
ask_which(L) :- length(L,N), N<9, N>0, screen_ask_which(L,L).

screen_ask_which([X|L],L2) :- length(L,N), length(L2,N2),
  N3 is N2 - N, write(N3), write(': '), questioncode(X,Q),
  write(Q), write('?'), nl, asserta(asked(X,no)),
  screen_ask_which(L,L2).
screen_ask_which([],L2) :-
  write('Give numbers of questions whose answer is yes.'),
  read(AL), create_facts(AL,L2), nl.

create_facts([N|L],L2) :- item(N,L2,I), assertz(fact(I)),
  retract(asked(I,no)), asserta(asked(I,yes)), create_facts(L,L2).
create_facts([N|L],L2) :- not(item(N,L2,I)), create_facts(L,L2).
create_facts([],L2).

item(1,[X|L],X).
item(N,[X|L],I) :- N>1, N2 is N-1, item(N2,L,I).


member(X,[X|L]).
member(X,[Y|L]) :- member(X,L).


length([],1).
length([X|L],N) :- length(L,N2), N is N2 + 1.
```

To implement a decision lattice, draw the lattice and label all the nodes with unique names. Write rules defining the branches with the **successor** predicate, for example

```
successor(n5,n9) :- askif(device_dead).
successor(n5,n15) :- askifnot(device_dead).
```

which says that if you're at node n5, go to node n9 if the user responds positively to the **device_dead** question, otherwise go to node n15. Then to run the decision lattice, call **diagnosis(D, <first-node>)**, which needs this definition:

```
diagnosis(D,Start) :- successor(Start,X), diagnosis(D,X).
diagnosis(Node,Node) :- not(successor(Node,X)).
```

KEYWORDS

> *diagnosis*
> *character string*
> *input coding*
> *output coding*
> *intermediate predicates*
> *menu*

EXERCISES

7-1. (R,A,P) Improve the appliance-diagnosis program given in Section 7.6 so it can reach the following new diagnoses:
- the motor has burned out, for appliances that have motors;
- something is blocking the mechanical operation (like something keeping the motor from turning), for mechanical appliances;
- some internal wiring is broken (possible if appliance was dropped recently, or some other jarring occurred).

Add new questions and perhaps intermediate predicates to handle these diagnoses. Show your new program working.

7-2. (A,P) Figure out a simple way to prevent repeated printing of the same diagnosis in the backward-chaining appliance program as in Section 7.7. Don't change every rule. Show your method working on the appliance program.

7-3. (E)

(a) Medical records often reference very high level and very low level concepts only, no intermediate concepts. Is this typical of other expert-system application areas?

(b) Suppose you must defend intermediate concepts in an expert system to your boss or representative of a funding agency. They could claim that intermediate concepts don't add capabilities to an expert system, just make its innards neater. Furthermore, intermediate concepts require extra design effort, and slow down operation by forcing reasoning to proceed by smaller steps. How would you reply in defense of intermediate predicates?

7-4. (P,H,G) Design a rule-based expert system to give debugging advice about Prolog programs. Use backward chaining in the manner of the appliance example, asking questions of the user. There is a lot of room for creativity in the choice of what the program knows about, but the program must help debug Prolog programs in some way. Be sure:

1. Your program is a rule-based expert system.

2. Your program contains at least 20 diagnosis rules (rules drawing a conclusion about what is wrong with a Prolog program), 12 of which have more than one kind of evidence "and"ed on their right side.

3. Your program uses at least three intermediate conclusions, conclusions that are neither equivalent to facts nor correspond to advice to the user.

4. Your program can reach at least seven different conclusions depending on the user's answers to the questions.

5. Three of the conclusions your program reaches appear on the left side of more than one rule (that is, there must be multiple paths to three conclusions).

6. Your program uses at least three kinds of history information, like how long the user has been programming Prolog, or whether parts of the user's program are already debugged.

7. The control structure of your program is not extensively "hard-wired" (for instance, there can't be a lot of branch specifications controlling where to go next).

8. As much as possible, all the variables and predicate names are semantically meaningful (that is, their function should be explained by their names; use numbers in your program only for (possibly) probabilities).

Use of probabilities or certainty factors is not necessary. Think about good ways to present your conclusions to the user.

7-5. (A) (For people who know something about probabilities.) Caching of facts in backward chaining is not always a good idea; it depends on the situation. Suppose we have rules for testing whether $a(X)$ is true for some X, rules that require R units of time to execute on the average. Suppose to speed things up we cache K values of X for which the a predicate holds. That is, we place facts for those values in front of the rules that calculate $a(X)$ as previously. Then to answer a query on the a predicate, we first sequentially search through all these cached facts, and use the rules only if we can't find a match in the cache.

(a) Suppose the probability is P that any one item in the cache matches an incoming query, and suppose this probability is mutually exclusive for each cache item. Under what approximate conditions will using the cache be preferable to not using the cache? Assume that $K < 0.1/P$, and assume that each cache access requires one unit of time.

(b) Now assume the items of the cache are not all equally likely to be used. Often a *Zipf's Law* distribution applies, for which the probability of the most common item is P, the probability of the second most common item is P/2, the probability of the third most common item is P/3, and so on. Again assume cache item probabilities are mutually exclusive. Again assume that each cache access requires one unit of time. Under what approximate conditions is caching desirable now? Hint: The sum of $1/I$ from $I = 1$ to K is approximately $\log_2(K + 1)$.

7-6. (P) Write a rule-based expert system to recommend cleaning methods for clothing. Obtain rules from a human "expert" on the subject. Use hybrid chaining in implementation for simplicity. Ask the user to give a single category that best describes the material they want to clean, and then ask additional questions as necessary to make its description more precise. Write at least twenty rules reaching at least ten different cleaning methods as conclusions. Use a lot of a_kind_of facts to classify the many kinds of clothing. You'll need to worry about rule order, and default rules will help.

7-7. The criteria for when to delete a rule in forward chaining were conservative: they miss other circumstances under which it would be good to delete rules. Define those circumstances, and explain how we could efficiently check for them.

7-8. (H,P) Write a program to diagnose malfunctions of a car using forward chaining in the pure form. Write at least fifty rules and use at least ten intermediate predicates. Use a repair manual as your source of expertise. Concentrate on some particular subsystem of the car to do a better job. Use the menu approach to defining facts. Provide for at least two invocations of forward chaining, and stop when one of a set of diagnosis facts is proved.

7-9. (H,P) Write a rule-based expert system to diagnose simple illnesses and medical problems (such as a "primary care" or "family practice" physician might handle). Use a medical reference book as your source of knowledge. Your program should be able to reach thirty different diagnoses, at least seven in more than one way, using at least five intermediate predicates. Run your rules with both backward chaining and forward chaining and compare performance. To do this, use the automatic conversion routines, or use the forward-chaining rule form and write your own backward-chainer. For forward chaining, let the user pick symptoms from a series of menus, and ask questions of the user directly for additional secondary facts. Show your rules working on sample situations.

7-10. (P) Write a rule-based expert system to choose a good way to graphically display data. Suppose as input this program loads a file of data facts of one argument, a list representing properties of some object. Suppose the output is a recommendation about whether to use bar graphs, pie graphs, two-dimensional plots, summary tables, etc., for particular positions in the data lists. For instance, a recommendation might be to plot all the first items of data lists as an X coordinate against second items as a Y coordinate, and to draw a bar graph showing all the first items against third items. These graphing recommendations will need to pick subsidiary information about ranges to be plotted, binning (what values get grouped together), approximate dimensions of the display, extra lines, unusual values (*outliers*) that have been left out, etc. Generally you can find some graphical display for every pair of data item positions, but only some of these will be interesting and worth recommending. Interestingness can be defined in various ways, but should emphasize the unpredictability of the data: a nearly straight line makes an uninteresting graph. It will be useful to define a number of processing predicates, including a **column** predicate that makes a list of all the data values in position K in the data list, and predicate that applies a standard statistical test (look one up in a statistics book) to see if the values in two such columns are associated or correlated. You may want to consult a book giving recommendations for graphical display.

7-11. (A) The definitions of the **forall** and **doall** predicates both use the built-in Prolog predicate **call**, which takes a predicate expression as argument and queries it. (This is useful because the argument can be a variable bound within a program.) Use **call** to implement the following:

   (a) or(P,Q) which succeeds whenever querying either P or Q succeeds.

   (b) if(P,Q,R) which succeeds whenever P succeeds then Q succeeds, or if P fails then R succeeds.

   (c) case(P,N,L) which succeeds whenever predicate expression number N of list L succeeds, where N is bound by executing predicate expression P (that is, N must be a variable in P that is bound by P).

7-12. (H,P) Implement the other hybrid of backward and forward chaining mentioned in Section 6.4, the hybrid that alternates between forward and backward chaining. Show your program working on some sample rules and facts.

7-13. (P) Implement meta-rules for pure forward chaining. Use a **prefer** predicate like the one used for rule-cycle hybrid meta-rules.

7-14. (P) Consider meta-rules with pure forward chaining (the implementation is considered in Exercise 7-13). Assume there are no variables in the rules.

   (a) Write a meta-rule to prevent the same conclusion from being reached twice.

   (b) Write a meta-rule, and a little additional code to that written for Exercise 7-13, to prevent the same rule from being used twice in a row.

7-15. Convert the fuse-blown, cord-break, and not-turned-on rules in the appliance-diagnosis program to a decision lattice. Try to minimize the number of questions required to a user. Use one-letter predicates, and assume omitted terms are false.

7-16. (H,P,G) Write a rule-based system that, given the syllables of an English sentence in phonemic representation, figures out which syllables to stress. Such stress rules are relatively straightforward and can be found in many linguistics books. You'll need list-processing techniques from Chapter 5, and you must worry about the order the stress rules are applied.

7-17. (P) Write a program to give simple navigation commands to a mobile robot moving across a battlefield. Assume the battlefield is divided into squares, designated by integer X and Y coordinates ranging from $X = 0$ to $X = 50$ and from $Y = 0$ to $Y = 50$; the robot is not allowed to leave this area. The robot starts at location somewhere on the $Y = 0$ line and it is trying to get to location (50,30). There are impassable bomb craters at (20,10), (10,25), and (20,40), all circles of radius 2. There is an impassable ravine extending along the $Y = 30$ line from $X = 10$ to $X = 50$.

The robot begins moving at time 0. The rule-based system to control it should order one of only four actions: move one unit north, move one unit south, move one unit east, and move one unit west. Each move takes one unit of time. At time $T = 15$ a bomb crater appears 4 units north of the robot; at $T = 25$ a crater appears 3 units west; at $T = 30$ a crater appears 3 units east; and at $T = 40$ a crater appears 4 units east.

The robot should not be able to "see" craters and ravines until it is just at their edges. But suppose the robot knows the coordinates of the goal location and its current coordinates at all times, so it always knows where it is. Try to specify the robot's actions in general terms that will work for any configuration of craters and ravines.

Try your program out with the robot starting at various locations along $Y = 0$.

7-18. (E) Like most rule-based expert systems, our appliance diagnosis system doesn't reason about causal chains. In other words, it knows that a certain pattern of symptoms signals an underlying cause, but it doesn't know *why* the cause leads to the symptoms, the exact chains of cause and effect that explain each particular symptom. For instance, it knows that when a device isn't working at all, there might be a short in the cord; but it doesn't know the reason is that a short causes the resistance of a cord to be significantly lowered, causing a lot of electricity to flow into the cord, causing a lot of electricity to flow through a fuse, causing the metal conductor in the fuse to heat up, causing it to melt, causing the metal to flow, causing it to break the electrical connection, causing no electricity to go to the appliance cord, causing the appliance to not work at all. For what kinds of appliances and diagnosis circumstances could this lack of causal-chain reasoning be a problem? (We should use a quite different rule-based system then.) In what sense can the appliance expert system of this chapter be seen as a simplification of a more general kind of expert system?

REPRESENTING UNCERTAINTY IN RULE-BASED SYSTEMS

Numbers are important in most areas of engineering and science. In artificial intelligence, one use of numbers is to quantify the *degree* to which we are certain about something, so we can rank our deductions. This lets us model the world more realistically. We'll show how these numbers can be easily added to rule-based systems in Prolog, and suggest ways—conservative, middle-of-the-road, and liberal—to manipulate them.

8.1 PROBABILITIES IN RULES

Rules in rule-based systems have so far been absolute: when things are absolutely true on the right side of a rule, then the thing on the left side is absolutely true. But in many real-world situations, inferences or even facts are to some degree uncertain or probabilistic. This is particularly true when facts in a rule-based system represent evidence, and rules represent hunches (hypotheses) explaining the evidence. Examples are the diagnosis rules for a car-repair expert system; many diagnoses can't be certain unless the car is taken apart, but suggestive evidence can be found from the way the car behaves.

Mathematicians have for a long time used probabilities to model degrees of uncertainty in the world. A probability is the fraction of the time we expect something will be true. Other numbers are used in artificial intelligence to represent uncertainty, but probabilities came first, so we'll prefer them here. Probabilities provide a strict ordering (ranking) of diagnoses or hypotheses.

As we mentioned in Section 2.10, we can add probabilities as a last argument to Prolog facts. So to say a battery in a randomly picked car is dead 3% of the time, we can put the fact

battery(dead,0.03).

in the Prolog database.[1] We can modify predicate expressions in rules similarly. For instance, if 20% of the time when the car won't start it is true the battery is dead, we could write

battery(dead,0.2) :- ignition(wont_start,1.0).

We can write different rules for inference of the same fact from different sources of evidence, each with its own probability. So if 50% of the time when the radio won't play the battery is dead:

battery(dead,0.5) :- radio(wont_play,1.0).

So if we want to reason about whether the battery is dead, we should gather all relevant rules and facts. Then somehow we must combine the probabilities from facts and successful rules to get a cumulative probability that the battery is dead. This we call the *or-combination* issue with probabilities, since you can think of rules with the same left-side predicate name as an implicit "or."

A second issue is that rules can be uncertain for a different reason than facts. Consider the preceding rule for the likelihood the battery is dead when the ignition won't start. Suppose we are not sure the ignition won't start—we've tried it a few times, and the car didn't seem to respond. (It might respond if we waited an hour to try it, which would be true if the engine is flooded.) What is our probability that the battery is dead? It must be less than the *rule probability* 0.2, because the new conditions worsen its likelihood, but how much less? It seems the 0.2 must be combined with the ignition-dead probability. We will call this the *rule probability with evidence probability combination* issue.

A third issue is that rules can have "and"s of several predicate expressions on

---

[1] Some Prolog implementations don't allow real (decimal) numbers. If yours doesn't, you can represent probabilities by the integer closest to a million times the probability. So 200,000 would represent a probability of 0.2. You'll also have to modify the formulas given later in this chapter so the math will work right. Use 1,000,000 wherever 1 occurs in formulas, and divide all products by 1,000,000, and multiply all two-number quotients by 1,000,000. Addition and subtraction don't have to be modified. Also, many Prolog implementations that do handle decimal numbers require digits both before and after the decimal point, so you have to say "0.03" instead of just ".03." We'll do that in this book.

their right sides, and if each has a probability, we must somehow combine those numbers to get a total probability for the right side—what we call the *and-combination* issue. Note this is quite different from the "or-combination," because weak evidence that any "and"ed expression is satisfied means weak evidence that the whole "and" is satisfied (a chain is as strong as its weakest link).

Probabilities often arise in artificial intelligence applications when reasoning backward. For instance, if the battery of a car is dead, the car will not start; and if there is a short in the electrical system of a car, the car will not start. Those things are absolutely certain. But if a car will not start, then we must reason backward to figure the likelihood that the battery is dead; we can't be completely certain because another cause like a short in the electrical system could also explain the failure to start. But reasoning backward from effects to causes has many important applications, so we must do it if we want computers to behave intelligently.

8.2 SOME RULES WITH PROBABILITIES

To show the flexibility of probabilities in rules, here are some examples. Suppose six times out of ten when the car won't start, the battery is dead. Then

    battery(dead,0.6) :- ignition(wont_start,1.0).

The rule probability 0.6 here is a *conditional probability*, a probability something happens supposing something else happens. We could also treat the right-side expression as something that couldn't possibly be uncertain, something that is either true or false. Then we could write the rule with a probability only on the left side:

    battery(dead,0.6) :- ignition(wont_start).

Now suppose the car won't start, and we measure the battery voltage with a voltmeter. Suppose we're not skilled at using a voltmeter. The following rule would apply:

    battery(dead,P) :- voltmeter(battery_terminals,abnormal,P).

This says that the battery is dead with the same probability that the voltmeter measurement is outside the normal range. Not being skilled, we might not be measuring the voltage properly (the terminals might be reversed, or the range setting on the voltmeter might be too low or too high, causing us to incorrectly read the voltage). So the uncertainty of the evidence (voltmeter measurement) is reflected in the conclusion. Note if P is 1 (if we are completely sure of our voltmeter measurement), then we are completely certain that the battery is dead too.

Suppose we want to rewrite the preceding rule to ignore very weak evidence for the conclusion; this will help avoid unnecessary computation on insignificant things. We can put in an arithmetic comparison:

```
battery(dead,P) :- voltmeter(battery_terminals,abnormal,P),
   P > 0.1.
```

This says that if the voltmeter reading is outside the normal range with probability P, and P is more than 0.1, then the battery is dead with that same probability P.

Now consider what to do when the evidence on the right side of a rule can be certain or uncertain, but when it is certain it does not imply certainty of the left side. This can happen when the right side is a conclusion itself. For instance

```
battery(dead,P) :- electrical_problem(P2), P is P2 * 0.5.
```

This says that half the time when the car has an electrical problem, the battery is dead. Mathematically, it takes the probability of an electrical problem and multiplies it by rule probability 0.5 to get the probability of the battery being dead.

Finally, here's an example of evidence and-combination. If there is an electrical problem and battery is old, then we suspect (with maybe a rule probability of 0.9, because the conclusion would be more sure than for the preceding rule) that the battery is dead. But suppose we're not sure of either contributing factor, the problem being electrical or the battery being old. We must somehow decrease the 0.9 by the uncertainty of the factors. One simple way (the probabilistic-independence-assumption method) is to take the product of 0.9 and the probabilities of the two factors, like this:

```
battery(dead,P) :- electrical_problem(P2), age(battery,old,P3),
   P is P2 * P3 * 0.9.
```

So if we believe there's an electrical problem with probability 0.7, and we're 80% sure the battery is old, an estimate of the probability that the battery is dead is 0.7 * 0.8 * 0.9 = 0.504.

All probabilities are estimates. We'll treat our probabilities as rough indications of certainty, mainly important relative to one another. We won't insist that all our probabilities of a certain kind sum to 1, because rarely can we feel we've covered all possibilities. For instance, an infinity of things can go wrong with your car, and it wouldn't be reasonable to compute the probability that your car won't start because mutant rats have eaten the engine. (We won't even insist that probabilities of a certain kind must sum to no more than 1, because it's hard to analyze the amount of overlap among probabilities.)

8.3 COMBINING EVIDENCE ASSUMING STATISTICAL INDEPENDENCE_____

The last section shows that combining probabilities in rule-based systems is very important. Surprisingly, there is no fully general mathematical approach to combining; the problem can be proved mathematically intractable. But we can give some formulas that hold under particular assumptions, and most artificial-intelligence work follows this route. Alas, people make frequent mistakes with probabilities, as shown by experiments, so it's a bad idea to look for guidance from the way people reason.

The easiest assumption we could make is that the different probabilities are probabilistically independent. That is, occurrence of one kind of event does not make another kind any more or less likely. This situation often happens when evidence comes by very different reasoning methods, and can't "interact." For instance, suppose we are writing an expert system to give advice about stock-market investments. We might have two rules:

1. If a quarterly report on economic indicators today says that interest rates will go up this year, then the stock market index will go down tomorrow with probability 0.7.

2. If the stock market index has gone up for three straight days, it will go down tomorrow with probability 0.4.

These two rules reflect quite different phenomena. So the success of the first rule won't make us believe the second is any more likely to succeed on the same day, and vice versa. (Maybe there is a little bit of influence—a stock market going down a lot might indirectly cause interest rates to go up—but the connection is pretty weak.) That's what we mean by probabilistic (or statistical) independence.

When statistical independence applies, probability theory says the probability of both of two uncertain events occurring is the product of the probabilities of each event occurring individually. In general, if events $A, B, C, \ldots$ are independent, then in mathematical notation

$$p \left[A \text{ and } B \text{ and } C \text{ and } \cdots \right] = p(A)p(B)p(C) \cdots$$

where $p(A)$ means "probability of event A," etc. This formula defines *and-combination* of the probabilities of the events with the assumption of probabilistic independence.

As for "or"s (unions) of events instead of "and"s (intersections), consider the *Venn diagram* in Figure 8-1. Let regions represent events, so areas of regions

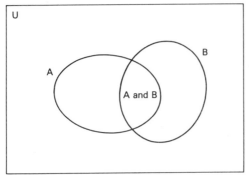

Figure 8-1. Venn diagram of two events A and B.

represent probabilities, and the area of region A is $p(A)$. Then the area of the region representing the "or" of A and B is the area of A plus that area of B, minus the area in common between both A and B (we counted the area in common twice, hence we must subtract it out once). So since areas correspond to probabilities

$$p(A \text{ or } B) = p(A) + p(B) - p(A \text{ and } B)$$

That last formula applies to *any* events. But when the independence assumption holds, we can think of the Venn diagrams as being drawn in a special way, so that events A and B correspond not to circles but to rectangular regions that cross at right angles. See the top diagram in Figure 8-2. Here the area of the whole square (representing the *universe* or all possible events) is 1, and the probabilities of A and B are each proportional to a distance along the side of the square. So the area of the upper left subrectangle is the probability $p(A \text{ and } B)$, and the area of a rectangle is its length times its width, or $p(A)p(B)$. Hence substituting in the preceding equation, we get the formula for "or-combination" of two probabilities with the independence assumption:

$$p(A \text{ or } B) = p(A) + p(B) - p(A)p(B)$$

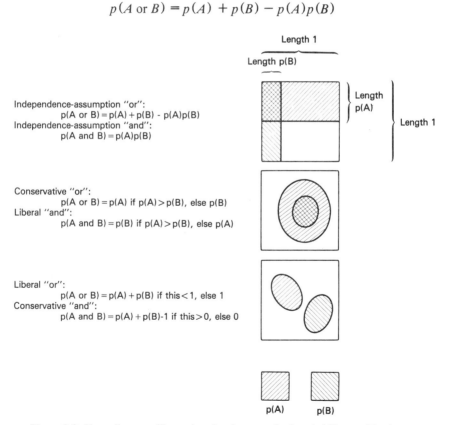

Independence-assumption "or":
    p(A or B) = p(A) + p(B) - p(A)p(B)
Independence-assumption "and":
    p(A and B) = p(A)p(B)

Conservative "or":
    p(A or B) = p(A) if p(A) > p(B), else p(B)
Liberal "and":
    p(A and B) = p(B) if p(A) > p(B), else p(A)

Liberal "or":
    p(A or B) = p(A) + p(B) if this < 1, else 1
Conservative "and":
    p(A and B) = p(A) + p(B)-1 if this > 0, else 0

Figure 8-2. Venn diagrams illustrating the three standard probability-combination methods, applied to two probabilities.

We can generalize this to the "or" of three events:

$$p(A \text{ or } B \text{ or } C) = p(A) + p(B) + p(C) - p(A \text{ and } B) - p(A \text{ and } C) - p(B \text{ and } C)$$

$$+ p(A \text{ and } B \text{ and } C)$$

$$= p(A) + p(B) + p(C) - p(A)p(B) - p(A)p(C) - p(B)p(C)$$

$$+ p(A)p(B)p(C)$$

Using mathematics we can prove the general formula for the "or-combination" of a set of probabilities assuming probabilistic independence:

$$p\left[A \text{ or } B \text{ or } C \text{ or } \cdots \right] = 1 - [(1 - p(A))(1 - p(B))(1 - p(C)) \cdots]$$

8.4 PROLOG IMPLEMENTATION OF INDEPENDENCE-ASSUMPTION "AND-COMBINATION"

We can define a predicate that implements the preceding independence-assumption "and-combination" formula. It will take two arguments: an input list of probabilities and an output number for the combined probability.

```
indep_andcombine([P],P).
indep_andcombine([P|PL],Ptotal) :- indep_andcombine(PL,P2), Ptotal is P2 * P.
```

We just call this predicate as the last thing on the right side of rules, to combine the "and"ed probabilities in a rule. If we had a rule without probabilities, like this

```
f :- a, b, c.
```

we would turn it into a rule with probabilities like this:

```
f(P) :- a(P1), b(P2), c(P3), indep_andcombine([P1,P2,P3],P).
```

That addresses the third issue discussed in Section 8.1. Interestingly, indep_andcombine can also address the second issue discussed in Section 8.1, that of combining rule with evidence probabilities. Suppose we have a rule

```
g(P) :- d(P1), e(P2), indep_andcombine([P1,P2],P).
```

The indep_andcombine handles uncertainty of d and e, but the rule itself may be uncertain, meaning that the conclusion g has a probability less than 1 even when P1 and P2 are both 1. We could characterize this rule uncertainty itself with a probability, the probability that the rule succeeds given complete certainty of all terms "and"ed on its right side. If this probability were 0.7 for instance, we could rewrite the rule as g(P) :- d(P1), e(P2), indep_andcombine([P1,P2,0.7],P).

In other words, rule uncertainty can be thought of as a hidden "and"ed predicate expression with an associated probability.

Here's an example. Suppose we have the following rule and facts:

f(P) :- a(P1), b, c(P2), indep_andcombine([P1,P2,0.8],P).
a(0.7).
b.
c(0.95).

Then for the query

?- f(X).

P1 will be bound to 0.7, and P2 to 0.95. Predicate indep_andcombine computes 0.7 * 0.95 * 0.8 = 0.532, and P is bound to that; so that's X, the total probability of predicate f.

For rules that refer only to things absolutely true and false, "and-combination" is unnecessary. The rule-strength probability need only be on the left side, as for instance

f(0.7) :- a, b, c.

8.5 PROLOG IMPLEMENTATION OF INDEPENDENCE-ASSUMPTION "OR-COMBINATION"_____

The remaining issue discussed in Section 8.1 was "or-combination" of probabilities. Independence-assumption "or-combination" can be defined analogously to independence-assumption "and-combination" but using the last formula in Section 8.3:

indep_orcombine([P],P).
indep_orcombine([P|PL],Ptotal) :- indep_orcombine(PL,P2),
  Ptotal is 1 - ((1-P) * (1-P2)).

"Or-combination" is needed when we have multiple evidence for the truth of predicate f, as for instance

f(0.5) :- a.
f(0.7) :- b, c.
f(0.8) :- d, not(e).

"Or-combination" is more awkward than "and-combination" because we must use a new predicate name to implement the combination. So for the preceding example we must define something like f_overall that represents the cumulative likelihood of f. This can use a special built-in predicate called bagof, used this way:

   f_overall(P) :- bagof(P2,f(P2),PL), indep_orcombine(PL,P).

We'll explain this bagof predicate (called findall in some dialects) more formally in Section 10.6. For now we'll note that bagof has three arguments: an unbound variable, a predicate expression containing that variable (an input), and a list of all values to which the variable in the expression can successfully be bound (an output). So the bagof example above says to make a list PL of all the P2 such that f(P2) succeeds. If the argument to f represents the probability of event f, the list PL will contain all the probabilities found for the predicate f by every possible use of rules and facts. These can be combined with the indep_orcombine. [2]
   As an example, suppose we have these rules and facts:

   g(0.7) :- a.
   g(P) :- b(P1), c(P2), indep_andcombine([P1,P2,0.9],P).
   g(0.3) :- a, d.
   a.
   b(0.8).
   c(0.9).
   d.

Then to combine evidence for the g predicate we need

   total_g(P) :- bagof(P2,g(P2),PL), indep_orcombine(PL,P).

and to use it we must query

   ?- total_g(X).

All three g rules will succeed with these facts, and P in the second g rule will be bound to $0.8*0.9*0.9 = 0.648$. So PL in the total_g rule will be bound to [0.7,0.648,0.3]. Now we must call on indep_orcombine. $1 - ((1 - 0.648)*(1 - 0.3)) = 1 - 0.352*0.7 = 0.7536$, and $1 - ((1 - 0.7) *(1 - 0.7536)) = 1 - 0.3*0.2464 = 0.92608$. Hence the argument P to total_g will be bound to 0.92608, and hence to X, the total probability that g is true.

---

[2] An alternative simpler implementation of indep_orcombine is possible in many dialects of Prolog with the "univ" feature (see Section 7.14) that converts from lists to predicate expressions, symbolized by " =..", where the left side is an expression and the right side is its component list of symbols. It's used like this:
   new_indep_orcombine(F,P) :- Pred =.. [F,P2], bagof(P2,Pred,PL), indep_orcombine(PL,P).

8.6 THE CONSERVATIVE APPROACH_____

Independence when combining probabilities is a strong assumption. It does not hold when one event causes another, or when two events are both caused by some other event. For instance with a small appliance, a totally nonfunctioning device suggests an electrical problem, and a frayed cord suggests an electrical problem. This could be represented as

    electrical_problem(0.5) :- doesnt_work.
    electrical_problem(0.6) :- frayed_cord.

If both rules succeed, the independence-assumption probability of an electrical problem is 0.8. But that's too high, because the cord problem could explain the not-working observation: the cord being frayed could cause the device not to work. So the true combined probability should be closer to 0.6, the number in the second rule.

One approach when independence does not hold is to be very conservative, very careful not to overestimate the cumulative probability. This *conservative* approach is sometimes called a *fuzzy set* approach, but actually it is more general than what is called "fuzzy set theory," representing a mathematically provable lower bound. Consider a "conservative orcombine." Whatever the total probability for some event with multiple positive evidence, it must be no worse than the probability of the strongest evidence: positive evidence shouldn't ever disconfirm other positive evidence. So we could define a "conservative orcombine" to operate on probability lists in place of **indep_orcombine**, to use whenever independence clearly doesn't hold between the probabilities:

    con_orcombine(PL,P) :- max(PL,P).
    max([P],P).
    max([P|PL],P) :- max(PL,P2), P > P2.
    max([P|PL],P2) :- max(PL,P2), not(P > P2).

The **max** definition is from Section 5.5. The middle diagram of Figure 8-2 is the Venn diagram for the "conservative-or" case.

For a corresponding "conservative andcombine," we could just give 0—that's always plenty conservative. But if the "and"ed probabilities are all large, we can prove a nonzero value. Consider the two probabilities 0.7 and 0.8 for two events; 30% of the time the first event must be false. That 80% for the second event can't all "fit" into 30%; only part of it can, with another 50% left over. So at least 50% of the time both events must occur; i.e., the minimum probability for the "and" is 0.5.

In general, the conservative value for $p(A$ and $B)$ is

$$\text{maxfunction}(p(A) + p(B) - 1,0)$$

where "maxfunction" is a mathematical function having a value (not a predicate like the previous max), and its value is the larger of its two arguments. We will define:

The value of maxfunction(X,Y) is the larger of the two numbers X and Y;

The value of minfunction(X,Y) is the smaller of the two numbers X and Y.

To generalize the "and" formula to any number of "and"ed expressions, we can define

```
con_andcombine([P],P).
con_andcombine([P|PL],0) :- con_andcombine(PL,P2), P + P2 < 1.0.
con_andcombine([P|PL],Ptotal) :- con_andcombine(PL,P2),
    P3 is P + P2, not(P3 < 1.0), Ptotal is P + P2 - 1.0.
```

The bottom diagram in Figure 8-2 is the Venn diagram for the conservative "and" case. So the diagram for conservative "or" is different from the diagram for conservative "and." In general, you should use the conservative "or" when there are strong positive correlations between evidence, and the conservative "and" when there are strong negative correlations.

To illustrate, let's use the same example of the last section but substitute in con_orcombine and con_andcombine:

```
total_g(P) :- bagof(P2,g(P2),PL), con_orcombine(PL,P).
g(0.7) :- a.
g(P) :- b(P1), c(P2), con_andcombine([P1,P2,0.9],P).
g(0.3) :- a, d.
a.
b(0.8).
c(0.9).
d.
```

The second g rule binds its P to $0.8 + (0.9 + 0.9 - 1) - 1 = 0.6$. Then PL is bound to [0.7,0.6,0.3], and P in total_g is bound to 0.7.

Note we don't have to pick the independence-assumption or conservative approach exclusively in a rule-based system. We can choose one in each situation based on our analysis of appropriateness.

The conservative "or-combination" is particularly useful for handling prior (or *a priori*) probabilities. These are "starting" probabilities for the likelihood of an event on general grounds. They are usually numbers close to 0, and they can be expressed in the Prolog database as *facts* (instead of rules) with probabilities. For instance, checking under the hood of a car for frayed wires is a lot of work, so an expert system for auto diagnosis might first try to diagnose an electrical problem without asking for such an inspection, using an a priori probability of 0.01 of any wire being frayed. The independence assumption is a poor idea for combining with an a priori probability because the latter represents a summary of many causes.

8.7 THE LIBERAL APPROACH AND OTHERS_____

There's also a *liberal* approach: compute the maximum probability possible with the evidence. This isn't as useful as the "conservative" approach, but applies for "and"s whenever one piece of evidence implies all the others, and applies for "or"s whenever pieces of evidence are disjoint (i.e., prove the same conclusion in ways that cannot hold simultaneously). Liberal formulas can be derived from the conservative formulas by relating "and" and "or," as with the formula for two variables:

$$p(A \text{ or } B) = p(A) + p(B) - p(A \text{ and } B)$$

which can also be written

$$p(A \text{ and } B) = p(A) + p(B) - p(A \text{ or } B)$$

Since $p(A)$ and $p(B)$ are known, the maximum value of the first formula occurs when $p(A \text{ and } B)$ has a minimum, and the maximum of the second formula occurs when $p(A \text{ or } B)$ has a minimum (note the important minus signs). These needed minima are given the conservative formulas. So the liberal bound on two-argument "or"s is

$$p(A) + p(B) - \text{maxfunction}(p(A) + p(B) - 1, 0) =$$

$$- \text{maxfunction}(-1, -p(A) - p(B)) = \text{minfunction}(1, p(A) + p(B))$$

and the liberal bound on "and"s is

$$p(A) + p(B) - \text{maxfunction}(p(A), p(B)) =$$

$$- \text{maxfunction}(-p(B), -p(A)) = \text{minfunction}(p(A), p(B))$$

To generalize, the liberal approach for "and-combination" is the minimum of the probabilities:

```
lib_andcombine(PL,P) :- min(PL,P).
min([X],X).
min([X|L],X) :- min(L,X2), X < X2.
min([X|L],X2) :- min(L,X2), not(X < X2).
```

(The min is like the max of Sections 5.5 and 8.6.) Similarly, the general "or-combination" is the sum of the probabilities, provided this number is not greater than 1:

```
lib_orcombine(PL,1.0) :- sumup(PL,P), P > 1.0.
lib_orcombine(PL,P) :- sumup(PL,P), not(P > 1.0).
sumup([P],P).
sumup([P|PL],Ptotal) :- sumup(PL,P2), Ptotal is P + P2.
```

The middle diagram in Figure 8-2 shows the liberal "and" case graphically, and the bottom diagram in Figure 8-2 illustrates the liberal "or." That is, they're the situations for the conservative "and" and "or" reversed. In general, you should use the liberal "and" when there are strong positive correlations between evidence, and the liberal "or" when there are strong negative correlations—just the opposite of the advice for the conservative formulas.

Consider the same example we have used before, but with lib_orcombine and lib_andcombine:

```
total_g(P) :- bagof(P2,g(P2),PL), lib_orcombine(PL,P).
g(0.7) :- a.
g(P) :- b(P1), c(P2), lib_andcombine([P1,P2,0.9],P).
g(0.3) :- a, d.
a.
b(0.8).
c(0.9).
d.
```

Now P in the second g rule will be bound to 0.8, the minimum of [0.8,0.9,0.9]. Then PL is bound to [0.7,0.8,0.3], and P in total_g is bound to 1.0.

Again, we can use the liberal approach wherever we like in a rule-based system, and the conservative and independence-assumption approaches elsewhere in the same system too. The formulas are summarized in Figure 8-3. (All the formulas are associative, so we can get the n-item formula from the two-item formula.) If we aren't sure any is best, we can take a weighted average of the three. Or we could invent our own formula. But we must be careful, because not all formulas make sense. Reasonable criteria are (1) smoothness, that the formula never makes abrupt jumps in value as input probabilities smoothly vary; (2) consistency, that it never gives values outside the range between the conservative and liberal values; (3) commutativity, that the order of binary combination doesn't matter; and (4) associativity, that the formula gives the same result no matter how the expressions are grouped (for example, combining p_1 with the combination of p_2 and p_3 must be the same as combining the combination of p_1 and p_2 with p_3).

	and-combination	*or-combination*
Independence assumption (reasonable-guess)	$p_1 p_2 \cdots p_n$	$1 - [(1 - p_1)(1 - p_2) \cdots (1 - p_n)]$
Conservative assumption (lower bound)	$\max(0,(p_1 + p_2 + \cdots + p_n) - n + 1)$	$\max(p_1,p_2, \cdots p_n)$
Liberal assumption (upper bound)	$\min(p_1,p_2, \cdots p_n)$	$\min(1,p_1 + p_2 + \cdots + p_n)$

Note: conservative "and" $\leq$ independence-assumption "and" $\leq$ liberal "and" $\leq$ conservative "or" $\leq$ independence-assumption "or" $\leq$ liberal "or"

Figure 8-3. Formulas for combination of probabilities.

8.8 NEGATION AND PROBABILITIES_____

Conditions in rules that something *not* be true cause problems for probabilities. For instance

    a :- b, not(c).

If a, b, and c are all uncertain and the rule itself has a certainty of 0.7, it won't do to just add extra arguments like this:

    a(P) :- b(P1), not(c(P2)), indep_andcombine([P1,P2,0.7],P).

because if there's any evidence for **c**, no matter how weak, the rule will fail. We want instead for weak evidence for **c** to *decrease* the probability of **a** in a small way. The way to handle this is to note the probability of something being false is one minus the probability of it being true. So instead

    a(P) :- b(P1), c(P2), inverse(P2,NegP2), indep_andcombine([P1,NegP2,0.7],P).

where **inverse** is defined as:

    inverse(X,IX) :- IX is 1 - X.

So we shouldn't use **nots** when probabilities are involved, but use this predicate **inverse** on the resulting probabilities. (But you must still be careful to remember that **p(0.0)** won't match **not(p)**.)

    Some artificial-intelligence systems don't follow this approach, however. They try to be more general by reasoning separately about events and their negations. They collect evidence for an event and combine it with probability combination rules, but they also collect evidence against an event and combine it separately. Then they combine these two cumulative probabilities somehow to get an overall likelihood measure. A simple way used in many expert systems is to take the difference of the probability for the event and the probability against it. This number ranges from 1.0 (complete certainty of truth) through 0.0 (complete indecision) to -1.0 (complete certainty of falsity).

8.9 AN EXAMPLE: FIXING TELEVISIONS_____

Now we'll give an example of a simple rule-based expert system using probabilities for diagnosis of malfunctioning equipment. Unfortunately, most expert systems (like most artificial-intelligence programs) must be big to do anything worthwhile; otherwise, human beings could do the job fine without them. So to avoid burdening you with an example ten pages long, we must pick something simple and not very useful. So here's an example of the few things wrong with a television set that you can fix yourself (television sets use high voltages so most malfunctions should be treated by trained service personnel).

When a television set is working improperly, one of two things may be improperly adjusted: the controls (knobs and switches) or the receiver (antenna or cable). So let's write an expert system to estimate probabilities of those two things. We'll assume these probabilities need not be very accurate, but their relative sizes provide a rough guide to where things are wrong.

Consider why the knobs might be adjusted wrong on a television. If it is old and requires frequent adjustment, that could be a reason. Similarly, if children use your set, and they play with the knobs, that could be a reason too, as well as anything strange you've done lately that required adjustment of the knobs (like taking a photograph of the television picture, requiring that the brightness be turned up very high). Let's write the rules. If a set requires frequent readjusting, then it's quite reasonable that the set is maladjusted today—let's say 50% sure:

maladjusted(0.5) :- askif(frequent_adjustments_needed).

(The askif predicate was defined in Section 7.3; it types out a question for the user and checks if the response is positive or negative.) For recent unusual usage of the television, it matters how you define "unusual." But let's say 50% to be reasonable, so the rule is

maladjusted(0.5) :- askif(recent_unusual_usage).

The rule for children must insist both that children hang around your house and that they would be inclined to mess around with the knobs on your television. That's the "and" of two conditions, so we need an "andcombine." When both conditions hold, it's quite likely the set is maladjusted, so we can give this rule a rule strength of 0.9. So the rule is

maladjusted(P) :- ask(children_present,P1),
   ask(children_twiddle_knobs,P2), andcombine([P1,P2,0.9],P).

Then to get the cumulative probability the set was recently adjusted, we need an orcombine:

recently_adjusted(P) :- bagof(P2,maladjusted(P2),PL), orcombine(PL,P).

This last predicate just summarizes predisposing evidence for a set maladjustment, but it doesn't incorporate the best evidence at all, observations of the television set. In other words, two major factors, past and present, must be combined. This could be either an "andcombine" or an "orcombine," but "andcombine" seems preferable because neither factor here implies strongly the diagnosis; it's only when both occur together that evidence is strong. That suggests

```
diagnosis('knobs on set require adjustment',P) :-
  recently_adjusted(P2), askif(operation(abnormal)),
  andcombine([P2,0.8],P).
```

(Remember, single quotation marks (') indicate character strings in Prolog; every-thing between two single quotation marks, including spaces, is treated as a unit.)

If there is some uncertainty about whether the television's behavior is normal, we could include a probability as another argument to the **operation** predicate, com-bining it in the "andcombine" too. Or we could characterize the operation with different words. For instance

```
diagnosis('knobs on set require adjustment',P) :-
  recently_adjusted(P2), askif(operation(mediocre)),
  andcombine([P2,0.5],P).
```

So we have a three-level expert system: an "and" of two expressions, one of which is an "or" of three expressions, one of which in turn is an "and" of two expressions. It's true we could simplify this into two levels by the laws of logic (see Appendix A), rewriting everything in disjunctive normal form or conjunctive nor-mal form (see Appendix A), but this isn't a good idea with rule-based systems. For one thing, extra levels let you group related concepts together to make the rule-based system easier to understand; in a normal form, widely different predicates can be thrown together. Grouping related terms together also enables easier deter-mination of probability values and easier choice of probability combination methods; it's difficult to pick a good combination method for twenty terms, since some of the "and"ed expressions must be considerably more related than others. Many-level rule-based systems also allow easier design and debugging, because they give lots of places to put checkpoints and tracing facilities.

Now let's turn to the other kind of television diagnosis we can make, that the antenna or cable connection to the television set is faulty. For this conclusion we will use the same **diagnosis** and **operation** predicates as before. But we'll need a new predicate to summarize contributing factors to the faultiness of the antenna or cable connection, **overall_source_problems**:

```
source_problems(0.8) :- askif(television(new)).
source_problems(0.95) :- askif(antenna(new)).
source_problems(0.95) :- askif(cable(new)).
source_problems(0.3) :- askif(recent_furniture_rearrangement).
overall_source_problems(P) :- bagof(P2,source_problems(P2),PL),
  orcombine(PL,P).
```

Let's assume that no one has both an antenna and a cable connection (or if they do, only one of them is operating). We'll use a **source_type** predicate to indicate whether the setup is an antenna or a cable. Then we have two rules for the two diagnoses:

```
diagnosis('antenna connection is faulty',P) :-
  askif(source_type(antenna)), askif(operation(abnormal)),
  overall_source_problems(P).
diagnosis('cable connection is faulty',P) :-
  askif(source_type(cable)), askif(operation(abnormal)),
  overall_source_problems(P).
```

So that's our simple expert system. To use it, we query

```
?- diagnosis(D,P).
```

And each answer that the Prolog interpreter finds to the query will bind **D** to a string representing a diagnosis and bind **P** to the corresponding probability. To find all diagnoses that there is some evidence for, we can repeatedly type semicolons.

8.10 GRAPHICAL REPRESENTATION OF PROBABILITIES IN RULE-BASED SYSTEMS_____

The logic-gate representation of an and-or-not lattice (see Section 6.10) is a useful graphical notation for simple rule-based systems. It can be used for rules with probabilities too. Associate every "andcombine" and "orcombine" with a logic gate in the representation. Indicate rule strengths next to their corresponding logic gates. For rules with only one expression on their right side, use special triangle gates (*attenuators*) with one input and one output. Then each line has an associated probability, computed by proceeding from the inputs through the network, applying the proper formula at each gate. Figure 8-4 shows the and-or-not lattice for the example of the last section.

8.11 GETTING PROBABILITES FROM STATISTICS_____

There's a more fundamental problem with probabilities than combining them, however: getting them in the first place. If probabilities are markedly incorrect, reasoning based on them can't be trusted. But getting good probabilities is often the hardest problem in building a rule-based system. Even when programmers can easily decide what the predicates should be, what things rules should cover, and how rules should be structured, they often have trouble estimating probabilities because it's hard to tell when an estimate is wrong. Two approaches are used: getting probabilities from statistics on data, and getting probabilities from human "experts."

Since people reason poorly about uncertainty, the first approach seems preferable. Often we have a lot of routinely collected data about the phenomena in a rule-based system, as when our rule-based system further automates human capabilities already partly automated. We can approximate needed probabilities by fre-

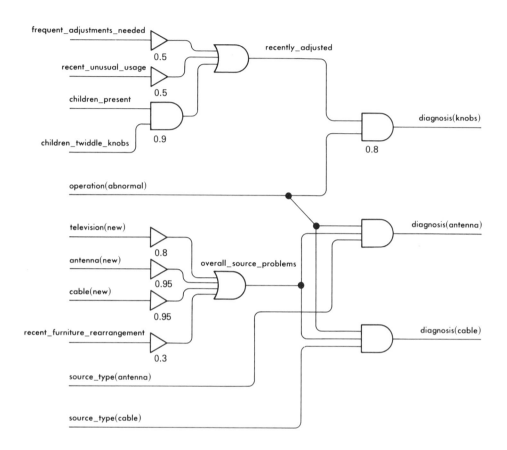

Figure 8-4. Example and-or-not lattice with probabilities.

quency ratios in the data. For instance, we can approximate rule-strength probabili-ties by the ratio of the number of times both sides of a rule were together satisfied to the number of times the right side was satisfied.

As an example, consider the repair of airplanes. They are expensive, so an organization that owns many of them must keep detailed repair and maintenance records to ensure quality work, to better allocate resources, and to track down trends in malfunctions. Most organizations today computerize these records, recording observed malfunctions, their eventually inferred causes, and what was done to fix them—just what we need to assign probabilities to an expert system for diagnosis. For instance, we can count how many times the radar system failed, and how many of those times the widget component was faulty, and take the ratio of the second to the first to fill in <strength> in the rule

faulty(widget, <strength>) :- failed(radar).

However, approximating a real number (a probability) by the ratio of two integers can be awkward, and the approximation is often poor when the integers are small. Suppose some event happens with probability 0.001, and we have data for 2000 occurrences. On the average we'll expect two events in those 2000, but the number could be 1, 0, 3, or 4 too, since the event is so rare. According to probability theory, random sets of size N, drawn from an infinite population with fraction F of its members possessing some property, will tend to show the same fraction F possessing the property with standard error (standard deviation of this fraction) approximately

$$\sqrt{F(1-F)/N}$$

(using the binomial-distribution approximation). This says how good a probability estimate is; the larger this number, the worse the estimate. As a rule of thumb, if the preceding is the same or larger than F, the F fraction should not be trusted.

As an example, suppose something happens 7 times out of 20 possible times. Then $N = 20$, $F = 0.35$, and the standard error by the formula is 0.105. This is significantly less than 0.35, so the probability estimate 0.35 looks OK.

8.12 PROBABILITIES DERIVED FROM OTHERS

If a probability is important to our rule-based system, yet the associated standard error of approximation from data is large, we may be able to better estimate the probability from other data. One way is Bayes's rule. Letting $p(A$ given $B)$ represent the probability of event A happening when event B also happens, we can say

$$p(A \text{ given } B) = p(A \text{ and } B)/p(B)$$

But switching A and B in that equation

$$p(B \text{ given } A) = p(A \text{ and } B)/p(A)$$

We can solve the second equation for $p(A$ and $B)$, and substitute in the first equation, obtaining the usual form of Bayes's rule:

$$p(A \text{ given } B) = p(B \text{ given } A)*p(A)/p(B)$$

This is useful when we have a rule

    a(P) :- b(P2), andcombine([P2,<strength>],P).

and we want to know what number to put for <strength>, the probability that a is true given that b is true. If we have enough data to compute the reverse—the probability that b is true given that a is true—then Bayes's rule can use that number, together with estimates of the overall probabilities of a and b, to give what we need. This is an especially good idea when a always *causes* b, because then the reverse probability that b is true given that a is true must be 1.0. For instance, a car absolutely will not start when its battery is dead, so we can approximate the probability that the battery is dead when the car won't start by the ratio of the overall probability the battery is dead to the overall probability the car won't start.

There are extensions of Bayes's rule, for instance:

$$p(A \text{ given } (B \text{ and } C)) = p((B \text{ and } C) \text{ given } A) * p(A) / p(B \text{ and } C)$$

Another trick to get rule probabilities is to use the independence assumption in a special way. Suppose we have

a(P) :- b(P1), c(P2), andcombine([P1,P2,<strength>],P).

Now there may be few situations in the data in which both b and c were true. But if there were many situations in which one of b and c was true, then we could estimate the probabilities of a given b, and a given c, and take the "or-combination" of these two numbers (yes, "or" not "and"; think about it) as an estimate of the rule strength needed. That is, we can precompile an "orcombine."

8.13 SUBJECTIVE PROBABILITIES

Even with these tricks we may not have enough data (or perhaps good enough data) to approximate probabilities very well. Then we must guess probabilities ourselves, or preferably, ask a human expert in the task or domain of the rule-based system. This isn't always easy: experts may be hard to find, or their time may be expensive, or they may not understand or feel comfortable with a rule formulation of their knowledge. But there may be no other choice.

As we've said, humans make many mistakes in probability estimation, as demonstrated by psychological experiments. One simple way to make things easier is to let people quantify uncertainty on a different numeric scale than 0.0 to 1.0. For instance, take *degrees of certainty* on a scale 0 to 100, and divide by 100 to get the probability. Better yet, do a nonlinear transformation of the probability scale, for instance with *odds* defined as $p/(1 - p)$. Odds range from 0 to positive infinity, so a probability of 0.9 is odds of 9, a probability of 0.5 is odds of 1, and a probability of 0.1 is odds of 0.111. The logarithm of the odds is also useful; it "flattens out" the curve more, and ranges from minus infinity to plus infinity.

Something that also helps is speaking of uncertainty nonnumerically. For instance, let them use the terms "certain," "almost certain," "likely," "suggestive," "possible," "not likely," and "impossible." Each term may map to a probability— say 1.00 for "certain," 0.99 for "almost certain," 0.8 for "likely," 0.5 for "suggestive," 0.2 for "possible," 0.05 for "not likely," and 0.0 for "impossible." If this isn't possible, perhaps different probabilities can be given for different contexts, so a "possible car problem" would be a 0.2 probability, but a "possible nuclear accident" would be 0.001 probability.

8.14 MAXIMUM-ENTROPY PROBABILITIES*_____

Bayes's rule extends the utility of both statistics and subjective probability estimates. We can generalize this idea to accept arbitrary probabilities from the
programmer—prior probabilities, conditional probabilities, and joint probabilities—
and make "reasonable guess" estimates of others, using some mathematics.

It can be shown mathematically that best guesses (based on certain postulates
for guess desirability) are those that maximize entropy, or minimize the *information content*, of probability assignments. This is a mathematical optimization problem, in which we want to maximize

$$\sum_{i=1}^{m} \left[-p(A_i)\log(p(A_i)) \right]$$

for some mutually exclusive set of probabilities $p(A_i)$ that sum to 1, subject to
given equality constraints in the form of probabilities already known. Optimization
problems like this can be attacked by many methods from operations research, and
computer packages are available. But they can take time since they usually iterate.

Sometimes we don't need to iterate to find maximum-entropy probabilities,
but we can use algebraic manipulations to get formulas. Here's an example for
those of you that know some calculus. Suppose we know the probabilities of two
events A and B, $p(A)$ and $p(B)$. Suppose we want to find the maximum-entropy
probability for $x = p(A \text{ and } B)$ (i.e., we want to do "and-combination" in a
maximum-entropy way). Then there are four mutually exclusive probabilities
involved: $p(A \text{ and } B), p(\bar{A} \text{ and } B), p(A \text{ and } \bar{B}), p(\bar{A} \text{ and } \bar{B})$, where we use $\bar{A}$ to
represent the exact opposite of A, so $p(\bar{A}) = 1 - p(A)$. Then

$$p(A \text{ and } B) = x, p(\bar{A} \text{ and } B) = p(B) - x, p(A \text{ and } \bar{B}) = p(A) - x$$

$$p(\bar{A} \text{ and } \bar{B}) = 1 - p(A) - p(B) + x$$

And the preceding summation formula for the entropy is

$$-x \log(x) - (p(B) - x)\log(p(B) - x) - (p(A) - x)\log(p(A) - x)$$

$$- (1 - p(A) - p(B) + x)\log(1 - p(A) - p(B) + x)$$

To find the maximum of this, we take the derivative with respect to x, and set this
to zero. Noting that the derivative of $y \log(y)$ with respect to x is
$(1 + \log(y))dy/dx$, we get

$$-\log(x) + \log(p(B) - x) + \log(p(A) - x) - \log(1 - p(A) - p(B) + x) = 0$$

$$\log[x(1 - p(A) - p(B) + x)/(p(A) - x)(p(B) - x)] = 0$$

$$x^2 - (p(A) + p(B))x + p(A)p(B) = x^2 + (1 - p(A) - p(B))x$$

$$x = p(A)p(B)$$

This is just the independence-assumption formula. So the formula we justified intuitively in Section 8.3 has a deeper justification. Formulas for more complicated situations can also be derived with the method.

8.15 CONSISTENCY*

Another problem with subjective probabilities (but also to a lesser extent with data-derived probabilities) is that they can be inconsistent (logically impossible) in a nonobvious way. This often happens when both a priori (unconditional) and conditional probabilities are specified by people. We should therefore run checks on user-given probabilities before entering them into a rule-based system.

As an example, note from the definition of conditional probability that

$$p(A \text{ given } B)p(B) = p(B \text{ given } A)p(A)$$

Hence, since probabilities are positive numbers no greater than one

$$p(A) \geqslant p(A \text{ given } B)p(B)$$

$$p(B \text{ given } A) \geqslant p(A \text{ given } B)p(B)$$

$$p(B) \geqslant p(B \text{ given } A)p(A)$$

$$p(A \text{ given } B) \geqslant p(B \text{ given } A)p(A)$$

so we can catch some inconsistencies from inequalities.

KEYWORDS

> *probability*
> *uncertainty*
> *or-combination*
> *and-combination*
> *rule probability*
> *conclusion probability*
> *independence assumption*
> *conservative assumption*
> *liberal assumption*
> *Bayes's rule*
> *scale transformations*
> *maximum-entropy estimates*

EXERCISES

8-1. Assume:
1. The battery is defective with certainty 0.5 when a car won't start.
2. The battery is defective with certainty 0.8 when the radio is functioning and the radio won't play.

3. You are not sure if your radio is functioning — the probability is 0.9 that it is functioning.

4. This morning your car won't start and the radio won't play.

What is the cumulative probability that your battery is defective this morning? Combine evidence assuming independence of probabilities.

8-2. Consider these rules (the arguments are all probabilities):

a(P) :- b(P2), P is P2 * 0.6.
a(P) :- c(P).

Suppose b is known to be absolutely certain, and c is 80% certain.

(a) What is the cumulative probability of a using the independence assumption?

(b) What is the cumulative probability of a using the conservative assumption?

(c) What is the cumulative probability of a using the liberal assumption?

8-3. (R,A) Suppose we want to fill in the <prob1> and <prob2> probability values in the following two rules that infer a flat tire on a car:

flat_tire(<prob1>) :- car_steers_strangely.
flat_tire(<prob2>) :- just_ran_over_something.

(a) Suppose we have statistics that say:

- In 200 situations in which the car steered strangely the tire was flat, out of 500 situations in which the car steered strangely.
- In 800 situations in which you just ran over something the tire was discovered to be flat, out of 1600 situations in which you just ran over something.
- A flat tire was observed in 1200 situations total.

Estimate <prob1> and <prob2> for these statistics.

(b) Suppose we also know that 70 times in which both the car steered strangely and you just ran over something the tire was then found to be flat, out of 101 times in which both those two things were observed. Which probability combination method (or-combination) for the preceding two rules is best confirmed here: conservative, independence-assumption, or liberal?

8-4. (A) Suppose you want to handle or-combination of uncertainties nonnumerically. Suppose the possible degrees of uncertainty are "definitely," "probably," "probably not," and "definitely not."

(a) Suppose the "orcombine" function of any two of those four terms is defined by the table in Figure 8-5. Each row and column represent a pair of values to be combined. Which of the numerical or-combination methods is this equivalent to: conservative, independence-assumption, liberal, or something else?

	definitely	probably	probably not	definitely not
definitely	definitely	definitely	definitely	definitely
probably	definitely	probably	probably	probably
probably not	definitely	probably	probably not	probably not
definitely not	definitely	probably	probably not	definitely not

Figure 8-5. One evidence combination method.

(b) Suppose the "orcombine" function of any two of those four terms is defined by the table in Figure 8-6. Which of the numerical or-combination methods is this equivalent to: conservative, independence-assumption, liberal, or something else?

(c) For the method of part (b), suppose you want to map "definitely," "probably," "probably not," and "definitely not" into probabilities. It makes sense to have "definitely" = 1.0 and "definitely not" = 0.0. Give probabilities for "probably" and "probably not" consistent with the table in part (b). (There are an infinite number of answers.)

	definitely	probably	probably not	definitely not
definitely	definitely	definitely	definitely	definitely
probably	definitely	definitely	definitely	probably
probably not	definitely	definitely	probably	probably not
definitely not	definitely	probably	probably not	definitely not

Figure 8-6. Another evidence combination method.

8-5. (A) Combination methods for probabilities use the Prolog is, which requires its arithmetic calculation to refer to only bound variables. Consider a rule-based system that uses rules with probabilities and calculates on those probabilities. Does the directionality of is mean that one of either backward chaining or forward chaining is impossible? Why?

8-6. (R,A) Consider the following way of doing or-combination of probabilities in an expert system: the cumulative probability is the fraction of the contributing probabilities that are greater than 0.5. So for instance the cumulative probability for contributing probabilities 0.3, 0.9, 0.66, 0.2, and 0.8 would be 0.6.

(a) Define a Prolog predicate **new_orcombine(PL,P)** that computes the cumulative probability **P** of a list **PL** using this method.

(b) Give two major disadvantages of this method, disadvantages not shared by the three methods discussed in the chapter, and explain why they are major.

8-7. Suppose we have R rules concluding D diagnoses such that there are the same number of rules concluding each diagnosis, R/D. Assume no intermediate predicates; have each diagnosis rule refer to facts. Suppose the probability of any rule succeeding in a random situation is P, and suppose this probability is independent of the success or failure of other rules.

(a) How many rules will succeed for a situation on the average?

(b) How many diagnoses will succeed for a situation on the average?

8-8. (G) Write ten or so Prolog rules to predict what the weather will be at 3 P.M. some day, reasoning at noon that day, using probabilities as an additional argument to all predicates that have uncertainty. The top-level rule should have a left side of the form predict(<weather>,<probability>), where <weather> is either sunny, partly_cloudy, or cloudy. Choose a good evidence-combination method. Assume the following predicates are available as the basis for your reasoning at noon. (Try to define some intermediate predicates based on these, which can then be combined to make predictions, to make things more interesting.)

> current_west_view(<weather>): whether the given weather is viewable from a west-facing window right now. The argument can be sunny, partly_cloudy, or cloudy.
>
> current_east_view(<weather>): same for east-facing window.
>
> raining(<degree>): whether it is raining to that degree right now. The <degree> can be light, steady_heavy, and cloudburst.
>
> weatherman_prediction(<weather>): whether the TV weatherman predicted that weather for 6 P.M. last night at 11 P.M.
>
> grandma_prediction(<weather>): whether Grandma predicted that weather this morning from how her joints hurt.
>
> grandma_memory: whether you remember anything Grandma said that morning.
>
> radio_prediction(<weather>): the weather predicted right now on the local radio news station.
>
> secretary_has_radio: you don't have a radio, but the secretary down the hall might.
>
> secretary_out_to_lunch: if they are out to lunch, the room is locked, and you can't get in.

8-9. (A,E) Consider the following argument: "Spending money on the lottery must be a good thing, because you constantly hear about people winning big bucks in the battery, in the newspapers and on television."

(a) What is the fallacy (reasoning error) here?

(b) What warning does this illustrate for using probabilities in rule-based systems?

8-10. Most students are adults (18 years old or more). Most adults are employed. We could write adult(X,P) :- student(X,P2), P is P2 * 0.95.

employed(X,P) :- adult(X,P2), P is P2 * 0.9.

Then if we knew that Joe was a student with complete certainty, these rules say that Joe is employed with 0.855 probability, a clearly fallacious conclusion because most students don't work at all, as any professor will tell you. This fallacy is due to a simplification that we have made to make our analysis in the chapter easier.

(a) Show how the problem can be fixed by writing one rule as two.

(b) Suppose we consider this rule rewriting as awkward and we wish to fix things by just changing the probability combination method. The previous method was independence-assumption combination. What happens to the probability of Joe being employed when we use the conservative assumption?

(c) The conservative assumption does not give a reasonable answer either. How can we solve this problem in a reasonably general way?

8-11. (E)

(a) In English, double negatives don't always mean what you expect them to mean. Explain why "not unhappy" is different from "happy."

(b) What warning does this suggest to the designer of a rule-based expert system using probabilities? In particular, for what sorts of English words should a designer be careful?

8-12. (P,G) Design a program to diagnose problems with cars. Many artificial intelligence applications involve diagnosis, and automatic diagnostic aids really help. We pick cars because almost everybody knows something about them, and we don't need to hire outside experts as with most expert systems. This diagnosis program should be usable by people who know virtually nothing about cars; it should use nontechnical words and familiar concepts. For instance, it shouldn't expect that a user knows what different sounds mean, and should try to describe sounds by analogies to everyday sounds.

An important part of the project will be the formal definition of concepts that may be concluded (e.g., "the car won't start"). Another part will be enumeration of things a user could be expected to know; in particular, try to use knowledge of the history of the car, what problems it has had in the past. Try not to get too technical; there are plenty of "commonsense" things about cars, particularly for the body and interior of the passenger compartment. For instance, one cause of a rattle in a car could be a baby's rattle under the seat.

Handle uncertain data and uncertain conclusions. Probably the easiest approach is independence-assumption combination. Decide initial values for probabilities, and how to treat evidence against something.

If this is a group project, one person should handle the control structure of

the program and provide utilities for everyone else. Other people can specialize in different systems of the car. For instance, someone should probably
handle the body and interior of the car, someone the electrical system, someone the engine and fuel system, etc. About thirty rules should be written by
each contributor. Emphasize quality of the rules, not quantity.

9

SEARCH

It's time for a change of pace. In this and the next two chapters, we'll cover a new class of artificial-intelligence techniques. These are good for reasoning about events in time and plans of action. Technically, "search".[1] We'll need a new vocabulary to talk about search problems—terms like "state," "operator," "search strategy," "evaluation function," and "branching factor."

Search problems appear in many application areas. Search relates to rule-based systems because they involve actions occurring over time. In fact, search is an abstraction of the concept of a control structure. So we'll be looking at rule-based systems in a new way.

9.1 CHANGING WORLDS

So far the facts in Prolog databases have rarely changed. We added facts through caching in forward chaining, but those facts were logically derivable from the other facts and rules all along. We rarely removed facts from a Prolog database—only in implementing a few special programs.

But Prolog databases usually model a situation in the world, and the world can change. In fact, the result of running an artificial-intelligence program may be

---

[1] Also called *heuristic search*, but that's misleading because you don't need heuristics to do it, and anyway the term "heuristic" is overused and much abused in artificial intelligence.

to recommend actions in the world, which are then taken, and then reflected in changes to the facts true about the world. Often an artificial-intelligence program is useless unless it does change something in the world. For instance, an automobile diagnosis program is not much help unless you can actually fix a car by its recommendations.

In many important applications, a problem can be solved only by a series of actions, not just one. Then the problem solver must track the changing situation in the world. Changing the facts appropriately can be complicated for such problems, and we need some new tricks.

9.2 STATES

A situation in the world described by some facts is a *state*. State is a fundamental concept in many areas of science and engineering. For instance, in physics a state is a set of measurable physical parameters fully describing some part of the universe; in simulation models of economics, a state is the set of values assigned to model parameters; and in computer systems programming, a processing state is a set of values currently in registers, buffers, and stacks. So a state is a "snapshot" of a process in time.

A state can be instantaneous or it can last for quite a while. In artificial intelligence (and computer science too) we only concern ourselves with noninstantaneous states, but where state changes (*branches* or *transitions*) are instantaneous. That is, state changes are *discrete* and not *continuous*. Loading a computer register is an example of a discrete state change. *Search* is the study of states and their transitions.

A state must include everything important about a situation in one bundle.[2] That means everything necessary to reason about it—and in artificial intelligence, that usually means a list of facts. These may be a lot of facts, and often we'll want to reason about many states, as when we try to figure how to achieve some desirable state. So two tricks often simplify state descriptions. First, we can record only the facts relevant to the very specific problem we're working on. For instance, if our problem is to fix a car when we know there is something wrong with the electrical system, we can ignore facts about the state of the engine (whether it is cold or warm, whether the timing is accurate, whether the oil has been changed recently, etc.) since they usually don't matter. Second, we can compress the fact representation by collapsing several predicates into one, like the "relational database" predicates of Section 2.9. For instance, if ten screws hold the battery onto the chassis of a car, we can write one fact with ten arguments where argument number K is the word "on" or the word "off" reflecting the status of screw number K.

---

[2] At least the states in this book. To make things easier, we deliberately ignore a class of searches performed using and-or-not lattices, for which states represent pieces of a problem. See other books under the topic of "searching and-or trees."

9.3 THREE EXAMPLES_____

Let's consider some examples of search problems. First, consider the problem of getting by car from one intersection to another in a city. There are different streets that you can take and different turns you can make. To complicate matters, some streets are one-way, and some turns are illegal. Also, you will probably want a short route rather than just any route. Considering this a search problem, a state is the position of a car in a city. We can represent this as the name of the intersection, since intersections are the only places where decisions must be made, and therefore the only locations that matter to reasoning. Solving a search problem means finding a series of states ending in some desired state, so the solution will be a sequence of intersections a car will traverse in order.

As a second example of search, consider the problem of car repair. Even if you know what's wrong, repair is rarely as simple as yanking the old part out and sticking the new part in. Usually you must unloosen fasteners (like screws and nuts) first, and move other parts out of the way to get to the part you want. You may need to run some tests on the suspect part to see if it is indeed faulty. Then you must reassemble everything, doing the reverse of the previous steps in the reverse order—and sometimes exact reversal is impossible, as when removing a cover is easy but refastening requires careful hole alignment. You must also worry about the difficulty of various actions if you want to get the job done efficiently; a sequence of actions that take half as much effort as another is better. For this problem, states are situations of partial disassembly (or assembly) of the car.

As a third example, consider the problem of smarter forward chaining for a rule-based expert system. Section 6.2 presented a simple general-purpose approach to forward chaining, using simple ideas like putting facts in a priority list in the order we find them (the focus-of-attention strategy). These ideas work for a wide class of applications. But for a specific application, a specific conflict-resolution policy may be better. For instance, we can keep the facts sorted by priorities of human experts (the experts' prestored hunches of relative importance), by analysis of the rules (like how many new conclusions a fact can lead to), by statistics on past runs of the rule-based system, or by dynamic features of the reasoning (like whether a certain fact has been proved yet). In general, intelligent forward chaining by intelligent fact sorting is a search problem with many options, each representing a fact to pursue, each leading to a different set of facts to choose from next, and so on. So a state for this problem is a set of unpursued and pursued facts.

We'll use these examples subsequently in the chapter. They were picked to symbolize three important applications of search: optimization problems, human and robot task planning, and expert systems.

9.4 OPERATORS_____

Our three examples involve many states. They can involve even more branches, ways directly from one state to another. It helps to group similar branches into categories called *operators*. Operators often correspond to verbs of English, the names of real-world actions.

Consider the three examples:

1. For finding routes in a city, the operators can be possible actions at an intersection, since states correspond to intersections. So the operators can be "go north," "go east," "go southwest," etc.
2. For car repair, the operators can be much more numerous, including every possible action that can be done on the car: unfasten, unscrew, remove, manipulate, replace, align, fasten, screw, and so on.
3. For smarter forward chaining for a rule-based system, there seems to be only one operator: remove a fact from the set of unexamined facts and pursue its implications.

Be careful though, because operators are not well-defined for many problems. We could, for instance, consider each screwing-in for every single screw as a separate operator; or we could consider each pursuit of a fact as a separate operator. But if operators get too specific, they lose their chief advantage of abstraction over many state transitions.

Preconditions and *postconditions* are frequently associated with operators. Preconditions for an operator are things that must be true before the operator can be applied, writable as predicate expressions. For instance, a precondition to the operator of removing the battery from a car is that all the screws fastening the battery to the chassis are removed. Analogously, postconditions are conditions that must be true after an operator has been applied. For instance, a postcondition of removing the battery from a car is that the car can't start when the ignition switch is turned. Preconditions are useful because they define what is necessary to apply an operator; postconditions are useful because they summarize the effect of an operator.

9.5 SEARCH AS GRAPH TRAVERSAL

The main reason for identifying states and operators is to let us plan in advance a solution to a search problem. By reasoning hypothetically about operator sequences, we can avoid blundering about in the real world. Planning can also ensure that we find the *best* solution to a problem, not just any solution.

For such advance planning, we can consider a search problem as a task of traversing a directed-graph data structure. Semantic networks (see Section 2.7) and decision lattices (see Section 6.8) are two kinds of directed graphs important in artificial intelligence, but there are several others too. Directed graphs consist of nodes (small named circles) and directed edges (named arrows) connecting nodes; we can equate nodes with states, the names on directed edges with operator names, and edges themselves with branches or operator applications. In a search problem, we are given a *starting* state and one or more finishing or *goal* states. On the search graph this means finding a path or traversal between a start node and one of a set of goal nodes. (Here we broaden the term "goal" beyond its meaning for rule-based systems, in which a "goal" was a predicate expression we want to prove; in search, a "goal" is any desired final state.)

Figure 9-1 shows an example route-planning problem. As we said, city-route planning is a search problem for which the states are intersections (intersections are the only places where we must make choices). Then a search graph can be drawn as in Figure 9-2. State a could be the start and state h the goal.

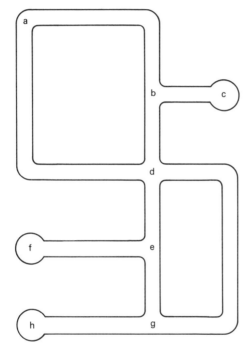

Figure 9-1. Some streets.

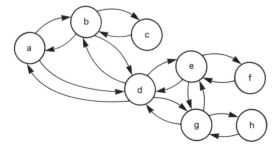

Figure 9-2. Equivalent search graph for Figure 9-1.

Figures 9-3 and 9-4 show similar example search graphs for the auto repair and the smarter-forward-chaining problems. The latter is interesting because we don't know the goal state in advance: we just keep searching until there are no more facts to pursue, and that's a goal state. If we knew what a goal state was in advance, we wouldn't need to do any work. An important class of search problems similarly defines goal states indirectly, in that they only can recognize one when they see one.

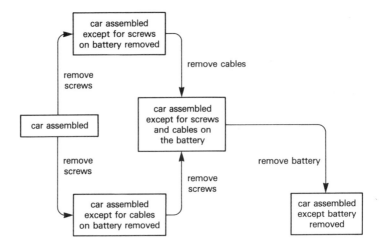

Figure 9-3. Part of a search graph for auto repair.

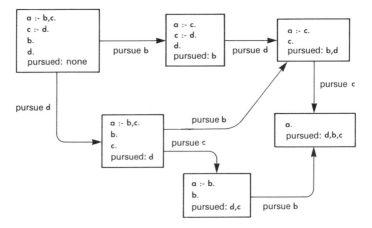

Figure 9-4. Complete search graph for generalized (any-fact-order) forward chaining from one particular set of facts and rules (rules no longer needed are deleted from states as search proceeds).

9.6 THE SIMPLEST SEARCH STRATEGIES: DEPTH-FIRST AND BREADTH-FIRST _____

There are many control structures for search; some of these *search strategies* are summarized in Figure 9-5. The two simplest are depth-first search and breadth-first search.

Name of search strategy	*Uses agenda?*	*Uses evaluation function?*	*Uses cost function?*	*Next state whose successors are found*
Depth-first search	no	no	no	A successor of the last state, else a successor of a predecessor
Breadth-first search	yes	no	no	The state on the agenda the longest
Hill-climbing (optimization)	no	yes	no	The lowest-evaluation successor of the last state
Best-first search	yes	yes	no	The state on the agenda of lowest evaluation value
Branch-and-bound	yes	no	yes	The state on the agenda of lowest total cost
A* search	yes	yes	yes	The state on the agenda of lowest sum of evaluation value and total cost

Figure 9-5. Classic search strategies (heuristics may be used with any of these).

With depth-first search, the start state is chosen (*visited*) to begin, then some *successor* (a state that we can reach by a single branch or state transition) of the start state, then some successor of *that* state, then some successor of that, and so on trying to reach a goal state. Usually the choice among successors of a state isn't arbitrary, but made by "heuristics," which we'll explain in Section 9.7. If depth-first search reaches a state S without successors, or if all the successors of a state S have been chosen (visited) and a goal state has not yet been found, then it "backs up." That means it goes to the immediately previous state or *predecessor*—formally, the state P whose successor was S originally. Depth-first search then takes the next-suggested successor choice of P. So "backing up" is just like Prolog backtracking.

An example will make this clearer (see Figure 9-6). The circled letters are states, and as before, the arrows are branches (operator applications). Suppose S is the start state and G is the only goal state. Suppose that vertical height of the state on the page is used to rank states when a choice is necessary, with higher states having higher rank. Depth-first search will first visit S, then A, then D. But D has no successors, so we must back up to A and try its second successor, E. But this doesn't have any successors either, so we back up to A again. But now we've tried all the successors of A and haven't found the goal state G, so we must back up to S.

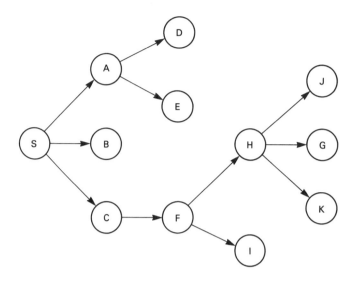

Figure 9-6. Example search lattice.

Now S has a second successor, B. But B has no successors, so we back up to S again and choose its third successor, C. C has one successor, F. The first successor of F is H, and the first of H is J. J doesn't have any successors, so we back up to H and try its second successor. And that's G, the only goal state. So we're done. The solution path to the goal is S, C, F, H, and G, and the states considered were in order S, A, D, E, B, C, F, H, J, G.

One problem with depth-first search is that it works fine when search graphs are trees or lattices, but can get stuck in an infinite loop on other graphs (see Appendix C for definitions of these terms). This is because depth-first search can travel around a cycle in the graph forever. One fix is to keep a list of states previously visited, and never permit search to return to any of them. We will do this in our depth-first program in the next chapter, but this check can require a lot of time since there may be lots of previous states, or states with long, complicated descriptions.

Breadth-first search does not have this danger of infinite loops. The idea is to consider states in order of increasing number of branches (*level*) from the start state. So we first check all the immediate successors of the start state, then all the immediate successors of these, then all the immediate successors of those, and so on until we find a goal state. For each level, we order states in some way as with depth-first search. For Figure 9-6, S is on level 0; A, B, and C are on level 1; D, E, and F, level 2; H and I, level 3; and J, G, and K, level 4. So breadth-first search, assuming the previously used vertical ordering among same-level states, will consider in order S, A, B, C, D, E, F, H, I, J, and G—and then stop because it's reached the goal state. But the solution path it will find is the same as depth-first's.

Breadth-first search is guaranteed to find a goal state if a path to one exists, unlike depth-first, but it may take a while. Cycles in the search graph will cause inefficiency (useless extra paths being considered) instead of infinite processing loops. If that inefficiency is bothersome, we can use the same trick in depth-first of storing a list of previously visited states and checking against it. Notice that by working by level, any later path we find to a state can be no shorter than the first path found to it, so the first path found to a state can be considered the best. However, breadth-first search does have one big disadvantage versus depth-first: it requires extra storage in the form of an *agenda* of states whose successors you have not yet found, as we will explain in Section 10.5.

Depth-first and breadth-first search often occur in disguise in artificial intelligence and computer science. The backward chaining, forward chaining, and rule-cycle hybrid chaining algorithms of Chapter 6 were really kinds of depth-first search, so they can be called *depth-first control structures*. Depth-first control structures are common in computer applications because of their intimate connection to stacks, an easy-to-implement data structure. Though we didn't discuss it in Chapter 6, we could do breadth-first backward chaining as a variant control structure, or breadth-first forward chaining. So be careful not to confuse the backward/forward chaining distinction with the depth-first/breadth-first search distinction—they're quite different things.

9.7 HEURISTICS

Depth-first and breadth-first search are easy to implement but often inefficient for hard problems. A top concern of artificial intelligence research has been finding better search strategies. Many of these better strategies are related to depth-first and breadth-first search. Two common variants are search using heuristics and search using evaluation functions.

Heuristics are any nonnumeric advice about what order to try the successors of a state for further search.[3] So their effects are "local": they give advice for a specific successor choice, not about the whole search strategy. Since both depth-first and breadth-first must make such choices, both can use heuristics, as well as the other search strategies we'll discuss in this chapter. Heuristics are like gardeners because they *prune* (eliminate) branches. Heuristics are a generalization of meta-rules (see Section 6.7), rules about rules. Like meta-rules, heuristics are good for only one operator application (branch), and must be reexamined at each new choice.

Usually heuristics are not guaranteed—that is, they represent reasonable advice about how to proceed and may be wrong. But if they're wrong a lot, there's no point in using them. Heuristics need not give a unique recommendation of what's best in every situation. At worst, we can choose at random among multiple recommendations. What if that's not a good idea? "Search" me.

Here are example heuristics:

- For city route planning, never turn right twice in a row, since this tends to make you go back in the direction you came from.

---

[3] Some authors say heuristics can be based on numeric calculations, but we'll call such things *evaluation functions* to prevent confusion.

- For city route planning, turn whenever you find you've left city limits.
- For car repair, never remove a part unless it is near another part you think is faulty.
- For car repair, take out small parts first.
- For smarter forward chaining, pursue facts that occur together with other known facts on the right side of a rule.
- For smarter forward chaining, pursue facts that led to useful conclusions on the ten most recent runs.

Heuristics are not all equally valuable.   Compare:

1. For car repair, do little jobs first.
2. For car repair, first take out small parts attached to objects you want to fix.
3. For car repair, first take out screws attached to objects you want to fix.
4. For car repair, if you must fix the alternator, take out its mounting screws first.
5. For car repair, if you must fix the alternator, take out its Right Front Mounting Screw first.

These heuristics span a spectrum from general to specific. Really general advice like #1 is hard to apply (it's hard to decide what's a "little job" and what isn't) and wrong in many cases (it would recommend equally the removal of any screw in the car, most of which are irrelevant). Such heuristics are "proverbs," like "Haste makes waste"; they sound nice, but they're nearly useless. At the other extreme, heuristics #4 and #5 are too specific to be helpful: they just apply to one action involving one screw in a car, and the effect could be had by just putting preconditions on the "fix-alternator" operator. And if we tried to use heuristics like #5 in a search problem, we'd need a lot of them—probably many more than the number of operators—so search efficiency would probably decrease, not increase as is the purpose of heuristics. Our best bets are heuristics like #2 and #3 that compromise between extremes; probably #3 is better because "small part" is hard to define.

9.8 EVALUATION FUNCTIONS

A big difficulty with heuristics is disagreements between them, situations for which two heuristics make contradictory recommendations. If one heuristic is known to be better than the other, then it should have priority, but the two can seem equally good. If such difficulties arise frequently, it's better to rate states numerically, then pick the state with the best number. A method for calculating such numbers is called an evaluation function. By convention the values of evaluation functions are nonnegative numbers such that the smaller the number, the better the associated state; and goal states usually have an evaluation function value of zero. Evaluation functions can be in any form and can use any available information about a state; they can also use a description of the goal states. (However, it's desirable that evaluation functions be "smooth"; that is, if they're calculated using numbers, they shouldn't ever jump abruptly in value when the numbers vary slightly.)

So:ne example evaluation functions:

- For city route planning, take the straight-line ("as the crow flies") distance between an intersection and the goal intersection (that is, prefer the successor state closest to the goal state along a straight line).

- For city route planning, take the straight-line distance to the goal plus one tenth of the number of streets crossed by that straight line (this helps you avoid stop signs and traffic lights).

- For car repair, take the number of parts removed from the car plus the number of faulty parts in the car (this will increase in the first half of the solution, but will decrease in the last half, and should be kept small anyway).

- For smarter forward chaining, take the current number of right-side expressions in rules minus the number of facts (proved and given) in some state. (This isn't likely to approach zero, but it does guide search helpfully.)

Evaluation functions make possible two new search strategies, summarized on the third and fourth rows in Figure 9-5. The evaluation-function variant of depth-first search is called *hill-climbing* (or sometimes *discrete optimization*) search; the evaluation-function variant of breadth-first search is called *best-first* search. However, best-first usually has an additional twist beyond breadth-first: the best-evaluation (lowest-evaluation) state of those *anywhere* in the search graph whose successors have not yet been found is picked, not just a state at the same level as the last state. So best-first search usually "jumps around" a lot in the search graph, always picking the minimum-evaluation state of all the unvisited states it knows about.

To illustrate best-first search, take the search graph of Figure 9-6 and assume the evaluation function values shown as circled numbers in Figure 9-7: S:12, A:7, B:8, C:8, D:6, E:4, F:7, H:4, I:5, J:2, G:0, and K:1. (Ignore the numbers in *squares* and the numbers beside the arrows for now.) As before, assume S is the starting state and G is the only goal state. Best-first search would start with S and would find and evaluate its successors A, B, and C, to discover that A is the minimum-evaluation one. So A is picked next, and its successors D and E evaluated. The states not yet examined to find successors (*visited*) are D, E, B, and C, with evaluation function values 6, 4, 8, and 8, respectively. E is the best, but it has no successors; D is the second best, but it has no successors.

We've got a tie between the two remaining unexamined states, B and C. In such cases, heuristics can decide (and perhaps for near-ties too). Assuming the vertical ordering heuristic used with the depth-first and breadth-first examples in Section 9.6, B should be picked next. But it has no successors, so C must be picked. It has one successor, F. F has two successors, H and I, with evaluation function values 4 and 5. The 4 is better, so H is better, and is picked next. H has successors J, G, and K with evaluation function values 2, 0, and 1. But G is a goal state, so we can stop. In summary, best-first search examined the states in the order S, A, E, D, B, C, F, H, G. That's different from both depth-first and breadth-first.

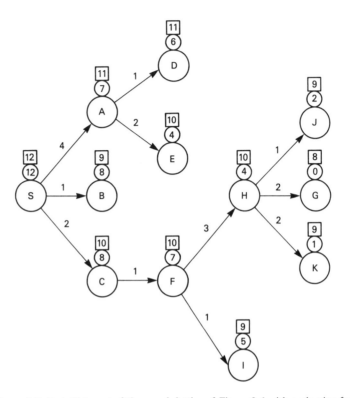

Figure 9-7. Embellishment of the search lattice of Figure 9-6 with evaluation function values and cost values.

9.9 COST FUNCTIONS

Evaluation function values are not the only numbers helpful in search. For some problems, we don't want just *any* path to a goal state, but a good or best path. We could assign costs to each operator, total up these costs along solution paths, and rate the paths. This requires a nonnegative *cost function* measuring something like the difficulty of going from one state to another.

Some example cost functions:

- For city route planning, the total length in meters of a path.
- For city route planning, the number of intersections in a path (since intersections slow you down).
- For car repair, the time in minutes needed to do a sequence of actions.
- For car repair, the amount of energy in calories needed to do a sequence of actions.
- For smarter forward chaining, the computer time in seconds required to pursue facts in a particular order.
- For smarter forward chaining, the amount of main-memory storage in bytes required to pursue facts in a particular order.

Cost functions and evaluation functions are easy to confuse. Remember that evaluation functions refer to the future, cost functions to the past. That is, evaluation functions guess how close a state is to a goal state, while a sum of cost functions measure how far a state is from the start state. So cost functions are more concrete than evaluation functions. A cost function often suggests an associated evaluation function, not the other way around, because (as we will see) it is useful to have them in the same units. So if a cost function measures in meters, its evaluation function should too.

9.10 OPTIMAL-PATH SEARCH

A search that must find the lowest-cost (*optimal*) path to a goal state, instead of just any path, needs a different search strategy from those so far considered. If we have a cost function but no good evaluation function and no good heuristics, we can use *branch-and-bound* search (see Figure 9-5). It's like best-first search but using costs instead: it always finds successors of the state whose path has lowest total cost from the start state. Such a strategy may "jump around" among states as best-first search does, but it has a nice property: the first path to the goal that it finds is guaranteed to be the lowest-cost path to the goal.

If we have both cost and evaluation functions, we can use an *A* search* strategy (that's pronounced "A-star"). The idea is to sum the cost and evaluation function value for a state to get a measure of overall worth, and use these numbers to select states in a best-first search algorithm, instead of just the evaluation function values. (This sum makes most sense when the cost function and evaluation function are in the same units.) So A* search is sort of a hybrid of best-first (using an evaluation function) and branch-and-bound search (using a cost function), incorporating information from both, and often giving better performance than both. As with branch-and-bound search, a certain guarantee applies to a solution found by A* search: if the evaluation function value for any state S is always no more than the subsequently found cost from S to the goal, then the first path to a goal found by A* search is the lowest-cost path to a goal. But A* is often still a good search strategy even when the guarantee doesn't hold.

Suppose we use the A* strategy instead of best-first on the search graph of Figure 9-7. Recall that the numbers in circles are the evaluation function values of states. Suppose the costs for path segments are shown by the numbers next to the arrows: 4 for A to S, 1 for A to D, 2 for A to 3, 1 for S to B, 2 for S to C, 1 for C to F, 3 for F to H, 1 for F to I, 1 for H to J, 2 for H to G, and 2 for H to K. The criterion number for a state is now the sum of the evaluation function value and the costs along the path leading to that state. For instance, the criterion number for state H is $4 + 3 + 1 + 2 = 10$. The other criterion values are S:12, A:11, D:11, E:10, B:9, C:10, F:10, I:9, J:9, G:8, and K:9; these numbers appear inside squares in Figure 9-7. A* search will work like best-first but use the numbers in the squares instead of the numbers in the circles, and it will visit the states in the order S, B, C, F, I, H, and G. (The evaluation function values are not a lower bound on the cost to the goal, but that isn't as important when there's only one path to the goal.)

9.11 A ROUTE-FINDING EXAMPLE

To better illustrate the differences between search programs, we show results from a program for one of our three standard examples, finding city routes. Figure 9-8 shows a portion of Monterey, California, USA, for which we stored street-intersection coordinates. The problem was to go from the point marked "start" to the point marked "goal." The evaluation function was the straight-line distance to the goal (computed from approximate coordinates of each intersection), and the cost function was the distance along the route (computed by summing straight-line distances between successive intersections); so the evaluation function was a lower bound on the cost, and the A* guarantee applied. Shown on the map are the results of three search strategies: breadth-first, best-first, and A* search. As you can see, the paths are different: A* finds the shortest path, breadth-first minimizes the number of intersections, and best-first tries to keep moving toward the goal. (Though not shown on the map, depth-first search wanders around stupidly.)

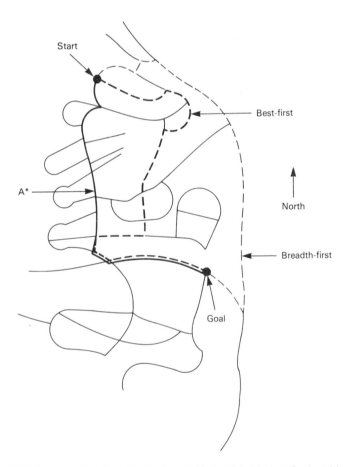

Figure 9-8. More complicated route-planning problem, with solutions for breadth-first, best-first, and A* search.

9.12 SPECIAL CASES OF SEARCH_____

Certain tricks sometimes make search problems easier. One trick often possible is reversing the search, working backward from goal states to the start state. For instance:

- For city route planning, find a path from the start to the goal by reasoning about states one away from the goal, then two away, etc.
- For car repair, solve the first half of the job by reasoning from the part P that must be fixed, deciding what other part P2 needs to be removed to get to P, what other part P3 must be removed to get to P2, and so on.

This does require you to know beforehand all goal states, something not possible for the smarter-forward-chaining problem and other important problems, in which finding a goal state is the whole point of the search (though backward chaining does represent something like a reverse of forward chaining). If you know more than one goal state, you can either try reverse search with each in turn, or make all the goal states the starting set of "unexamined" states for those strategies that use them.

Be careful you don't confuse backward search with a forward search from a goal state to the start state. For instance, in city route planning, the backward search would be reasoning about what places one intersection away from the goal you should come from to reach the goal, then what places one intersection away from there you should come from, and so on; that's a different problem from driving a car forward from the goal to the start. That's because what might be a legal right turn in one direction would be an illegal left turn in the other direction, so the forward goal-to-start path might be quite different from the forward start-to-goal path.

Whenever backward search is good, an even better idea is parallel forward and backward search on the same problem—*bidirectional search*. Run both searches independently (either on two processors or time-sharing on a single processor), and stop whenever they meet (or reach the same state). As illustration, compare the top and middle diagrams in Figure 9-9. Bidirectional search often finds a solution much faster than either forward or backward search alone, because the number of search states usually increases quickly as we move farther from the starting point, and with two searches we're searching half as deep. But it does have a serious danger: if we use a poor search strategy for both searches, like best-first with a poor evaluation function or, often, depth-first search, the two searches may "bypass" one another instead of meeting in the middle.

Another trick we can often use to make search easier is *decomposition*, breaking the search problem into several simpler subsearches, each of which can be solved independently. This usually means finding an intermediate state through which the search must go.[4] Then we solve two separate search problems: getting

---

[4] A starting state usually has several branches from it. But each branch isn't considered a "decomposition" of the problem—the whole search problem isn't made any simpler by looking at it this way, as it usually is by decomposition around intermediate states.

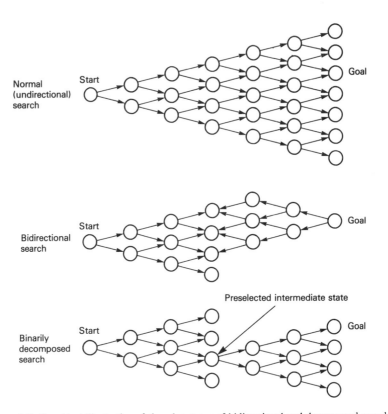

Normal (undirectional) search

Bidirectional search

Preselected intermediate state

Binarily decomposed search

Figure 9-9. Graphical illustration of the advantages of bidirectional and decomposed search.

from the start to the intermediate state, and getting from the intermediate state to a goal state. As illustration, compare the top and bottom diagrams in Figure 9-9. You can also decompose a problem into more than two pieces, if you can figure out more than one intermediate state that the search must go through.

For city route planning, if the goal is a place on the other side of a river, and only one bridge crosses the river, you must use that bridge. So you can simplify the problem by decomposition into two subproblems: getting from your start to the bridge, and getting from the bridge to the goal. For car repair, a good decomposition is into three pieces: getting the faulty part out, fixing the faulty part, and then reassembling the car. Decomposability of search depends on the problem, but whenever it's possible it's usually a good idea because shallow search problems can be a lot easier than deep search problems.

Another useful feature of a search problem is *monotonicity*. If whenever an operator can be applied from a state S, that same operator can be applied from any state reachable from S (by a sequence of successors), then the search problem is monotonic. Often we don't need to be so careful in choosing an operator in a monotonic search problem, because we can can get much the same effect by applying the overlooked operator later, and hence we don't need terribly good evaluation functions and heuristics. But monotonic search problems aren't common. Only the third of our three standard examples is monotonic, the smarter forward-chaining problem when the operators are assumed to be "pursue fact a," "pursue fact b," and so on (since a postponed pursuit of some fact F is always doable later). Many searches for proving things are monotonic, since provable things usually don't stop being provable later (what is called *monotonic logic*). One word of warning: mono-tonicity depends on the operator definitions, and different operators can be defined for the same search problem, so a search problem monotonic for one set of opera-tors may not be for another.

9.13 HOW HARD IS A SEARCH PROBLEM?

It helps to know the difficulty of a search problem before tackling it so you can allocate time and space resources. Sometimes what seems an easy problem can be enormously difficult, or a problem very similar to a really difficult one can be easy. So people try to estimate the number of states that need to be studied to solve a search problem. Two methods can do this: bounding the size of the *search space*, and calculating the average *branching factor* or fanout of successive states.

The first method takes as an upper bound on the number of states that need to be examined to solve a problem the number of possible states in the entire prob-lem. This set of all possible states is called the *search space*, and what's needed is the size of the search space. (Don't confuse the term "search space" with the amount of memory needed to search: "space" is used abstractly here, the way mathematicians use "vector space.") For some problems, the size of the search space is easy to see from the description of the problem, as for city route planning in which it's the number of intersections in the city, something we can count. For other problems, we can use what mathematicians call *combinatorial methods*. For instance, for car repair we can describe the condition of every part in the car as either in the car and faulty, in the car and OK, out of the car and faulty, or out of the car and OK. So if there are 1000 parts in the car, the size of the search space is 4 to the 1000th power—a lot! That means heuristics or an evaluation function is necessary to solve this problem, because we'll never succeed if we try operators at random.

The size-of-the-search-space method of estimating search difficulty can't always estimate the size of the search space so easily, as in smarter forward chain-ing when we can't tell in advance which or even how many facts we'll prove. Also, the method calculates only an upper bound on difficulty. Alternatively, we can reason how the number of states increases with each level of search, and figure how many levels deep we'll go. The number of successors (usually, previously unvisited successors) of a state is called its *branching factor*. (Caution: Don't confuse the branching factor with the number of *operators* that can generate successors, a smaller number.) If the branching factor doesn't differ much between states, we can speak of an *average branching factor* for the whole search problem. Then we can estimate the number of states at level K in the search graph as B^K, B the aver-age branching factor. Notice that this exponential function gets large very fast as K increases—the so-called *combinatorial explosion*. So if we can estimate the level of a goal (the length of branches from the starting state to it), we can estimate the number of states that will be visited by breadth-first search, summing up the estimate for the number of states at each level. This is also a good approximation for best-first search, branch-and-bound search, and A* search when evaluation and cost functions aren't very helpful in guiding search.

As an example, the average branching factor for the city route problem is around three, since there are usually three branches (new directions of travel) at an intersection. Suppose we know we are about ten blocks from where we want to go. Then for a breadth-first search there are approximately 3 states at level 1, 9 states at level 2, 27 at level 3, and so on up to 3^{10} for level 10. So the total number of states of level 10 or less, assuming no multiple paths to the same state, is approximately the sum of a geometric series:

$$1 + 3 + 9 + 27 + \cdots = (3^{11} - 1)/(3 - 1) = (3^{11} - 1)/2 = 88{,}573$$

In general, in a search problem with an average branching factor of B, the number of states up to and including those at level K is $(B^{K+1} - 1)/(B - 1)$. If B is large (say 5 or more), this can be approximated by B^K, the number of states at the deepest level. These formulas help quantify the advantages of bidirectional search and search decomposition. If you divide a problem whose solution is R states long into two approximately even halves, each half is about $R/2$ states long. If the average branching factor B is large and the same in both directions, the number of states examined in the two half-problems is probably much less than the number of states examined without decomposition or bidirectional search, because

$$B^{R/2} + B^{R/2} \text{ is much less than } B^R$$

because, dividing both sides by $B^{R/2}$,

$$2 \text{ is much less than } B^{R/2}$$

The effect of heuristics and evaluation functions is to rule out certain successors for particular states in preference to other successors. So in effect, heuristics and evaluation functions decrease the average branching factor. This means we can get farther down into the search graph faster. So the usefulness of heuristics and evaluation functions can be quantified as a ratio of average branching factors with and without them.

9.14 BACKWARD CHAINING VERSUS FORWARD CHAINING*

Analysis of search-problem difficulty lets us quantify for the first time differences between the control structures discussed in Chapter 6. Take for instance this rule-based system:

```
t :- a, b.
t :- c.
u :- not(a), c.
u :- a, d.
v :- b, e.
```

And further assume the facts a, e, and d only are true, and given in that order.

Backward chaining will try the first three rules, which fail, and then the fourth, which succeeds. Basic backward chaining without caching involves eight total queries: top-level predicates t and u, a (which succeeds), b (which fails), c (which fails), a again (which succeeds), a again, and finally d (which succeeds). The time to do this is approximately proportional to the number of queries made because each query requires an index lookup of nearly equal time.

Pure forward chaining will match fact a to expressions in the first and fourth rules, then match e to an expression in the last. Finally, it matches d in the fourth rule, and u is proved. So four matches are made. The time to do this is approximately proportional to the number of matches because each requires an index lookup of nearly equal time. Now we just compare eight queries to four matches to decide whether backward or forward chaining is better for this very specific situation. Though this is a comparison of different units ("apples with oranges"), we can usually conduct experiments to equate both queries and matches to time units.

The main problem with this analysis is that it's hard to generalize: we may not know which or how many facts are going to be true in a situation, and there are many possible situations. Simulations are one approach. But we can also use probabilities in mathematical analysis, as we'll now show.

Let's consider backward chaining first, still using the previous example. Suppose that potential facts a, b, c, d, and e have independent probabilities P of truth. Then the probability of the first rule t :- a, b. succeeding is P^2, the probability of the second succeeding is P, the third $(1 - P)P$, and the fourth and fifth P^2. The expected number of queries generated when the rules are in this order is a long, tricky formula because we don't need to fully evaluate a rule to have it fail:

$$3P^2 + 3(1 - P)P + 4P(1 - P)P + 8P(1 - P)^2P$$

$$+ 10(1 - P)P(1 - P)P + 10P(1 - P)^3 + 9(1 - P)^3 + 10(1 - P)P(1 - P)^2$$

We got this formula by reasoning about the search lattice, which was actually more like a decision lattice, for the situations possible (see Figure 9-10). Here are the rules again:

    t :- a, b.
    t :- c.
    u :- not(a), c.
    u :- a, d.
    v :- b, e.

The first term in the above formula corresponds to success of the first rule, terms 2 and 3 to the success of the second, no terms to the third (there's no way the third rule can succeed given the second fails), term 4 to the success of the fourth rule, term 5 to the success of the fifth, and the remaining terms to the three different cases in which all the rules fail. To get this formula, we separately considered cases with a true and with a false.

Given the rule set:

       t :- a, b.
       t :- c.
       u :- not(a), c.
       u :- a, d.
       v :- b, e.

Then this is a decision lattice implementing it:

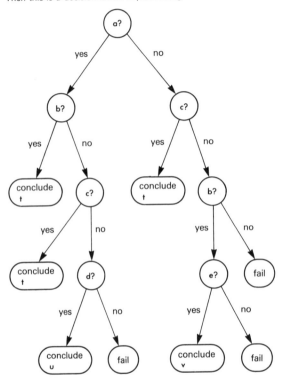

Figure 9-10. Decision lattice for backward chaining on an example rule set.

We can reason similarly about forward chaining when facts are always taken in some order and each has the same probability P of occurrence (see Figure 9-11). Suppose the order is **a** before **b**, **b** before **c**, **c** before **d**, and **d** before **e**. The formula for the number of fact-rule matches is

$$1P(1 - P) + 3P^2 + 3P^2(1 - P) + 3P^2(1 - P)^2 + 4P^2(1 - P)^3$$

$$+ 3P(1 - P)^4 + 4P^3(1 - P)^2$$

$$+ 4P^2(1 - P)^3 + 3P^2(1 - P)^3 + 3P(1 - P)^4 + 3P^2(1 - P)^3$$

$$+ 2P(1 - P)^4 + 2P(1 - P)^4 + 1(1 - P)^5$$

Knowing the ratio of the cost of a backward-chaining query to the cost of a forward-chaining match, we can compare the two formulas for a specific value of P to decide whether backward or forward chaining is better.

Assume the rules:

t :- a, b.
t :- c.
u :- not(a), c.
u :- a, d.
v :- b, e.

And assume the only possible facts are a, b, c, d, and e, provided for a database in order of priority a, c, b, d, and e.   Assume each has an independent probability of occurrence P. Situations to consider:

a?	c?	b?	d?	e?	Probability	Number of matches	Conclusion reached
false	true	—	—	—	$P(1 - P)$	1	t
true	true	—	—	—	P^2	3	t
true	false	true	—	—	$P^2(1 - P)$	3	t
true	false	false	true	—	$P^2(1 - P)^2$	3	u
true	false	false	false	true	$P^2(1 - P)^3$	4	—
true	false	false	false	false	$P(1 - P)^4$	3	—
false	false	true	true	true	$P^3(1 - P)^2$	4	v
false	false	true	true	false	$P^2(1 - P)^3$	4	—
false	false	true	false	true	$P^2(1 - P)^3$	3	v
false	false	true	false	false	$P(1 - P)^4$	3	—
false	false	false	true	true	$P^2(1 - P)^3$	3	—
false	false	false	true	false	$P(1 - P)^4$	2	—
false	false	false	false	true	$P(1 - P)^4$	2	—
false	false	false	false	false	$(1 - P)^5$	1	—

Figure 9-11. Analysis of the cost of forward chaining on the rule set.

9.15 USING PROBABILITIES IN SEARCH*

Since probabilities are numbers, they can guide hill-climbing, best-first, branch-and-bound, and A* searches. For instance, the probability that a state is on a path to a goal can be used as an evaluation function. Or in search during forward chaining, facts can be ranked for selection by 1 million minus the reciprocal of their a priori probability, so unusual facts are followed up first. In backward chaining using rules with uncertainty like those in Chapter 8, rules can be selected by the reciprocal of their rule probability (the probability of their conclusion under the most favorable conditions.)

9.16 ANOTHER EXAMPLE:
VISUAL EDGE-FINDING AS SEARCH*

Computer vision is an important subarea of artificial intelligence. It's complicated, and its methods are often quite specialized, since two-dimensional and three-dimensional information seems at first to be quite different from predicate expressions. But it also exploits many of the general-purpose techniques described in this book, including search.

One role search plays is in edge-finding and edge-following, as a kind of "constructive" search that actually builds something as it performs a search. But first we must give some background. Most computer vision systems start from a digitized image, a two-dimensional array representing the brightness of dots in a television picture. The picture is first "cleaned up" and "smoothed out" to make it easier to analyze, using some mathematical tricks. Any remaining sharp contrasts between adjacent parts in the picture are important—contrasts in brightness, color, and the "grain" or *texture* of small adjacent regions. These contrasts can be used to make a line drawing (a drawing consisting only of lines) of the picture, where lines correspond to boundaries of high contrast between regions of mostly homogeneous characteristics; the lines are called *edges*. So a line drawing can be a kind of data compression of the original picture. Line drawings provide a basis for most visual analysis techniques, techniques that try to figure out what the picture is showing.

But edge-finding isn't as easy as it may seem. The problem is that for various reasons, things in the real world that you'd think would make edges don't. Consider Figure 9-12. Different surfaces may coincidentally be the same brightness and color along part of their edge, or an edge may lie in shadow, or glares and reflections may cover the edge, or the resolution of the picture may be insufficient to pick up small details of edges. So usually only some edges and parts of edges in a picture can be recognized, meaning line drawings with gaps. Human beings can easily fill in these gaps, because they have strong expectations about what they will see and their vision automatically fills in details. But computers must be taught how.

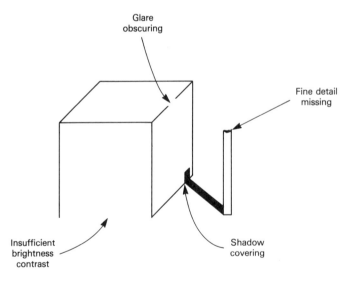

Figure 9-12. Obstacles to visual edge-finding.

A good first step is to quantify the "edgeness" of each dot in the picture. Several mathematical formulas can be used, but we'll show here a simple one that only examines the brightness of its cell and its immediate neighbors. (Edges between regions of different color can be found by looking at brightness of the picture viewed through colored filters.) Suppose we represent the picture as a two-dimensional array $b(i,j)$ of numbers representing light intensities. Then the *magnitude of the gradient* for each dot is defined as

$$g(i,j) = \sqrt{(b(i+1,j) - b(i-1,j))^2 + (b(i,j+1) - b(i,j-1))^2}$$

This is a measure of "edgeness" for every dot. The larger this number is, the more the brightnesses around some dot in the picture differ among themselves.

Now we're ready to formulate edge-finding as a search problem. A state can be represented as a two-dimensional bit array $e(i,j)$ (that is, an array of things with Boolean or true/false values) with an entry for every dot in the picture. A "true" means that in the corresponding picture the dot lies on an edge; in the starting state, every dot is marked "false." A branch between states changes a single element from "false" to "true," meaning we've decided an edge is there. There's only one operator: mark $e(i,j)$ as "true" for some i and some j.

Given this array of edgeness measures for a picture array $g(i,j)$:

0	1	0	8	2
1	2	7	3	1
3	1	5	2	0
2	2	3	3	1
2	5	2	1	3
1	7	1	2	1
3	6	2	2	1

Inference: There's a continuous edge running north-northeast to south-southwest, though it's hard to see, toward the center of the picture. That's the interpretation array $e(i,j)$:

false	false	false	true	false
false	false	true	false	false
false	false	true	false	false
false	false	true	false	false
false	true	false	false	false
false	true	false	false	false
false	true	false	false	false

Figure 9-13. Example arrays for finding visual edges.

However, there is no well-defined goal for this problem. It's more like an optimization problem in operations research. We want to maximize the number of "good" edges identified, so it sounds like a best-first search with an evaluation function. Several things can be considered in an evaluation function:

- the number of dots with edgeness more than some number C, of those for which $e(i,j)$ is false (this measures the completeness of the edge assignments);
- the total number of approximately straight line segments formed by the dots marked "true" (this measures the "elegance" of the edge assignments);
- the sum of the average curvatures for all such approximately-straight line segments (this measures straightness of segments);
- the number of true-marked dots with exactly two true-marked immediate neighbors (this measures narrowness of edges);
- the negative of the average edgeness measure of all true-marked dots (this measures the selectivity of true-marking).

Whenever several different measures like these describe progress in a search problem, a good idea is to take a weighted average of these and make that the evaluation function. (Or if all the numbers are positive, take the product.) That seems good here, but we would need to experiment to find the proper weightings.

Despite the lack of a goal per se, it helps to invent one to prevent working forever. A simple but effective criterion is to stop at state S if no state under consideration whose successors are unvisited is better than D worse than the evaluation of S, for some fixed constant D.

Notice how this search problem differs from city-route planning: the edge-finder will rarely mark adjacent cells in succession. In fact, it's likely to jump around considerably, since a good heuristic is to mark the cell with the highest "edgeness" among those not yet marked "true." With that heuristic, we're unlikely to mark adjacent cells in succession. This nonlocality of processing appears in many different vision applications, and reflects the concurrency apparently present in much human vision.

KEYWORDS

search
state
branch
operator
precondition
postcondition
starting state
goal state
search strategy

depth-first search
breadth-first search
hill-climbing search
best-first search
heuristic
pruning
evaluation function
cost function
optimal-path search
branch-and-bound search
A* search
backward search
bidirectional search
decomposability
monotonicity
monotonic logic
search space
branching factor
combinatorial explosion

EXERCISES

9-1. (E) Explain why none of the following are states as we define the term for search.

(a) All the important events that happen in an organization in one day.

(b) The current temperature of a room.

(c) The mental condition of a person's mind.

9-2. (A,E) Explain how using inheritance to find a value of the property of some object is a kind of search.

9-3. The search graphs in this chapter have all been *planar*—that is, none of the branches crossed. Is this necessarily true of all search graphs?

9-4. (a) Modify the description of the algorithm for pure forward chaining, given in Section 6.2, to work in a breadth-first way.

(b) Explain how a breadth-first backward chaining might work.

9-5. Consider the problem of driving by car from one place in a city to another. Assume you do not know the way. Consider this as a search problem with three operators:

> A: travel to the next intersection and keep going straight, if legal
> B: travel to the next intersection and turn right, if legal
> C: travel to the next intersection and turn left, if legal

(a) Suppose you are driving a car without a map. Which control strategy is better, depth-first or breadth-first? Assume you can use simple heuristics (like "turn around if you're in the country") to stay near the goal.

(b) Suppose you planned a route with a map, and the map was slightly wrong (for instance, a street is closed for repairs). How could you prepare to better handle such occurrences?

9-6. Consider the complete search graph for some problem shown in Figure 9-14. Suppose state "a" is the starting state, and the states shown are the only possible states (and none of the states shown is the goal). Numbers written next to states represent the evaluation function at those states, and numbers written next to branches represent the cost function on those branches. (Some of this information may be irrelevant.)

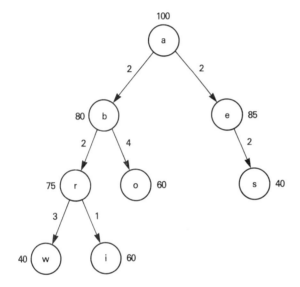

Figure 9-14. Picture for Exercise 9-6.

(a) Which is the fourth state whose successors are attempted to be found by a depth-first search using the heuristic that states whose names are vowels (a, e, i, o, or u) are preferred to states whose names are not?

(b) Which is the fourth state whose successors are attempted to be found by a best-first search?

9-7. (a) For the search graphs of Figures 9-6 and 9-7 we imposed a heuristic that states be ordered when necessary by vertical height on the page from top to bottom. Explain how this can be considered either a heuristic or an evaluation function.

(b) An evaluation function is just a way to assign nonnegative numbers to states (not necessarily a continuous function on any variable). Explain how an evaluation function can always be constructed to duplicate the effect of any set of (nonnumeric) heuristics for a search problem.

(c) Now consider the reverse direction. In a search problem, can you always go from an evaluation function for that problem to a finite set of (non-numeric) heuristics that have the same meaning?

9-8. (E) (For people who know something about music) Explain how harmonizing a melody is a kind of search. What are the states and operators? What are some good heuristics? Why is backing up to previous states necessary?

9-9. (a) Consider A* search in which the evaluation function is zero for every state. What is the name for this search?

    (b) Consider A* search in which the cost function is zero for every state. What is the name for this search?

    (c) Consider A* search in which the evaluation function is zero for every state, and the cost function is the length of the path to the state. What is the best name for this search, besides the name for part (a)?

9-10. (A) Suppose for some search problem for which you want to use the A* search you have found an evaluation function that never overestimates the cost to a goal state by more than K units. How can you get a guaranteed-optimal solution from A* search?

9-11. (R,A) Suppose for a search problem there are three operators, Op1, Op2, and Op3. Suppose in the starting state you can apply any of the three. Then suppose if the first operator was not Op3 you can apply a different operator for the second action than the first operator. Assume no other operator applications are possible. No goal is given, so a search must eventually explore every possible state.

    (a) Suppose you do breadth-first search using the heuristic that Op1 branches are preferred to Op2 branches, and Op2 to Op3. Draw the state diagram, and label the states in the order in which you try to find their successors. Use labels a, b, c, d, e, f, g, and h.

    (b) Suppose you do best-first search for which the evaluation function is

        6 after Op1 then Op2
        4 after Op1 then Op3
        9 after Op2 then Op1
        11 after Op2 then Op3
        8 after Op1
        7 after Op2
        5 after Op3
        10 for the starting state

    List the states in the order in which you try to find their successors.

    (c) Suppose you do A* search for which the evaluation function in part (b) and the cost function is

        2 for Op1
        5 for Op2
        9 for Op3

    List the states in the order in which you try to find their successors.

9-12. (H) Suppose we have computer terminals we wish to move to different floors of a three-floor building. Suppose at the start:

1. One terminal on the third floor belongs on the second floor.
2. One terminal on the second floor belongs on the first floor.
3. Two terminals on the first floor belong on the third floor.
4. Another terminal on the first floor belongs on the second floor.

In the starting state, the elevator is on the first floor. In the goal state, each terminal is on the floor where it belongs. Assume there are two operators:

> A: take one terminal from floor X to floor Y, X different from Y.
> B: take two terminals from floor X to floor Y, X different from Y.

Suppose the cost function is the sum over all steps in the solution of a number that is 1 for trips between adjacent floors, and 1.2 otherwise.

(a) Give a heuristic (nonnumeric reason) for choosing branches during search.

(b) Give a lower-bound evaluation function for use with A*.

(c) Would bidirectional search be a good idea for this and similar problems? Why?

(d) Approximate the size of the search space for T terminals and F floors.

(e) Draw the state graph after the first three states have had their successors found in the solution of the given problem using A*. Use the evaluation function you gave, but not the heuristic. Don't allow returns to previous states. Draw the evaluation plus the cost of a state next to it. If ties arise, use a heuristic to choose, and say what heuristic you're using. (*Hint*: Use a compact notation for the state, so you don't have to write a lot.)

9-13. (A) Consider this problem:

> A farmer wants to get a lion, a fox, a goose, and some corn across a river. There is a boat, but the farmer can only take one passenger in addition to himself on each trip, or else both the goose and the corn, or both the fox and the corn. The corn cannot be left with the goose because the goose will eat the corn; the fox cannot be left with the goose because the fox will eat the goose; and the lion cannot be left with the fox because the lion will eat the fox. How does everything get across the river? Assume animals do not wander off when left alone.

(a) What is the search space?

(b) Give the starting and ending states.

(c) Give the operators.

(d) Draw the first two levels of the search graph. That's two besides the starting state.

(e) What is the average branching factor for these two levels? Disregard branches back to previous states.

(f) Give an upper bound on the size of the search space.

(g) Is this problem decomposable about an intermediate state?

9-14. Consider the two tasks of solving jigsaw puzzles and solving integration problems symbolically. For each, answer the following.

(a) What is the search space?

(b) What are the operators?

(c) What is the starting state?

(d) What are the final states?

(e) Is the task decomposable (breakable into subproblems that can be solved independently) about an intermediate state?

(f) Are the operators monotonic (applicable at any time, if applicable once)?

(g) Is one solution needed or the best solution?

(h) What is the initial branching factor?

(i) How (approximately) does the branching factor vary as the task proceeds?

9-15. (R,A) Consider the problem of designing electrical connections between places on the surface of a two-dimensional integrated circuit. Group the surface into square regions with a square grid. Consider this a search problem (a single search problem, not a group of search problems) in which there is only one operator: coat with metal the grid cell [X,Y] where X and Y are integers representing Cartesian coordinates. No grid cells have any metal coating in the starting state. In the goal state, electrical connections exist between each pair of a specified list of cell pairs; "electrical connection" means an unbroken sequence of adjacent coated grid cells linking a cell pair, while at the same time not linking them to any other cell pair. So for instance the goal might be to connect [10,20] to [25,29], and simultaneously [3,9] to [44,18], but not [10,20] to [3,9]. It's desired to find the coating pattern that uses the least amount of metal in achieving the goal connections.

(a) What is the search space?

(b) Is bidirectional search a good idea? Why?

(c) How does the branching factor vary as forward search proceeds?

(d) Give a heuristic for limiting forward search in this problem.

9-16. Consider the allocation of variables to registers done by an optimizing compiler for a programming language. Consider this as a search with just one operator: assign (allocate) occurrence N of variable V on line L of the program to be in register R. (Assume that variables must be in registers to use them in programs.) Since computers have a small fixed number of registers, and a poor allocation requires a lot of unnecessary instructions for moving data between registers and main memory, it's important to choose a good allocation if you want a compiler that generates the fastest possible code. For this problem, assume you do want to generate the fastest possible code. And assume this means the code with the fewest number of instructions, to make this simpler. Notice that you can calculate speed for partial allocations of variables, not just complete allocations. That is, for all unbroken segments of code that mention register-assigned variables, you can count the number of instructions in the segments. Those numbers for those code segments can't change as new allocations of other variables are made, because one register allocation can't affect another.

(a) Which is the best search strategy?

    (i)   Depth-first search

    (ii)   Breadth-first search

    (iii)   Best-first search

    (iv)   A* search

(b) Which is a heuristic for this problem? (only one answer is correct)

    (i)   "Count the number of machine instructions generated by a solution."

    (ii)   "Allocate registers to real-number variables first."

    (iii)   "Prefer forward chaining to backward chaining when there are few facts and many conclusions."

    (iv)   "Don't figure a register allocation of the same variable occurrence in a particular line twice."

(c) How does the branching factor change as the search proceeds (that is, with level in the search)? (choose only one answer)

    (i)   It decreases

    (ii)   It decreases or stays the same, depending on the state

    (iii)   It stays the same

    (iv)   It increases

9-17. Consider the task of proving a theorem from a set of postulates and assumptions. Suppose postulates, assumptions, and theorems are all either in the form of "A implies B" or just "A," where A and B are simple logical statements about the world. Suppose there is a way of taking any two postulates, assumptions, or previously derived theorems to get a conclusion, if any. For instance, if one statement says "A implies B" and another statement says "A," then we get a conclusion "B"; if one statement says "A implies B" and another statement says "B implies C," then we get a conclusion "A implies C."

(a) What is the search space?

(b) What is the branching factor, as a function of the number of steps taken?

(c) Give a search heuristic.

(d) Give a rough evaluation function for guiding search.

(e) Is the search monotonic?

(f) Is the search decomposable about an intermediate state?

(g) Is this a better problem for heuristics or for evaluation functions? Explain.

(h) Assuming we had a good approximate evaluation function, would the A* algorithm work well here? Explain.

(i) Would best-first search be a good idea here?

(j) Would bidirectional search be a good idea here?

9-18. Search has some surprising applications to numeric calculations. Consider the search for a numeric formula that approximates the value of some *target* variable from mathematical operations on a set of *study* variables. To test the accuracy of our approximation formula, we are given a set of *data points*, Prolog facts of the form

data_point([<study-variable-value-1>,<study-variable-value-2>, ...], <target-variable-value>).

That is, the study variable values for a data point are stored in a list. Now think of this search problem as one of creating new list entries whose values match more closely the target variable values. To get these new study variables, we will do simple arithmetic operations on the old study variables. For example, take these data points:

data_point([1,2],6).
data_point([2,5],14).
data_point([3,2],10).

Then if we take the sum of the two study variables we can get a third study variable:

data_point([1,2,3],6).
data_point([2,5,7],14.)
data-point([3,2,5],10.)

And if we double those new values we can get

data_point([1,2,3,6],6).
data_point([2,5,7,14],14).
data_point([3,2,5,10],10).

and we have "explained" the value of the target variable as twice the sum of the original two study variables. In general, assume the following arithmetic operations are permissible on study variables:

● multiplying by a constant or adding a constant to values of some study variable;

● taking the negatives, squares, square roots, logarithms to the base 2 or powers of 2 of the values of some study variable;

● taking the sum, difference, product, or quotient of the corresponding values for two different study variables of the same data point for all data points.

(a) Considered as a search problem, what is the search space?

(b) What are the operators?

(c) What is the branching factor from any state?

(d) For the following starting data points, draw the first two levels (not counting the starting state as a level) of the search graph for the portion including only the "squaring" operation (that is, multiplying values by themselves).

data_point([1,2],1).
data_point([2,0],16).
data_point([3,1],81).

(e) Give an evaluation function for this problem (the problem in general, not just the data points in part (e)).

(f) If the variable values represent experimental measurements, it will be difficult for a formula to match the target variable exactly. What then would be a reasonable goal condition?

(g) Give a general-purpose heuristic (nonnumeric way) for choosing branches well for this general problem (for any set of data points, not just those in part (d)).

(h) Is bidirectional search a good idea for this problem? Why?

(i) Is A* search a good idea for this problem? Why?

(j) Explain why preconditions are necessary for some of the operators.

(k) Is the problem decomposable about an intermediate state? Why?

(l) Professional statisticians often do this sort of analysis. They claim they don't use search techniques very often. If so, how (in artificial intelligence terminology) must they be solving these problems?

9-19. (E)

(a) Explain how playing chess or checkers requires search.

(b) How is this kind of search fundamentally different from those that we have considered in this chapter?

10

IMPLEMENTING
SEARCH

We have postponed consideration of search implementation to this chapter to better focus on the quite different issues involved. We will present programs for several kinds of search, working from a search problem described in an abstract way. We'll also use search as a springboard to discuss some advanced features of Prolog, including set-collection and "cut" predicates, and more of the wild and wacky world of backtracking.

10.1 DEFINING A SIMPLE SEARCH PROBLEM

First, we need a way to describe a search problem precisely. We ask the programmer to define the following predicates, the last two optional depending on the desired search strategy:

- successor(<old-state>,<new-state>): rules and facts defining this predicate give all possible immediate branches or state transitions. It's a function predicate with its first argument an input, a state, and second argument an output, a successor state. Both arguments are state descriptions. We emphasize that <new-state> must be an *immediate* successor.

- goalreached(<state>): rules and facts defining this predicate give the stopping conditions for the search. The argument is an input, a state. Multiple goal states are possible.

- eval(<state>,<evaluation>): rules and facts defining this predicate give the evaluation function. This is a function predicate taking an input state as first argument, and binding its second argument, an output, to an estimate of how close that state is to the nearest goal state.
- cost(<state-list>,<cost>): rules and facts defining this predicate give the cost function. This is a function predicate taking an input list of states as first argument, and binding its second argument, an output, to some nonnegative number representing the sum of the costs along the path through those states.

Of these four, the first is generally the hardest: it must define all the operators, incorporating their necessary conditions and describing precisely how they modify a state-description list. (The successor definitions may also include heuristics about operator use, though Section 10.11 will show a more general way to handle heuristics.) Successor rule definitions turn a search problem into a rule-based system, so we can steal ideas from Chapter 7.

Then to actually start searching, we ask that you query something like

?- search(<starting-state>,<answer-state-list>).

where the first argument is an input, the starting state (written in the format handled by the successor rules), and the second argument is an output, the discovered sequence of states, usually in reverse order (that is, from the goal state back to the start state).

As an example of this Prolog-style definition of a search problem, let's return to the example of Figure 9-1, redrawn as Figure 10-1. This is a city route planning problem in which our starting location is a and our goal location is h. States are the labeled intersections, so to define successor we must write a fact for every pair of intersections that connect directly:

successor(a,b).
successor(a,d).
successor(b,c).
successor(b,a).
successor(b,d).
successor(c,b).
successor(d,a).
successor(d,b).
successor(d,e).
successor(d,g).
successor(e,d).
successor(e,f).
successor(e,g).
successor(f,e).
successor(g,d).
successor(g,e).
successor(g,h).
successor(h,g).

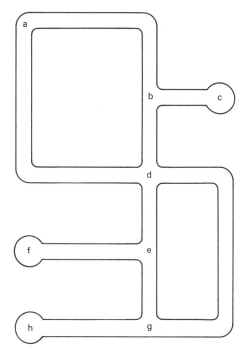

Figure 10-1. Reprise of Figure 9-1.

For the **goalreached** condition we need:

    goalreached(h).

And to start the program out, we will query a particular search predicate, like

    ?- depthsearch(a,Path).

to do depth-first search from start state **a**. (The search predicates we'll define in this chapter are **depthsearch**, **breadthsearch** (breadth-first), **bestsearch** (best-first), and **astarsearch** (A* search).) When search is done, the variable **Path** is bound to the list of intersections (states) we must travel through. We can use evaluation and cost functions to improve search if we like. A good evaluation function for this problem would be the straight-line distance to the goal (measuring on the map with a ruler), giving approximate distances for Figure 10-1 of

    eval(a,8).
    eval(b,7).
    eval(c,8).
    eval(d,5).
    eval(e,3).
    eval(f,1).
    eval(g,2).
    eval(h,0).

The cost definition can be the sum of actual distances along roads, which we can approximate from Figure 10-1 with

cost([X],0).
cost([X,Y|L],E) :- piece_cost(X,Y,E2), cost([Y|L],E3), E is E2 + E3.

piece_cost(a,b,3).
piece_cost(a,d,5).
piece_cost(b,c,1).
piece_cost(b,d,2).
piece_cost(d,e,2).
piece_cost(d,g,3).
piece_cost(e,f,2).
piece_cost(e,g,1).
piece_cost(g,h,2).
piece_cost(X,Y,C) :- piece_cost(Y,X,C).

A cost definition will often need recursion to handle paths of unknown length.

10.2 DEFINING A SEARCH PROBLEM WITH FACT-LIST STATES

Now let's try representing a different kind of search problem, one more typical. The previous example was easy because states could be represented by letters. But often you can't name states in advance, as when you don't know what states are possible, and you must describe them by lists of facts.

Here's an example. This search concerns a very small part of car repair: putting nuts and washers onto bolts in the right way. Suppose we have two bolts. In the starting state (the top picture in Figure 10-2), nut a, washer b, and nut c are on the left bolt in that order, and nut d, washer e, and nut f are on the right bolt in that order. The goal is to get nut c on top of washer e (as for example in the bottom picture in Figure 10-2). To do this, we must work on one nut or washer at a time. We can remove one from the top of the nuts and washers on a bolt, place one on the top of the stack of nuts and washers on a bolt, or just place one alone on the flat surface around the bolts. The bolts themselves can't be moved. The four nuts and two washers are the only parts available.

The only facts that change during the search are those about what parts (nuts or washers) rest on what other parts. Let's use on(<part-1>,<part-2>,<bolt>) facts for this, where <part-1> and <part-2> are codes for parts, and <part-1> is on the bolt named <bolt> directly above <part-2>. To keep track of parts *not*

on the bolts, we'll represent them with on facts too, by on(<part>,surface,none);
parts can only rest on other parts when both are on bolts. To keep track of the
names of empty bolts, we'll use two additional permanent facts, bolt(bolt1) and
bolt(bolt2). So any state can be represented as a list of eight predicate expressions,
six specifying the location of each of the six parts, and two giving bolt names. For
instance, the starting state (the top picture in Figure 10-2) can be written

> [on(a,b,bolt1),on(b,c,bolt1),on(c,surface,bolt1),on(d,e,bolt2),
>   on(e,f,bolt2),on(f,surface,bolt2),bolt(bolt1),bolt(bolt2)]

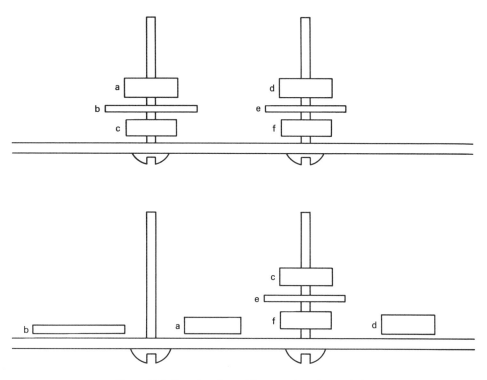

Figure 10-2. Two situations with nuts and washers on bolts.

In other words, like a Prolog database on its side. We could start a depth-first
search by querying

> ?- depthsearch([on(a,b,bolt1),on(b,c,bolt1),on(c,surface,bolt1),
>   on(d,e,bolt2),on(e,f,bolt2),on(f,surface,bolt2),
>   bolt(bolt1),bolt(bolt2)],Answerpath).

The example final state in Figure 10-2 can be written

> [on(a,surface,none),on(b,surface,none),on(c,e,bolt2),
>   on(d,surface,none),on(e,f,bolt2),on(f,surface,bolt2),bolt(bolt1),bolt(bolt2)]

But let's say we're not so fussy about where every part ends up. Let's say we only want part **c** to be on part **e**. Then we can define the goal state by

> goalreached(S) :- member(on(c,e,bolt2),S).

That is, we can stop in state **S** whenever the facts true for **S** include on(c,e,bolt2). The member predicate was defined in Section 5.5 and is true whenever some item is a member of some list:

> member(X,[X|L]).
> member(X,[Y|L]) :- member(X,L).

Successor rules like the preceding that work on fact lists usually just insert and delete facts from the list describing one state to get the list describing another. Typically, they only insert and delete a few. So to specify the effect of an operator, we need only list the fact *changes* made by an operator—everything else can be assumed constant. In problems with complicated state descriptions, it may be hard to figure which facts stay the same, because of "side effects." This is called the *frame problem* in artificial intelligence (not to be confused with the knowledge-partitioning "frames" we'll discuss in Chapter 12).

By referring to variables, just three successor rules are needed for the bolts problem, as shown in the following code. The first handles removing parts from bolts, and the second handles placing parts on bolts. (The intermediate predicate cleartop simplifies the rules.) The first successor rule says that if in some state the part **X** (1) is on a bolt and (2) doesn't have another part on it, then a successor state is one in which **X** is removed from the bolt and placed on the surface. Further-more, the rule says that we can get the successor state from the old state by removing the old fact about where part **X** was (with the delete predicate), and adding a new fact that **X** is alone on the surface (with the stuff in brackets on the rule left side, the last thing done before the rule succeeds). The second successor rule says that if in some state the part **X** (1) doesn't have another part on it, and (2) another part **Z** doesn't have anything on it either, and (3) **Z** is on a bolt, and (4) **Z** is different from **X**, then a possible successor state has **X** placed on **Z**. And we can get a description of the new state by removing the old location of **X** and adding the new location. The third successor rule says that if a bolt is empty in some state, we can put any part with a clear top on it.

```
successor(S,[on(X,surface,none)|S2]) :- member(on(X,Y,B),S),
  not(B = none), cleartop(X,S), delete(on(X,Y,B),S,S2).
successor(S,[on(X,Z,B2)|S2]) :- member(on(X,Y,B),S),
  cleartop(X,S), member(on(Z,W,B2),S), not(B2 = none),
  cleartop(Z,S), not(X = Z), delete(on(X,Y,B),S,S2).
successor(S,[on(X,surface,B2)|S2]) :- member(on(X,Y,B),S),
  cleartop(X,S), member(bolt(B2),S), not(member(on(Z,W,B2),S)),
  delete(on(X,Y,B),S,S2).
```

```
cleartop(Part,State) :- not(member(on(X,Part,B),State)).

delete(X,[X|L],L).
delete(X,[X|L],L2) :- delete(X,L,L2).
delete(X,[Y|L],[Y|L2]) :- not(X = Y), delete(X,L,L2).
```

In the preceding, **cleartop** just checks that there's nothing resting on a part. The **delete** predicate comes from Section 5.6: it removes all occurrences of its first argument (an input) from the list that is its second argument (an input), binding the resulting list to the third argument (the output).

10.3 IMPLEMENTING DEPTH-FIRST SEARCH _____

Prolog interpreters work depth-first, so it isn't hard to implement a general depth-first search facility in Prolog. As with the programs in Chapter 7, we'll divide code for a search into two files: a problem-dependent or "problem-defining" file containing the **successor**, **goalreached**, **eval**, and **cost** definitions discussed in Section 10.1, and a problem-independent file containing search machinery. Here is the problem-independent depth-first-search file in its entirety: [1]

```
/* Problem-independent code for depth-first search */
depthsearch(Start,Ans) :- depthsearch2(Start,[Start],Ans).

depthsearch2(State,Statelist,Statelist) :- goalreached(State).
depthsearch2(State,Statelist,Ans) :- successor(State,Newstate),
  not(member(Newstate,Statelist)),
  depthsearch2(Newstate,[Newstate|Statelist],Ans).

member(X,[X|L]).
member(X,[Y|L]) :- member(X,L).
```

Predicate **depthsearch** is the top level. Its first argument is an input, bound to a description of the starting state, and its second argument is the output, bound when search is done to the solution path in reverse order. The **depthsearch** rule just initializes a third argument (the middle one) for the predicate **depthsearch2**.

The recursive **depthsearch2** predicate does the real work of the program. Let's first explain it mostly declaratively; the next section will explain it mostly procedurally. Its three arguments are the current state (an input), the path followed to this state (an input), and the eventual path list found (an output). The first **depthsearch2** rule says that if the current state is a goal state, the output (third argu-

---

[1] When using all the programs in this chapter, be careful not to redefine or duplicate definitions of the predicate names used here, or you can get into serious trouble. That particularly applies to duplication of the classic list-predicate definitions **member**, **length**, and **append**.

ment) is the second argument, the list of states we went through to get here. Otherwise, the second rule says for some successor of the current state not previously encountered on the path here (that is, avoiding infinite loops), put this successor on the front of the path list, and recursively search for the goal from the new state. The **member** predicate is from the last section.

The key to this program is the **successor** predicate expression in the second **depthsearch2** rule. Backing up in a search problem means backtracking to that expression. Whenever a state has no successors, or all its successors have been tried and found not to lead to a goal, the second **depthsearch2** rule fails. Since it's the *last* **depthsearch2** rule, the program returns to where it was called—or it "backs up." If the call of **depthsearch2** was (as usually) a recursive one from the same second **depthsearch2** rule at the next highest level of recursion, backtracking goes to the **not** (which like all **not**s, can never succeed on backtracking), and then immediately to the **successor** expression. If another successor can be found for this earlier state, it is then taken. Otherwise, *this* invocation of the rule also fails, and backing up and backtracking happens again.

10.4 A DEPTH-FIRST EXAMPLE

Let's simulate the depth-first program on an example, to illustrate its procedural interpretation. The previous city-route example is a little too complicated for a good show, so let's try the following. Suppose in some city (see Figure 10-3) that two-way streets connect intersection **a** to intersection **b**, intersection **b** to intersection **d**, and intersection **d** to intersection **e**. Suppose also that one-way streets connect intersection **b** to intersection **c**, and intersection **a** to intersection **d**. Then the following **successor** facts hold; assume they're put in this order.

```
successor(a,b).
successor(b,c).
successor(a,d).
successor(b,d).
successor(d,b).
successor(d,e).
successor(e,d).
successor(b,a).
```

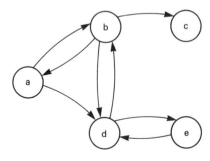

Figure 10-3. Simpler route-planning problem.

Assume for this problem that the starting state is a, and there is only one goal state
e. Then the problem-definition file must also include

goalreached(e).

Now let's follow what happens when we query

?- depthsearch(a,Answer).

and the problem-independent file of the last section is loaded too. The action is
summarized in Figure 10-4.

1. The predicate **depthsearch** is called with its first argument bound to a and its
   second argument unbound. So predicate **depthsearch2** is called with first
   argument a, second argument [a], and third argument unbound.
2. The goal is not reached in state a, so the second rule for **depthsearch2** is
   tried.
3. In the **successor** facts, the first successor of state a is b, and b is not a
   member of the list of previous states, [a]. So **depthsearch2** is recursively
   called with first argument b, second argument [b,a], and third argument
   unbound.
4. For this second level of **depthsearch2** recursion, the state b is not a goal state;
   the first successor listed for b is c, and c isn't in the list of previous states,
   [b,a]. So we recursively call **depthsearch2**, now with first argument c, second
   argument [c,b,a], and third argument unbound.
5. For this third level of recursion, new state c is not a goal state nor does it
   have successors, so both rules for **depthsearch2** fail. We must backtrack,
   "backing up" to the previous state b at the second level, and hence to the
   recursive **depthsearch2** call in the last line of the last **depthsearch2** rule.
6. The **not** fails on backtracking, as all **not**s do, so we backtrack further to the
   successor predicate in the second rule for **depthsearch2**, which chooses successors. Backtracking to here means we want a different successor for state b
   than c. And the only other successor of b is d. So we resume forward progress through the second **depthsearch2** rule with **Newstate** bound to d. This d
   is not in the list of previously visited states [b,a], so we recursively call **depth-
   search2** with first argument d, second argument [d,b,a] (c was removed in
   backtracking), and third argument unbound.
7. For this new third-level call, the new state d is not a goal, so we find a successor of it. Its first-listed successor is b, but b is a member of the list of previous states [d,b,a], so we backtrack within the rule to find another successor.
8. The only other successor fact for d mentions state e. This isn't a member of
   [d,b,a], so we recursively call **depthsearch2** with the e as first argument,
   [e,d,b,a] as second argument, and an unbound variable (still) as third argument.
9. But for this fourth level of recursion, state e is a goal state, and the **goalreached** predicate succeeds. So the first rule for **depthsearch2** succeeds, bind-

ing the third argument **Statelist** (finally!) to the list of states visited on the path here in reverse order, [e,d,b,a]. Now all other levels of **depthsearch2** recursion succeed because the recursive call was always the last predicate expression in the rule (in other words, we always did tail recursion).

10. So query variable **Answer** is bound to [e,d,b,a].

Step number in text	depthsearch2 first call	depthsearch2 second call	depthsearch2 third call	depthsearch2 fourth call
1	called with state a			
2	first rule fails			
3	second rule tried	called with state b		
4		first rule fails, second tried	called with state c	
5			both rules fail on c	
6		backtrack to not, then to successor; choose d		
7			called with state d; first rule fails; second rule picks new state b, which fails not	
8			choose e as new state	called with state e
9				first rule succeeds with path list [e,d,b,a]
			succeeds	
		succeeds		
	succeeds			

Figure 10-4. Summary of the depth-first search example.

Notice this is not the shortest solution to the problem. This is a common defect of depth-first search.

10.5 IMPLEMENTING BREADTH-FIRST SEARCH

We can write code for problem-independent breadth-first search to load as an alternative to the depth-first problem-independent code. Recall from the last chapter that breadth-first search finds states level by level (that is, by distance in number of branches·from the starting state). To do this, it must keep facts about all states found but whose successors haven't yet been found. Those states are an *agenda*; each represents further work to do. One simple way to implement breadth-first search is to make the agenda a queue (see Appendix C), a data structure for which the first thing added is always the first thing removed. We begin with a queue consisting of just the starting state; anytime we need a new state, we pick it from the front of the queue, and anytime we find successors, we put them on the end of the queue. That way we are guaranteed to not try (find successors of) any states at level N until all states at level $N - 1$ have been tried.

We can implement agendas in Prolog by facts with predicate name **agenda**, one for each unexplored (successors-not-found) state. To get the effect of a queue, we can put new states at the end of the agenda by the built-in predicate **assertz** (introduced in Section 6.1), so the first fact will always be the one that has been on the agenda the longest, and the first we'll find when we query the **agenda** predicate. This **agenda** can have two arguments: a state, and the path followed to reach it. As with depth-first search, the second argument is needed because (1) checking states against it prevents some of the possible cycles (returns to previous states), and (2) its value for the goal state is the answer to the search problem.

We also should keep **oldagenda** facts. These, with the same two arguments as **agenda** facts, can record "exhausted" states, states for which we have found all successors. Checking against **oldagenda** facts before adding a new **agenda** fact prevents other cycles. This checking also ensures that any path given in the agenda fact for a state **S** has the minimum number of branches of any path to **S**, because it was found first and breadth-first works level by level.

Here is the problem-independent breadth-first search code,[2] whose predicate hierarchy is given in Figure 10-5. (Those strange exclamation points "!" will be explained in Section 10.7, and the **bagof** in Section 10.6.)

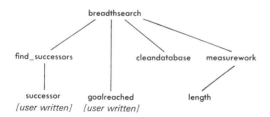

Figure 10-5. Rule-predicate hierarchy for the breadth-first search (**breadthsearch**) program.

[2] This won't work for some Prolog dialects, those that can't handle dynamic additions of new backtracking points with **assertz**. For such implementations, we can get breadth-first search from the best-first search program **bestsearch** given later in this chapter, by including two extra lines with it:

```
eval(S,T) :- time(T), retract(time(T)), T2 is T + 1, asserta(time(T2)).
eval(S,0) :- not(time(T)), asserta(time(1)).
```

```
/* Problem-independent breadth-first search */
breadthsearch(Start,Ans) :- cleandatabase,
  asserta(agenda(Start,[Start])), agenda(State,Oldstates),
  find_successors(State,Oldstates,Newstate),
  goalreached(Newstate), agenda(Newstate,Ans),
  retract(agenda(Newstate,Ans)),
  asserta(oldagenda(Newstate,Ans)), measurework.

find_successors(State,Oldstates,Newstate) :-
  successor(State,Newstate), not(State = Newstate),
  not(agenda(Newstate,S)), not(oldagenda(Newstate,S)),
  assertz(agenda(Newstate,[Newstate|Oldstates])).
find_successors(State,Oldstates,Newstate) :-
  retract(agenda(State,Oldstates)),
  asserta(oldagenda(State,Oldstates)), fail.

cleandatabase :- abolish(oldagenda,2), abolish(agenda,2), !.
cleandatabase :- abolish(agenda,2), !.
cleandatabase.

measurework :- bagof([X,Y],agenda(X,Y),Aset), length(Aset,Len),
  bagof([X2,Y2],oldagenda(X2,Y2),A2set), length(A2set,Len2),
  write(Len), write(' incompletely examined state(s) and '),
  write(Len2),write(' examined state(s).'),!.
measurework :- bagof([X,Y],oldagenda(X,Y),Aset),
  length(Aset,Len), write('no incompletely examined states and '),
  write(Len), write(' examined state(s).'),!.

length([],0).
length([X|L],N) :- length(L,N2), N is N2 + 1.
```

The predicate **breadthsearch** starts by removing any **agenda** and **oldagenda** facts remaining from previous searches. It "seeds" or starts the agenda with a single item, the starting state. The program then spends most of its time bouncing back and forth between the next three predicate expressions **agenda**, **find_successors**, and **goalreached**. The **agenda** retrieves an agenda state, **find_successors** finds a successor of it (as explained in a moment), and **goalreached** checks whether it's done. Most of the time it won't be. So most of the time it backtracks to the **find_successors** call to find another successor, or if there aren't any more, it backtracks to the **agenda** call to pick the next state on the agenda. Otherwise if a goal state is found, it cleans up the agenda, and binds the answer variable (the second argument to **breadthsearch** as with **depthsearch**) to the path used to get there. Finally, it prints the size of the agenda and the oldagenda to show how much work it did.

The two **find_successors** rules are the key to the program. Function predicate **find_successors** has three arguments: the current state (an input), the path there (an input), and a successor state (an output). The right side of the first **find_successors** rule calls first on the **successor** definition, just as in the depth-first search program. If a successor is found, it is checked to be (1) not the current state, (2) not on the agenda, and (3) not on the oldagenda. Only if these tests succeed is the new successor added to the agenda. The first **find_successors** rule is repeatedly backtracked into to generate all the successors of a state; this backtracking is forced by the usually failing **goalreached** expression in **breadthsearch**.

The second **find_successors** rule applies whenever the first fails, or whenever no further successors can be found for a state. It removes the "exhausted" state from the agenda and adds it to the oldagenda. Then by a **fail**, it forces the top-level predicate **breadthsearch** to pick a new state to find successors of. As we explained before, the next state picked will always be the oldest remaining agenda fact because of the **assertz**.

If the agenda ever becomes empty (that is, there are no new states to be found), then the **agenda** in **breadthsearch** fails, and then the **asserta** fails (there's never a new way to assert something), and then the **cleandatabase** fails (though we can't explain why this last for several pages yet). So the interpreter would type **no**.

As an example, here is the result of running the breadth-first program on the bolts problem defined in Section 10.2. Three solution paths were found, differing only in when part **e** is removed relative to the removals of parts **a** and **b**. (Carriage returns have been added to improve readability.)

```
?- breadthsearch([on(a,b,bolt1),on(b,c,bolt1),on(c,surface,bolt1),
   on(d,e,bolt2),on(e,f,bolt2),on(f,surface,bolt2),
   bolt(bolt1),bolt(bolt2)],Answer).
81 incompletely examined state(s) and 1 examined state(s).
Answer =
[[on(c,e,bolt2),on(d,surface,none),on(b,surface,none),
   on(a,surface,none),on(e,f,bolt2),on(f,surface,bolt2),
   bolt(bolt1),bolt(bolt2)],
 [on(d,surface,none),on(b,surface,none),on(a,surface,none),
   on(c,surface,bolt1),on(e,f,bolt2),on(f,surface,bolt2),
   bolt(bolt1),bolt(bolt2)],
 [on(b,surface,none),on(a,surface,none),on(c,surface,bolt1),
   on(d,e,bolt2),on(e,f,bolt2),on(f,surface,bolt2),
   bolt(bolt1),bolt(bolt2)],
 [on(a,surface,none),on(b,c,bolt1),on(c,surface,bolt1),
   on(d,e,bolt2),on(e,f,bolt2),on(f,surface,bolt2),
   bolt(bolt1),bolt(bolt2)],
 [on(a,b,bolt1),on(b,c,bolt1),on(c,surface,bolt1),
   on(d,e,bolt2),on(e,f,bolt2),on(f,surface,bolt2),
   bolt(bolt1),bolt(bolt2)]] ;
```

108 incompletely examined state(s) and 2 examined state(s).
Answer =
[[on(c,e,bolt2),on(b,surface,none),on(d,surface,none),
  on(a,surface,none),on(e,f,bolt2),on(f,surface,bolt2),
  bolt(bolt1),bolt(bolt2)],
 [on(b,surface,none),on(d,surface,none),on(a,surface,none),
  on(c,surface,bolt1),on(e,f,bolt2),on(f,surface,bolt2),
  bolt(bolt1),bolt(bolt2)],
 [on(d,surface,none),on(a,surface,none),on(b,c,bolt1),
  on(c,surface,bolt1),on(e,f,bolt2),on(f,surface,bolt2),
  bolt(bolt1),bolt(bolt2)],
 [on(a,surface,none),on(b,c,bolt1),on(c,surface,bolt1),
  on(d,e,bolt2),on(e,f,bolt2),on(f,surface,bolt2),
  bolt(bolt1),bolt(bolt2)],
 [on(a,b,bolt1),on(b,c,bolt1),on(c,surface,bolt1),
  on(d,e,bolt2),on(e,f,bolt2),on(f,surface,bolt2),
  bolt(bolt1),bolt(bolt2)]] ;

161 incompletely examined state(s) and 3 examined state(s).
Answer =
[[on(c,e,bolt2),on(b,surface,none),on(a,surface,none),
  on(d,surface,none),on(e,f,bolt2),on(f,surface,bolt2),
  bolt(bolt1),bolt(bolt2)],
 [on(b,surface,none),on(a,surface,none),on(d,surface,none),
  on(c,surface,bolt1),on(e,f,bolt2),on(f,surface,bolt2),
  bolt(bolt1),bolt(bolt2)],
 [on(a,surface,none),on(d,surface,none),on(b,c,bolt1),
  on(c,surface,bolt1),on(e,f,bolt2),on(f,surface,bolt2),
  bolt(bolt1),bolt(bolt2)],
 [on(d,surface,none),on(a,b,bolt1),on(b,c,bolt1),
  on(c,surface,bolt1),on(e,f,bolt2),on(f,surface,bolt2),
  bolt(bolt1),bolt(bolt2)],
 [on(a,b,bolt1),on(b,c,bolt1),on(c,surface,bolt1),
  on(d,e,bolt2),on(e,f,bolt2),on(f,surface,bolt2),
  bolt(bolt1),bolt(bolt2)]]]

10.6 COLLECTING ALL ITEMS THAT SATISFY A PREDICATE EXPRESSION

A feature of the **breadthsearch** program we haven't explained is the **bagof** predicate in the **measurework** rules. This predicate we used before in Chapter 8 to implement "or-combination," and it is built-in in most Prolog dialects (though it can be defined in Prolog); it is sometimes called **findall**. It collects into a list all the values for some variable that satisfy a predicate expression, much like the **forall** (defined in Section 7.12) in reverse. Predicate **bagof** takes three arguments: an input variable, an input predicate expression containing that variable, and an output list to hold all possible bindings of that variable which satisfy that expression. (Some variants of **bagof** delete duplicates in the result.)

Here's an example. Suppose we have this database:

```
boss_of(mary,tom).
boss_of(mary,dick).
boss_of(dick,harry).
boss_of(dick,ann).
```

Suppose we want a list of all people that Mary is the boss of. We can type

```
?- bagof(X,boss_of(mary,X),L)
```

and the interpreter will type

```
L = [tom,dick]
```

and X won't be printed because it's just a placeholder.

We can put, within the expression that is the second argument to **bagof**, variables besides the one we are collecting; the interpreter will try to bind them too. So if, for the preceding database, we type

```
?- bagof(X,boss_of(Y,X),L).
```

the interpreter will type

```
Y = mary, L = [tom,dick]
```

for its first answer. If we then type a semicolon, it will type

```
Y = dick, L = [harry,ann]
```

for its second answer.

The first argument to **bagof** can be a list. That is, we can search for a set of values satisfying a predicate instead of just one value. For instance, we can query

```
?- bagof([X,Y],boss_of(X,Y),L).
```

and receive the answer

```
L = [[mary,tom],[mary,dick],[dick,harry],[dick,ann]]
```

This query form is used in the **measurework** rules in the **breadthsearch** program.

The **bagof** predicate can be defined this way to operate on single-variables predicates (provided you have no predicate named **zzz** in your program):

bagof(X,P,L) :- asserta(zzz([])), fail.
bagof(X,P,L) :- call(P), zzz(M), retract(zzz(M)),
  asserta(zzz([X|M])), fail.
bagof(X,P,L) :- zzz(L), retract(zzz(L)).

10.7 THE CUT PREDICATE

We still must explain those strange exclamation points (the "!") in the **breadth-search** program. These are a special built-in predicate of no arguments called the *cut*, whose meaning is exclusively procedural. The cut always succeeds when the interpreter first encounters it, but has a special side effect: it prevents backtracking to it by throwing away the necessary bookkeeping information. This can improve the efficiency of Prolog programs, and can be necessary to make some programs work properly, those for which backtracking just doesn't make sense.

Usually the cut predicate expression is last in a rule, as in **cleandatabase** and the two **measurework** rules in the **breadthsearch** program. It can be paraphrased as: "Don't ever backtrack into this rule. What's more, don't ever try another rule to satisfy the goal that this rule tried to satisfy. That goal is dead. So fail it." (Note that a cut has no effect on the next call of the rule, even a call with the same arguments as before: the prohibition of backtracking just applies to the call in which the cut was encountered.) So a cut symbol forces behavior more like that of a subprocedure in a conventional programming language, in that once a subprocedure is done it can only be reentered by a different call—except that a Prolog "subprocedure" is all the rules with the same left-side predicate name, not just a single rule.

So a cut at the end of a rule means you want only one solution to the query of that rule. This often is true for "existential quantification" queries in which we check existence of something of a certain type, and we don't care what. For instance, the **member** predicate from Section 5.5

member(X,[X|L]).
member(X,[Y|L]) :- member(X,L).

is often used this way, when it is queried with both arguments bound. For instance

?- member(b,[a,b,c,b,e,a,f]).

Recursion will find the first **b** in the list and the interpreter will type **yes**. If we were to type a semicolon, recursion would find the second occurrence of **b** and the interpreter would type **yes** again. But finding that second occurrence doesn't make sense in most applications; the answer to the query is the same, after all. A backtracking **member** is useless in our depth-first and breadth-first search programs,

where **member** is enclosed in a **not**, since the Prolog interpreter doesn't backtrack
into **not**s. And backtracking into **member** is unnecessary whenever there can't be
duplicates in a list. (But we do need a backtracking **member** in the bolts example
of Section 10.2, to choose alternative parts to move by querying **member** with an
unbound first argument.) A nonbacktracking **member** can be obtained by just
inserting a cut symbol in the backtracking **member**:

```
singlemember(X,[X|L]) :- !.
singlemember(X,[Y|L]) :- singlemember(X,L).
```

We don't need a cut symbol at the end of the second rule, because when it fails no
more possibilities remain.
    We don't actually need a cut symbol to define **singlemember**, for we could say
equivalently (if both arguments are always bound in queries)

```
singlemember(X,[X|L]).
singlemember(X,[Y|L]) :- not(X = Y), singlemember(X,L).
```

But this is slower because the extra expression not(X = Y) must be tested on every
recursion; the cut predicate expression is done at most once for any query.
    A related use of the cut predicate is to do something only once instead of
repeatedly. For instance, here's the predicate from Section 5.6 that deletes all
occurrences of an item X from a list L:

```
delete(X,[],[]).
delete(X,[X|L],M) :- delete(X,L,M).
delete(X,[Y|L],[Y|M]) :- not(X = Y), delete(X,L,M).
```

Suppose we want a predicate that deletes only the first X from list L. We can
remove the recursion in the second rule, remove the not(X = Y) in the third rule,
and insert a cut symbol:

```
deleteone(X,[],[]).
deleteone(X,[X|L],L) :- !.
deleteone(X,[Y|L],[Y|M]) :- deleteone(X,L,M).
```

The cut symbol is important here, because if we just omit it like this:

```
deleteone(X,[],[]).
deleteone(X,[X|L],L).
deleteone(X,[Y|L],[Y|M]) :- deleteone(X,L,M).
```

then **deleteone** will give a correct first answer, but wrong subsequent answers on
backtracking, just like the similar mistake-making **delete** discussed in Section 5.6.
    The cut predicate can also be used merely to improve efficiency. Recall the
definition of the maximum of a list in Section 5.5:

```
max([X],X).
max([X|L],X) :- max(L,M), X>M.
max([X|L],M) :- max(L,M), not(X>M).
```

When the first two rules fail, the computation of the maximum of a list is done twice: once in the second rule, and once in the third rule. This is wasteful. So we can define it as

```
max([X],X) :- !.
max([X|L],M) :- max(L,M), not(X>M), !.
max([X|L],X).
```

Here we've changed the order of the last two rules and removed the redundant max call. The cuts guarantee no backtracking inside max, so we won't start taking the third rule when the second rule was taken before and thereby get wrong answers.

A cut predicate can be put in the middle of a rule. Then it means that backtracking is allowed to the right of it, but that if the interpreter ever tries to backtrack to its left, both the rule and the goal that invoked it will fail unconditionally. But usually cuts should go last in a rule.

Nothing in life is free, so it's not surprising that the efficiency advantages of the cut predicate have the associated disadvantage of restricting multiway use (see Section 3.3) of predicate definitions. That's because the cut is a purely procedural feature of Prolog, with no declarative meaning. If you're sure you'll only query a definition with one particular pattern of bindings, multiway use is not an issue, and cut predicates can be used freely to improve efficiency. But cuts can be easily abused; for instance, putting cuts in every rule of a rule-based expert system is poor programming, and there's always a better alternative.

10.8 ITERATION WITH THE CUT PREDICATE*

The cut predicate provides a way to write iterative Prolog programs in a way more general than the forall and doall of Section 7.12 and bagof of Section 10.6. It gives a sometimes better way to repeat things than by backtracking, since backtracking does things in reverse order, and that can be confusing or even wrong.

To get a true "do-until," or in other words to repeatedly query some predicate expression Pred until some other predicate expression done holds, query predicate iterate with argument Pred:

```
iterate(Pred) :- repeat, iterate2(Pred), done.
iterate2(Pred) :- call(Pred), !.
repeat.
repeat :- repeat.
```

Here repeat is a predicate that always succeeds, and what's more, always succeeds on backtracking (unlike 1 = 1 which always succeeds once, but fails on backtracking because it can't succeed in a new way). The **repeat** is built-in in many Prolog dialects, but it's easy to define as you see.

Predicate **iterate** will hand the expression **Pred** to **iterate2** for execution using the **call** predicate explained in Section 7.12. Then **iterate** checks the **done** condition, which usually fails. At this point, the cut in **iterate** is important, because it prevents backtracking into **iterate2** and **Pred**. So **iterate2** fails, and the interpreter returns to the **repeat**. But **repeat** always succeeds anew on backtracking (it just recurses once more as a new way to succeed), and so the interpreter returns to **iterate2**, and **Pred** is executed again *in the forward direction.* So the cut predicate forces the interpreter to call **Pred** like within a loop in a conventional programming language: always forward. (Note that **Pred** can contain arguments.)

One disadvantage of the preceding is that **iterate** can never fail. This would mean an infinite loop if **done** has a bug preventing it from ever succeeding. So we might distinguish **donegood** and **donebad** conditions, both user-defined, for when the iteration should stop with success and failure, respectively:

```
iterate(Pred) :- repeatcond, iterate2(Pred), donegood.
iterate2(Pred) :- call(Pred), !.
repeatcond.
repeatcond :- not(donebad), repeatcond.
```

Another kind of iteration increases a counter at each iteration, like the "FOR" construct in Pascal and the "DO" construct in Fortran which iterate for $K = 1$ to N:

```
foriterate(Pred,N) :- asserta(counter(0)), repeat, counter(K),
  K2 is K + 1, retract(counter(K)), asserta(counter(K2)),
  iterate2(Pred), K2 > = N, retract(counter(K2)), !.
iterate2(Pred) :- (call(Pred), !), 1 = 1.
repeat.
repeat :- repeat.
```

To access the counter at any time inside the rules invoked by calling **Pred**, you query predicate **counter**.

10.9 IMPLEMENTING BEST-FIRST SEARCH* _____

Now we can show our best-first search program. To use it you need (besides **successor** and **goalreached** definitions) a definition of a function predicate **eval** of two arguments. As we said in Section 10.1, the first argument to **eval** is an input state, and its second is an output number, a nonnegative evaluation of that state.

The best-first program keeps an agenda of states like the breadth-first program, but each agenda fact has a third argument holding the evaluation function value for the state. (It makes sense to compute this when we put the state on the agenda, so we only do it once per state.) And when we select a state from an agenda with the **pick_best_state** predicate, we must take the state with the minimum evaluation function value, not just the first one on the agenda. Our best-first search program also has iteration in several places where the breadth-first search program used recursion, so it's a more efficient program. Here's the program, whose predicate hierarchy appears in Figure 10-6:

```
/* Problem-independent best-first search */
bestsearch(Start,Goalpathlist) :- cleandatabase,
  add_state(Start,[]), repeatifagenda,
  pick_best_state(State,Pathlist),
  add_successors(State,Pathlist), agenda(State,Goalpathlist,E),
  retract(agenda(State,Goalpathlist,E)), measurework.

pick_best_state(State,Pathlist) :-
  asserta(beststate(dummy,dummy,dummy)),
  agenda(S,SL,E), beststate(S2,SL2,E2), special_less_than(E,E2),
  retract(beststate(S2,SL2,E2)), asserta(beststate(S,SL,E)), fail.
pick_best_state(State,Pathlist) :- beststate(State,Pathlist,E),
  retract(beststate(State,Pathlist,E)), not(E = dummy), !.

add_successors(State,Pathlist) :- goalreached(State), !.
add_successors(State,Pathlist) :- successor(State,Newstate),
  add_state(Newstate,Pathlist), fail.
add_successors(State,Pathlist) :-
  retract(agenda(State,Pathlist,E)),
  asserta(usedstate(State)), fail.

add_state(Newstate,Pathlist) :- not(usedstate(Newstate)),
  not(agenda(Newstate,P,E)), eval(Newstate,Enew),
  asserta(agenda(Newstate,[Newstate|Pathlist],Enew)), !.
add_state(Newstate,Pathlist) :- not(eval(Newstate,Enew)),
  write('Warning: your evaluation function failed on state '),
  write(Newstate), nl, !.


/* Utility functions */
repeatifagenda.
repeatifagenda :- agenda(X,Y,Z), repeatifagenda.

special_less_than(X,dummy) :- !.
special_less_than(X,Y) :- X<Y.

cleandatabase :- checkabolish(agenda,3), checkabolish(usedstate,1),
  checkabolish(beststate,1), checkabolish(counter,1).

checkabolish(P,N) :- abolish(P,N), !.
checkabolish(P,N).
```

```
measurework :- countup(agenda(X,Y,Z),NA), countup(usedstate(S),NB),
  write(NA), write(' incompletely examined state(s) and '),
  write(NB),write(' examined state(s)'), !.

countup(P,N) :- asserta(counter(0)), call(P), counter(K),
  retract(counter(K)), K2 is K + 1, asserta(counter(K2)), fail.
countup(P,N) :- counter(N), retract(counter(N)), !.
```

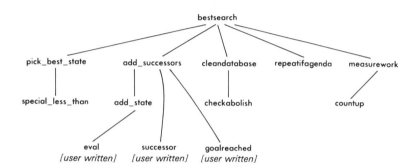

Figure 10-6. Rule-predicate hierarchy for the best-first search (bestsearch) program.

The top-level **bestsearch** predicate iterates by repeatedly picking a state from the agenda. It initializes and cleans up around a kernel of commands repeatedly invoked. But the iteration is done differently from the **breadthsearch** program, with the **bestsearch** bouncing among a **repeatifagenda** on the left, the **pick_best_state**, and an **add_successors** on the right. The **repeatifagenda** is an instance of the **repeatcond** in the last section.

The **pick_best_state** chooses the minimum-evaluation state by iterating over the agenda states; the cut predicate at the end of its definition ensures that it finds only one such state per call. The **add_successors** checks whether some state S is a goal state (then succeeding), and otherwise adds all the acceptable successors of S to the agenda (then failing); the predicate **add_state** runs the necessary acceptance checks on a new state before adding it to the agenda. When **add_successors** finally succeeds, its path argument must be the solution, so this is retrieved and bound to the answer **Goalpathlist**.

As an example, let's use best-first search on the bolts problem of Section 10.2. We need an evaluation function. Our goal is to get part **c** on part **e**, so we could take the sum of the number of parts on top of both **c** and **e**. That is, we could measure the degree of "burial" of each. But then some non-goal states have evaluation zero. Instead, let's try

```
eval(S,0) :- goalreached(S).
eval(S,N) :- burial(c,S,N1), burial(e,S,N2), N is N1 + N2 + 1.

burial(P,S,0) :- cleartop(P,S).
burial(P,S,N) :- member(on(X,P,B),S), burial(X,S,N2), N is N2 + 1.
```

Running bestsearch on the same starting state as before, we get the third answer for breadth-first search:

```
?- bestsearch([on(a,b,bolt1),on(b,c,bolt1),on(c,surface,bolt1),
   on(d,e,bolt2),on(e,f,bolt2),on(f,surface,bolt2),
   bolt(bolt1),bolt(bolt2)],A).
23 incompletely examined state(s) and 4 examined state(s)
A = [[on(c,e,bolt2),on(b,surface,none),on(a,surface,none),
   on(d,surface,none),on(e,f,bolt2),on(f,surface,bolt2),
   bolt(bolt1),bolt(bolt2)],
   [on(b,surface,none),on(a,surface,none),on(d,surface,none),
   on(c,surface,bolt1),on(e,f,bolt2),on(f,surface,bolt2),
   bolt(bolt1),bolt(bolt2)],
   [on(a,surface,none),on(d,surface,none),on(b,c,bolt1),
   on(c,surface,bolt1),on(e,f,bolt2),on(f,surface,bolt2),
   bolt(bolt1),bolt(bolt2)],
   [on(d,surface,none),on(a,b,bolt1),on(b,c,bolt1),
   on(c,surface,bolt1),on(e,f,bolt2),on(f,surface,bolt2),
   bolt(bolt1),bolt(bolt2)],
   [on(a,b,bolt1),on(b,c,bolt1),on(c,surface,bolt1),
   on(d,e,bolt2),on(e,f,bolt2),on(f,surface,bolt2),
   bolt(bolt1),bolt(bolt2)]]]
```

But look how many fewer states were found: 25 (21 + 4) versus 82. That's more efficient search.

10.10 IMPLEMENTING A* SEARCH*

A* search is like best-first except we must add path cost to the evaluation function. So as we said, the user must define a cost function predicate with two arguments, an input path and an output holding the computed cost of that path.

Our A* program is intended to be forgiving. So it still works if you don't give it a lower-bound cost function, though you may need to type semicolons to get the right (lowest-cost) answer. Also without a lower-bound evaluation function, the first path found to any state S may not be lowest cost; so if we find a lower-cost path to S later, we must revise the path lists of everything on the agenda mentioning S.

Here's the program (whose predicate hierarchy is summarized in Figure 10-7):

```
/* Problem-independent A* search code. */
/* Note: "cost" must be nonnegative. The "eval" should be a lower */
/* bound on cost in order for the first answer found to be */
/* guaranteed optimal, but the right answer will be reached */
/* eventually otherwise. */
```

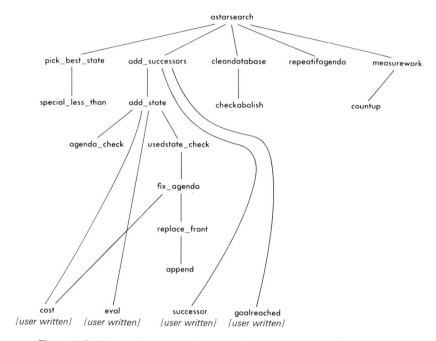

Figure 10-7. Rule-predicate hierarchy for the A* search (astarsearch) program.

astarsearch(Start,Goalpathlist) :- cleandatabase,
  add_state(Start,[]), repeatifagenda,
  pick_best_state(State,Pathlist),
  add_successors(State,Pathlist), agenda(State,Goalpathlist,C,D),
  retract(agenda(State,Goalpathlist,C,D)), measurework.

pick_best_state(State,Pathlist) :-
  asserta(beststate(dummy,dummy,dummy)),
  agenda(S,SL,C,D), beststate(S2,SL2,D2), special_less_than(D,D2),
  retract(beststate(S2,SL2,D2)), asserta(beststate(S,SL,D)), fail.
pick_best_state(State,Pathlist) :- beststate(State,Pathlist,D),
  retract(beststate(State,Pathlist,D)), not(D = dummy), !.

add_successors(State,Pathlist) :- goalreached(State), !.
add_successors(State,Pathlist) :- successor(State,Newstate),
  add_state(Newstate,Pathlist), fail.
add_successors(State,Pathlist) :-
  retract(agenda(State,Pathlist,C,D)),
  asserta(usedstate(State,C)), fail.

/* If you are sure that your evaluation function is always
/* a lower bound on the cost function, then you can delete the */
/* first rule for "agenda_check" and the first rule for */

```
/* "usedstate_check," and delete the entire definitions of */
/* "fix_agenda," "replace_front," and "append." */
add_state(Newstate,Pathlist) :- cost([Newstate|Pathlist],Cnew), !,
  agenda_check(Newstate,Cnew), !,
  usedstate_check(Newstate,Pathlist,Cnew), !,
  eval(Newstate,Enew), D is Enew + Cnew,
  asserta(agenda(Newstate,[Newstate|Pathlist],Cnew,D)), !.
add_state(Newstate,Pathlist) :-
  not(cost([Newstate|Pathlist],Cnew)),
  write('Warning: your cost function failed on path list '),
  write(Pathlist), nl, !.
add_state(Newstate,Pathlist) :- not(eval(Newstate,Enew)),
  write('Warning: your evaluation function failed on state '),
  write(Newstate), nl, !.

agenda_check(S,C) :- agenda(S,P2,C2,D2), C<C2,
  retract(agenda(S,P2,C2,D2)), !.
agenda_check(S,C) :- agenda(S,P2,C2,D2), !, fail.
agenda_check(S,C).

usedstate_check(S,P,C) :- usedstate(S,C2), C<C2,
  retract(usedstate(S,C2)), asserta(usedstate(S,C)), !,
  fix_agenda(S,P,C,C2).
usedstate_check(S,P,C) :- usedstate(S,C2), !, fail.
usedstate_check(S,P,C).

fix_agenda(S,P,C,OldC) :- agenda(S2,P2,C2,D2),
  replace_front(P,S,P2,Pnew), cost(Pnew,Cnew),
  Dnew is D2 + C-OldC, retract(agenda(S2,P2,C2,D2)),
  asserta(agenda(S2,Pnew,Cnew,Dnew)), fail.

replace_front(P,S,P2,Pnew) :- append(P3,[S|P4],P2),
  append(P,[S|P4],Pnew), !.

/* Utility functions */
repeatifagenda.
repeatifagenda :- agenda(X,Y,Z,W), repeatifagenda.

special_less_than(X,dummy) :- !.
special_less_than(X,Y) :- X<Y.

cleandatabase :- checkabolish(agenda,4), checkabolish(usedstate,2),
  checkabolish(beststate,1), checkabolish(counter,1).

checkabolish(P,N) :- abolish(P,N), !.
checkabolish(P,N).
```

```
measurework :- countup(agenda(X,Y,C,D),NA),
   countup(usedstate(S,C),NB), write(NA),
   write(' incompletely examined state(s) and '),
   write(NB),write(' examined state(s).'), !.

countup(P,N) :- asserta(counter(0)), call(P), counter(K),
   retract(counter(K)), K2 is K + 1, asserta(counter(K2)), fail.
countup(P,N) :- counter(N), retract(counter(N)), !.

append([],L,L).
append([I|L1],L2,[I|L3]) :- append(L1,L2,L3).
```

10.11 IMPLEMENTING SEARCH WITH HEURISTICS* _____

Heuristics define a policy for choosing things from the agenda in search. So searching with heuristics can be implemented by redefining the pick_best_state in the best-first program, and leaving the rest of the program unchanged. Specifically, a search-with-heuristics program should pick the first state on the agenda for which no other state is preferred by heuristics (prefer rules):

```
pick_best_state(State,Pathlist) :-
   agenda(State,Pathlist,E), not(better_pick(State,Pathlist,E)), !.
better_pick(X,Y,E) :- agenda(X2,Y2,E2), not(X = X2), prefer(X2,Y2,E2,X,Y,E).
```

This same idea was used to implement meta-rules in Section 7.16, and a heuristic *is* a kind of meta-rule, a rule guiding usage of successor rules. We'll broaden the concept of a heuristic here to allow use of evaluation functions in its decision, to be fully general. Such *extended heuristics* can be defined with a prefer predicate of six arguments: two groups of three where the first group represents an agenda item preferred to an agenda item represented by the second group. Each group represents the three arguments to agenda facts: state, path list, and evaluation-function value. (The last can be left unbound and ignored if numeric evaluation is hard.) So

```
prefer(X1,Y1,E1,X2,Y2,E2) :- E1 < E2.
```

implements best-first search, and

```
prefer(X1,Y1,E1,X2,Y2,E2) :- length(Y1,L1), length(Y2,L2), L1 < L2.
length([],0).
length([X|L],N) :- length(L,N2), N is N2 + 1.
```

implements breadth-first search, and

```
prefer(X1,Y1,E1,X2,Y2,E2) :- fail.
```

(or equivalently, no **prefer** rule at all) implements depth-first search. (Then the first agenda item will always be picked; it will always be the successor found most recently, thanks to the **asserta** in **add_state.**) These **prefer** rules can also refer to quite specific characteristics of a search problem, though then they can't be reused in other search problems as much. For instance for the bolts problem, we want part **c** on part **e**, so a heuristic would be to prefer a state in which the top of **e** is clear:

> prefer(X1,Y1,E1,X2,Y2,E2) :- cleartop(e,X1), not(cleartop(e,X2)).

We can have several extended heuristics for a problem, and they will be tried in the order given. For instance we can do a best-first search with a breadth-first criterion to break ties between states with the same evaluation-function value:

> prefer(X1,Y1,E1,X2,Y2,E2) :- E1 < E2.
> prefer(X1,Y1,E,X2,Y2,E) :- length(Y1,L1), length(Y2,L2), L1 < L2.
> length([],0).
> length([X|L],N) :- length(L,N2), N is N2 + 1.

We could also combine breadth-first and best-first search in a different way:

> prefer(X1,Y1,E1,X2,Y2,E2) :- Ep1 is E1 + 1, Ep1 < E2.
> prefer(X1,Y1,E1,X2,Y2,E2) :-
>   length(Y1,L1), length(Y2,L2), L1 < L2.

This says to prefer states according to the evaluation function if they are more than one unit apart, but otherwise pick the state closest to the start.

Sets of heuristics or extended heuristics can exhibit complex behavior; they can be an extensive rule-based system on their own. The most important heuristics (**prefer** rules) should be first, then general-purpose heuristics, and finally default heuristics. As rule-based system rules go, heuristics can be powerful because they can be quite general: we can often reuse the same heuristic in many different problems.

The preceding extended heuristics choose among states. Other heuristics choose among branches of (operators applied to) a state, but these can often be transformed into the first kind by having them reference characteristics of the result of the desired branch.

10.12 COMPILATION OF SEARCH*

Since a search problem can be seen as a rule-based system with **successor** rules, it isn't surprising that we can use compilation techniques for rule-based systems to make search faster. We can exploit all the "compiled forms" in the lower half of Figure 6-1, except virtual facts and decision lattices which require questioning (this is uncommon in search).

Caching is helpful and simple to apply. An agenda is one form of a cache, but we can extend an agenda to include entries from previous related problems (together with descriptions of those problems). So as we solve problems, we gradually build up a library of solutions, some to full problems and some to subproblems, to make new problems easier. If this creates a large agenda, we can index or hash items for fast lookup. If this is still too slow or requires too much storage, we can cache selectively, using as criterion the amount of work needed to compute the item and perhaps statistics on how often it was used in problems. Caching criteria can also be suggested by the problem itself, as in route planning in a city for which it makes sense to cache routes between landmarks.

Partitioning or modularization is important in many areas of computer science, and search is no exception. Groups of related operators can be put into partitions, each loaded as needed. File loads can be done by a **consult** last in a **successor** rule. Partitions are essential for a system with many **successor** rules, like a general-purpose car repair system, for which quite different parts of the car require quite different repair techniques, so many operators have narrow applicability.

Parallelism can increase the speed of successor rules too. All four types of parallelism discussed in Section 6.9 can be used: partition parallelism, "and" parallelism, "or" parallelism, and variable-matching parallelism. Actual concurrency in execution is essential for speed in real-time applications. Good examples are the lattices used for high-performance speech-understanding systems, a kind of and-or-not lattice representing parallelism taken to the maximum extent. For a fixed vocabulary of words, the lattice corresponds to every possible sequence in which sounds can occur to express grammatical utterances using those words. Each node in the lattice represents a sound, and each branch represents a transition to a possible next sound. The speech to be understood is first broken into small varying-length segments representing homogeneous (constant-nature) intervals in the speech. A cost function is used that measures the "distance" any segment comes to some "ideal" sound. Speech recognition then becomes an optimal-path search problem, in which we want to find a path through a lattice that minimizes the sum of the branch costs. Such precompiled search lattices have many other real-time applications.

KEYWORDS

frame problem
agenda of states
the **bagof** *predicate*
the cut predicate
iteration

EXERCISES

10-1. (R,A,P)

(a) Improve the depth-first search program to print out the answer path list in the forward (opposite) order. Print one state per line.

(b) Suppose we want a search answer to include names of operators used at each step in the solution. Explain how you can do this by writing the problem-dependent files in a certain way without making any changes at all to the problem-independent files.

(c) Suppose states are lists of facts in which the order of the facts doesn't matter — that is, states are described by *sets* of facts, not lists. Modify the depth-first search program to prevent going to "permutation" states that have the same facts as an already examined state but in a different order.

10-2. (P) Country X and country Y are carefully negotiating an arms agreement. Each has missiles of varying strengths, each strength summarized by a single number. Each step in the negotiation does one of two things: (1) eliminates from both sides a single missile of the same numerical strength, or (2) eliminates from one side a missile of strength S and from the other side two missiles whose strength sums to S. Write a program that figures out a sequence of such negotiation steps that will eliminate all the missiles entirely from one or both of the sides, but making sure in the process that no side ever has more than one more missile than the other.

Use the depth-first program to do searching. Assume to start:

Country X: missile strengths 9, 11, 9, 3, 4, 5, 7, 18

Country Y: missile strengths 12, 2, 16, 5, 7, 4, 20

Type semicolons to your program to get alternative solutions. Hints: Use the **member** and **delete** predicates from Sections 5.5 and 5.6, and define a **twomembers** which says two things are different items from the same list.

10-3. Suppose we modify the bolts problem in Section 10.2 a bit. Suppose we have the same operators and starting state, but our goal is to get part **b** and part **c** on bolt 1, with **c** on **b** instead of vice versa.

(a) Give the **goalreached** definition.

(b) Give a corresponding **eval** definition.

(c) What answer will breadth-first search find first?

10-4. (P) We didn't show the bolts problem being solved with depth-first search, and there's a good reason: it takes a long time to solve it, a thousand times more perhaps than breadth-first.

(a) Study the program running to see why it's taking so much time for such a simple problem. Warning: don't duplicate **member** in the database.

(b) One possible reason is the lack of unordered sets as opposed to lists in Prolog. Explain why this is a problem. Then explain how you would change the problem-independent code for depth-first search to eliminate this problem. Do so and see if efficiency improves.

(c) Another suggestion is to use heuristics to control the depth-first search. But the implementation of heuristics given in Section 10.11 isn't very helpful. Why not?

(d) Explain how, in place of meta-rules or heuristics, additional successor rules can be written. Do this for the bolts program and analyze the improvement in performance.

10-5. (R,A,P) Load into the Prolog interpreter the breadth-first program given in Section 10.5 and the following additional code:

```
glassesdepth(Cap1,Cap2,Goal,Ans) :- checkretract(cap1(C1)),
  checkretract(cap2(C2)), checkretract(goalvolume(G)),
  checkassert(cap1(Cap1)), checkassert(cap2(Cap2)),
  checkassert(goalvolume(Goal)), !, depthsearch([0,0],Ans).

glassesbreadth(Cap1,Cap2,Goal,Ans) :- checkretract(cap1(C1)),
  checkretract(cap2(C2)), checkretract(goalvolume(G)),
  checkassert(cap1(Cap1)), checkassert(cap2(Cap2)),
  checkassert(goalvolume(Goal)), !, breadthsearch([0,0],Ans).

goalreached([Goalvolume,V2]) :- goalvolume(Goalvolume).
goalreached([V1,Goalvolume]) :- goalvolume(Goalvolume).

successor([V1,V2],[Vsum,0]) :- V2 > 0, Vsum is V1 + V2,
  cap1(Cap1), Vsum = < Cap1.
successor([V1,V2],[0,Vsum]) :- V1 > 0, Vsum is V1 + V2,
  cap2(Cap2), Vsum = < Cap2.
successor([V1,V2],[Cap1,Vdiff]) :- V2 > 0, V1 > = 0,
  cap1(Cap1), Vdiff is V2 - ( Cap1 - V1 ), Vdiff > 0.
successor([V1,V2],[Vdiff,Cap2]) :- V1 > 0, V2 > = 0,
  cap2(Cap2), Vdiff is V1 - ( Cap2 - V2 ), Vdiff > 0.
successor([V1,V2],[Cap1,V2]) :- cap1(Cap1).
successor([V1,V2],[V1,Cap2]) :- cap2(Cap2).
successor([V1,V2],[0,V2]).
successor([V1,V2],[V1,0]).

checkassert(S) :- call(S), !.
checkassert(S) :- asserta(S).

checkretract(S) :- call(S), retract(S), fail.
checkretract(S).
```

This code defines a famous puzzle known as the water-glass problem. You have two empty glasses of capacities C1 and C2, a faucet to fill the glasses with water, and a drain. The glasses are not marked along the sides so you can't fill them directly to a specified partial amount. The goal is to get a certain fixed quantity of liquid. To do this you can fill the glasses, empty the glasses, pour all of one glass into another, or fill one glass from the other. To run the program, type

```
?-glassesbreadth
  (<capacity-glass-1>,<capacity-glass-2>,<goal-amount>,<answer>).
```

for which the first three arguments are inputs, numbers you must fill in, and the last is the output.

(a) First study the situation in which you have two glasses of sizes 5 and 7. Call the predicate **glassesbreadth** with goal amounts equal to 0, 1, 2, 3, 4, 5, 6, 7, and 8, and construct a diagram of all possible states and their connections. Type the semicolon to obtain all distinct solutions. Note that <answer> represents a stack (i.e., it's in reverse chronological order). Describe the overall pattern in the diagram.

(b) Now use the depth-first program given in the chapter. Invoke it with

```
?- glassesdepth
   (<capacity-glass-1>,<capacity-glass-2>,<goal-amount>,
   <answer>).
```

Try it on all the situations considered previously, and draw its state diagram. Describe how the diagram is different from that for breadth-first search. In particular, how does the depth-first state diagram relate to the breadth-first diagram?

(c) Explain what each of the eight **successor** rules does.

(d) Modify the preceding code defining the operators so that the solutions found will have the desired quantity in the left glass (that is, the glass with the first-mentioned capacity). Test your code with the breadth-first search code.

10-6. (H,P) *Beam search* is a more efficient kind of breadth-first search, a sort of cross between breadth-first search and best-first search. Rather than putting all the successors of a given state on the agenda, it only puts the *K* best successors according to an evaluation function. Modify the breadth-first search program to do beam search.

10-7. (A,P) Modify the A* search program to do a branch-and-bound search.

10-8. In the city-route planning example of Section 10.1, the last line of the **piece_cost** function definition seems very dangerous: it would seem to define an infinite loop. Such definitions of commutativity for predicates always have such dangers.

(a) What advantage is gained by having such a line in the definitions?

(b) Why can the danger be ignored for this particular cost function definition used with the A* search program?

(c) Suppose we are doing route planning in which the routes are highways and the nodes are cities. If you can go from city X to city Y along route R you can also go from Y to X backward along R. So state transitions would be commutative, and we could write a single commutativity rule to state this, like the commutativity rule in the cost function definition. Why wouldn't this be a good idea, when it generally is a good idea with costs?

10-9. (R,P)

(a) Consider a housekeeping robot that must clean a two-room suite (Figure 10-8). It must vacuum the floors, dust, and empty the trash baskets. Vacuuming the floor generates dust that goes into the trash basket of the room it is in. Emptying the trash baskets in each room requires a trip to the trash chute. Dusting puts dust on the floor, requiring vacuuming.

Assume the following energy costs:

10 units to vacuum a single room (assume the robot has a built-in vacuum);

6 units to dust a room (assume the robot has a built-in device for removing dust);

3 units to pick up a trash basket (assume the robot can hold more than one);

1 unit to put down a trash basket;

3 units to travel between the two offices;

8 units to travel between an office and the trash chute (assume there are doors to the trash chute from both rooms);

5 units to dispose of the contents of a trash basket down the trash chute.

Use the following reasonable preconditions for actions (and no others):

- It doesn't make sense to vacuum or dust if the room isn't vacuumable or dusty respectively.
- It doesn't make sense to vacuum if a room is dustable.
- It doesn't make sense to pick up a trash basket if a room is vacuumable or dusty.
- It doesn't make sense to put down something you just picked up.

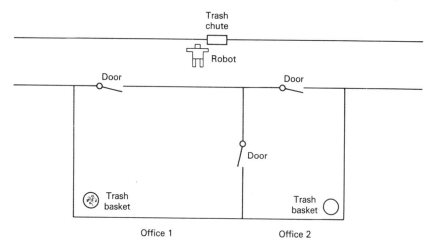

Figure 10-8. Picture for Exercise 10-9.

For the starting state, assume the robot is at the trash chute. Assume that both rooms need dusting. Office 1 has trash in its trash basket, but Office 2 doesn't; and the carpet in Office 1 does not need vacuuming, while the carpet in Office 2 does. The goal is to get everything dusted, every carpet vacuumed, and every basket emptied. The robot must finish at either room but not at the trash chute.

Set this problem up for the A* search program for this chapter. Give appropriate definitions, including a good evaluation function, one that gives a lower bound on the cost to a goal state. You may find you run out of space; if so, revise the program to eliminate unnecessary successors. Run the program and show your results.

Hints: Make the first item in each state represent the last operator applied, or "none" for the starting state. Have the cost function use these to assign costs. You don't need append or = anywhere in your program; use the left sides of rules to get their effect. And in defining successor, it may improve efficiency to rule out new states in which the facts are just permutations (ignoring the last-operator-applied item) of the facts in some other state already on the agenda or already visited, as in Exercise 10-1(c).

10-10. (A,P)

(a) Combining chemicals to react and make new chemicals is a kind of search. Find a good way to represent states and successor functions for operations including these:

   If we combine one mole of Cl_2 and one mole of H_2O, you get one mole of $HClO$ and one mole of HCl.

   If you combine one mole of $CaCO_3$ with two moles of HCl, you get one mole of $CaCl_2$, one mole of CO_2, and one mole of H_2O.

   If you combine two moles of H_2O_2 and one mole of MnO_2, you get two moles of H_2O, one mole of O_2, and one mole of MnO_2 (that is, manganese dioxide is only a catalyst).

   If you combine one mole of H_2 and one mole of Cl_2, you get two moles of HCl.

   If you combine four moles of HCl with one mole of MnO_2, you get one mole of $MnCl_2$, two moles of H_2O, and one mole of Cl_2.

   Hint: Represent states by lists of lists.

(b) Write Prolog code, and try it with the depth-first program. Do the problem of making 1 mole of $CaCl_2$ from a starting state consisting of 2 moles of Cl_2, 1 mole of MnO_2, 1 mole of $CaCO_3$, and 2 moles of H_2O_2. That is, find a sequence of operations that could lead to a mole of $CaCl_2$ being formed—not necessarily the only way it could be formed. Hint: Use the **member** predicate of Section 5.5 and the **delete** predicate of Section 5.6 or the **deleteone** of Section 10.7.

(c) Describe a cost function that would be meaningful for this kind of search problem, and describe a corresponding evaluation function.

(d) The Prolog interpreter's conflict-resolution method (trying rules in the order they appear) is not good for chemical-reaction rules. Explain why, and suggest (describe) a better conflict-resolution method from ideas in Chapter 6.

10-11. Suppose you are doing a best-first search in a search space of N states.

    (a) Suppose only one state in the search space satisfies the condition for a goal state. What is the smallest maximum size of the agenda during the finding of this goal state?

    (b) For the same situation as part (a), what is the largest maximum size of the agenda during the finding of the goal state?

    (c) Now suppose there is no goal state in the search space and we must search to confirm this. What is now the smallest maximum size of the agenda in this process of confirmation?

    (d) For the situation in part (c), what is the largest maximum size of the agenda?

10-12. (A) Suppose a search space can be represented as a complete (filled-in) and balanced binary tree of 31 states on four levels (not counting the starting state as a level). Suppose there is a single goal state that does lie in the search space.

    (a) Suppose we are doing a breadth-first search. What is the maximum possible size of the agenda?

    (b) Suppose we are doing a best-first search. What is the maximum possible size of the agenda?

10-13. When a search problem has a solution, breadth-first search, best-first search, and A* search cannot get into an infinite loop. So it's not strictly necessary to check for previously visited states—that just improves the efficiency of search. There are also searches for which the added overhead of checking isn't worth it, and we'd like to define some criteria for recognizing such situations.

    (a) Suppose for some search problem there are B successors of every state on the average, fraction P of which are previously visited (either on the agenda or the oldagenda) on the average. How many states can we expect in the search lattice up to and including level K for both visited-state pruning and no pruning at all?

    (b) Suppose on the average visited-state checking requires E units of time while all the other processing required of a state (finding it and adding it to the agenda) requires C units on the average. Give an inequality for deciding when visited-state checking pays off.

    (c) Now suppose that visited-state checking is not constant time but increases proportionately to the level in the search lattice; let's say the dependency is AK, K the level. What now is the inequality for deciding whether visited-state checking pays off?

10-14. **(a)** Consider the following program. Suppose it is only used when the first two arguments are bound (inputs) and the third argument is unbound (an output). Could a cut predicate improve efficiency? If so, under what circumstances, and where would you put it? Assume the rules are in a data-base in the order listed.

```
countup(I,[I|L],N) :- countup(I,L,N2), N is N2 + 1.
countup(I,[X|L],N) :- countup(I,L,N), not(I = X).
countup(I,[],0).
```

(b) Discuss why the cut predicate is often so tricky and hard to use.

10-15. (A,P) The Micro-Prolog dialect of Prolog has an interesting built-in feature: you can ask it to find and match the Kth rule or fact that is able to match some query. Implement this feature in the "standard" Prolog of this book, using **asserta**. Assume you are given a predicate expression P that is to be queried K times, and assume that P has no side effects so that it is OK to query the previous K - 1 matches to it.

10-16. Another kind of iteration not yet considered occurs with the "mapcar" feature of Lisp and the vector-processing features of APL. Something similar can be provided for every two-argument function predicate in Prolog. Suppose we have a function predicate f(X,Y). We would want to define a new predicate f_of_list(L,FL) such that FL is a list created by applying the f function to every element of the L list in turn. For example, suppose we had a defined predicate **double**:

```
double(X,Y) :- Y is 2 * X.
```

then querying

```
?- double_of_list([1,3,4],L).
```

will result in

$$L = [2,6,8]$$

Write a Prolog definition of **double_of_list**. Explain how the idea can be generalized to other predicates.

10-17. Implement each of the following heuristics in the way described in Section 10.11 using a six-argument **prefer** predicate. Assume they are called on by something like the best-first search program **bestsearch**.

  (a) Prefer a state whose fact-list description includes an predicate named **zzxxy** of one argument.

  (b) Prefer the state about which the fewest facts are true, assuming states are represented as lists of facts true in them.

  (c) Prefer the state whose path list involves the fewest fact additions and deletions along its course. (Assume states are described as lists of facts true in them.)

  (d) Prefer any state to one that was a successor to the last state selected.

10-18. Redo Exercise 5-12, but this time have the third argument be the *minimum* distance between two things. Allow for the possibility of cycles in the facts and more than one route between things.

10-19. (E) Suppose we defined a search problem in Prolog, and we now want to try searching backward, as perhaps when the forward search didn't work well.

To make things easier, assume there is a single goal state known beforehand.

(a) Give a simple way the definition of the cost function can be modified to provide a cost function for the new backward search.

(b) Give a simple way the evaluation function can be modified to provide an evaluation function for the new problem of searching backward.

(c) Describe in general terms how the successor predicate definitions must be modified. Note that some definitions are easier to use backward than others, so explain which ones these are.

10-20. (P) The program following[3] plays the game of Reversi. In this game, two players take turns placing pieces on a checkerboard; their pieces are indicated by the symbols X and O. Players place pieces so as to surround part of a row, column, or diagonal containing an unbroken string of the opponent's pieces; the pieces so surrounded are "captured" and become the opposite (surrounding player's) pieces. A player must always move so as to capture at least one opposing piece; if a player can't move, they forfeit their turn. The game is over when neither player can move; then the player with the most pieces on the board wins. Here's an example of the program output, in which first a human player makes a move, and then the computer.

```
8 X X X X X X _
7 0 0 0 0 X 0 _ _
6 X 0 X X X 0 _ _
5 X 0 0 X X 0 _ _
4 X 0 0 0 X 0 _ _
4 X 0 0 X 0 0 _ _
2 _ 0 0 X X 0 _ _
1 _ _ 0 0 X 0 _ _
  1 2 3 4 5 6 7 8
Give move:76.
8 X X X X X X _
7 0 0 0 0 X X _ _
6 X 0 X X X X _
5 X 0 0 X X X _ _
4 X 0 0 0 X 0 _ _
3 X 0 0 X 0 0 _ _
2 _ 0 0 X X 0 _ _
1 _ _ 0 0 X 0 _ _
  1 2 3 4 5 6 7 8
Evaluation of move 12 is 2
Evaluation of move 74 is 193
Evaluation of move 75 is 191
Evaluation of move 86 is 144
Evaluation of move 77 is 178
Evaluation of move 87 is 266
I make move 12
```

----

[3] This and other major programs in this book are available on tape from the publisher.

In the program, the board is stored as an 8-item list of 8-item lists, where a 0 element means a blank board position, a 1 element means a board position occupied by the human player, and a -1 element means a board position occupied by the computer player. States are represented as 10-item lists: the player who last moved, the move they took, and the eight rows of the resulting board position.

(a) The program shown following uses a simple evaluation function. Redefine pick_best_move so it uses nonnumeric heuristics to select a move. That is, don't use any numbers for move selection except to look up board positions by row and column number.

(b) Now change gamesearch so the computer can play against itself, using your heuristics for player 1 and its evaluation function for player -1. Make sure by your heuristics that player 1 wins—improve the heuristics as necessary. Then use the heuristics for player -1, and the evaluation function for player 1, and further improve the heuristics as necessary so that player -1 wins.

(c) Now change the pick_best_move rules for player -1 so it looks ahead one move to anticipate what the other player will do, and chooses the move leading to the best result assuming player 1 always makes the best choice available to them. Run this smarter player against the heuristics from part (b) used for player 1. Who wins?

(d) Probably player -1 won in part (c), but the comparison wasn't fair because player 1 doesn't look ahead. But they don't need to if they just have better heuristics. Demonstrate this.

```
/* Top-level routines */
go :-
  write('This program plays the game of Reversi (X is you, O is me).'),
  nl, start_state(SS), gamesearch(SS).

start_state([-1,none,Z,Z,Z,[0,0,0,1,-1,0,0,0],[0,0,0,-1,1,0,0,0],Z,Z,Z])
  :- zero_row(Z).
    zero_row([0,0,0,0,0,0,0,0]).

  gamesearch(State) :- goalreached(State), print_win(State), !.
  gamesearch([-1,M|B]) :- not(get_move(B,1,S,NB)),
    write('You cannot move so I get another turn.'), nl, !,
    gamesearch([1,M|B]).
  gamesearch([-1,OM|B]) :- print_board(B), write('Give move:'),
    repeatread(Movecode), move_decode(Movecode,Move),
    get_move(B,1,Move,NB), !, gamesearch([1,Move|NB]).
  gamesearch([1,M|B]) :- print_board(B),
    pick_best_move([1,M|B],Newstate),
    write_move(Newstate), !, gamesearch(Newstate).
  gamesearch([1,M|B]) :- not(get_move(B,-1,S,NB)),
```

```
    not(get_move(B,1,S,NB)), print_win([1,MIB]), !.
gamesearch([1,MIB]) :- not(get_move(B,-1,S,NB)),
  write('I cannot move so you get another turn.'),
  nl, !, gamesearch([-1,MIB]).
gamesearch(S) :- print_win(S), !.


/* Intermediate routines */
pick_best_move(S,NS) :- asserta(ebest(none,1000000)), successor(S,S2),
  eval(S2,E2), write_eval(S2,E2), ebest(S1,E1), E2<E1,
  retract(ebest(S1,E1)), asserta(ebest(S2,E2)), fail.
pick_best_move(S,NS) :- ebest(NS,E), retract(ebest(NS,E)).


goalreached([X,YIB]) :- not(somezero(B)).


somezero(B) :- member(R,B), member(0,R).


successor([OP,LastmoveIOldboard],[P,MINewboard]) :-
  opposite(OP,P), get_move(Oldboard,P,M,Newboard).


opposite(1,-1).
opposite(-1,1).


repeatread(M) :- read(M).
repeatread(M) :- write('Invalid move.  Try again:'),
  nl, repeatread(M).
move_decode(M,[X,Y]) :- X is M//10, Y is M mod 10.


/* Printing routines */
write_move([P,[X,Y]IB]) :- Move is (10*X)+Y, write('I make move '),
  write(Move), nl, !.
write_eval([P,[X,Y]IB],E) :- write('Evaluation of move '),
  Movecode is (10*X)+Y, write(Movecode), write(' is '),
  write(E), nl, !.


print_win([P,MIB]) :- print_board(B),
  countup(1,B,N1), countup(-1,B,N2), print_win2(N1,N2).
print_win2(N1,N2) :- N2<N1, write('Congratulations! You win.'), nl.
print_win2(N1,N2) :- N2>N1, write('Sorry—I win.'), nl.
print_win2(N,N) :- write('The game is a draw.'), nl.


countup(I,[],0) :- !.
countup(I,[RIB],N) :- countrow(I,R,N2), countup(I,B,N3), N is N2+N3.


countrow(I,[],0) :- !.
countrow(I,[IIL],N) :- countrow(I,L,N2), N is N2+1, !.
countrow(I,[JIL],N) :- countrow(I,L,N).
```

```
print_board(B) :- reverse(B,RB), print_board2(RB,8), !.
print_board2([],N) :- write('  1 2 3 4 5 6 7 8'), nl.
print_board2([Row|Board],N) :- write(N), print_row(Row), N2 is N-1,
  print_board2(Board,N2).
print_row([]) :- nl.
print_row([I|Row]) :- decode(I,DI), write(' '), write(DI),
  print_row(Row).

decode(0,'_').
decode(1,'X').
decode(-1,'O').

/* Move generation */
get_move(B,P,[X,Y],NB) :- get_move2(B,[X,Y],FR,BR,FI,BI),
  fix_key_row_half(P,FI,NFI), fix_key_row_half(P,BI,NBI),
  fix_rows(FR,X,P,NFR), fix_rows(BR,X,P,NBR),
  not(nochange(FI,NFI,BI,NBI,FR,NFR,BR,NBR)),
  reverse(NFI,RFI), reverse(NFR,RFR),
  append(RFI,[P|NBI],Row), append(RFR,[Row|NBR],NB).

nochange(X,X,Y,Y,A,B,C,D) :- samefront(A,B), samefront(C,D).

samefront([],[]) :- !.
samefront([X|L],[X|M]).

get_move2(B,M,FR,BR,FI,BI) :- get_move3(B,1,[],M,FR,BR,FI,BI).

get_move3([R|B],Y,FR,[X,Y],FR,B,FI,BI) :- get_move4(R,1,[],X,FI,BI).
get_move3([R|B],Y,FR,M,FRF,BR,FI,BI) :- Y2 is Y + 1,
  get_move3(B,Y2,[R|FR],M,FRF,BR,FI,BI).

get_move4([O|R],X,FI,X,FI,R).
get_move4([I|R],X,FI,XF,FIF,BI) :- X2 is X + 1,
  get_move4(R,X2,[I|FI],XF,FIF,BI).

/* Board update for a particular move */
fix_key_row_half(P,R,NR) :- fix_key_row_half2(P,R,NR), !.
fix_key_row_half(P,R,R) :- !.

fix_key_row_half2(P,[],[]) :- !, fail.
fix_key_row_half2(P,[O|L],[O|L]) :- !, fail.
fix_key_row_half2(P,[P|L],[P|L]) :- !.
fix_key_row_half2(P,[OP|L],[P|L2]) :- opposite(P,OP),
  fix_key_row_half2(P,L,L2).
```

```
fix_rows([],X,P,[]) :- !.
fix_rows([R],X,P,[R]) :- !.
fix_rows(B,X,P,NB) :- Xm1 is X-1, Xp1 is X + 1, opposite(P,OP),
    fix_rows2(B,OP,NB,Xm1,X,Xp1,VL,VM,VR), !.
fix_rows2(B,OP,B,dead,dead,dead,VL,VM,VR).
fix_rows2([],OP,[],XL,XM,XR,VL,VM,VR) :- topfix(OP,VL),
    topfix(OP,VM), topfix(OP,VR).
fix_rows2([R|B],OP,[NR|NB],XL,XM,XR,VL,VM,VR) :-
    fix_rowL(R,OP,1,NR,XL,XM,XR,VL,VM,VR,NXL,NXM,NXR),
    fix_rows2(B,OP,NB,NXL,NXM,NXR,VL,VM,VR).

topfix(OP,OP) :- !.
topfix(OP,V).

fix_rowL(R,OP,X,NR,dead,dead,XR,VL,VM,VR,dead,dead,NXR) :-
    fix_rowR(R,OP,X,NR,XR,VR,NXR).
fix_rowL(R,OP,X,NR,dead,XM,XR,VL,VM,VR,dead,NXM,NXR) :-
    fix_rowM(R,OP,X,NR,XM,XR,VM,VR,NXM,NXR).
fix_rowL(R,OP,X,NR,0,XM,XR,OP,VM,VR,dead,NXM,NXR) :-
    fix_rowM(R,OP,X,NR,XM,XR,VM,VR,NXM,NXR).
fix_rowL([0|R],OP,X,[0|NR],X,XM,XR,OP,VM,VR,dead,NXM,NXR)
    :- Xp1 is X + 1, fix_rowM(R,OP,Xp1,NR,XM,XR,VM,VR,NXM,NXR).
fix_rowL([OP|R],OP,X,[VL|NR],X,XM,XR,VL,VM,VR,Xm1,NXM,NXR) :-
    Xp1 is X + 1, Xm1 is X-1,
    fix_rowM(R,OP,Xp1,NR,XM,XR,VM,VR,NXM,NXR).
fix_rowL([P|R],OP,X,[P|NR],X,XM,XR,P,VM,VR,dead,NXM,NXR) :-
    Xp1 is X + 1, opposite(OP,P),
    fix_rowM(R,OP,Xp1,NR,XM,XR,VM,VR,NXM,NXR).
fix_rowL([I|R],OP,X,[I|NR],XL,XM,XR,VL,VM,VR,NXL,NXM,NXR) :-
    Xp1 is X + 1,
    fix_rowL(R,OP,Xp1,NR,XL,XM,XR,VL,VM,VR,NXL,NXM,NXR).

fix_rowM(R,OP,X,NR,dead,XR,VM,VR,dead,NXR) :-
    fix_rowR(R,OP,X,NR,XR,VR,NXR).
fix_rowM([0|R],OP,X,[0|NR],X,XR,OP,VR,dead,NXR) :- Xp1 is X + 1,
    fix_rowR(R,OP,Xp1,NR,XR,VR,NXR).
fix_rowM([OP|R],OP,X,[VM|NR],X,XR,VM,VR,X,NXR) :- Xp1 is X + 1,
    fix_rowR(R,OP,Xp1,NR,XR,VR,NXR).
fix_rowM([P|R],OP,X,[P|NR],X,XR,P,VR,dead,NXR) :- Xp1 is X + 1,
    opposite(OP,P), fix_rowR(R,OP,Xp1,NR,XR,VR,NXR).
fix_rowM([I|R],OP,X,[I|NR],XM,XR,VM,VR,NVM,NXR) :- Xp1 is X + 1,
    fix_rowM(R,OP,Xp1,NR,XM,XR,VM,VR,NVM,NXR).
    fix_rowR(R,OP,X,R,dead,VR,dead).
    fix_rowR(R,OP,X,R,9,OP,dead).
```

```
fix_rowR([0|R],OP,X,[0|R],X,OP,dead).
fix_rowR([OP|R],OP,X,[VR|R],X,VR,Xp1) :- Xp1 is X + 1.
fix_rowR([P|R],OP,X,[P|R],X,P,dead) :- opposite(OP,P).
fix_rowR([I|R],OP,X,[I|NR],XR,VR,NXR) :- Xp1 is X + 1,
  fix_rowR(R,OP,Xp1,NR,XR,VR,NXR).

/* Evaluation function */
eval([P,[X,Y],A,B,C,D,E,F,G,H],Ev) :- eval2s(A,B,Ev1),
  eval2s(H,G,Ev2), eval2m(C,Ev3), eval2m(D,Ev4),
  eval2m(E,Ev5), eval2m(F,Ev6),
  Ev is -P*(Ev1 + Ev2 + Ev3 + Ev4 + Ev5 + Ev6), !.

eval2m([A,B,C,D,E,F,G,H],Ev) :-
  Ev2 is ((30*A) + (-15*B) + C + D + E + F + (-15*G) + (30*H)),
  sc(A,B,C1), sc(H,G,C2), Ev is Ev2 + C1 + C2, !.

sc(0,B,0).
sc(A,0,0).
sc(1,1,30).
sc(1,-1,20).
sc(-1,-1,-30).
sc(-1,1,-20).

eval2s([A,B,C,D,E,F,G,H],[I,J,K,L,M,N,O,P],Ev) :-
  Ev2 is
    (200*A) + (-50*B) + (30*C) + (30*D) + (30*E) + (30*F) + (-50*G) + (200*
  Ev3 is
    -((50*I) + (100*J) + (15*K) + (15*L) + (15*M) + (15*N) + (100*O) + (50*
  sc2(A,I,J,B,Ev4), sc2(H,G,O,P,Ev5), sc(C,K,Ev6), sc(D,L,Ev7),
  sc(E,M,Ev8), sc(F,N,Ev9),
  Ev is Ev2 + Ev3 + Ev4 + Ev5 + Ev6 + Ev7 + Ev8 + Ev9, !.

sc2(0,B,C,D,0).
sc2(A,B,C,D,Ev) :- sc(A,B,E1), sc(A,C,E2), sc(A,D,E3),
  Ev is 3*(E1 + E2 + E2 + E3).

/* Utility functions */
reverse(L,RL) :- reverse2(L,[],RL), !.

reverse2([],L,L).
reverse2([X|L],L2,RL) :- reverse2(L,[X|L2],RL).

append([],L,L) :- !.
append([X|L],L2,[X|L3]) :- append(L,L2,L3).

member(X,[X|L]).
member(X,[Y|L]) :- member(X,L).
```

11

![chapter heading banner]

ABSTRACTION
IN SEARCH

When people solve without computers the search problems discussed in the last two chapters, they only use the techniques so far described as a last resort. Instead, they try to reason about abstractions, what's known as *hierarchical reasoning*.

Abstraction is simplifying your model of the world so you can reason more easily about it. Intermediate predicates for rule-based systems (see Section 7.5) are one form of abstraction, since they summarize a category of data and provide a handle on that summarization. Abstraction is essential in organizing and managing large numbers of facts, as we will see in the next chapter. Abstraction is also a way to simplify large search problems. Search abstraction works best when a problem is decomposable, and exploits the preconditions and postconditions of operators.

11.1 MEANS-ENDS ANALYSIS

The classic technique for solving search problems by abstraction is means-ends analysis. It applies to those decomposable search problems (see Section 9.12), and some nondecomposable ones, for which clear "major operators" or "recommended operators" on the solution path can be identified in advance. To specify these operators for specific situations, means-ends analysis needs something like a table. Usually these tables refer to the difference between the current state and the goal state, and are thus called *difference tables*.

Difference tables describe operators in terms of their preconditions and postconditions (see Section 9.4). So they're akin to the **successor** definitions of Chapter 10, but with one big difference: difference tables only *recommend* an operator appropriate to a state and a goal, with no concern if the operator can actually be applied to the state. Difference tables provide a way of decomposing a problem into three, hopefully, simpler subproblems: a subproblem of getting from the current state to a state in which we can apply the recommended operator, a subproblem of applying the operator, and a subproblem of going from there to the goal state. Formally, a search from a starting state S to some goal state G is decomposed into:

1. Satisfying the preconditions (prerequisites) for some recommended operator O when starting from S, by going to state S2.
2. Applying operator O to S2 resulting in state S3 (by postconditions).
3. Going from S3 to the goal state G.

The first and third steps are search problems themselves, possibly requiring additional decompositions of their own by the difference table. So means-ends analysis is recursive search. Means-ends analysis is also hierarchical reasoning because we start with big wholes and try to gradually reason down to little details. The ends truly justify the means.

Complete and correct specification in the difference table of preconditions and postconditions of operators is essential for means-ends analysis. In particular, you must carefully distinguish preconditions from the looser conditions recommending operators. Both could be mixed together in the **successor** rules of Chapter 10, but that won't work here.

11.2 A SIMPLE EXAMPLE

Means-ends analysis is useful for many human "planning" activities. Here's a simple example of planning for an office worker. Suppose we have a difference table of three rules (see Figure 11-1), written informally as

If in your current state you are hungry, and in your goal state you are not hungry, then either the "visit_cafeteria" or "visit_vending_machine" operator is recommended.

If in your current state you do not have change, and if in your goal state you have change, then the "visit_your_office" operator or the "visit_secretary" operator is recommended.

If in your current state you do not know where something is, and in your goal state you do know, then either the "visit_your_office," "visit_secretary," or "visit_colleague" operator is recommended.

We need preconditions and postconditions for the preceding operators:

Preconditions of visit_cafeteria: you know where the cafeteria is.

Postconditions of visit_cafeteria: you are no longer hungry.

Preconditions of visit_vending_machine: you know where the vending machine is and you have change.

Postconditions of visit_vending_machine: you are no longer hungry.

Preconditions of visit_your_office: none (we assume everyone knows where his or her office is).

Postconditions of visit_your_office: you have change and you know where everything is (since you can look it up in, say, the phone directory).

Preconditions of visit_secretary: you know where the secretary is and the secretary is available.

Postconditions of visit_secretary: you have change, and you know where everything is.

Preconditions of visit_colleague: none.

Postconditions of visit_colleague: you know where everything is.

Since we will implement difference tables in Prolog, we'll follow the usual top-to-bottom and left-to-right conventions about order of action. So we will try difference-table rules in the order listed, try operator alternatives in the order listed, and try to satisfy preconditions and postconditions in the order listed. So the order of rows and columns in Figure 11-1 is significant.

Let's illustrate means-ends analysis for the situation in which you are hungry, you have no change, a secretary is available, and you are new and don't know

Desired situation	Should you visit? cafeteria?	Should you visit vending machine?	Should you visit your office?	Should you visit? secretary?	Should you visit colleague?
You want to be not hungry, and you're hungry now	yes	yes	no	no	no
You want to have change, and you don't now	no	no	yes	yes	no
You want to know where something is	no	no	yes	yes	yes

Figure 11-1. Tabular representation of the operatior recommendations (difference table) for the office-worker problem.

where anything is besides your own office; and your goal is any state in which you are not hungry. (Other things can be true of your final state besides being not hungry, but hunger relief is what you insist on.)

1. The first recommendation rule succeeds, so you want to visit the cafeteria.
2. This has the precondition that you know where the cafeteria is, and since you don't, you must recursively call on means-ends analysis to find a way to change that discrepancy (difference).
3. Only the third recommendation rule can handle this kind of a difference between a state and a goal, so you try to apply the first operator suggested, visit_your_office. (That is, you will look through the telephone directory to locate the cafeteria.)
4. There are no preconditions for visit_your_office (everybody knows where his or her office is), so it can be applied without further recursion. And the state after visit_your_office satisfies the preconditions of visit_cafeteria as you hoped—no postconditions will interfere.
5. The postcondition of visit_cafeteria is that you are no longer hungry, and the goal of the problem was to make this become true. So you're done. So the operator sequence found to solve the problem is visit_your_office and then visit_cafeteria.

To show the importance of difference-table order, suppose we switch the order of visit_cafeteria and visit_vending_machine in the first rule, switch the order of visit_your_office and visit_secretary in the second rule, put visit_colleague first in the third rule, and switch the second and third recommendation rules, so we have (see Figure 11-2)

If in your current state you are hungry and in your goal state you are not hungry, then either the "visit_vending_machine" or "visit_cafeteria" operator is recommended.

If in your current state you do not know where something is, and in your goal state you do know, then either the "visit_colleague," "visit_your_office," or "visit_secretary" operator is recommended.

If in your current state you do not have change and if in your goal state you have change, then the "visit_secretary" operator or the "visit_your_office" operator is recommended.

Let's redo the problem in which you are hungry, you need change, a secretary is available, and you don't know anything, and you want to get to a state in which you are no longer hungry. Means-ends analysis finds a different, but equally valid, solution:

1. The first rule succeeds, so it is recommended that you first try to visit a vending machine. This has two preconditions: that you know where one is and you have change.
2. You recursively call on means-ends analysis to satisfy these preconditions. The starting state is the original starting state, and the new goal is any state

in which you know where a vending machine is and you have change.

3. The first rule won't help this difference, but the second rule will, the one that recommends visiting a colleague (to ask where a vending machine is). This has no preconditions, so you can directly apply it.

4. After applying the postconditions of visit_colleague, you must still get to a state in which we have change; remember, visit_vending_machine had two preconditions. (All my colleagues are poor and never have any change—or so they tell me.) So you need a recursive "postcondition search" to accomplish this, from the state in which you are hungry, you need change, a secretary is available, and you know everything. For this difference the third rule is recommended, and the recommended operator is visit_secretary.

5. This has two preconditions: that you know where the secretary is and that secretary is available. Both conditions hold in the current state (the first condition since the beginning, and the second condition was just accomplished by visit_colleague). So you can directly apply visit_secretary.

6. Now taking into account the postconditions of visit_secretary, you're in a state in which you are hungry, you have change, a secretary is available, and you know where everything is. This satisfies all the conditions of the visit_vending_machine operator, so you apply it. Examining its postconditions, you see you've reached a goal state.

7. So the overall operator sequence is to visit your colleague to find out where a vending machine is and where the secretary is, visit the secretary to get change, and then visit a vending machine.

Desired situation	Should you visit vending machine?	Should you visit cafeteria?	Should you visit colleague?	Should you visit secretary?	Should you visit your office?
You want to be not hungry, and you're hungry now	yes	yes	no	no	no
You want to have change, and you don't now	no	no	no	yes	yes
You want to know where something is	no	no	yes	yes (but try third)	yes (but try second)

Figure 11-2. Different difference table for the office-worker problem. (Note: You must try the third row before the second.)

This example didn't require backtracking, but you may need it when your first choice for a rule or operator doesn't pan out, just as with depth-first search. A choice doesn't pan out when no way can be found to satisfy some preconditions or to handle some postconditions. However, the more "intelligent" nature of means-ends analysis compared to the other search methods means that it backtracks a lot less than they do on nicely decomposable problems.

This example of means-ends analysis is highly simplified. If we wanted to realistically model the way people solve daily problems like the preceding, we would need a lot more operators, preconditions, and postconditions. Nevertheless, many psychologists argue that something like means-ends analysis underlies much human activity.

11.3 PARTIAL STATE DESCRIPTION

In the preceding example, we described goal states by giving a few facts that must be true in them. For instance, we said the overall goal was a state in which you are no longer hungry. This *partial state description* is very common with means-ends analysis, because it's hard to define a goal achievement predicate, like the goal-reached in Chapter 10, when each precondition decomposition has a different goal.

Since means-ends analysis is driven by differences between states, we must be careful in defining this difference for partial state descriptions. Basically, we can go through the list of facts describing the goal G and "cross out" facts also true for current state S. Here's the definition:

difference([ ],S,[ ]).
difference([P|G],S,G2) :- singlemember(P,S), !, difference(G,S,G2).
difference([P|G],S,[P|G2]) :- difference(G,S,G2).

(Predicate singlemember was defined in Section 10.7 and checks only once whether an item is a member of a list; the ! (cut symbol) was explained in Section 10.7 too.) Then we write difference-table rules to refer to these differences.

So for instance:

?-difference
    ([on(b,c),on(e,f),on(a,e)],[on(a,b),on(b,c),on(d,e),on(e,f)],D).
D = [on(a,e)]

11.4 IMPLEMENTATION OF MEANS-ENDS ANALYSIS

With these details out of the way, implementation of means-ends analysis is straightforward. We represent the difference table with rules and/or facts defining

recommended(<difference>,<operator>)

where <difference> is some result (binding of the third argument) of the difference predicate defined in the last section, and <operator> is the name of a recommended operator. Each operator will have at least one **recommended** definition.

Preconditions are best expressed as two-argument facts. The first argument can be the operator, and the second argument the list of associated preconditions, predicate expressions that must be present in a state description for the operator to be used in that state:

precondition(<operator>,[<predexpr1 >, <predexpr2> ,...]).

But postconditions are tricky. An operator cannot only make certain conditions true, but can make certain other true conditions become false—otherwise, we couldn't undo anything. So we'll distinguish two kinds of postconditions:

addpostcondition(<operator>,[<predexpr1 >, <predexpr2>...]).
deletepostcondition(<operator>,[<predexpr1 >, <predexpr2>...]).

By the way, operators can have arguments just as in Chapter 9, and these arguments can be referenced in the precondition and postcondition lists. Variable arguments bound in the **recommended** facts and rules can be referenced in the preconditions and postconditions. [1]

That covers the format of the problem-dependent part of means-ends analysis; now for the problem-independent part. We'll use *double recursion*, which sounds like a horrible disease but just means a self-referencing program that self-references twice. Our top-level rule will be a recursive means_ends predicate of four arguments:

State, a complete list of facts true in the starting state (an input);

Goal, a list of those facts that must be true in the goal state, or a partial description of the goal state (an input);

Oplist, the list of operators that will get you from the starting state to the goal state (an output);

Goalstate, the complete list of facts true in the goal state (an output).

Here's the program:

```
/* Problem-independent means-ends analysis */
means_ends(State,Goal,[],State) :- difference(Goal,State,[]), !.
means_ends(State,Goal,Oplist,Goalstate) :-
  difference(Goal,State,D),
  recommended(Dsub,Operator), subset(Dsub,D),
  precondition(Operator,Prelist),
  means_ends(State,Prelist,Preoplist,Prestate),
  deletepostcondition(Operator,Deletepostlist),
  deleteitems(Deletepostlist,Prestate,Prestate2),
  addpostcondition(Operator,Addpostlist),
  union(Addpostlist,Prestate2,Postlist),
  means_ends(Postlist,Goal,Postoplist,Goalstate),
  append(Preoplist,[Operator|Postoplist],Oplist).
```

[1] Except in Turbo Prolog.

This recursive program has a single basis step (the first line), which says we don't need any operators to solve a problem in which the starting state includes all the goal facts. The rest of the lines are a single induction step, which you'll note has two recursive calls: the first for the preconditions, the second for the postconditions. The lines say to first compute the list of facts different between **State** and **Goal**, and find a recommended operator for some subset of those facts. Look up the preconditions of the operator and recursively call **means_ends** to figure how to satisfy them. Then look up the deletion postconditions and delete them from the final state resulting from the precondition recursion; look up the addition postconditions, and add them to that state. Now we have the state after application of the original recommended operator. So recursively call **means_ends** to figure how to get from here to the original goal. The final operator list for the whole problem is the appending together of the precondition-recursion operator list, the recommended operator, and the postcondition-recursion operator list.

The **means_ends** program requires five utility functions: **singlemember**, **subset**, **append**, **union**, and **deleteitems**. The **singlemember** (defined in Section 10.7) checks whether an item is a member of a list; it is written to always fail on backtracking into it. The **subset** (defined in Section 5.7) says whether every item in its list first argument is also a member of its list second argument. The **append** (defined in Section 5.6) glues two lists together to create a new list. The **union** is like the **append** except it removes duplicates from the result. The **deleteitems** removes all members of one list from another list, and uses the **delete** predicate of Section 5.6. To improve efficiency, cut symbols (!) appear in some of these definitions.

```
/* Utility functions for means-ends analysis */
singlemember(X,[X|L]) :- !.
singlemember(X,[Y|L]) :- singlemember(X,L).

subset([],L).
subset([X|L],L2) :- singlemember(X,L2), subset(L,L2).

append([],L,L).
append([X|L],L2,[X|L3]) :- append(L,L2,L3).

union([],L,L).
union([X|L1],L2,L3) :- singlemember(X,L2), !, union(L1,L2,L3).
union([X|L1],L2,[X|L3]) :- union(L1,L2,L3).

deleteitems([],L,L).
deleteitems([X|L],L2,L3) :- delete(X,L2,L4), deleteitems(L,L4,L3).

delete(X,[],[]).
delete(X,[X|L],M) :- !, delete(X,L,M).
delete(X,[Y|L],[Y|M]) :- delete(X,L,M).
```

To make the means-ends program more user-friendly, it's helpful to put in some error checking. This goes after the two original rules for **means_ends**.

```
means_ends(State,Goal,Oplist,Goalstate) :-
  difference(Goal,State,D), recommended(Dsub,Operator),
  subset(Dsub,D), not(precondition(Operator,Prelist)),
  write('Bug found: no preconditions given for operator '),
  write(Operator), nl, !, fail.
means_ends(State,Goal,Oplist,Goalstate) :-
  difference(Goal,State,D),
  recommended(Dsub,Operator), subset(Dsub,D),
  not(deletepostcondition(Operator,Deletepostlist)),
  write('Bug found: no deletepostconditions given for operator '),
  write(Operator), nl, !, fail.
means_ends(State,Goal,Oplist,Goalstate) :-
  difference(Goal,State,D),
  recommended(Dsub,Operator), subset(Dsub,D),
  not(addpostcondition(Operator,Addpostlist)),
  write('Bug found: no addpostconditions given for operator '),
  write(Operator), nl, !, fail.
```

11.5 A HARDER EXAMPLE: FLASHLIGHT REPAIR

Car repair is often a decomposable search problem and thus appropriate for means-ends analysis, but it's too complicated to use as an example here. So let's consider repair of a flashlight, the kind shown in Figure 11-3. This flashlight has two batteries inside a case touching a light bulb. To reach the batteries you must disassemble the case, and to reach the light bulb you must disassemble the top as well as disassembling the case. We'll use the following facts to describe states in flashlight repair (which mean what they suggest):

```
defective(batteries).
ok(batteries).
defective(light).
ok(light).
open(case).
closed(case).
unbroken(case).
broken(case).
open(top).
closed(top).
inside(batteries).
outside(batteries).
```

We'll assume the following operators: replace_batteries, replace_light, disassemble_case, assemble_case, disassemble_top, assemble_top, turn_over_case, and smash_case.

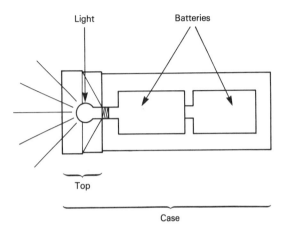

Figure 11-3. Typical flashlight, assembled.

Now let's apply our means-ends program to the flashlight-repair problem. First we need a difference table (summarized in Figure 11-4), stating recommended operators with facts of the predicate name **recommended**:

```
recommended([ok(batteries)],replace_batteries).
recommended([ok(light)],replace_light).
recommended([open(case)],disassemble_case).
recommended([open(case)],smash_case).
recommended([open(top)],disassemble_top).
recommended([open(top)],smash_case).
recommended([closed(case)],assemble_case).
recommended([closed(top)],assemble_top).
recommended([outside(batteries)],turn_over_case).
recommended([outside(batteries)],smash_case).
```

As you may recall, the first argument to **recommended** is part of the difference of the goal from the current state, and the second argument is the recommended operator. So the first argument is what we want to become true, what isn't true in the current state. So read the first fact as "If you want to get the batteries to be OK because they aren't now, try the replace_batteries operator." All these recommendations refer to single-fact desires, but that's only because it's hard to do two things at once with one action on a flashlight; other kinds of repair may be different.

The order of the **recommended** rules is important, because they'll be considered by the Prolog interpreter in that order, and the first one applying to the given state-goal difference will be the first one used. So we've put in front those for the most important operators, the "replace_batteries" and "replace_light" operators. Several situations suggest the "smash_case" operator besides another operator, but we want to make "smash_case" a last resort, and hence we put the lines mentioning it after the corresponding lines for the alternatives. Now for the preconditions:

Desired situation	Should you replace batteries?	Should you replace light?	Should you disassemble case?	Should you disassemble top?	Should you assemble case?	Should you assemble top?	Should you turn over case?	Should you smash case?
You want batteries OK, when they aren't	yes	no	no	no	no	no	no	no
You want light OK, when it isn't	no	yes	no	no	no	no	no	no
You want case open, when it isn't	no	no	yes	no	no	no	no	yes
You want top open, when it isn't	no	no	no	yes	no	no	no	yes
You want case closed, when it isn't	no	no	no	no	yes	no	no	no
You want top closed, when it isn't	no	no	no	no	no	yes	no	no
You want batteries outside, when they aren't	no	no	no	no	no	no	yes	yes

Figure 11-4. Difference table for flashlight repair.

```
precondition(replace_batteries,
   [open(case),outside(batteries),unbroken(case)]).
precondition(replace_light,[open(top)]).
precondition(disassemble_case,[closed(case)]).
precondition(assemble_case,
   [open(case),closed(top),unbroken(case)]).
precondition(disassemble_top,[open(case),closed(top)]).
precondition(assemble_top,[open(top)]).
precondition(turn_over_case,[open(case)]).
precondition(smash_case,[]).
```

Notice we don't need to list everything that must be true for an operator to be applied, only the major conditions that imply everything else. For instance, the precondition for "replace_light" that the top be open implies that the case be open first, but we can find this in looking up the preconditions to the disassemble_top operator anyway. So means-ends analysis lets us put preconditions in the places that make our programs clearest.

Now for the postconditions. Often the facts deleted by postconditions (deletepostconditions) are just the preconditions, and often the facts added by postconditions (addpostconditions) are just the opposites of the deletepostconditions. So postconditions are often easy to write. But this isn't true when operators have "side effects," like the "smash_case" operator that does several things simultaneously—and that's one of the reasons it's not a very good operator.

```
deletepostcondition(replace_batteries,
  [outside(batteries),defective(batteries)]).
deletepostcondition(replace_light,[defective(light)]).
deletepostcondition(disassemble_case,[closed(case)]).
deletepostcondition(assemble_case,[open(case)]).
deletepostcondition(disassemble_top,[closed(top)]).
deletepostcondition(assemble_top,[open(top)]).
deletepostcondition(turn_over_case,[inside(batteries)]).
deletepostcondition(smash_case,
  [unbroken(case),closed(case),closed(top),inside(batteries)]).

addpostcondition(replace_batteries,
  [inside(batteries),ok(batteries)]).
addpostcondition(replace_light,[ok(light)]).
addpostcondition(disassemble_case,[open(case)]).
addpostcondition(assemble_case,[closed(case)]).
addpostcondition(disassemble_top,[open(top)]).
addpostcondition(assemble_top,[closed(top)]).
addpostcondition(turn_over_case,[outside(batteries)]).
addpostcondition(smash_case,
  [broken(case),open(case),open(top),outside(batteries)]).
```

Note that even if some **deletepostcondition** facts are not true for a state, no harm is done—those facts will just be ignored—because the **delete** predicate and hence the **deleteitems** predicate always succeed, even when they don't delete anything.

11.6 RUNNING THE FLASHLIGHT PROGRAM

Let's run our flashlight and means-ends analysis code for the situation in which the batteries are defective and we want to get the flashlight working again. The correct solution is shown in Figure 11-5. Let's assume the flashlight is assembled and unbroken when we start out, so the starting state is

```
[closed(case),closed(top),inside(batteries),defective(batteries),
  ok(light),unbroken(case)].
```

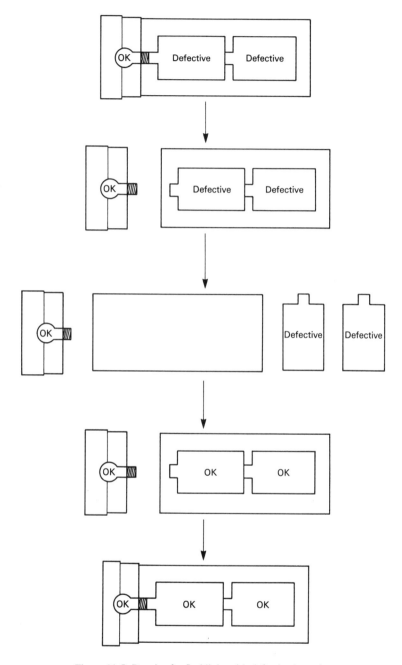

Figure 11-5. Repair of a flashlight with defective batteries.

The goal is any state in which the following facts are true (i.e., this partial goal description holds):

[ok(batteries),closed(case),closed(top)].

(A flashlight isn't much good unless it's put back together again, hence the last two conditions.) To do means-ends analysis, we supply the preceding two lists as inputs (the first two arguments) to means_ends, leaving the last two arguments unbound:

> ?- means_ends([closed(case),closed(top),inside(batteries),
>   defective(batteries),ok(light),unbroken(case)],
>   [ok(batteries),closed(case),closed(top)], Operators, Final_state).

What will happen is summarized in Figures 11-6 (an overview) and 11-7 (the details). In the latter figure the four arguments to means_ends (State, Goal, Oplist, and Goalstate) are listed for each call, plus the local variable Operator. The calls are drawn like the predicate hierarchies of Figures 10-5, 10-6, and 10-7; be careful not to confuse Figures 11-6 and 11-7 with search graphs, which are superficially similar. Oplist and Goalstate are the outputs bound as a result of reasoning, so the values shown for them are their final bindings.

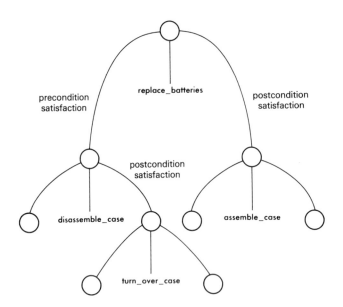

Figure 11-6. Form of the solution of the dead-batteries flashlight problem by means-ends analysis (Figure 11-7 gives a more detailed picture).

In more detail, here's what Figure 11-7 recounts. Fasten your seat belts.

1. The **difference** function is applied to the original goal and the starting state. The last two facts in the goal cancel out, leaving only [ok(batteries)]. For this difference, "replace_batteries" is the recommended operator. The problem can then be recursively divided into three parts: satisfying the preconditions of replace_batteries, applying it, and going from there to the original goal.

2. The three preconditions of replace_batteries are that the case is open, the batteries are outside the case, and the case is unbroken. So we recursively call the predicate **means_ends** with first argument the original starting state, and second argument (partial goal description) the precondition list

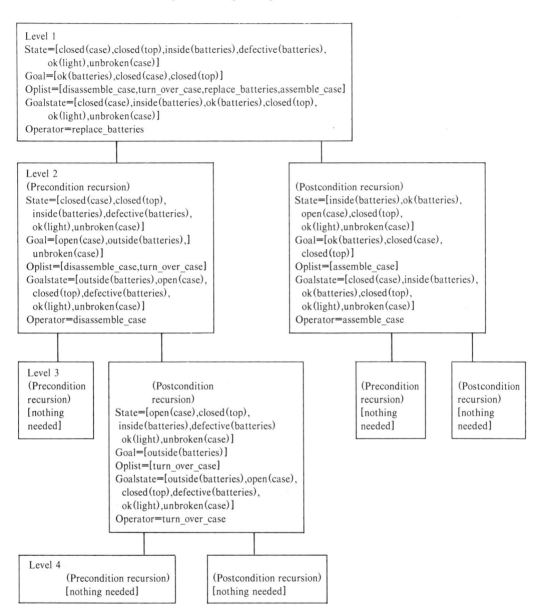

Level 1
State=[closed(case),closed(top),inside(batteries),defective(batteries),
     ok(light),unbroken(case)]
Goal=[ok(batteries),closed(case),closed(top)]
Oplist=[disassemble_case,turn_over_case,replace_batteries,assemble_case]
Goalstate=[closed(case),inside(batteries),ok(batteries),closed(top),
     ok(light),unbroken(case)]
Operator=replace_batteries

Level 2
(Precondition recursion)
State=[closed(case),closed(top),
  inside(batteries),defective(batteries),
  ok(light),unbroken(case)]
Goal=[open(case),outside(batteries),]
  unbroken(case)]
Oplist=[disassemble_case,turn_over_case]
Goalstate=[outside(batteries),open(case),
  closed(top),defective(batteries),
  ok(light),unbroken(case)]
Operator=disassemble_case

(Postcondition recursion)
State=[inside(batteries),ok(batteries),
  open(case),closed(top),
  ok(light),unbroken(case)]
Goal=[ok(batteries),closed(case),
  closed(top)]
Oplist=[assemble_case]
Goalstate=[closed(case),inside(batteries),
  ok(batteries),closed(top),
  ok(light),unbroken(case)]
Operator=assemble_case

Level 3
(Precondition
recursion)
[nothing
needed]

(Postcondition
recursion)
State=[open(case),closed(top),
  inside(batteries),defective(batteries)
  ok(light),unbroken(case)]
Goal=[outside(batteries)]
Oplist=[turn_over_case]
Goalstate=[outside(batteries),open(case),
  closed(top),defective(batteries),
  ok(light),unbroken(case)]
Operator=turn_over_case

(Precondition
recursion)
[nothing
needed]

(Postcondition
recursion)
[nothing
needed]

Level 4
       (Precondition recursion)
       [nothing needed]

(Postcondition recursion)
[nothing needed]

Figure 11-7. Recursive calls in the dead-batteries flashlight problem, with bindings eventually found for Oplist, Goalstate, and Operator.

[open(case),outside(batteries),unbroken(case)].

3. The difference between this new goal and the original starting state is

[open(case),outside(batteries)].

For this, either the "disassemble_case," "smash_case," or "turn_over_case" operator is recommended. We always try the first recommendation first. That's disassemble_case, and its only precondition is that the case be closed.

4. So we do a third level of recursive call with the same starting state and the goal

   [closed(case)].

But this fact is already true in the starting state. So the difference is [], and no work must be done to solve this recursion. We succeed with the first **means_ends** rule (the basis step), setting the third argument (the operator list) to [] and the fourth argument (the final state) to the starting state. Such trivial search problems are indicated in Figure 11-7 by the words "nothing needed."

5. Now we return to the second level of recursion where we are trying to apply the recommended "disassemble_case" operator. We just discovered that no work is needed to satisfy preconditions, so we just figure out the consequences of disassemble_case. The facts to be deleted (the deletepostconditions) are [closed(case)], and the facts to be added (the addpostconditions) are [open(case)]. So the state after applying disassemble_case (the **Postlist** variable) is

   [open(case),closed(top),inside(batteries),defective(batteries),
      ok(light),unbroken(case)]

6. Now we recurse (to the third level) to find how, from this new state, we can satisfy the second-level partial goal description

   [open(case),outside(batteries),unbroken(case)].

The difference is

   [outside(batteries)].

so now only one fact is different. For this difference, two operators are recommended: turn_over_case and smash_case, in that order. We try the first one first.

7. Turn_over_case has precondition

   [open(case)].

which is already true. So the precondition recursion for turn_over_case succeeds trivially. Using the deletepostconditions and addpostconditions, the new state after turn_over_case is

[outside(batteries),open(case),closed(top),
   defective(batteries),ok(light),unbroken(case)]]

We now compare this to the second-level goal of

[open(case),outside(batteries),unbroken(case)].

and the second-level goal is satisfied. So a postcondition recursion for turn_over_case succeeds trivially. The third level of means_ends recursion binds its third argument (answer operator list) to [turn_over_case], and its fourth argument (final state) to the just-mentioned state.

8. We return to the second level, and can complete its job with third argument (answer operator list)

[disassemble_case,turn_over_case].

so we can bind the fourth argument (final state) to the same state list as previously.

9. We finally return to the first level, where we have satisfied the preconditions of replace_batteries. We now figure out the result of replace_batteries. The deletepostcondition is

[outside(batteries),defective(batteries)].

and the addpostcondition is

[inside(batteries),ok(batteries)].

so the new state is

[inside(batteries),ok(batteries),open(case),
   closed(top),ok(light),unbroken(case)]]

10. We now must determine how to go from this new state to the original (first-level) goal of

[ok(batteries),closed(case),closed(top)].

We recursively call means_ends to do this. The only difference is [closed(case)], for which the recommended operator is assemble_case. The preconditions of assemble_case are satisfied by the last-mentioned state, so we just work out the postconditions of the operator. This gives the new state

[closed(case),inside(batteries),ok(batteries),
   closed(top),ok(light),unbroken(case)]]

This state matches the goal, so no postcondition recursion is necessary at the second level. So the postcondition recursion for replace_batteries (the top level) finishes with third argument (operator list) being [assemble_case] and fourth argument (new state) the preceding state.

11. To summarize, we have for the replace_batteries operator a precondition-satisfying operator list [disassemble_case,turn_over_case] and a postcondition handling operator list of [assemble_case]. So the complete operator list for this problem is

> [disassemble_case,turn_over_case,replace_batteries,assemble_case].

and the final state is what we just found,

> [closed(case),inside(batteries),ok(batteries),
>   closed(top),ok(light),unbroken(case)]

You can see that means-ends analysis is a little tricky, but it all makes sense when you follow through the steps carefully. Curiously, the operator sequence found seems "obvious" to people. This is another one of those situations mentioned at the beginning of Chapter 2: things that seem obvious at first, but aren't so obvious when you examine them carefully. Getting computers to understand language and interpret pictures are also surprisingly difficult problems.

It's interesting to see what happens if for step 3 we try smash_case instead of disassemble_case to get the case open. The smash_case operator doesn't have any prerequisites, but it has the serious postcondition (actually, addpostcondition) that the case is broken. None of the operators can replace a broken(case) fact by the unbroken(case) we need for the goal state, so further progress is impossible. So if we ever selected smash_case, we would fail and backtrack.

11.7 MEANS-END VERSUS OTHER SEARCH METHODS_____

The flashlight example illustrates the advantages of means-ends analysis over the classical search methods of Chapters 9 and 10. Consider what those earlier methods would do on the same problem. They would have considered every action possible in the starting state, then every next action, and so on until they reached the goal. Such a search is mostly "local" in not having an overall plan of attack, just moving like an ant one step at a time. Heuristics, evaluation functions, and cost functions are just tools to make better local decisions about which branches are most likely to lead to the goal.

Means-ends analysis, on the other hand, reasons top-down from abstractions, gradually filling in details of a solution. It's "global" since it always has an overall idea of what it's trying to do. It uses recursion to decompose a problem in an intelligent way, a way more like how people solve problems. It does require that you identify explicit and complete preconditions and postconditions for each operator; when this is impossible, means-ends won't work.

   Another advantage of means-ends analysis is its explainability. Search results in a list of operators to apply in the real world. When this list is long, it's hard to understand and follow, leading to mistakes. But if you can group ("chunk") operators as means-ends analysis does, like saying that a sequence of four operators accomplishes some single overall goal, then a long string is more comprehensible. We'll talk more about explanations in Chapter 15.

11.8 MODELING REAL-WORLD UNCERTAINTY*_____

Means-ends analysis plans a solution to (operator sequence for) a search problem; actually using its solution in the real world is another thing altogether. Difficulties occur when assumptions on which the plan is based are violated. For instance, you may assume the flashlight batteries are defective, but discover when you've replaced them that it really was the light that was defective. Or while you were assembling the case, the batteries may fall out. With cases (pun intended) like this we don't need to start over, but we can replan from the unexpected state; that is, do a new means-ends analysis with this unexpected state as the starting state, and goal the same. Do this anytime you find inconsistency between the real-world state and the state anticipated by planning at some point. So even though means-ends analysis is top-down reasoning from abstract goals, you can handle some mistakes and imperfections in the world.

11.9 PROCEDURAL NETS*_____

All the search methods in this and the last two chapters find a sequence of states or operators to solve a problem, on the assumption you can do only one action at a time. But this may be false: you may have a multiarm robot, or you may have several people to help you, or actions not requiring supervision can be started simultaneously. As we discussed in Section 10.12, concurrency can speed up search.

   Concurrency in an operator sequence can be expressed with the *PERT chart*, a kind of lattice often used in operations research. Figure 11-8 gives an example, one way of replacing both the batteries and light in a flashlight. Each box represents an operator; an operator to the right of another must wait for the first to finish, and vertically parallel operator sequences can be done concurrently. Much work in operations research has studied good ways to design and use such PERT charts efficiently.

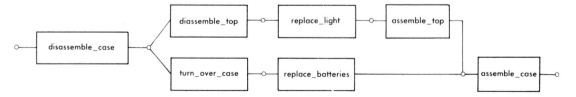

Figure 11-8. Example procedural net for repair of both the light and batteries of a flashlight.

PERT charts are often used in artificial intelligence under the name of *procedural nets*. The algorithms used are similar to means-ends analysis but result in a procedural net, by noting multiple differences between a state and the goal that can be eliminated simultaneously by parallel activities. But a major headache with concurrency is possible conflict between simultaneous activities. The postconditions of one concurrent operator might undo the preconditions for another, for instance. So several different conflict-handling approaches have been proposed for procedural nets. They're too complicated to explain in detail here, but involve intersection checks on preconditions and postconditions of operators appearing in parallel; when conflicts are found, the operators are rearranged into a sequence. This may involve removing part or all of the concurrency, or finding a new concurrency. A rule-based system can summarize such fixes.

KEYWORDS

> *means-ends analysis*
> *difference table*
> *recursive decomposition*
> *double recursion*
> *hierarchical reasoning*
> *abstraction*
> *planning*
> *partial state description*
> *procedural net*

EXERCISES

11-1. (A) Newspapers often run *household hints* like:

> To remove egg from plastic, use grapefruit juice.
> Wrap sandwiches in lettuce to keep them fresher.
> To make a cauldron bubble faster, use some eye of newt.

What part of means-ends analysis do these correspond to?

11-2. (E) As described, means-ends analysis decomposes a problem into three parts. Explain why a useful variant might be to decompose a problem into five parts. Generally speaking, how could such a variant be implemented in Prolog?

11-3. You are a character in a British murder mystery. You have endured enough of Sir Reginald Finch-Stratton. Not only is he an unbearable egotist, but his bad advice has caused you to lose your life savings on unsound business ventures. Now you hear of his sordid liaison with your daughter, an affair that has left her a broken woman. Clearly the man deserves to die.

(a) Set this up for the means-ends analysis program. Assume his room is next to yours and he keeps the door locked. Assume the operators are to stab him with a knife, to pick up the knife, to hide the knife, to go from a room to the corridor or vice versa, to knock on his door, and to wait until the corridor is empty. Needless to say, you don't want to be caught in this foul deed, so you don't want anyone to see you or to find the murder weapon. Assume in the starting state that you are in your room, there are people in the corridor, you are not holding the murder weapon (knife), Sir Reginald is alive, Sir Reginald is in his room, and the door is locked.

(**b**) Trace through informally the operation of means-ends analysis on this problem. What is the final operator sequence found?

(**c**) Some of the things assumed in this problem are hard to know in advance, like whether there will be people in the corridor or not. How in general can means-ends analysis be modified to handle such randomness in facts?

11-4. (R,A,P) In many flashlights the top consists of three parts instead of the two assumed in this chapter: a holder, a transparent plate, and a light bulb that screws into the holder underneath the plate. Modify the flashlight repair program to handle flashlights with these three parts, in which only the light is ever defective. You'll need to define new operators **remove_plate** and **replace_plate**; the plate must be removed before the light can be removed, and the plate must be replaced before the top can be assembled. You'll also need some new predicates to include in states. Try it out on the same repair situation given in the chapter.

11-5. (P) Consider using the flashlight repair program for the situation in which both the light and the batteries are defective.

(**a**) What does the program in this chapter give as an answer operator list? (Use a computer if you have one.)

(**b**) The order of the **recommended** rules can make a lot of difference. Suppose you move the second **recommended** rule (the one about replacing the light) to the end of the others. What answer do you get now? Why?

(**c**) Suppose you instead move the first **recommended** rule (the one about replacing the batteries) to the end of the others. What answer do you get now? Why?

11-6. (A,E) Auto repair manuals often suggest laying out the parts removed in order in a line on a flat surface. Assuming that people do auto repair by something close to means-ends analysis, explain in artificial-intelligence and computer-science terms why this way of laying out is a good idea.

11-7. (A) So far, preconditions and postconditions have been lists of predicate expressions "and"ed together. This seems limiting. Suppose some operator has two alternative sets of preconditions, either of which can be satisfied to make the operator usable. Give an easy way to represent such situations when using the mean-ends analysis program in this chapter.

11-8. (E) The means-ends analysis program of this chapter works in a depth-first way: it figures out how to satisfy the preconditions of a recommended operator, possibly requiring more recursions, and then it figures out how to go from the result of the operator to the goal, possibly requiring more recursions. So it's depth-first in style, with a branching factor of 0, 1, or 2 at each node (each invocation of the means_ends predicate). But this is not strictly necessary.

(a) Explain how a breadth-first means-ends analysis might work.

(b) Why do you think we used the depth-first approach in this chapter?

11-9. (E) Discuss the application of means-ends analysis to improve the user friendliness of networks of computers. Give an example.

11-10. (E) Discuss the similarities and differences between means-ends analysis and the top-down parsing of strings of words as discussed at the end of Chapter 6.

11-11. (H) Machines now exist to synthesize pieces of DNA (deoxyribonucleic acid) under microprocessor control. Chemical reactions take place in a single test tube. The following actions are possible:

1. Add plastic beads to the test tube.

2. Add one of four similar "bases" to the tube (symbolized by A + X, C + X, G + X, and T + X).

3. Add a chemical that strips the X off bases (for instance, A + X becomes A).

4. Add a chemical that binds the left ends of bases to beads.

5. Neutralize the chemical that binds the left ends of bases to beads.

6. Add a chemical that detaches the left ends of bases (or strings of bases) from beads.

The following conditions apply:

1. The right end of a base will attach to the left end of another base, but only if there is no X on the right end of the first base.

2. If an X is removed from a base and the base is not used immediately, it will decompose into a different (useless) chemical.

For this problem, use means-ends analysis to find a plan to synthesize the chemical A + C + G (and only that chemical, no other combinations). That is, accomplish both the operations "attach C to right end of A" and "attach G to right end of C." Modify the means-ends program as necessary.

12

ABSTRACTION OF FACTS

Abstractions of search problems were considered in the last chapter. We'll now look at abstractions on groups of facts: *frames*. Frames are invaluable when you've got lots of facts because they organize them. We'll discuss the different kinds of frames, the features of frames, and new issues in inheritance with frames.

12.1 PARTITIONING FACTS

Frames—sometimes called *classes*, sometimes *prototypes*, and sometimes *structured-object descriptions* (which doesn't necessarily mean "objects" with physical presence)—partition facts in an artificial-intelligence system. Partitioning of large programs into subroutines and procedures is done everywhere in computer science; Section 6.6 mentioned partitioning rules into groups by topic. But we can also partition data (facts). The computer language Smalltalk exploits extensive fact partitioning. The usual way is to group together facts about the same thing (or *object*).

Prolog dialects usually already have built-in fact partitioning in their indexing together of the facts with the same predicate name. But frames usually work differently: they group facts with the same *argument values*. So these facts

a_kind_of(enterprise,carrier).
a_kind_of(vinson,carrier).
location(enterprise,san_diego).
location(vinson,san_francisco).
color(enterprise,gray).
color(vinson,gray).
east_of(vinson,enterprise)

can provide material for two frames (partitions): one of facts about the Enterprise (the first, third, fifth, and seventh facts) and one of facts about the Vinson (the second, fourth, sixth, and seventh facts). With the built-in Prolog indexing by predicate name, there would be four implicit partitions: the two a_kind_of facts, the two location facts, the two color facts, and the east_of fact. The first way seems more like how people organize facts in their heads.

Frames, like semantic networks, are intended for two-argument predicates. This includes the Chapter 2 categories of relationship predicates (in which both arguments are objects) and property predicates (in which the first argument is an object, the second argument a property of that object). (If you have more than two arguments to your facts, you must convert them to relationships and properties somehow.) Relationship-predicate facts are generally stored only with the first-argument frame; then for the second-argument frame, a different "reverse" predicate name is used. For instance, for a_kind_of(X,Y), a_generalization_of(Y,X) is the reverse; for part_of(X,Y), contains(Y,X) is the reverse.

Note that frames aren't necessarily disjoint. For instance, the Enterprise could be both an example for the ship frame and an example for the "American-things" frame.

12.2 FRAMES AND SLOTS

A frame is more than a collection of facts; it is an abstraction in its own right. Often we feel that certain facts are the only essential ones about some object, the ones giving descriptive *completeness*. For instance, for a ship the name, identification number, type of ship, nationality, tonnage, and location might be the important features. We should make sure we always put those facts in a frame for a ship.

There's a problem, however: we may want to describe sets of objects with a frame, not just a single object. Why? We might want a frame to generalize about certain groups or classes of objects, identifying properties each group shares. Then we can't always fill in all the essential facts in such a frame since different objects may have different facts true. For instance, a frame for American ships: each ship has a different identification number, so we can't assert a single identification-number fact for the entire frame.

But identification number is still a *potential* fact for the frame. The terminology is that frames have *slots* that can be *unfilled* or *filled*; filled slots represent facts. For instance, ships vary in location, so frames for "ship" and "carrier" should leave the "location" slot unfilled; but the "transport medium" slot of ships should always be filled with the word "water." Some slots are so important to fill that their frames don't make sense otherwise. Such slots are *definitional*, part of the definition of the frame. For instance, the "nationality" slot of the frame for "American ships" must be filled in with the value "American," because that's what the frame is all about. Many pairs of frames having a_kind_of relationships have such slots, which come about when the more general frame is restricted in some slot to create the more specific frame.

Inference rules can fill unfilled slots, especially inheritance rules (Section 4.9). That is, to fill a slot in a frame F, find a related frame F2, and take the value for the same-named slot in F2 provided the slot inherits across the relationship between F and F2. For example, if all carriers are gray, that color fact can be stored with the "carrier" frame and inherited via a_kind_of to the frames for the carriers "Enterprise" and "Vinson." Inheritance can be overridden by putting explicit values into normally-unfilled slots, stating the exceptions to general principles. For instance, the few carriers that are not gray can have an explicit color value in their "color" slot.

12.3 SLOTS QUALIFYING OTHER SLOTS

Slots may have more than a value attached to them: they can have information that explains or qualifies that value. Slots with numeric values can have associated information about the units of measurement and its accuracy. Slots with non-numeric values can have a format (a formal description of what the values look like). Slots representing real-world data can have an associated location, time, and observer. Slots can have default or "usual" values. Slots may have associated sets of permissible values, given by a list if the number of such values is finite or by a range if values are numeric. Slots may also have sets of "unusual" values that should generate a warning if seen.

For instance, a slot for the current latitude of a ship can have as explanatory or qualifying information:

- an indication that the format is a one-digit or two-digit number followed by the letter N or S;
- the units "degrees";
- the time a ship was at that position;
- who reported it;
- a note that the number must be less than 91;
- a note that it's unusual for the number to be more than 60;
- a default value that is the latitude of Norfolk (a default for U. S. Navy ships, anyway).

Such *slot qualification* information can be considered as slots itself, and we'll call them *qualifying slots*. They can inherit like regular slots. For instance, the restriction that the latitude be less than 91 holds for anything on the surface of the earth, not just a ship, and so could inherit from the corresponding information in a more general frame like "vehicle_on_earth" or "physical_object_on_earth." The values in qualifying slots generally inherit from a higher-generalization frame than do the values in the slots they describe, when both inherit.

12.4 FRAMES WITH COMPONENTS

Frames can represent things with components. For instance, a ship frame can indicate as components the hull, the engine, and the bridge. Often just listing component names is insufficiently descriptive. Instead we should have a separate frame for each component, and **contains** slots in the frame for the whole whose values are pointers to the component frames. This has several advantages:

- We can distinguish properties of components not shared by the whole (inheritance can always be used otherwise).
- We can describe relationships of the components to one another, like the relative location of parts of a physical object or the relative time of subevents of an action. Frames for which components can be put in a sequence are called *scripts*.
- We can distinguish multiple or optional occurrences of a component, as instances of some component-type frame, whose variation in occurrence is described by qualifying slots of the **contains** slots. For instance, a wheel is part of a car, and cars have four of them, each with their own properties; and a sunroof is an optional part of a car, occurring either zero or one times in every car.
- We only need to identify the most important, "top-level" components in our main frame. The frames for these components can describe subcomponents, and so on.

12.5 FRAMES AS FORMS: MEMOS

Frames have many applications to management of paperwork, because frames are a lot like forms. For instance, consider memos used for communication in organizations. Figure 12-1 shows some memo frames linked in an **a_kind_of** lattice. All memo frames have certain slots: author, intended readers (addressees), date written, subject, type (formal or informal), and text. Often the first four are even written on paper to look like slots, with the symbols TO, FROM, DATE, and RE followed by colons.

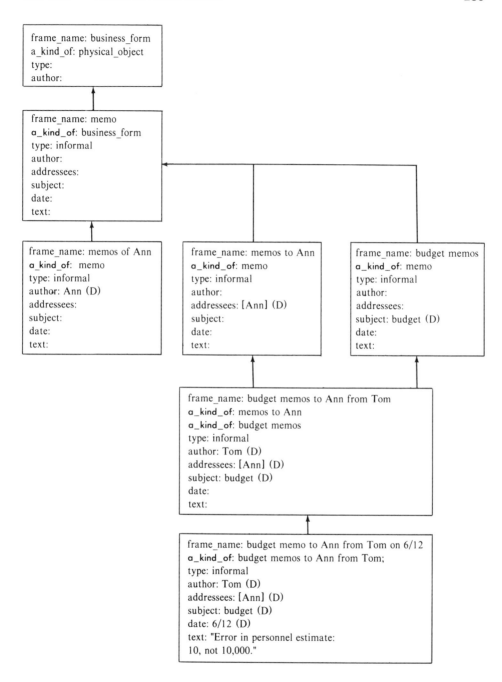

Note: Each box is a frame, and arrows represent **a_kind_of** facts. Slot names are given, then a colon, and then the slot value; a (D) means the value follows by the definition of the frame.

Figure 12-1. Some frames about memos.

The general memo frame has many (not necessarily exclusive) sub-frames, each linked by a_kind_of(X,memo) facts. Examples are a frame for all the memos written by Ann, a frame for all the memos received by Ann, and a frame for all memos about the budget. These last two have, among others, a sub-frame in common: all memos received by Ann from Tom about the budget. And this might happen to have another sub-frame, for a specific memo Ann got from Tom on this subject the other day. Of course, there are many other memo sub-frames. Just considering sub-frames restricting the values in the "subject" slot, there are "policy" memos, "announcement" memos, and "personal" memos. Considering sub-frames restricting the "date" slot, there are memos of yesterday, last month, and last year. Finally, note that the "memo" frame itself is a sub-frame of a "business form" frame.

Since memo components appear in sequence down a page, their frames are scripts. But organizations do differ in these orders, so the component sequence is inherited from frames specific to each organization.

The author, addressee, and text slots shown are special to memos because they must be filled in for every specific memo *instance* (that is, real-world memo), though not for every memo frame (which can represent classes of memos), with new slots added at various levels in the lattice of memo frames. This is a special type of "cardinality" information for those slots, which can be expressed in qualifying slots.

12.6 SLOT INHERITANCE

All memos have a text slot, but this isn't filled in unless we're talking about a specific real-world memo; nearly every memo's text is different, obviously. But you must agree that since the general "memo" frame has a "text" slot, the "memos to Ann" frame must have a "text" slot too. This is inheritance, but of a fundamentally different sort than any in this book so far: it's inheritance of the mere *concept* of a slot, and not the value in a slot. We'll call this *slot inheritance*, and the regular kind *value inheritance*. In one sense, slot inheritance is more limited than value inheritance in that it usually only works with the a_kind_of relationship. That is, situations when some frame F has a slot S, saying then anything that is "a kind of" F also has slot S. But in another sense, slot inheritance is more general than value inheritance because it applies higher up in frame hierarchies, to slots that don't yet have values filled in.

Usually slot inheritance tells us most of the slots that must be in a sub-frame given the slots in a frame. But some slots may be unique to the sub-frame. For instance, carrier ships have airplanes, whereas ships in general don't. So slots referring to airplanes, like those indicating number and types, are unique to the "carrier" frame. But slots in a frame can't "disappear" in a sub-frame.

12.7 PART-KIND INHERITANCE

Besides value and slot inheritance there is a third fundamental kind of inheritance: part-kind inheritance. It occurs in the interaction between a_kind_of and part_of (see the example in Figure 12-2). A ship has decks, a hull, and a propulsion system. So the ships Enterprise and Vinson have those things. But the Enterprise's hull is *different* from the Vinson's hull. It may have different properties: it may be damaged while the Vinson's hull or the hull of ships in general isn't. Some kind of inheritance is happening from the "hull" frame, but it's not inheritance of values or slots because "hull" isn't either a value or slot but a frame itself. We'll call this *part-kind inheritance*. Formally, it's the inheritance of a component FC of some frame F of which another frame FK is "a kind of"; the inherited frame becomes a component of FK, inheriting slots and values from both FK and FC. Part-kind inheritance means you don't need to define every frame in advance for which you want to assert slot values: some frames must exist because others exist. Part-kind inheritance is often signaled in English by possessives, like "Enterprise's" in the phrase "the Enterprise's hull."

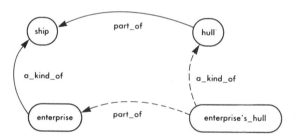

Figure 12-2. Example of part-kind inheritance.

12.8 EXTENSIONS VERSUS INTENSIONS

Philosophers make an important distinction between abstract concepts (what they call *intensions* or *meanings* of concepts) and real-world things that frames correspond to (what they call *extensions*). (Don't confuse this first word with the more common but differently spelled one "intention.") For instance, the intension of "carrier" is an abstract specification of what it means for something to be a carrier. One extension of "carrier" is the set of all currently existing carriers, another the set of all carriers that existed a year ago, another the set of all carriers ever built, and another the set of all carriers that will exist ten years from now (the "world" of the extension may be hypothetical).

Extensions and intensions generally require separate frames, linked by "extension" and "intension" pointers to one another, because the slots can be filled differently. For instance, it's technically incorrect to say that the Enterprise is at 14N42W, only that the extension of the Enterprise for the current instant of time has a location value of 14N42W. So only extensions of movable things, not their intensions, can have a location. In general, extensions can have statistics while intensions cannot. So if you want to be technically correct in filling a slot with something that's usually true or true on the average, you need an extension frame. For instance, if you want to say "most tankers are Liberian," you're making a statement about the nationality statistics of some extension of the abstract concept of "tankers." The bottom frame in Figure 12-1 can be alternatively viewed as an extension of the frame above it.

Properties of extensions usually inherit from their intensions: an abstract concept constrains the examples of it. For instance, the fact that ships float on water by definition (i.e., as a property of their intension) means that existing ships (i.e., an extension) float on water. But statistical properties of extensions rarely inherit in any direction. For instance, the average length of a memo in some organization isn't likely to be the average length of a policy memo in that organization. Weak inferences are sometimes possible between sets and their subsets, if the condition of statistical independence holds; sampling theory from statistics can help us recognize such situations.

12.9 PROCEDURAL ATTACHMENT

Inference rules (or inference procedures) can be values in slots. Usually they appear in qualifying slots, and represent a way to fill the value in the main slot from other accessible values. This is *procedural attachment*, and the rules are sometimes called *if-needed rules*. Unlike the rules in Prolog databases, these are "local": they apply initially to just one slot of one frame. However, rules can inherit just like other slot values, so we can often specify a rule useful in many slots in many frames with a single value entry.

Extensive or exclusive use of procedural attachment in an artificial-intelligence system leads to a whole new style of programming, *object-oriented programming*. We mentioned it back in Section 6.9, as one interpretation of parallelism in rule-based systems. Object-oriented programming is especially useful for writing simulations. The simulation is divided into *objects*, each with its own frame, data, and rules running independently. This is a sort of opposite to the *procedure-oriented programming* using Prolog that is emphasized in this book, for which procedures (rules) call on data; with object-oriented programming, data (in frames) calls on procedures. As such, object-oriented programming requires a whole different mindset or programming philosophy than procedure-oriented programming, and it's hard to intermingle it with the other things we discuss in this book. If you're interested, take a look at the Smalltalk literature.

12.10 FRAMES IN PROLOG

Frames are best implemented in Prolog with software modules where each module has its own local facts, rules, and indexing scheme. Unfortunately, only some of the currently available Prolog dialects provide true module-making capability with features such as special storage management and referential locality. But some of the meaning of frames can be captured by identifying them with files, making each frame a separate file.

Filled slots in a frame can just be facts in the file, with the usual predicate names. Unfilled slots can be represented by facts of the form

    slot(<object>,<slot-name>).

assuming slot is not a slot name itself. This special predicate can inherit by slot inheritance from whatever that object is a kind of.

Qualifying information (like units, bounds, and measurement accuracy) can be implemented as special property facts where the predicate name is the name of the qualifying slot, the first argument is name of the slot qualified, and the second argument is the value in the qualifying slot. For instance

    units(length,meters).

Ordering between parts can be modeled by additional relationship facts besides those designating the parts themselves. For instance

    beneath(engine_room,flight_deck,carrier).

which says that the engine room part of a carrier is beneath the flight deck part.

12.11 EXAMPLE OF A FRAME LATTICE_____

Here are some interrelated frames (files) about cars; Figure 12-3 shows their relationships. To make inference rules simpler, we use triples to represent slot values instead of the usual two-argument predicates. The syntax is value(<object>,<slot>,<value>), which means that the <slot> of the <object> has the <value>.

Physical-object frame:

    slot(physical_object,weight).
    slot(physical_object,name).
    slot(physical_object,use).

    units(physical_object,weight,kilograms).

Vehicle frame:

    value(vehicle,a_kind_of,physical_object).
    value(vehicle,use,transportation).
    value(vehicle,has_a_part,propulsion_system).

```
slot(vehicle,owner).
slot(vehicle,dealers).
slot(vehicle,year).
slot(vehicle,age).
slot(vehicle,propulsion_method).

units(vehicle,age,years).
units(vehicle,year,years).
```

Car frame:

```
value(car,a_kind_of,vehicle).
value(car,propulsion_method,internal_combustion_engine).
value(car,has_a_part,electrical_system).
value(car,extension,cars_on_road).

slot(car,make).
slot(car,model).

possible_values(car,make,
    [gm,ford,chrysler,amc,vw,toyota,nissan,bmw]).
```

Electrical-system frame:

```
value(electrical_system,part_of,car).
value(electrical_system,has_a_part,battery).
value(electrical_system,has_a_part,starter).
```

VW-Rabbit frame:

```
value(vw_rabbit,a_kind_of,car).
value(vw_rabbit,make,vw).
value(vw_rabbit,model,rabbit).
```

Cars-on-the-road-now frame:

```
value(cars_on_road,intension,car).

statistic(cars_on_road,mean,age,6.4).
```

Joe's-VW-Rabbit frame:

```
value(joes_rabbit,a_kind_of,vw_rabbit).
value(joes_rabbit,extension,joes_rabbit_now).
value(joes_rabbit,owner,joe).
value(joes_rabbit,year,1976).
```

Joe's-VW-Rabbit-now frame:

    value(joes_rabbit_now,contained,cars_on_road).
    value(joes_rabbit_now,intension,joes_rabbit).

    statistic(joes_rabbit_now,size,none,1).

Joe's-VW-Rabbit-battery frame:

    value(joes_rabbits_battery,extension,joes_rabbits_battery_now).
    value(joes_rabbits_battery,part_of,joes_rabbit).

Joe's-VW-Rabbit-battery-now frame:

    value(joes_rabbits_battery_now,intension,joes_rabbits_battery).
    value(joes_rabbits_battery_now,within,joes_rabbit_now).
    value(joes_rabbits_battery_now,status,dead).

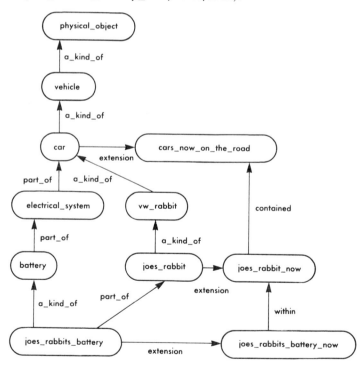

Figure 12-3. Semantic network for the frames in the cars example.

Now for some inference rules applying to these frames. We first define a single general-purpose value-inheritance rule that can do inheritance for arbitrary

predicate names. This makes inheritance implementation a lot simpler since we don't have to write a separate rule for each predicate that inherits. Technically, we've implemented something close to a *second-order logic*, something that reasons about predicate names as well as arguments, as we'll explain more in Chapter 14.

```
has_value(Object,Slot,V) :- value(Object,Slot,V), !.
has_value(Object,Slot,V) :- inherits(Slot,Relation),
  value(Object,Relation,Superconcept),
  has_value(Superconcept,Slot,V).

inherits(S,a_kind_of) :-
  member(S,[use,
    propulsion_method,dealers,year,age,make,model,has_a_part,part_of]).
inherits(S,part_of) :-
  member(S,[owner,dealers,year,age,make,model]).
```

Slot inheritance must be defined separately:

```
has_slot(Object,Slot) :- slot(Object,Slot), !.
has_slot(Object,Slot) :- value(Object,a_kind_of,Superconcept),
  has_slot(Superconcept,Slot).
```

Qualifying slot values also inherit downward. For instance, units of a slot:

```
has_units(Object,Slot,U) :- units(Object,Slot,U), !.
has_units(Object,Slot,U) :- value(Object,a_kind_of,Superconcept),
  has_units(Superconcept,Slot,U).
```

Here's a rule that says to get a slot value of an extension, get the corresponding slot value (possibly inherited) in the intension.

```
has_value(Extension,Slot,V) :- value(Extension,intension,I),
  has_value(I,Slot,V).

has_slot(Object,Slot) :- value(Object,intension,I), has_slot(I,Slot).
```

As we said, statistics can sometimes inherit from one extension to another, if an "independence" condition holds:

```
statistic(Extension,Statname,Slot,Value) :-
  has_value(Extension,contained,Bigextension),
  independent(Extension,Bigextension),
  statistic(Extension,Statname,Slot,Value).
```

And the contained relationship holds between two extensions whenever their intensions have an a_kind_of relationship:

```
has_value(Extension,contained,Bigextension) :-
  value(Extension,intension,I), has_value(I,a_kind_of,Bigl),
  value(Bigl,extension,Bigextension).
```

Also, some redundant slots may have their values defined in terms of other slot values. The has_a_part relationship can be defined as the opposite of the part_of relationship:

```
value(X,has_a_part,Y) :- value(Y,part_of,X).
```

And the age slot value can be defined from the year slot value (note the following fact must be changed every year):

```
value(Object,age,A) :- value(Object,year,Y), current_year(Y2),
  A is Y2 - Y.
```

```
current_year(1987).
```

Here are some sample queries run with the preceding facts and rules:

```
?- has_value(joes_rabbit_now,use,U).
U = transportation
```

```
?- has_value(joes_rabbits_battery_now,age,A).
A = 11
```

```
?- has_slot(joes_rabbit_now,name).
yes
```

```
?- has_value(joes_rabbit_now,contained,X).
X = cars_on_road
```

12.12 EXPECTATIONS FROM SLOTS

An important applications of frames is to modeling and reconstruction of stereotypical situations in the world from incomplete knowledge. Empty slots in a frame have "expectations" about what should fill them: from inheritance, from qualifying-slot information (possible values and permissible values), and from extension statistics. Such expectations can support type checking of user-entered slot values. They can also support weaker inferences. Consider purchasing of equipment for a bureaucratic organization, which usually involves many steps and many details; if we know some of the details (slot values) of the purchase, then other details (slot values) are often obvious. For instance, an arriving order was probably ordered six to three weeks ago; orders from accounting-supplies companies are for the Accounting Department; orders that come by express mail are probably for management and should be delivered immediately.

12.13 FRAMES FOR NATURAL LANGUAGE UNDERSTANDING* _____

People must exploit expectations to understand natural languages, because speakers and writers try to avoid wordiness. So it's not surprising that frames are very helpful for natural-language understanding by computers, for the *semantics* or meaning-assignment subarea (as opposed to the *syntax* or parsing subarea we discussed in Section 6.12). That is, with a good frame representation we can efficiently capture the meaning of some natural-language sentences so as to answer questions about it.

Usually the objective in interpretation of a sentence or sentences is to get a set of interrelated frames, in which each frame represents a verb or noun and its associated modifiers. Verbs and nouns can be frames, and modifiers can be slots or have something to do with slots. So for instance the sentence

> Yesterday we sent headquarters by express mail the budget memo that Tom drew up for Ann on 6/12.

can be represented by three frames as in Figure 12-4: an instance or sub-frame of a "sending" frame, an instance of a "memo" frame (like those in Figure 12-1), and an instance of a "drawing-up" frame. These three are linked by the uses of their names as slot values. Some implications of the sentence are also filled in; for instance, the person a memo is drawn up for is assumed an addressee of the memo. Note that if we know more about the sending, drawing up, or the memo itself from other sentences, we could fill in additional slots in the frames without necessarily requiring more frames.

```
frame_name: sending8347
a_kind_of: sending
actor: we
object: memo72185
time: yesterday
destination: headquarters
method: express mail
```

```
frame_name: memo72185
a_kind_of: memo
author: Tom
addressees: [Ann]
origin: drawingup20991
```

```
frame_name: drawingup20991
a_kind_of: drawingup
actor: Tom
object: memo72185
beneficiary: Ann
time: 6/12
```

Figure 12-4. Frame representation of the meaning (semantics) of the sentence "Yesterday we sent headquarters by express mail the budget memo that Tom drew up for Ann on 6/12."

Filling in frames the right way to capture the meaning of a sentence can involve search. To be sure, the parse of the sentence (see Section 6.12) helps us considerably by identifying the grammatical categories of each word. But there are many ambiguities that can't be resolved by a parse. For instance, compare the previous sentence to

> Yesterday we sent several times by 4 P.M. the budget memo that Tom drew up for practice on the plane.

Here we have "several times" instead of "headquarters," "by 4 P.M." instead of "by express mail," "for practice" instead of "for Ann," and "on the plane" instead of "on 6/12." In all cases we've substituted something similar grammatically. But the functions of the substitutions are different: "several times" describes the style of the sending, not the place we sent to; "by 4 P.M." is a time limit, not how we sent; "for practice" is a purpose, not a beneficiary; and "on the plane" is a location, not a time. We must figure these things out by making guesses about words, drawing from their possible meanings, and checking the resulting interpretation of the whole sentence for reasonableness by trying to build frames for it.

12.14 MULTIPLE INHERITANCE

We haven't discussed how to handle "multiple inheritance" paths for some slot of a frame. For instance, a policy memo from your boss is simultaneously a memo from your boss and a policy memo. Things are fine if only one path provides an inheritance for a slot, or if the paths all agree on some value. But if different paths give different values for a slot, we must do something. If we can assign priorities to paths, we can take the value from the path with highest priority. Or we can compromise or find a middle ground between different values. Or we can decide certain values are wrong. The next section presents an example application.

12.15 A MULTIPLE INHERITANCE EXAMPLE: CUSTOM OPERATING SYSTEMS*

Frames are valuable in managing large software systems. As an example, take the operating system of a computer, the top-level program that runs other programs on your orders. Operating systems are standardized for an average computer user, with not too many things you can adjust. Users would prefer operating systems more custom-fitted to their needs.

One way is by a hierarchy of user models. Think of each user model as a frame holding information about defaults for a user or class of users, defaults about how they need or prefer to use particular programs and facilities. Some possible slots are:

- default terminal setting parameters;
- storage and time allocations (different programs and facilities have quite different requirements);
- the project for which this computer time should be charged;
- default nonfile parameters of the program or facility itself (like in printing, whether output is double-spaced);
- protection information for any input and output files (to prevent reading non-meaningful files or overwriting valuable files);
- additional character strings (extensions) to be automatically added to the names of input and output files (like "pro" for all Prolog programs);
- interrupt-condition handling (like what to do on arithmetic overflow);
- common misspellings (so they can be recognized);
- common bugs (so they can be caught before damage is done);
- pointers to documentation;
- names of default editors, document handlers, and programming languages (so the user can just type short words like "edit" and the operating system will know what they mean).

The interesting thing about this application is the three independent inheritance hierarchies (see Figure 12-5). First, there's a hierarchy of user classes: frames for Tom, frames for people in Tom's project group above that, and frames for everybody using the operating system above that. This hierarchy may be a lattice, because Tom may belong to more than one project group, each with different associated projects. Second, there's a hierarchy on programs and facilities of the operating system: a frame for Tom using the Prolog interpreter, and a frame above that for Tom using any programming language, and a frame above that for Tom doing anything under the operating system. This hierarchy could be a lattice too, since for example a Prolog interpreter is both a Prolog-related facility and an interpreter. Third, there's a hierarchy on time: Tom's use of the Prolog interpreter today is below a frame for Tom's use of the Prolog interpreter anytime.

So there are at least three independent dimensions of frame generalization for the frame representing Tom using the Prolog interpreter today, the bottom frame in Figure 12-5. We can represent them by a three-dimensional lattice (which Figure 12-5 tries to suggest) in which the first (user-class) dimension runs northwest, the second (facility-class) dimension runs northeast, and the third (time) dimension runs straight north. Though the examples drawn from each of the three hierarchies in the figure form linear sequences, they form a lattice when put together, since there are many routes between the top frame and the bottom frame.

The big problem is thus multiple inheritance: there are three different directions to reason. This doesn't affect slot inheritance for which nothing conflicts, but it is a serious problem for value inheritance. One approach is to give the a_kind_of link for each hierarchy a different name, like a_kind_of_1, a_kind_of_2, and a_kind_of_3. Then for every slot, designate one of these as preferred for inheritance, and store this in a qualifying slot of the original slot. For instance

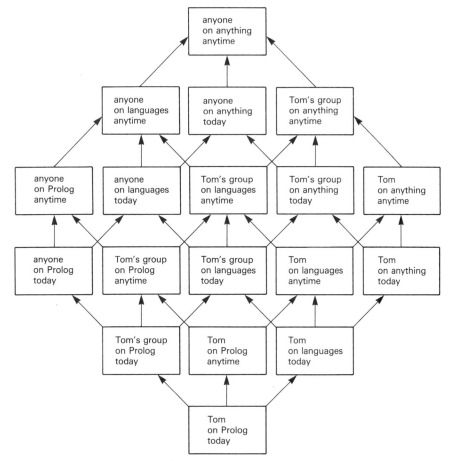

Note: "languages" means "programming languages," "Prolog" means "Prolog interpreter"; all arrows represent "a_kind_of"

Figure 12-5. Three-dimensional inheritance hierarchy of user model frames.

- inherit a value for the "sponsoring projects" slot via the user-class hierarchy, since projects are composed of people;
- inherit terminal settings from the program and facility class hierarchy;
- inherit program storage allocation from the time hierarchy, the typical allocation in the past.

Now consider what to do when a user wants to override defaults. For instance, suppose user Tom wants to override default terminal settings for the Prolog interpreter, obtained from traveling up the program-class hierarchy (the default direction) to "Tom on languages today," and suppose Tom wants this override for all time (that is, Prolog programs might benefit from consistently unconventional settings). So he should place the overriding settings in the frame above him in the time dimension ("Tom on Prolog anytime") representing all his uses of the Prolog interpreter for all time. But now we must prevent inheritance along the program dimension. A fix is to store for each slot a sequence of inheritance predicates that should be tried to find the value of the slot—for this example perhaps the sequence of the time dimension, the program dimension, and the user-class dimension. Each slot can have a possibly different associated sequence, and this can inherit.

This approach to inheritance is general, but sometimes unwieldy. For particular slots we may be able to do something simpler. For instance, we may be absolutely certain that values won't conflict because of the way we've built the frames hierarchy. Or for slots with numeric values, we can apply a numeric function to the values inherited along different dimensions to get a "compromise" number. For example, for a storage allocation slot, we could take the maximum of the storage allocation values found along the three dimensions, because each dimension represents a different requirement that must be met. For the time allocation slot (the amount of time given to a running program before asking the user if they want to continue), we could take the average of values, since each number is just a rough guess about an intuitive parameter. This idea of a compromise value applies to non-numeric slots too. For example, if Tom's project group insists on putting its name at the end of every file created by that group, while a Prolog compiler insists on putting "procomp" at the end of the name of every file compiled from Prolog code, a compromise would be putting first the project name, then "procomp." Such specialized multiple-inheritance strategies (not to be confused with "conflict-resolution" strategies for rule-based systems) can be flagged by a special "multiple-inheritance method" qualifying slot. And this slot can inherit too.

KEYWORDS

object-based representation
frame
class
slot
filling a slot
definitional slots
qualifying slots
script
value inheritance
slot inheritance
part-kind inheritance
intension
extension
procedural attachment
semantics
multiple inheritance
frame lattice

EXERCISES

12-1. Consider a frame representing any class meeting at any university (that is, a generalized class hour).

(a) Give two example slots that are always filled with values and what those filled values are.

(b) Give a superconcept frame (a frame that this frame is a kind of) and a subconcept frame (a frame that is a kind of this frame).

(c) Give a slot that inherits from your superconcept frame and one that does not.

(d) Describe a script associated with a class meeting frame.

12-2. (E) People dealing with bureaucracies are constantly filling in the same information on forms over and over again. Discuss the use of inheritance to lighten this burden. In particular, explain how inheritance could have a concrete physical meaning.

12-3. (R,A) Consider a frame representing any purchase order (a form ordering the buying of something).

(a) Give an example of value inheritance from a value in this frame to a value in some other frame.

(b) Consider the "units" slot associated with some slot S in the purchase order frame (so if S is the cost slot, units would be "dollars"). Suppose S inherits its value from the same slot S of some other frame P2. What does this tell you about from where the "units" slot inherits?

12-4. (A) Different slots in a frame system require different qualifying slots to accompany them. But every time we use a slot with a particular name, we want it to have the same qualifying slots, and the same values in those qualifying slots that have values filled in. We can't always just inherit this information from a higher (more general a_kind_of) frame because, say, two different uses of a "length" slot might be in frames having no common ancestor having a "length" slot. (This is especially a problem when different people are building different frames for a big system.) Suggest an elegant way to handle this sort of problem.

12-5. (R,A) Every computer has a manufacturer's name and an ID number. Every computer has a CPU as a component. Consider the frame representing any computer sold by Floodge Manufacturing, Inc.

(a) Give an example of downward value inheritance from this frame.

(b) Give an example of downward slot inheritance from this frame.

(c) Give an example of downward part-kind inheritance involving this frame.

12-6. Contrast the intension and extension of the concept "memo."

12-7. Draw a semantic network representing the following facts. Represent property values by nodes too (though this isn't always a good idea). Represent what these mean, not what they literally say.

Wrenches are tools.

Hammers are tools.

Tools have handles.

The handle of a hammer is hard.

Wrenches are hard.

Most hammers have a steel handle.

Wrenches are 10 inches long on the average.

12-8. Names of frames often correspond to nouns. For instance, a ship frame corresponds to the meaning of the English word "ship."

(a) What, in frame terminology, does an adjective modifying the noun name of a frame often correspond to? For instance, the adjectives "big," "American," and "merchant" in the description "big American merchant ships."

(b) What, in frame terminology, does a preposition in a prepositional phrase modifying the name of a frame often correspond to? For instance, the prepositions "in" and "at" in the description "ships in the Mediterranean at noon yesterday."

12-9. (A) Consider the following example of reasoning by modus ponens:

Given: Military organizations are widely dispersed geographically.

Given: The Navy is a military organization.

Hence the Navy is widely dispersed geographically.

That conclusion makes sense. But consider:

Given: Navy organizations are widely dispersed geographically.

Given: The Naval Postgraduate School is a Navy organization.

Hence The Naval Postgraduate School is widely dispersed geographically.

That is an incorrect inference assuming the "Given"'s are true. Discuss why the two situations are different. (To get full credit, you must show depth of understanding, not just cite a superficial difference.)

12-10. Represent the meaning of the following letter with a group of interlinked frames.

Dear Fly-by-Nite Software,

I tried your product "Amazing Artificial Intelligence Software" and it doesn't work. I tried Example 5 shown in the manual, and it crashed on an attempt to divide by zero. I next tried Example 7, and the line-printer printed 100,000 line feeds. Then when I exited your program, I found it had destroyed all my files. I want my money back.

Sincerely,

Irate Programmer

12-11. Some slots are easier to handle with multiple inheritance than others.

(a) Consider associated with a nonnumeric slot a qualifying slot that lists all the conceivable values that first slot could have. Formulate a multiple inheritance policy for this qualifying slot.

(b) Consider associated with a numeric slot a qualifying slot that lists the maximum and minimum conceivable values for that first slot. Formulate a multiple inheritance policy for this qualifying slot.

12-12. For the user-model hierarchy example, formulate conflict-handling methods for multiple inheritance of the following.

(a) The directory to which output files go.

(b) A bit indicating whether the user should be warned before the operating system executes a command whose side effect is to destroy a file.

(c) The "CPU intensity" of usage, defined as the expected ratio of CPU time to login-connection time.

12-13. (A) Suppose that for our user model frames example we have qualifying slots describing how to resolve multiple inheritance on other slots. These qualifying slots could have qualifying slots themselves explaining how to resolve their own multiple inheritance problems, and these could have qualifying slots themselves, and so on. Why shouldn't we worry about an infinite loop?

12-14. (E) Chapter 7 considered the building of an expert system for appliance repair. Suppose instead of one general expert system we would like a set of expert systems, one for each kind of appliance. Many rules are common to different appliances, but some rules must be deleted, some added, and some modified in going from one appliance to another. Discuss how it might be useful to define an appliance's rules as a frame and do inheritance. What slots would be necessary and useful in the frames, and how would you fill in their values?

12-15. (E) Discuss the use of a frames hierarchy to represent a contract negotiation between management and labor. Each frame will represent a particular offer or proposal. Some of these can be grouped together. State what slots can be useful for these frames. Provide a good representation of negotiation so that later analysis can more easily pick out patterns in the style of negotiation such as flexibility.

12-16. (H,E) Reasoning by analogy is a fundamentally different kind of reasoning than any so far considered in this book. It has similarities to inheritance, but it's really something else entirely: it involves four things instead of two. It's easiest to understand in terms of frames and slots. Suppose you want to know about the slots or slot values in some frame D. You could find frames A, B, and C such that the relationship of A to B is very similar to the relationship of C to D, the frame of interest. For instance, A might be a frame representing the circulatory system of the human body, and B a frame representing the medical emergency of a heart attack; then C might represent the cooling system of a car and D the serious malfunction of complete coolant blockage. Using the analogy, we might be able to infer that the "number of previous attacks" in frame B should correspond to a slot "number of previous blockages" in frame D. Furthermore, the value in the "immediate treatment" slot of frame B of "inject anticoagulants into the system" could have an analogy in a slot "immediate treatment" of frame D of "add anticorrosives." Give a general strategy for finding such analogous slots and analogous slot values in reasoning-by-analogy situations.

13

PROBLEMS WITH MANY CONSTRAINTS

Some problems have lots of conditions or *constraints* that must be satisfied. When expressed as Prolog queries, these problems appear as many predicate expressions "and"ed together. Processing these queries can be awfully slow if we don't do it right.

Special techniques are often used for such many-constraint problems. We'll talk about three such ideas in this chapter: rearranging queries to make them easier to solve, smarter ("dependency-based") backtracking, and relaxation (reasoning about possibility lists).

13.1 TWO EXAMPLES

Two good examples of many-constraint applications are automatic scheduling and computer vision.

Suppose we want to schedule a class to meet five hours a week. Assume meeting times must be on the hour, from 9 A.M. to 4 P.M., and on weekdays. Suppose we have ten students, each of which is taking other already-scheduled classes, and we can't have our class meet when any of those meets. Furthermore, suppose we don't want our class to meet two successive hours on any day, and we don't want our class to meet more than two hours total on any day. Figure 13-1 gives an example situation and an example solution; "occupied" represents times that aren't available because of the other commitments of the ten students, and "class" represents a solution time proposed for our class. (Blank spaces are available times we don't need to use.)

Time	Monday	Tuesday	Wednesday	Thursday	Friday
9	occupied	occupied	occupied		occupied
10	occupied	occupied	occupied	occupied	occupied
11	class	occupied	occupied	class	occupied
12	occupied	occupied	occupied	occupied	occupied
1	class	class	occupied	class	occupied
2	occupied		occupied		occupied
3	occupied	occupied	occupied	occupied	occupied
4	occupied	occupied	occupied		occupied

Figure 13-1. Example scheduling problem, with an example solution symbolized by "class."

This problem can be stated as a query finding values of five variables T1, T2, T3, T4, and T5, each value of which is a two-item list [<day>,<hour>] representing a class time, so [tuesday,3] means a meeting on Tuesday at 3 P.M. Each variable represents a different chosen meeting time. Suppose meeting times of other classes are represented as occupied([<day>,<hour>]) facts. Then the following query would solve our problem:

```
?- classtime(T1), classtime(T2), classtime(T3),
   classtime(T4), classtime(T5),
   not(occupied(T1)), not(occupied(T2)), not(occupied(T3)),
   not(occupied(T4)), not(occupied(T5)),
   not(two_consecutive_hours([T1,T2,T3,T4,T5])),
   not(three_classes_same_day([T1,T2,T3,T4,T5])),
   not(duplication([T1,T2,T3,T4,T5])).
```

For this we need the following definitions:

```
classtime([Day,Hour]) :-
   member(Day,[monday,tuesday,wednesday,thursday,friday]),
   member(Hour,[9,10,11,12,1,2,3,4]).

two_consecutive_hours(TL) :- member([Day,Hour1],TL),
   member([Day,Hour2],TL), H2 is Hour1 + 1, H2 = Hour2.

three_classes_same_day(TL) :- member([Day,Hour1],TL),
   member([Day,Hour2],TL), member([Day,Hour3],TL),
   not(Hour1 = Hour2), not(Hour1 = Hour3), not(Hour2 = Hour3).

duplication([X|L]) :- member(X,L).
duplication([X|L]) :- duplication(L).

member(X,[X|L]).
member(X,[Y|L]) :- member(X,L).
```

Here we use the backtracking version of the **member** predicate to both generate class times and to check conditions in a bound list.

Computer vision often involves applying many constraints to interpret some picture. Preliminary visual processing (for example, the techniques of Section 9.16) groups parts of a picture into regions (creates edges) based on similarities of brightness, color, and texture. The remaining problem is to decide what each region of the picture represents. For this, variables correspond to regions, and values of the variables correspond to labels (from a finite label set) for the identity of each region. Additional constraints (conditions) affect which regions can border others, or be above others, or be inside others.

Consider the aerial photograph shown in Figure 13-2. Assume regions can be labeled either **grass, water, pavement, house,** or **vehicle.** Let's give some reasonable constraints about relationships of regions in an aerial photo.

- a region cannot border or be inside a region with the same label (else we couldn't see the boundary edge);
- houses and vehicles cannot be next to or surrounded by water regions (we assume no water is deep enough for boats in this part of the world);
- vehicles must be next to or surrounded by pavement, but pavement cannot be inside them;
- vehicles cannot be inside houses;
- grass cannot be inside vehicles or houses;
- pavement cannot be completely inside another region (pavement nearly always connects to other pavement);
- only houses, vehicles, and pavement are regular (straight-edged) regions;
- only grass and water are irregular regions;
- on a scale of 1 inch = 150 feet for Figure 13-2, vehicles cannot exceed an area of one twenty-fifth of a square inch.

These constraints might be violated, but aren't likely to be—remember, artificial intelligence programs don't try to be perfect, just "intelligent." We'll know when constraints must be violated by being unable to find a solution to a problem. Then we can remove the most questionable constraint and try again, and then the second most questionable, and so on until we do find a solution.

Examining the photo in Figure 13-2, we see five regions; we've written names on them for convenience. R5 is the only small region. Regions R3 and R5 are the only regions that are definitely regular; regions R1 and R2 are definitely irregular; but R4 is hard to classify so we won't state that it is either regular or irregular. R1 borders R2, and R2 borders R4; R3 is inside R2, and R5 is inside R4. So the photo interpretation problem can be described in a query this way:

```
?- label(R1), label(R2), label(R3), label(R4), label(R5),
   borders(R1,R2), borders(R2,R4), inside(R3,R2), inside(R5,R4),
   large(R1), large(R2), large(R3), large(R4),
   regular(R3), regular(R5), irregular(R2), irregular(R1).
```

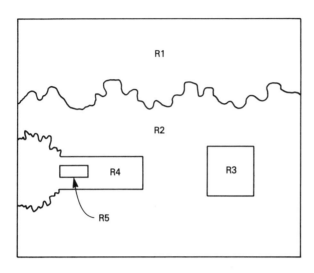

Figure 13-2. Example aerial photograph.

with the following definitions:

    label(grass).
    label(water).
    label(pavement).
    label(house).
    label(vehicle).

    borders(A1,A2) :- not(A1 = A2), not(water_constraint(A1,A2)),
      not(vehicle_constraint(A1,A2)).

    inside(A1,A2) :- not(A1 = A2), not(water_constraint(A1,A2)),
      not(vehicle_constraint2(A1,A2)),
      not(grass_constraint(A1,A2)), not(A1 = pavement).

    water_constraint(water,house).
    water_constraint(water,vehicle).
    water_constraint(house,water).
    water_constraint(vehicle,water).

    vehicle_constraint(A1,vehicle) :- not(A1 = pavement).
    vehicle_constraint(vehicle,A2) :- not(A2 = pavement).
    vehicle_constraint2(A1,vehicle).
    vehicle_constraint2(vehicle,A2) :- not(A2 = pavement).

    grass_constraint(grass,house).
    grass_constraint(grass,vehicle).

    large(A) :- not(A = vehicle).

regular(house).
regular(vehicle).
regular(pavement).

irregular(grass).
irregular(water).

Here water_constraint, vehicle_constraint, and grass_constraint predicates specify impermissible combinations of adjacent regions.

13.2 REARRANGING LONG QUERIES WITHOUT LOCAL VARIABLES

Before giving the Prolog interpreter a long query, we can often rearrange it into a more efficient form. It's usually best in an "and" to put first the predicate expressions hardest to satisfy. We can use probabilities to explain why. Take the query

?- a, b, c.

and suppose a is true with probability 0.9, b with probability 0.5, and c with probability 0.8. Assume these probabilities are independent of each other. Then the preceding query has a probability of success of 0.9 * 0.5 * 0.8 = 0.36, and a probability of failure of 0.64. So it will more often fail than succeed. When it does fail, we would like to know as soon as possible. With the order as given, 0.1 of the time we will recognize a failure from evaluating just the a, and 0.9 * 0.5 = 0.45 from evaluating both a and b. That's a total of 0.55. But if we rearrange the query as

?- b, c, a.

then 0.5 of the time we will know a failure from examining the first predicate expression, and 0.5 * 0.2 = 0.1 from examining the first two. That's a total of 0.6. So we're finding the failure earlier, meaning a little less work for us.

In general, if we have a bunch of predicate expressions "and"ed together, we should order them by *increasing* probability of success. (Even when complete independence of the probabilities does not hold, this is a good heuristic.) That way, if the whole thing is going to fail, we find out as soon as possible. This also applies to all rules with parameter variables but without local variables. For instance

f(X) :- b(X), c(X), a(X).

If for a random X, b succeeds with probability 0.5, c with probability 0.8, and a with probability 0.9, and these probabilities are all independent of each other, then this is the best arrangement of the right side of the rule for all queries of f with a bound argument, as for example

?- f(foo).

There is a corresponding idea for "or"s (rules "or"ed together). Consider

    r :- a.
    r :- b.
    r :- c.

Here we should try the rule most likely to succeed first, because if it succeeds then we're done. And we should try second the rule second-most-likely to succeed. The same applies to the rules

    r(X) :- a(X).
    r(X) :- b(X).
    r(X) :- c(X).

provided r is only queried with X bound. So we should order "or"s by *decreasing* probability of success, just the opposite of "and"s.

13.3 SOME MATHEMATICS

We can give general mathematical formulas for this rearrangement problem. They apply to any queries or rules without local variables, without "side effect" predicates like asserta and consult, and for which the success probabilities of expressions are independent.

First, suppose we have some expressions "and"ed together, where each has a probability of success p_i and an execution cost c_i (measured in arbitrary nonnegative units, perhaps time, perhaps the number of database queries made). Number the expressions from left to right. Consider two adjacent ones i and $i + 1$. Interchanging them will improve computation cost if

$$c_i + p_i c_{i+1} > c_{i+1} + p_{i+1} c_i$$

Manipulating the inequality we get:

$$(1 - p_{i+1})c_i > (1 - p_i)c_{i+1}$$

or

$$(1 - p_i)/c_i < (1 - p_{i+1})/c_{i+1}$$

In other words, we can use the ratio of probability of failure to the execution cost as a sorting criterion for adjacent expressions. Since repeated interchanges of adjacent expresssions are sufficient to sort a list (this is how the famous "bubble sort" sorting algorithm works), we should sort the expressions by this criterion to get the best order in an "and."

A similar formula applies to "or"s. We should interchange adjacent expressions i and $i + 1$ in an "or" if

$$c_i + (1 - p_i)c_{i+1} > c_{i+1} + (1 - p_{i+1})c_i$$

or

$$p_i/c_i < p_{i+1}/c_{i+1}$$

Here's an example. Take the query

   ?- a, b.

where a has probability 0.6 of success, and b has probability 0.8. If it costs the same amount of time to query either, a should be first. We can see this with the "and" formula because

$$(1 - 0.6)/1 > (1 - 0.8)/1 \quad \text{or} \quad 0.4 > 0.2$$

But suppose (without changing its probability) that a is defined as

   a :- c, d.

where c and d are only expressible as facts. Now it requires more work to find the truth of a: a query of a, followed by queries of c and d. If each query costs about the same, that's three times as much work. So now

$$(1 - 0.6)/3 < (1 - 0.8)/1 \quad \text{since} \quad 0.1333 < 0.2$$

and b is better to put first in the original query.

13.4 REARRANGING QUERIES WITH LOCAL VARIABLES_____

Local variables cause problems for the preceding reasoning. Consider

   ?- a(X), b(X).

Here X is local to the query, and will be bound in a; a isn't expected to fail. But if we try to rearrange the query to

   ?- b(X), a(X).

b is now the predicate that binds X, and it becomes unlikely to fail. So predicate expressions that bind local variables to values must be analyzed specially.

   For certain expressions we can ignore this problem, those that require bound variable values. Consider

   ?- a(X), b(Y), X>Y.
   ?- a(X), Y is X*X.
   ?- a(X), square(X,Y).

where square in the last query is defined by

   square(X,Y) :- Y is X*X.

In each of these queries, putting last predicate expression first will cause an error message about trying to refer to an unbound variable. Things are almost as bad with

?- a(X), b(Y), not(c(X,Y)).

which, while not giving an error message, gives different answers when the last expression is put first (see a similar use in the **done** predicate for forward chaining in Chapter 7):

?- not(c(X,Y)), a(X), b(Y).

The first predicate expression here asks whether there are any two-argument c facts, and doesn't connect its X and Y to those in the a and b predicates.

But assuming we *can* move expressions to a front binding position, which should we put there? Consider

?- a(X), b(X).

Suppose there are only a finite number of X values satisfying this query, say 5. Suppose predicate a is satisfied by 20 values of X, and predicate b by 100 values. If we put first a, then 5 of its 20 solutions will subsequently satisfy b. But if we put first b, then 5 of its 100 solutions will subsequently satisfy a. So if X values occur in a random way, we'll need more backtracking to answer the query the second way than the first. The amount of backtracking is the important criterion, because probabilities and costs don't apply here. Probabilities aren't relevant because we don't usually expect a variable-binding predicate to fail, and costs aren't relevant because binding a variable doesn't cost much.

To summarize: when you have several predicate expressions in an "and" that could bind variables were they moved to the left in a query, move the one with the fewest possible bindings total for those variables. Then sort the remaining expressions by increasing probability of success, as before.

13.5 REARRANGING QUERIES BASED ON DEPENDENCIES

Besides the preceding criteria, we should also use *dependencies* as criteria for rearranging queries. A dependency holds between two predicate expressions if they share a variable. Generally speaking, you should try to maximize the number of dependencies between adjacent expressions in an "and," while staying consistent with the previous criteria. This is because when two adjacent expressions don't have variables in common, the variable bindings in the first are irrelevant to the success or failure of the second, and later backtracking may be wasting its time going from the second to the first.

For example, consider

?- a(X), b(Y), c(X), e(X,Y), d(X), f(Y), g(Y).

Here the b expression has no dependency on the a expression, the c none on the b, and the f none on the d, though the other adjacent expressions do have dependencies. A better (not necessarily the best) rearrangement would be (assuming that this has about the same average overall cost due to expression probabilities and costs)

?- a(X), c(X), d(X), b(Y), e(X,Y), f(Y), g(Y).

where there is only one nondependency between adjacent expressions, between d and b. Now when g fails, backtracking only needs to go back three expressions, whereas before it needed to go back five.

13.6 SUMMARY OF GUIDELINES FOR OPTIMAL QUERY ARRANGEMENTS

We can summarize what we have concluded about query and rule rearrangement by the following guidelines. (They're like heuristics because they can be wrong.)

1. For an "and" that does not bind local variables, sort the predicate expressions by decreasing values of the ratio of the failure probability for the expression to its execution cost.

2. For either an "or" or for rules with the same left side (an implicit "or"), sort them by decreasing values of the ratio of the success probability for the rule to its execution cost.

3. For an "and" that binds local variables, choose to make binding for each variable the predicate expression that mentions it, among those that can bind it both legally and without changing the predicate meaning, that has the fewest database matches when queried alone. Then rearrange the rest of the expressions by guidelines 1 and 4 while freezing the position of these binding expressions.

4. Maximize the number of dependencies between adjacent expressions in an "and" as long as you don't violate the binding choices made according to guideline 3, or significantly violate the probability-cost ratio ordering in guideline 1.

Let's apply these guidelines to the scheduling example of Section 13.1. It originally looked like this:

```
classtime(T1), classtime(T2), classtime(T3),
  classtime(T4), classtime(T5),
  not(occupied(T1)), not(occupied(T2)), not(occupied(T3)),
  not(occupied(T4)), not(occupied(T5)),
  not(two_consecutive_hours([T1,T2,T3,T4,T5])),
  not(three_classes_same_day([T1,T2,T3,T4,T5])),
  not(duplication([T1,T2,T3,T4,T5])).
```

For guideline 3 the question is which expressions should bind variables **T1, T2, T3, T4,** and **T5.** But every expression besides the **classtime** ones has a **not** in front of it, so this arrangement will satisfy the conditions of guideline 3.

To better satisfy guideline 4, we can move the **not** expressions to immediately after the expressions binding them.

```
classtime(T1), not(occupied(T1)),
classtime(T2), not(occupied(T2)),
classtime(T3), not(occupied(T3)),
classtime(T4), not(occupied(T4)),
classtime(T5), not(occupied(T5)),
not(two_consecutive_hours([T1,T2,T3,T4,T5])),
not(three_classes_same_day([T1,T2,T3,T4,T5])),
not(duplication([T1,T2,T3,T4,T5])).
```

It's hard to guess success probabilities here—this varies enormously with the number of **occupied** facts we have—so we can just use computation cost to order by guideline 1. So we should keep the last three expressions last because they involve computation (calls to rule definitions), and the other **not** expressions don't. Similarly, **two_consecutive_hours** should precede **three_classes_same_day** because the first has four expressions in its definition, the second six. And **duplication** should go last because it involves some complicated processing.

13.7 REARRANGEMENT AND IMPROVEMENT OF THE PHOTO INTERPRETATION QUERY _____

The photo interpretation query of Section 13.1 requires more care to rearrange. Here it is:

```
?- label(R1), label(R2), label(R3), label(R4), label(R5),
   borders(R1,R2), borders(R2,R4), inside(R3,R2), inside(R5,R4)
   large(R1), large(R2), large(R3), large(R4),
   regular(R3), regular(R5), irregular(R2), irregular(R1).
```

All five variables (**R1, R2, R3, R4,** and **R5**) are bound locally in this query. So apply guideline 3 to decide which expressions to put first. The definitions of **borders, inside,** and **large** all have **nots** containing variables that would become unbound if those expressions were put first in the query. So the only expressions that can bind variables are those for **label, regular,** and **irregular.** Among them, **irregular** is best by guideline 3 because it has only two argument possibilities, **regular** is second best with three possibilities, and **label** is third with five (see Figure 13-3). That suggests this rearrangement:

```
?- irregular(R2), irregular(R1), regular(R3), regular(R5),
   label(R1), label(R2), label(R3), label(R4), label(R5),
   borders(R1,R2), borders(R2,R4), inside(R3,R2), inside(R5,R4)
   large(R1), large(R2), large(R3), large(R4).
```

Value	Satisfies label?	Satisfies large?	Satisfies regular?	Satisfies irregular?
grass	yes	yes	no	yes
water	yes	yes	no	yes
pavement	yes	yes	yes	no
house	yes	yes	yes	no
vehicle	yes	no	yes	no

Figure 13-3. Summary of the single-argument predicates in the photo interpretation example.

But now label can never fail for R2, R1, R3, and R5 (see Figure 13-3); any value bound in the first line will satisfy the label predicate. So we can eliminate four predicate expressions to give the equivalent shorter query

> ?- irregular(R2), irregular(R1), regular(R3), regular(R5),
>   label(R4), borders(R1,R2), borders(R2,R4), inside(R3,R2),
>   inside(R5,R4) large(R1), large(R2), large(R3), large(R4).

(We must still keep label(R4) because there's no regular or irregular fact to bind R4.)

So now the first line does all the variable binding. Let's now apply guideline 1 (the probability-to-cost ratio ordering) to the rest of the query, as suggested in the discussion of guideline 3. To simplify analysis, we'll assume all labels are equally likely, and we'll measure processing cost by the number of queries needed. Predicate large (see Figure 13-3) succeeds except if its argument is vehicle, so it succeeds with probability 0.8; it requires two query lookups. This means a guideline 1 ratio of $(1 - 0.8)/2 = 0.1$. Predicates borders and inside require more complicated analysis, however. Here again are their definitions:

> borders(A1,A2) :- not(A1 = A2), not(water_constraint(A1,A2)),
>   not(vehicle_constraint(A1,A2)).
> inside(A1,A2) :- not(A1 = A2), not(water_constraint(A1,A2)),
>   not(vehicle_constraint2(A1,A2)), not(grass_constraint(A1,A2)),
>   not(A1 = pavement).

Counting both left and right sides of rules, borders requires four query lookups for its four expressions, and inside requires six. (We'll ignore the added complication of lowered cost due to incomplete rule processing for some rule failures.) From Figure 13-4, we can estimate the probability of success of borders as $12/25 = 0.48$, and the probability of success of inside as $7/25 = 0.28$. Then the ratios needed for guideline 1 are $(1 - 0.48)/4 = 0.13$ for borders and $(1 - 0.28)/6 = 0.12$ for inside. By these rough numbers, borders expressions should come first, then inside expressions, and then large expressions. So the query should be rearranged to

> ?- irregular(R2), irregular(R1), regular(R3), regular(R5),
>   label(R4), borders(R1,R2), inside(R3,R2), borders(R2,R4),
>   inside(R5,R4), large(R1), large(R2), large(R3), large(R4).

A1 value	A2 value	*Satisfies* borders(A1,A2)?	*Satisfies* inside(A1,A2)?
grass	grass	no	no
grass	water	yes	yes
grass	pavement	yes	yes
grass	house	yes	no
grass	vehicle	no	no
water	grass	yes	yes
water	water	no	no
water	pavement	yes	yes
water	house	no	no
water	vehicle	no	no
pavement	grass	yes	no
pavement	water	yes	no
pavement	pavement	no	no
pavement	house	yes	no
pavement	vehicle	yes	no
house	grass	yes	yes
house	water	no	no
house	pavement	yes	yes
house	house	no	no
house	vehicle	no	no
vehicle	grass	no	no
vehicle	water	no	no
vehicle	pavement	yes	yes
vehicle	house	no	no
vehicle	vehicle	no	no

Figure 13-4. Summary of the two-argument predicates in the photo interpretation example.

Studying Figure 13-3, we see that **large** succeeds whenever **irregular** succeeds. So we can eliminate the **large(R1)** and **large(R2)** to get an equivalent query:

    ?- irregular(R2), irregular(R1), regular(R3), regular(R5),
       label(R4), borders(R1,R2), borders(R2,R4), inside(R3,R2),
       inside(R5,R4), large(R3), large(R4).

Now we can apply guideline 4, trying to group expressions mentioning the same variable together. One way is to move the **inside**, **borders**, and **large** expressions back into the first line, preserving their order at the expense of the order of the first line (since guideline 1 order is more important than guideline 3 order):

    ?- irregular(R2), irregular(R1), borders(R1,R2),
       label(R4), borders(R2,R4), regular(R3),
       inside(R3,R2), regular(R5), inside(R5,R4),
       large(R4), large(R3).

Here we've had to move **regular(R5)** considerably to the right, but that's the only expression moved significantly right.

So now we've probably got a much faster query. We emphasize "probably" since we had to make a number of simplifying assumptions about probabilities and costs. (If these assumptions seemed too much, we could do a more careful analysis using conditional probabilities and more subcases.)

13.8 DEPENDENCY-BASED BACKTRACKING

Our second technique for handling long queries is *dependency-based backtracking.*
Consider the query

?- a(X), b(X,Y), c(Z), d(X,Z), e(X).

Suppose the probability of any predicate expression succeeding is 0.1, and that
these probabilities are independent of the success or failure of other expressions.
On the average we'll need to generate 10 X values before we find one that works, 10
Y values, and 10 Z values. But for each X value we must try about 10 Y values, for
about 100 Y values in all; and for each Y value we must try about 10 Z values, for
about 1000 Z values in all. So there will be a lot of backtracking to answer this
query with Prolog's standard backward-chaining control structure.

An alternative is *nonchronological* or *dependency-based* backtracking. That
is, backing up to the expression that did the last variable binding that could have
affected the failure, and finding a new binding there. That's not necessarily the previous expression, so dependency-based backtracking is "smarter" backtracking,
backtracking that notices and takes obvious shortcuts. Dependencies (indications of
which expressions have common variables) help this considerably, so that's why
they're in the name of the technique. Prolog interpreters don't provide
dependency-based backtracking, but there are programs for it.

Let's apply dependency-based backtracking to the previous query. First, we
need to tabulate the predicate expressions in the query that bind, and what expressions have dependencies on what other expressions; see Figure 13-5. Assume as a
database for this query

a(1).
a(2).
a(3).
b(A,B) :- B is 3*A.
c(4).
c(1).
d(A,B) :- A>B.
e(3).

Predicate expression	Variables bound	Dependencies to previous predicate expressions	Dependencies that bind a common variable
a(X)	X	none	none
b(X,Y)	Y	a(X)	a(X)
c(Z)	Z	none	none
d(X,Z)	none	a(X),b(X,Y),c(Z)	a(X),c(Z)
e(X)	none	a(X),b(X,Y),d(X,Z)	a(X)

Figure 13-5. Summary of dependencies in an example query.

Then what happens in executing the query with dependency-based backtracking is shown in Figure 13-6. Notice that it's identical to regular Prolog backtracking except at three places, after steps 7, 14, and 16:

- After step 7, we backtrack from the third predicate expression directly to the first, since variable X must be responsible for the earlier failure of the fourth expression, and variable Y has nothing to do with that failure.
- After step 14, we backtrack from the last expression directly to the first, since variable X is the only possible cause of the failure, and the first expression binds it.
- After step 16, we skip over the third expression in moving back to the right, since it didn't fail and it doesn't include any variables whose values were changed since the last time it was visited.

So the effect of dependency-based backtracking is to save us 5 actions (right and left movements) out of 24 total. That's not much, but other queries show more dramatic savings.

Given the query:

?- a(X), b(X,Y), c(Z), d(X,Z), e(X).

Given the database:

a(1).
a(2).
a(3).
b(A,B) :- B is 3*A.
c(4).
c(1).
d(A,B) :- A > B.
e(3).

This is what happens in dependency-based backtracking:

Step	a(X)	b(X,Y)	c(Z)	d(X,Z)	e(X)
start	active	active	active	active	active
1	X bound to 1	active	active	active	active
2	inactive	Y bound to 3	active	active	active
3	inactive	inactive	Z bound to 4	active	active
4	inactive	inactive	inactive	fails	active
5	active	inactive	Z bound to 1	active	active
6	active	inactive	inactive	fails	active
7	active	inactive	fails	active	active
8	X bound to 2	active	active	active	active
9	inactive	Y bound to 6	active	active	active
10	inactive	inactive	Z bound to 4	active	active
11	inactive	inactive	inactive	fails	active
12	active	inactive	Z bound to 1	active	active
13	active	inactive	inactive	succeeds	active
14	active	inactive	inactive	inactive	fails
15	X bound to 3	active	inactive	active	active
16	inactive	Y bound to 9	inactive	active	active
17	inactive	inactive	inactive	succeeds	active
18	inactive	inactive	inactive	inactive	succeeds

Figure 13-6. Dependency-based backtracking example.

Here's an algorithm for dependency-based backtracking:

1. Mark every predicate expression in the query as "active." Set P to the left-most predicate in the query.

2. Execute repeatedly until you reach the right end of the query, or backtrack off the left end:

   (a) Execute expression P, and mark it as "inactive."

   (b) If P succeeds and does not bind variables, set P to the next expression to the right that is marked "active."

   (c) If P succeeds and binds variables, mark as "active" all other query expressions to the right containing those variables if (1) they are not so marked already and (2) the values are different from the previous values of those variables. Set P to the next expression to the right that is marked "active."

   (d) If P fails, mark as "active" all the expressions to the left of P that bind variables mentioned in P. Set P to the first expression to the left that is currently marked "active" (which is not necessarily one just marked, for it may have been marked previously).

There are further improvements on dependency-based backtracking that we don't have space for here. The theory is quite elegant, and this is an active area of research, also called *truth maintenance*.

13.9 REASONING ABOUT POSSIBILITIES

There's a third way to efficiently handle long queries. The idea is to abandon considering variable bindings one at a time, and to reason about the set of possibilities for each variable. Consider the query of the last section:

?- a(X), b(X,Y), c(Z), d(X,Z), e(X).

Suppose there are only a finite number of ways to satisfy each predicate expression. We could figure out all the possible values for X that satisfy a(X), and then check which of them also satisfy e(X). Then for each remaining choice we could check which could satisfy b(X,Y), eliminating those that can't. Then we could figure out the possible values of Z that satisfy c(Z), and determine which of those have a corresponding X value remaining that can satisfy d(X,Z). Sherlock Holmes might put the approach this way: when you have eliminated the impossible, whatever remains, however improbable, must include the truth.

Why reason about sets of possibilities for variables? So we don't need to work as hard to answer the query. Early elimination of impossible values for variables reduces fruitless backtracking in a later Prolog-style query execution. Sometimes we can even reduce possibilities to one for each variable, and we don't need to do any further work. Possibility reasoning is called *relaxation*—a technical term that has nothing to do with vacations on beaches. Artificial intelligence uses in particular *discrete relaxation*, relaxation involving variables with finitely large possibility sets.

13.10 USING RELAXATION FOR THE PHOTO
INTERPRETATION EXAMPLE‗‗‗‗‗‗‗‗‗‗‗‗‗‗‗‗‗‗‗‗‗‗‗‗

We'll present an algorithm for relaxation in Section 13.12. It's a little complicated. To work our way up to it, let's see how we can reason about possibility lists for the photo interpretation problem of Section 13.1, the one with the query

    ?- label(R1), label(R2), label(R3), label(R4), label(R5),
       borders(R1,R2), borders(R2,R4), inside(R3,R2), inside(R5,R4),
       large(R1), large(R2), large(R3), large(R4), regular(R3),
       regular(R5), irregular(R2), irregular(R1).

To get possibility lists for each variable, we must extract the single-variable expressions referring to each variable:

    variable R1: label(R1), large(R1), irregular(R1).
    variable R2: label(R2), large(R2), irregular(R2).
    variable R3: label(R3), large(R3), regular(R3).
    variable R4: label(R4), large(R4).
    variable R5: label(R5), regular(R5).

Reexamining Figure 13-3, we can see what values (labels) are consistent with the restrictions. The possible labels are grass, water, pavement, house, and vehicle. The large predicate rules out the vehicle label. The regular predicate specifies house, vehicle, or pavement, and irregular specifies grass or water. So the initial possibility lists are

    variable R1: grass or water
    variable R2: grass or water
    variable R3: house or pavement
    variable R4: house or pavement or grass or water
    variable R5: house or vehicle or pavement

Now let's eliminate or "cross out" possibilities using the remaining multivariable predicate expressions (constraints) of the original query:

    borders(R1,R2), borders(R2,R4), inside(R3,R2), inside(R5,R4)

We can pick a variable and a possibility, and check if the possibility works. Suppose we pick R1 and grass. The borders(R1,R2) mentions R1, so we see if some R2 value will work with R1 = grass—that is, whether there's some label that could border grass. Yes, R2 = water works. Check the definition of borders:

    borders(A1,A2) :- not(A1 = A2), not(water_constraint(A1,A2)),
       not(vehicle_constraint(A1,A2)).

For A1 = grass and A2 = water, A1 is not equal to A2. The water_constraint only applies when one label is a house or vehicle, as you can see from its definition:

    water_constraint(water,house).
    water_constraint(water,vehicle).
    water_constraint(house,water).
    water_constraint(vehicle,water).

And vehicle_constraint only applies when A1 or A2 is a vehicle:

    vehicle_constraint(A1,vehicle) :- not(A1 = pavement).
    vehicle_constraint(vehicle,A2) :- not(A2 = pavement).

So R1 = grass will work for at least one value of R2, which is all we need to keep us from crossing grass out.

But if we examine a different variable or value, things can be different. Suppose we pick the R2 variable and water. The inside(R3,R2) constraint mentions R2. But there's no way to label R3 to satisfy the second expression on the right side of the inside definition. Here's that definition:

    inside(A1,A2) :- not(A1 = A2), not(water_constraint(A1,A2)),
        not(vehicle_constraint2(A1,A2)), not(grass_constraint(A1,A2)),
        not(A1 = pavement).

The only possibilities for R3 from the single-variable constraints are house and pavement, and water_constraint succeeds for the first. Hence the not fails, and inside fails too because this is the only rule for inside. In other words, a house can't be inside water, a reasonable assumption for most pictures, though you can probably imagine a few exceptions. But R3 cannot be pavement either by the last expression in the inside definition. So R2 cannot be water. The only remaining possibility is grass, so R2 must be grass.

Once we've eliminated possibilities for a variable, we can often eliminate possibilities for other variables appearing in constraints with it. Consider variable R1 which we didn't have any success with originally. Now it's no longer possible that R1 is grass, because then R1 would be the same as R2, and the first condition in the borders definition prohibits that. It says two adjacent regions can't have the same label (since we couldn't then see the boundary). There's only one remaining label for R1, water, so R1 must be that.

Our possibility lists are now:

    variable R1: water
    variable R2: grass
    variable R3: house or pavement
    variable R4: house or pavement or grass or water
    variable R5: house or vehicle or pavement

Now consider **R3**. It can't be pavement because **R3** is inside **R2**, and the last condition in the definition of **inside** says that the thing inside can't be pavement. That is, pavement must connect to other pavement—a reasonable, though sometimes false, assumption. So **R3** must be a house.

Consider **R4**. It can't be grass because it borders **R2**, and **R2** is already grass. It can't be water because water can't contain (as **R5**) a house or a vehicle by **water_constraint**, and water can't contain pavement by the last condition in the **inside** definition. That leaves house or pavement for **R4**. Now consider **R5**. It can't be pavement because pavement can't be contained in anything. So it must be a house or vehicle.

Now consider **R4** again. Suppose it's a house. Then **R5** can't be a house too because that would make two adjacent regions with the same label. But **R5** couldn't be a vehicle either, because a vehicle can't be inside a house by the **vehicle_constraint2** definition. So **R4** can't be a house, and must be pavement.

No further eliminations can be done, so the final possibility lists are:

variable **R1**: water
variable **R2**: grass
variable **R3**: house
variable **R4**: pavement
variable **R5**: house or vehicle

13.11 QUANTIFYING THE EFFECT*

To show the savings in considering possibility lists instead of individual values, let's use some numbers. Suppose there are n_Y possibilities for a variable **Y**. Suppose the expression $d(X,Y)$ is satisfied by fraction p of all possible **XY** pairs. If we can assume satisfaction pairs for **d** are randomly distributed over all **XY** pairs, then the probability that some **X** value r has at least one corresponding **Y** that satisfies **d** can be approximated by the binomial series:

$$1 - (1 - p)^{n_Y} = n_Y p - n_Y(n_Y - 1)p^2/2 + n_Y(n_Y - 1)(n_Y - 2)p^3/6 - \cdots$$

And the expected number of such matched **X** values in the n_X values for **X** will be just n_X times this. Figure 13-7 shows the probability computed for sample values of p and n_Y. When p is small (as a rule of thumb, whenever $p < 0.2$) we can approximate the binomial distribution by the Poisson distribution, and the probability is

$$1 - e^{-n_Y p}$$

And the expected number of **X** values remaining from n_X originally, after examining predicate $d(X,Y)$ which has probability of success p and n_Y values of **Y** that can match it is

$$n_X(1 - e^{-n_Y p})$$

The smaller this number, the better is reasoning about possibilities first before working Prolog-style.

n	p	Probability
5	0.25	0.76
10	0.25	0.94
20	0.25	1.00
50	0.25	1.00
5	0.1	0.4
10	0.1	0.65
20	0.1	0.88
50	0.1	0.99
5	0.01	0.05
10	0.01	0.10
20	0.01	0.18
50	0.01	0.39
100	0.01	0.63

Figure 13-7. Probability that at least one item in a list will be possible, for an n-item list with independent probabilities P for each item that it will be impossible.

If several constraints mention a variable, each can independently eliminate possibilities, further reducing their number. Consider this query:

?- a(R), b(S), c(T), d(R,S), e(S,T).

Suppose there are 10 ways to satisfy predicate a, 20 ways to satisfy b, and 50 ways to satisfy c. Suppose further that the probability is 0.1 that a random pair of values satisfy d, and 0.01 that a random pair of values will satisfy e, and that probabilities are all independent. Then:

- From Figure 13-7 and our formula we can expect $10*0.88 = 8.8$ possibilities remaining for R that satisfy d, on the average.
- And we can expect $50*0.39 = 19.5$ possibilities remaining for T that satisfy e, on the average.
- S occurs in both the two-argument predicates d and e. For the occurrence in d we can expect $20 * (1 - e^{-8.8*0.1}) = 11.7$ possibilities remaining.
- The predicate e can only remove further S possibilities of these. If satisfaction of e is probabilistically independent of satisfaction of d, for instance, we expect $11.7 *(1 - e^{-19.5*0.01}) = 2.1$ possibilities remaining for S. That's a lot better than the initial 20.

13.12 FORMALIZATION OF PURE RELAXATION

Here's an algorithm for the simplest kind of relaxation method for answering "and"ed-constraint queries: *pure* relaxation. It can be summarized as three embedded loops that pick first a variable, then a value, and then a constraint. Note for efficiency in this algorithm that it's important to index all variable names appearing in constraint expressions.

1. Create possibility lists for each variable using all single-variable query predicate expressions. (Single-argument expressions with a variable argument are single-variable, but others like p(X,a,X) can be too.) In Prolog, **bagof** will help do this.

2. Mark each variable in the original query as "active."

3. Do the following step repeatedly until no more "active" variables remain.

   (a) Choose some "active" variable A. (Heuristics may help choose, like "focus-of-attention" heuristics.) For each current possible value V for A:

   > For each constraint C mentioning variable A:
   >
   > > Check to see if when variable A has value V, constraint C can be satisfied some way (binding other variables of C as necessary). If not, skip the other constraints and remove V from the possibility list for A; otherwise do nothing. Throw away previous bindings in other constraints when considering each new constraint (this makes the relaxation "pure").

   (b) Mark variable A as "inactive," and if any of A's possibilities were eliminated, mark as "active" all variables that are (i) mentioned in constraints with A, and (ii) marked "inactive," and (iii) have more than one possibility remaining. If A has only one possibility remaining, substitute that value in all constraints mentioning A, and eliminate any constraints without variables.

4. If there is now a unique possibility for each variable, stop and give those values as the query answer. Otherwise, run the Prolog interpreter on the original query, drawing values from the possibility lists.

We emphasize that for every constraint we consider, we ignore bindings of its variables made when those variables occurred in other constraints. This "pure" relaxation idea may seem wasteful, but it avoids most backtracking, and if we didn't do it we would just be doing Prolog-style backward chaining in disguise. But compromises between the two approaches are possible, like the *double relaxation* we'll show later.

One nice thing about this relaxation algorithm is its good potential for concurrency. We can work in parallel on different constraints, values, or variables.

13.13 ANOTHER RELAXATION EXAMPLE: CRYPTARITHMETIC

No artificial-intelligence book would be complete without an analysis of a good puzzle problem. Analysis of "brain-teaser" puzzles stimulated much of the early development of the field.

A classic application of relaxation is to puzzles in which numbers are represented by letters (*cryptarithmetic*). Here the variables are the letters and the possibility lists are numbers those letters can be (often, the possibilities are restricted to single digits). Constraints come from arithmetic relationships between the digits. Here's a famous example, where every letter stands for a different digit, and every occurrence of a letter is the same digit.

```
    S E N D
 +  M O R E
 ----------
  M O N E Y
```

Note that's the letter "O," not the number zero. To make the problem easier, suppose we are told that E=5. (Otherwise we can't solve it completely with pure relaxation.)

So from the single-variable constraints, initial possibility lists for this problem are (representing 8,100,000 combinations):

M: [1,2,3,4,5,6,7,8,9]
S: [1,2,3,4,5,6,7,8,9]
O: [0,1,2,3,4,5,6,7,8,9]
E: [5]
N: [0,1,2,3,4,5,6,7,8,9]
R: [0,1,2,3,4,5,6,7,8,9]
D: [0,1,2,3,4,5,6,7,8,9]
Y: [0,1,2,3,4,5,6,7,8,9]

Each letter represents a variable for this problem. Note M and S cannot be 0 because they are the first digits in numbers, and numbers don't start with 0. On the other hand, we can't cross out the 5's yet because we need to use a multi-variable constraint for them.

But there are also some important additional variables buried in the problem: the carries from each column. We'll label these C1, C10, and C100, representing the carries out of the 1's column, the 10's column, and the 100's column respectively. Their possibilities for two-number addition are:

C1: [0,1]
C10: [0,1]
C100: [0,1]

Here are the constraints on the variables. They're written in equation notation instead of Prolog to make them clearer. The first four come from the rules of column addition, and the last says that digit assignments must be unique. While these constraints could also be satisfied for integers greater than 9 or real numbers, the initial possibility lists will prevent such happenings.

Con1: D + E = Y + (10 * C1)
Con2: N + R + C1 = E + (10 * C10)
Con3: E + O + C10 = N + (10 * C100)
Con4: S + M + C100 = O + (10 * M)
Con5: all_different_numbers(S,E,N,D,M,O,R,Y)

Since E=5 we can substitute that value into the constraints to simplify them:

```
Con1: D + 5 = Y + (10 * C1)
Con2: N + R + C1 = 5 + (10 * C10)
Con3: 5 + O + C10 = N + (10 * C100)
Con4: S + M + C100 = O + (10 * M)
Con5: all_different_numbers(S,5,N,D,M,O,R,Y)
```

That covers step 1 of the relaxation algorithm, so we proceed to step 2 and mark every letter and carry as "active." Now we start step 3, the big step. We will follow a "leftmost-first" heuristic that says to work on the active variable representing the digit or carry that is farthest left in the sum display.

1. We pick M as the first variable according to our heuristic. Only constraints Con4 and Con5 mention M. And the only value of M satisfying Con4 is 1, since 0 is not on M's original possibility list, and a value for M of 2 or greater would make the right side of Con4 at least 20, and there's no combination of S and C100 drawn from their possibility lists whose sum plus 2 (for M=2) could equal or surpass 20. We mark M inactive.

2. Using our "leftmost active" choice heuristic, we pick S next. It's only mentioned in Con4 and Con5. The only way to satisfy Con4 is if S is 8 or 9, because M is 1 and the right side is at least 10. Con5 doesn't further eliminate possibilities for S. We mark S inactive.

3. We pick O next. It's mentioned in Con3, Con4, and Con5. We can't do anything with Con3, but by Con4 we see O must be 0 or 1 since M=1 and S is either 8 or 9. But turning now to Con5, O cannot be 1 (with M already 1). So O=0. We mark S active and O inactive.

4. We pick S next. We can't conclude anything about it, so we mark it inactive. (Nothing is marked active because we didn't rule out any possibilities.)

5. We pick C100 next. It's mentioned in Con3 and Con4. It must be 0, since 5 + 0 + C10 < 7. We mark S active, and C100 inactive.

6. We pick S next. Now by Con4 it must be 9, since 9 + 1 + 0 = 0 + (10*1). S is marked inactive. Current possibility lists and activity markings are:

```
M: [1] inactive
S: [9] inactive
O: [0] inactive
E: [5] inactive
N: [0,1,2,3,4,5,6,7,8,9] active
R: [0,1,2,3,4,5,6,7,8,9] active
D: [0,1,2,3,4,5,6,7,8,9] active
Y: [0,1,2,3,4,5,6,7,8,9] active
C1: [0,1] active
C10: [0,1] active
C100: [0] inactive
```

And the sum looks like:

```
  9 5 N D
+ 1 0 R 5
---------
1 0 N 5 Y
```

And the constraints are:

Con1: $D + 5 = Y + (10 * C1)$
Con2: $N + R + C1 = 5 + (10 * C10)$
Con3: $5 + C10 = N$
Con4: $10 = 10$
Con5: all_different_numbers(9,5,N,D,1,0,R,Y)

We can ignore Con4 from now on because it no longer has variables.

7. Pick N next. It's mentioned in Con2, Con3, and Con5. Con2 doesn't help, but Con3 says N must be 5 or 6. And then Con5 says N can't be 5 since E is already, so N=6. Mark N inactive.

8. Pick C10. It's mentioned in Con2 and Con3. But for Con3 it must be 1 since N=6. Mark C10 inactive.

9. Pick R. It's mentioned in Con2 and Con5. In Con2, $6 + R + C1 = 5 + 10*1$, so R is 8 or 9. But by Con5, R cannot be 9 because S is already 9. So R=8. Mark R inactive.

10. Pick C1. It's mentioned in Con1 and Con2. By Con2, it must be 1. Mark C1 inactive.

11. Pick D. It's mentioned in Con1 and Con5. By Con1, $D + 5 = Y + 10*1$. This means $D = Y + 5$, so D can only be 5, 6, 7, 8, or 9. But by Con5, the values 5, 6, 8, and 9 are ruled out because variables already have those values. So D=7. Mark D inactive.

12. Pick Y. By Con1, it must be 2. Mark Y inactive. Now every variable is marked inactive, so we can stop.

The final solution is:

$M = 1, S = 9, O = 0, E = 5, N = 6, R = 8, D = 7,$
$Y = 2, C1 = 1, C10 = 1, C100 = 0$

```
  9 5 6 7
+ 1 0 8 5
---------
1 0 6 5 2
```

Notice relaxation is much like iterative methods for solving mathematical equations: "convergence" or progress towards the solution may be slow at times, but things speed up as the solution approaches. At any rate, the solution can be reached much faster this way than with backward-chaining Prolog, considering the 8,100,000 initial combinations of valid values.

13.14 IMPLEMENTATION OF PURE RELAXATION* _____

We can implement relaxation as we implemented the chaining programs (Chapter 7) and search programs (Chapter 10): with a problem-independent file and a problem-dependent file. The latter must specify the constraints. In it we'll require the following definitions (as either facts or rules):

- choices(<variable_name>,<possible_value>)—gives initial possibilities for <variable_name>, incorporating all the single-variable constraints
- constraint(<type>,<argument_list>)—gives multivariable constraints, classifying by type and arguments
- satisfiable(<type>,<argument_list>,<bindings_found>)—determines whether a multivariable constraint of a given type is actually satisfiable by some set of variable bindings

To circumvent the Prolog interpreter's usual binding of variables, "variable names" here must actually be constants (written in lower case). Note that because constraints have a type as an argument, all constraints of the same type can be checked by a single satisfiable predicate definition. Another reason for having both constraint and satisfiable is that relaxation can notice common variables between constraints without having to test constraints.

Here's an example problem-dependent file, the definitions for the photo interpretation problem considered earlier. Much of the code remains the same as before.

```
choices(R,CL) :- member(R,[r1,r2,r3,r4,r5]),
  bagof(C,choice(R,C),CL).

choice(R,grass) :- irregular(R).
choice(R,water) :- irregular(R).
choice(R,pavement) :- regular(R).
choice(R,house) :- regular(R).
choice(R,vehicle) :- regular(R), not(large(R)).
choice(R,L) :- not(regular(R)), not(irregular(R)), label(L).

label(grass).
label(water).
label(pavement).
label(house).
label(vehicle).

large(r1).
large(r2).
large(r3).
large(r4).
```

```
regular(r3).
regular(r5).

irregular(r2).
irregular(r1).

constraint(borders,[r1,r2]).
constraint(borders,[r2,r4]).
constraint(inside,[r3,r2]).
constraint(inside,[r5,r4]).

satisfiable(borders,Args,[A1,A2]) :- some_bindings(Args,[A1,A2]),
   not(A1 = A2), not(water_constraint(A1,A2)),
   not(vehicle_constraint(A1,A2)).
satisfiable(inside,Args,[A1,A2]) :- some_bindings(Args,[A1,A2]),
   not(A1 = A2), not(water_constraint(A1,A2)),
   not(vehicle_constraint2(A1,A2)),
   not(grass_constraint(A1,A2)), not(A1 = pavement).


water_constraint(water,house).
water_constraint(water,vehicle).
water_constraint(house,water).
water_constraint(vehicle,water).


vehicle_constraint(A1,vehicle) :- not(A1 = pavement).
vehicle_constraint(vehicle,A2) :- not(A2 = pavement).
vehicle_constraint2(A1,vehicle).
vehicle_constraint2(vehicle,A2) :- not(A2 = pavement).


grass_constraint(grass,house).
grass_constraint(grass,vehicle).
```

The problem-independent code implements the algorithm given in Section
13.12. Figure 13-8 gives the predicate hierarchy. The top-level predicate is **relax** of
no arguments. It firsts converts all **choices** definitions into possibility lists. It then
repeatedly chooses an **active** variable, until no more such variables exist. For that
variable, it retrieves the possibility list and checks each possibility in turn, making a
list of those possibilities that are satisfiable, using the **bagof** predicate defined in
Section 10.6. If any previous possibilities are now impossible (meaning that the
possibility list is shortened), it marks all variables in constraints with this one as
active, and makes this variable inactive. If only one possibility remains for the variable, then (predicate **check_unique**) that value is substituted into the constraints.
Any constraints no longer having variables in them, just constants, are removed.

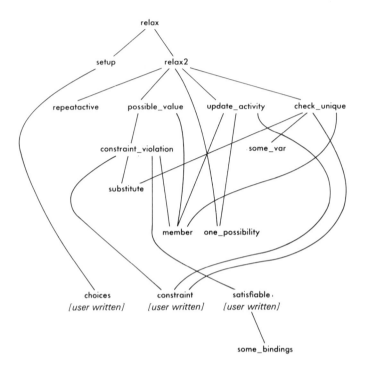

Figure 13-8. Predicate hierarchy for the pure-relaxation program.

Checking of possibilities is done by **possible_value** and **constraint_violation**. The first generates possibilities, and the second substitutes them into the constraints and calls **satisfiable** to check for satisfiability. Only constraints containing the variable under study are accessed. Note it's important we look for constraint violation and not constraint satisfaction; as soon as we find a constraint that can't be satisfied, we can stop and cross out a possibility.

Here's the program for pure relaxation:

```
/* Top-level routines */
relax :- setup, relax2.
relax :- listing(choice_list).
```

```
relax2 :- repeatactive, choice_list(O,CL), active(O),
  retract(active(O)), not(one_possibility(CL)),
  write('Studying variable '), write(O), nl,
  bagof(V,possible_value(O,CL,V),NCL), not(CL = NCL),
  retract(choice_list(O,CL)), asserta(choice_list(O,NCL)),
  write('Possibilities for '), write(O), write(' reduced to '),
  write(NCL), nl, update_activity(O), check_unique(O,NCL), fail.
```

```
/* Creation of the initial possibility lists */
setup :- abolish(choice_list,2), fail.
setup :- choices(O,VL), assertz(choice_list(O,VL)),
  assertz(active(O)), fail.
setup.

/* Analysis of a particular variable value */
possible_value(O,CL,V) :- member(V,CL),
  not(constraint_violation(V,O)).

constraint_violation(V,O) :- constraint(Type,Args), member(O,Args),
  substitute(O,V,Args,Args2), not(satisfiable(Type,Args2,Newargs)).

update_activity(O) :- constraint(T,A), member(O,A),
  member(O2,A), not(O2 = O), choice_list(O2,L), not(active(O2)),
  not(one_possibility(L)), asserta(active(O2)), fail.
update_activity(O).

check_unique(O,[V]) :- constraint(Type,Args), member(O,Args),
  substitute(O,V,Args,Args2), retract(constraint(Type,Args)),
  some_var(Args2), asserta(constraint(Type,Args2)), fail.
check_unique(O,L).

/* Utility routines */
some_var([X|L]) :- choice_list(X,CL), !.
some_var([X|L]) :- some_var(L).

one_possibility([ZZZ]).

repeatactive.
repeatactive :- active(X), repeatactive.

member(X,[X|L]).
member(X,[Y|L]) :- member(X,L).

substitute(X,Y,[],[]).
substitute(X,Y,[X|L],[Y|L2]) :- substitute(X,Y,L,L2), !.
substitute(X,Y,[Z|L],[Z|L2]) :- substitute(X,Y,L,L2).

/* Note—the following is not necessary to run the program, but */
/* is provided as an aid to user definition of "satisfiable" */
some_bindings([],[]).
some_bindings([Arg|Args],[Substarg|Substargs]) :-
  choice_list(Arg,CL), !, member(Substarg,CL),
  substitute(Arg,Substarg,Args,Args2),
  some_bindings(Args2,Substargs).
some_bindings([Arg|Args],[Arg|Substargs]) :-
  some_bindings(Args,Substargs).
```

Here's the program working on our photo interpretation problem:

```
?- relax.
Studying variable r1
Studying variable r2
Possibilities for r2 reduced to [grass]
Studying variable r3
Possibilities for r3 reduced to [house]
Studying variable r4
Possibilities for r4 reduced to [pavement]
Studying variable r5
Possibilities for r5 reduced to [house,vehicle]
Studying variable r1
Possibilities for r1 reduced to [water]

choice_list(r1,[water]).
choice_list(r5,[house,vehicle]).
choice_list(r4,[pavement]).
choice_list(r3,[house]).
choice_list(r2,[grass]).

yes
```

13.15 RUNNING A CRYPTARITHMETIC RELAXATION*_____

Here's a similar problem-dependent file defining the "send more money" cryptarithmetic problem:

```
choices(D,[0,1,2,3,4,5,6,7,8,9]) :- member(D,[n,d,r,o,y]).
choices(D,[1,2,3,4,5,6,7,8,9]) :- member(D,[s,m]).
choices(e,[5]).
choices(C,[0,1]) :- member(C,[c1,c10,c100]).

constraint(sum,[s,m,c100,o,m]).
constraint(sum,[e,o,c10,n,c100]).
constraint(sum,[n,r,c1,e,c10]).
constraint(sum,[d,e,0,y,c1]).
constraint(unique,[s,e,n,d,m,o,r,y]).

satisfiable(sum,L,[D1,D2,Carryin,Sum,Carryout]) :-
  some_bindings(L,[D1,D2,Carryin,Sum,Carryout]),
  S is D1 + D2 + Carryin,
  S2 is Sum + (Carryout * 10), S = S2.
satisfiable(unique,L,VL) :- not(duplication(L)),
  unique_values(L,VL,[]).
```

```
duplication([X|L]) :- member(X,L), !.
duplication([X|L]) :- duplication(L).

unique_values([],[],KL).
unique_values([O|L],[V|L2],KL) :- choice_list(O,VL), !,
   unique_values(L,L2,KL), member(V,VL), not(member(V,L2)),
   not(member(V,KL)).
unique_values([K|L],[K|L2],KL) :- unique_values(L,L2,[K|KL]),
   not(member(K,L2)).
```

The satisfiable rule with sum as first argument checks column-sum constraints, and the satisfiable rule with unique checks unique-assignment constraints.

Here's a run. We've inserted extra blank lines for readability. Notice that the order of considering variables is different than for the problem analysis of Section 13.13, so possibility eliminations come in a different order.

```
?- relax.
Studying variable n
Possibilities for n reduced to [0,1,2,3,4,6,7,8,9]
Studying variable d
Possibilities for d reduced to [0,1,2,3,4,6,7,8,9]
Studying variable r
Possibilities for r reduced to [0,1,2,3,4,6,7,8,9]
Studying variable o
Possibilities for o reduced to [0,1]
Studying variable y
Possibilities for y reduced to [1,2,3,4,6,7,8,9]
Studying variable s
Possibilities for s reduced to [8,9]
Studying variable m
Possibilities for m reduced to [1]
Studying variable c1
Studying variable c10
Studying variable c100
Possibilities for c100 reduced to [0]
Studying variable s
Possibilities for s reduced to [9]
Studying variable y
Possibilities for y reduced to [2,3,4,6,7,8]
Studying variable o
Possibilities for o reduced to [0]
Studying variable r
Possibilities for r reduced to [2,3,4,6,7,8]
Studying variable d
Possibilities for d reduced to [2,3,7,8]
Studying variable n
Possibilities for n reduced to [6]
```

Studying variable c1
Possibilities for c1 reduced to [1]
Studying variable c10
Possibilities for c10 reduced to [1]

Studying variable d
Possibilities for d reduced to [7,8]
Studying variable r
Possibilities for r reduced to [8]
Studying variable y
Possibilities for y reduced to [2,3]
Studying variable d
Possibilities for d reduced to [7]
Studying variable y
Possibilities for y reduced to [2]

```
choice_list(y,[2]).
choice_list(d,[7]).
choice_list(r,[8]).
choice_list(c10,[1]).
choice_list(c1,[1]).
choice_list(n,[6]).
choice_list(o,[0]).
choice_list(s,[9]).
choice_list(c100,[0]).
choice_list(m,[1]).
choice_list(e,[5]).
```

13.16 IMPLEMENTING DOUBLE RELAXATION* _____

But pure relaxation can't solve the "send more money" problem unless we're told E=5 in advance. A better relaxation program could consider pairs of constraints together when it stops making progress analyzing single constraints. That is, a program could use the same bindings for variables common to two constraints. This "double relaxation" will be slower than pure relaxation, since there are more pairs than singles and it's doing more work with each pair, so it should only be used as a last resort. Only when both methods fail should relaxation stop.

```
/* Top-level routines */
relax :- setup, relax2.

relax2 :- single_pred_relax.
relax2 :- done.
relax2 :- double_pred_relax.
relax2 :- active(X), relax2.
relax2 :- not(active(X)), listing(choice_list).
```

```
done :- not(possibilities_remain), listing(choice_list).

possibilities_remain :- choice_list(O,CL),
  not(one_possibility(CL)).

single_pred_relax :- write('Single predicate relaxation begun.'),
  nl, repeatactive, choice_list(O,CL), active(O),
  retract(active(O)), not(one_possibility(CL)),
  write('Studying variable '), write(O), nl,
  bagof(V,possible_value(O,CL,V),NCL), not(CL = NCL),
  new_possibilities(O,CL,NCL), fail.

double_pred_relax :- write('Double predicate relaxation begun.'),
  nl, choice_list(O,CL), not(one_possibility(CL)),
  write('Studying variable '), write(O), nl,
  bagof(V,possible_value2(O,CL,V), NCL),
  not(CL = NCL), new_possibilities(O,CL,NCL), fail.

new_possibilities(O,CL,NCL) :- retract(choice_list(O,CL)),
  asserta(choice_list(O,NCL)), write('Possibilities for '),
  write(O), write(' reduced to '), write(NCL), nl,
  update_activity(O), check_unique(O,NCL).

/* Creation of the initial possibility lists */
setup :- abolish(choice_list,2), fail.
setup :- choices(O,VL), assertz(choice_list(O,VL)),
  assertz(active(O)), fail.
setup.

/* Single-relaxation analysis of a particular value for a particular
variable */
possible_value(O,CL,V) :- member(V,CL),
  not(constraint_violation(V,O)).

constraint_violation(V,O) :- constraint(Type,Args),
  member(O,Args), substitute(O,V,Args,Args2),
  not(satisfiable(Type,Args2,Newargs)).

update_activity(O) :- constraint(T,A), member(O,A), member(O2,A),
  not(O2 = O), choice_list(O2,L), not(active(O2)),
  not(one_possibility(L)), asserta(active(O2)), fail.
update_activity(O).

check_unique(O,[V]) :- constraint(Type,Args), member(O,Args),
  substitute(O,V,Args,Args2), retract(constraint(Type,Args)),
  some_var(Args2), asserta(constraint(Type,Args2)), fail.
check_unique(O,L).
```

```
some_var([X|L]) :- choice_list(X,CL), !.
some_var([X|L]) :- some_var(L).


one_possibility([ZZZ]).


/* Double-relaxation analysis of a particular value */
/* for a particular variable */
possible_value2(O,CL,V) :- member(V,CL),
  bagof([T,A],constraint(T,A),ConL),
  not(constraint_violation2(V,O,ConL)).


constraint_violation2(V,O,ConL) :-
  twoconstraints(ConL,Type,Args,Type2,Args2),
  member(O,Args), argsoverlap(Args,Args2),
  substitute(O,V,Args,XArgs),
  substitute(O,V,Args2,XArgs2),
  not(double_satisfiable(Type,XArgs,Type2,XArgs2)).


double_satisfiable(Type,Args,Type2,Args2) :-
  constraint_preference(Type2,Type),
  !, double_satisfiable(Type2,Args2,Type,Args).
double_satisfiable(Type,Args,Type2,Args2) :-
  satisfiable(Type,Args,Newargs),
  bind(Args,Newargs,Args2,Result),
  satisfiable(Type2,Result,Newargs2).


twoconstraints([[T,A]|ConL],T,A,T2,A2) :- member([T2,A2],ConL).
twoconstraints([[T,A]|ConL],T1,A1,T2,A2) :-
  twoconstraints(ConL,T1,A1,T2,A2).


argsoverlap(L1,L2) :- member(X,L1), member(X,L2),
  choice_list(X,CL), !.


bind([],[],A2,A2).
bind([V|A],[V|NA],A2,R) :- bind(A,NA,A2,R), !.
bind([O|A],[V|NA],A2,R) :- substitute(O,V,A2,NA2),
  bind(A,NA,NA2,R), !.


/* Utility functions */
repeatactive.
repeatactive :- active(X), repeatactive.


member(X,[X|L]).
member(X,[Y|L]) :- member(X,L).
```

```
substitute(X,Y,[],[]).
substitute(X,Y,[X|L],[Y|L2]) :- substitute(X,Y,L,L2), !.
substitute(X,Y,[Z|L],[Z|L2]) :- substitute(X,Y,L,L2).

some_bindings([],[]).
some_bindings([Arg|Args],[Substarg|Substargs]) :-
  choice_list(Arg,CL), !, member(Substarg,CL),
  substitute(Arg,Substarg,Args,Args2),
  some_bindings(Args2,Substargs).
some_bindings([Arg|Args],[Arg|Substargs]) :-
  some_bindings(Args,Substargs).
```

And here's the script of a run on the "send more money" problem, using the problem-dependent file of the last section, without E=5, and plus one additional fact which says sum constraints should be used before unique constraints (since sum requires less computation to check):

```
constraint_preference(sum,unique).
```

Extra blank lines were inserted in the following printout to make it easier to read.

```
?- relax.
Single predicate relaxation begun.
Studying variable e
Studying variable n
Studying variable d
Studying variable o
Possibilities for o reduced to [0,1]
Studying variable r
Studying variable y
Studying variable s
Possibilities for s reduced to [8,9]
Studying variable m
Possibilities for m reduced to [1]
Studying variable c1
Studying variable c10
Studying variable c100

Studying variable s
Studying variable o
Possibilities for o reduced to [0]
Studying variable e
Possibilities for e reduced to [2,3,4,5,6,7,8,9]
Studying variable n
Possibilities for n reduced to [2,3,4,5,6,7,8,9]
```

Studying variable d
Possibilities for d reduced to [2,3,4,5,6,7,8,9]
Studying variable r
Possibilities for r reduced to [2,3,4,5,6,7,8,9]
Studying variable y
Possibilities for y reduced to [2,3,4,5,6,7,8,9]
Studying variable c1
Studying variable c10
Studying variable c100
Possibilities for c100 reduced to [0]

Studying variable r
Studying variable d
Studying variable n
Studying variable e
Studying variable s
Possibilities for s reduced to [9]
Studying variable c10
Studying variable y
Possibilities for y reduced to [2,3,4,5,6,7,8]
Studying variable r
Possibilities for r reduced to [2,3,4,5,6,7,8]
Studying variable d
Possibilities for d reduced to [2,3,4,5,6,7,8]
Studying variable n
Possibilities for n reduced to [2,3,4,5,6,7,8]
Studying variable e
Possibilities for e reduced to [2,3,4,5,6,7,8]
Studying variable c1
Studying variable c10

Studying variable n
Studying variable d
Studying variable r
Studying variable y
Double predicate relaxation begun.
Studying variable e
Possibilities for e reduced to [2,3,4,5,6,7]
Studying variable n
Possibilities for n reduced to [3,4,5,6,7,8]
Studying variable d
Studying variable r
Studying variable y
Studying variable c1
Studying variable c10
Possibilities for c10 reduced to [1]

Single predicate relaxation begun.
Studying variable n
Studying variable e
Studying variable d
Studying variable r
Possibilities for r reduced to [3,4,5,6,7,8]
Studying variable y
Studying variable c1
Studying variable n
Studying variable e
Studying variable d

Double predicate relaxation begun.
Studying variable r
Possibilities for r reduced to [8]
Studying variable n
Possibilities for n reduced to [4,5,6,7]
Studying variable e
Possibilities for e reduced to [3,4,5,6]
Studying variable d
Possibilities for d reduced to [2,3,4,7]
Studying variable y
Possibilities for y reduced to [2,3,5,6,7]
Studying variable c1
Possibilities for c1 reduced to [1]

Single predicate relaxation begun.
Studying variable y
Possibilities for y reduced to [2,3]
Studying variable d
Possibilities for d reduced to [7]
Studying variable e
Possibilities for e reduced to [5,6]
Studying variable n
Possibilities for n reduced to [6]
Studying variable e
Possibilities for e reduced to [5]
Studying variable y
Possibilities for y reduced to [2]

```
choice_list(y,[2]).
choice_list(e,[5]).
choice_list(n,[6]).
choice_list(d,[7]).
choice_list(c1,[1]).
choice_list(r,[8]).
```

```
choice_list(c10,[1]).
choice_list(s,[9]).
choice_list(c100,[0]).
choice_list(o,[0]).
choice_list(m,[1]).
```

yes

KEYWORDS

constraint
label
dependency
dependency-based backtracking
possibility list
relaxation
active variable

EXERCISES

13-1. (A) Suppose in an expert system written in Prolog we have the following rules for proving that some person X is an a:

```
a(X) :- b(X), c(X).
a(X) :- d(X).
a(X) :- e(X).
```

Suppose:

  b is true with probability 0.8;

  c is true with probability 0.7;

  d is true with probability 0.1;

  e is true with probability 0.6;

  b, c, d, and e are probabilistically independent of one another.

Rearrange the three rules, and perhaps the expressions in the first rule, to give the fastest (most efficient) execution of the query

```
?- a(george).
```

13-2. Rearrange the query given in Figure 13-6 for most efficient execution using the suggested rearrangement guidelines. How does regular Prolog interpretation of the rearranged query compare with dependency-based backtracking on the original query?

13-3. (E) For some queries it is better to rearrange the query than to do dependency-based backtracking, but for other queries dependency-based backtracking will almost always result in fewer backtracks than any rearrangement of the query. Explain why the following exemplifies the latter situation:

$$?\text{-} \; a(X), \; b(Y), \; c(Z), \; d(X,Y), \; e(X,Z), \; f(Y,Z).$$

13-4. (A) Suppose we are doing relaxation for picture interpretation. It would be nice if we had unique variable assignments when done; that would be strong evidence that we found the correct interpretation of the picture. But what can we conclude if we get instead:

(a) No possible final interpretations?

(b) Two possible final interpretations?

(c) One million possible final interpretations?

13-5. (E) Discuss why relaxation might have more application to artistic creation than any of the other control structures we have discussed in this book.

13-6. (R,A) Budget General Hospital must schedule meals for its patients. Budget tries to save its patients money, so its food is cheap and tastes terrible, and there are only three meals offered:

   Meal m1: gruel
   Meal m2: dehydrated eggs
   Meal m3: leftovers from nearby restaurants

Assist the hospital by scheduling six meals for a patient. The six meals are breakfast, lunch, and dinner on each of the two days. The following constraints apply:

   C1. Breakfast on the first day must be Meal m1, since the patient will still be queasy from their operation.

   C2. No two meals in succession may be the same—you don't want the patients to realize how cheap you are.

   C3. Meal m3 is the most expensive, so it must only occur once. (It requires a trip to a restaurant.)

   C4. Every meal on the second day must have a higher number than the meal at the corresponding time on the first day. For instance, lunch on the first day could be Meal m1 and lunch on the second day Meal m2. (This is because patients are harder to fool as they recover.)

Find a meal plan for the six meals using pure relaxation. After obtaining initial possibility lists, check the possibilities for breakfast on the second day, and proceed from there. Write out each step of your solution, giving constraints used and how they were used.

13-7. (E) Develop a relaxation approach to analyzing pictures like Figure 13-9. This picture was produced by a camera mounted on a robot moving around outdoors. The picture only indicates line boundaries between visual regions of

abruptly different brightness. Assume all the lines represent sharp boundaries, and the camera was focussed far away so that everything seen was
more than 30 feet away. Assume the camera was oriented so that horizontal
is one third of the way down from the top of the picture.

(a) Define ten permissible labels for regions based on their shapes, the ten
most reasonable ones you can think of.

(b) List impossible relationships between regions based on these labels (what
regions cannot be next to a particular region, etc.) Use **above, left-of,**
and **inside** for relationships, and any others you think useful. Treat combinations that are possible only rarely as impossible; don't worry about
minor exceptions.

(c) Use your constraints to assign as narrow an interpretation as possible to
the picture.

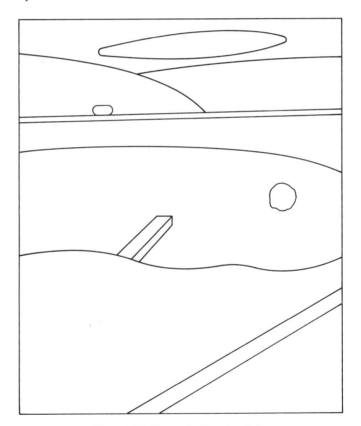

Figure 13-9. Picture for Exercise 13-7.

13-8. Relaxation can be used to solve an immensely important problem of large
organizations: interpretation of acronyms. The full names of many organizations are so long that it's impossible to avoid abbreviating them, yet no one
can keep track of all these acronyms. Sophisticated computer programs are
maybe necessary. Suppose for each letter of the alphabet we have a list of

words that the letter could represent, in the context of names of government organizations. Suppose:

> N can be national, naval, new, name
>
> S can be school, staff, science
>
> C can be center, committee, computer, crazy

Here are the constraints:

C1. A word at the right end of an acronym must be a noun. The nouns are "name," "science," "school," "staff," "center," "committee," and "computer."

C2. A word anywhere else must be an adjective. The adjectives are "national," "naval," "new," "science," "computer," and "crazy."

C3. The same word cannot occur twice in an acronym.

C4. "National" and "naval" cannot be in the same acronym with "crazy" (no one ever admits something national or naval is crazy, even when it is).

C5. "Staff" cannot be in the same acronym with "naval," "national," or "name."

C6. "New" cannot be in the same acronym with "science."

Interpret the acronym "NCSS" using these constraints.

(a) Use relaxation to reduce the possibilities as much as you can. Write out each step. Then write out the possible interpretations remaining.

(b) Suppose we assign probabilities to every word possibility, representing how likely they are to occur in an acronym. So "national" might be 0.5 and "new" might be 0.02 (rarely is anything new in government organizations). Describe a good way to combine these probabilities to choose the "best" one of several interpretations of some acronym, "best" according to a single derived number (give or refer to a formula).

13-9. (H) Try to interpret Figure 13-10 (label the regions) using constraint propagation. You won't be able to find a unique interpretation, but do as much as you can. Initial region labels are as follows:

> The five small regions are either airplanes or ships; anything else is either water, marsh, land, or a cloud.

You have the following constraints:

C1. Airplane regions are the only ones that can be within cloud regions, but airplane regions can be within any region.

C2. Ship regions can only be within water regions.

C3. Two small regions touching one another must be ships.

C4. A "T" vertex (where three line segments meet, and two of them form an angle of approximately 180 degrees) not involving a ship or airplane means either

> **(a)** that the region with the 180 degree angle is a cloud, or
>
> **(b)** the region with the 180 degree angle is land and the other two regions are water and marsh.

C5. Every marsh region must have such a T vertex somewhere on its border.

C6. Water regions cannot border water regions.

C7. Marsh regions cannot border marsh regions.

C8. Land regions cannot border land regions.

C9. The outer (border) region is not a cloud.

Give every step in your relaxation.

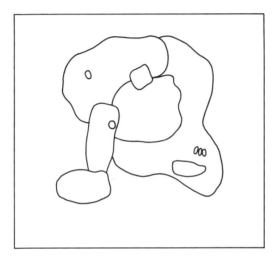

Figure 13-10. Picture for Exercise 13-9.

13-10. (a) Suppose in relaxation there are ten variables with initially eight possible labels each. Suppose there is a unique solution. What is the size of the search space?

(b) Suppose each step that chooses a variable eliminates half the possibilities for that variable, on the average. What is approximately the average number of steps to reach the unique solution?

13-11. Consider a picture as a graph. Regions border edges, and there are vertices where edges meet. Suppose you do relaxation to interpret the picture, and constraints specify what labels adjacent regions can have. Suppose you draw another graph for which the vertices represent variables in the relaxation, with connections between vertices representing that the two variables both occur together in at least one constraint. What is the relationship of this new graph to the original picture graph?

13-12. (E) Suppose we are certain that there is one and only one solution to a relaxation problem. Suppose when we run this relaxation problem with all the constraints we can think of, we get several hundred possible interpretations. Suppose we can also formulate some "reasonable restrictions," restrictions usually but not always true (their probability being close to 1). Then we can try to get a solution by taking (assuming) some of the "reasonable restrictions" as constraints, and seeing if we get a unique solution to the relaxation. But we want to assume as few restrictions as possible, and we prefer to assume those that are most certain. Explain how finding a unique solution to a relaxation problem by assuming "reasonable restrictions" can be considered a search problem. Describe its characteristics, and recommend an appropriate search strategy.

13-13. (R,A,P) Consider the query:

?- n(X), n(Y), n(Z), X>Y, not(f(X,X)), g(X,Y,Z).

Suppose the database is:

n(1).
n(2).
n(3).
n(4).
n(5).

f(2,2).
f(2,4).
f(3,1).

g(1,3,2).
g(2,3,3).
g(3,3,4).
g(4,3,5).

(a) How many times does this query backtrack to get its first answer? Count each right-to-left movement from predicate expression to predicate expression as one backtrack.

(b) Rearrange the query in a form that leads to the fewest backtracks. How many times does it backtrack now? Show the query you used.

(c) Suggest a way to do dependency-based backtracking to answer the original query. Simulate it without the computer. How many times do you backtrack now?

(d) Now answer the original query by doing relaxation without the computer. Assume the standard form of relaxation that tries to satisfy each multivariable constraint separately, throwing away previously found bindings. Write out your steps.

13-14. (A) The demonstration of the pure relaxation program on the cryptarithmetic problem takes a considerable amount of time on the first few variables, then speeds up considerably. If instead of specifying E=5 we say that E is either 0 or 5, the program runs faster and reaches a solution faster.

(a) What accounts for this paradox?

(b) Suggest code that can be eliminated from the definition of this cryptarithmetic problem to significantly lessen or eliminate the paradoxical behavior.

(c) The code that you eliminated in part (b) must have been there for a reason. What was it?

13-15. (P) Suppose you have an eight-digit number whose digits are all different. Suppose that when you multiply this number by its rightmost (least) digit, you get a nine-digit number whose digits are all the leftmost (highest) digit of the original number. Suppose further that the second-highest digit of the original number is 2. Set this problem up in a problem-dependent file to run with the pure relaxation program. Run it and see what you get.

13-16. (H,P) Generalize the "double relaxation" program to "N-relaxation." In other words, take three constraints together if you don't get anywhere with two constraints together, and four constraints together if you don't get anywhere with three, and so on up to the total number of constraints. This will require recursion. The program should degrade to standard Prolog querying in the worst case. Try your program on the cryptarithmetic problem CROSS + ROADS = DANGER.

13-17. (H,P) Besides double relaxation, there is an alternative improvement on pure relaxation: keep possibility lists for pairs, triples, etc. of variables instead of single variables. So you can solve harder problems this way than with pure relaxation, but you need more possibility lists. Write a "pair-relaxation program" that reasons about pairs of values this way.

13-18. (A) We can see relaxation as a search problem with a single operator: picking a variable and a value, and trying to verify that value is still possible.

(a) What is the search space for this problem? Remember, a state for a search problem must include everything about the problem in one bundle.

(b) Which search strategy, of those mentioned in Chapter 9, is most like that used by the algorithm?

(c) Is this search decomposable about intermediate states into simpler sub-problems?

(d) How does the branching factor change as search proceeds?

(e) Give an upper bound on the size of the search space.

14

A MORE GENERAL LOGIC PROGRAMMING

Prolog is a language for *logic programming*. That is, it's a programming language that looks and works somewhat like formal logic. To be efficient and easy to use, Prolog omits some important features of logic. We'll discuss now these omissions, and present a more general and powerful—but slower—approach to logic programming. This approach is called *resolution*, and it emphasizes declarative (instead of procedural) meanings of logical formulas.

14.1 LOGICAL LIMITATIONS OF PROLOG

Prolog can do many things. But it has four fundamental logical weaknesses:

1. Prolog doesn't allow "or"d (disjunctive) facts or conclusions—that is, statements that one or more of several things is true, but you don't know which. For instance, if a light does not come on when we turn on its switch, we can conclude that either the bulb is burned out or the power is off or the light is disconnected.

2. Prolog doesn't allow "not" (negative) facts or conclusions—that is, direct statements that something is false. For instance, if a light does not come on when we turn on its switch, but another light in the same room comes on when we turn on *its* switch, we can conclude that it is false that there is a power failure.

3. Prolog doesn't allow most facts, conclusions, or rules having existential quantification—that is, statements that there exists some value of a variable, though we don't know what, such that a predicate expression containing it is true. (Prolog does have a limited form of existential quantification for local variables in rules, as discussed in Section 4.1.) For instance, if we know that something is wrong with an appliance, then there exists a component X of the appliance such that X has a fault in it.

4. Prolog doesn't directly allow *second-order logic*, predicate names as variables—that is, statements about P where P stands for any predicate name. We can get something close with the trick of the inherits predicate in the car frame hierarchy of Section 12.11, the idea of rewriting facts to include extra predicate-name arguments. You can also approach second-order logic using the built-in clause predicate discussed in Section 7.13. So this weakness of Prolog is less serious than the others, and we won't say anything further about it in this chapter.

Notice that these are logical issues, not efficiency issues. Chapter 6 discussed how Prolog isn't an efficient control structure for reasoning about some problems. But these four points are deeper and more serious weaknesses: they represent things Prolog can't do at all even working slowly.

14.2 THE LOGICAL (DECLARATIVE) MEANING OF PROLOG RULES AND FACTS

To better understand Prolog's limitations and how to get around them, let's examine more carefully what Prolog rules and facts mean. Chapter 4 explained how rules and facts all go into a Prolog database of true statements. Alternatively, a Prolog database can be seen as a single logical statement representing the conjunction ("and"ing) of the statements of each rule and fact. We'll now show how the declarative or logical meaning (not the same as the procedural meaning) of any Prolog database can be expressed entirely as a set of statements using only "or"s and "not"s.

To do this we must first remove the ":-" symbol from rules, because that is not a logic symbol. In Section 4.1 we said to think of it as a backward arrow or backward implication. In logic, an implication (or, strictly speaking, a *material implication*) is equivalent to an "or" (a disjunction, symbolized in Prolog by ";") of the pointed-to side of the arrow with the negation of the other side of the arrow. So the rule

    a :- b.

is equivalent in logical (declarative) meaning to

    a; not(b).

which reads as "a or not b." Figure 14-1 shows the truth table for the two forms, to better convince you.

a	b	a; not (b)	Is the rule a :- b. *consistent* *(uncontradicted)?*	*Justification*
true	true	true	yes	b proves a
true	false	true	yes	a could be proved by another rule, and that wouldn't violate the truth of this one
false	true	false	no	b proves a by the rule, a contradiction
false	false	true	yes	The rule doesn't apply, and there may be no other rule to prove a

Figure 14-1. Demonstration that an equivalent logical (declarative) meaning of the Prolog rule a :- b is a;not(b).

An immediate generalization comes from taking predicate b to be an "and" (conjunction) itself. For instance

a :- c, d, e.

is equivalent to

a; not(c,d,e).

which by DeMorgan's Law is the same as:

a; not(c); not(d); not(e).

So we can express the logical equivalent of any Prolog rule by "or"ing the left side with the nots of each expression that is "and"ed on the original right side. This is called the *clause form* of the rule. But logical equivalence is not complete equivalence of meaning because it only covers the declarative meaning of rules. Prolog rules also have the "procedural" interpretation of "If you believe that these things hold, then believe that this thing holds." So rules also involve a causation, a moving from a cause (a belief in several things) to an effect (a belief in something else); and the effect comes after the cause in time. Causations imply a direction of reasoning, while an "or" doesn't necessarily. For instance,

a :- b.

models a causation from b to a. But its logical equivalent in clause form

a; not(b).

can also be used from a to b: if we are told a is false, then b must be false too so the "or" will be true. That's the *contrapositive* direction of reasoning, and Prolog rules can't be used that way even though it's logically valid.[1]

The second limitation on reasoning of Prolog interpreters mentioned in Section 14.1 concerned nots: they mean "impossible to prove," not "proved false." But when we write things in clause form we can interpret nots more precisely, to reach new conclusions not otherwise possible. For instance, in the previous contrapositive reasoning example, when a is false, b is proved false, not just proved to be impossible to succeed. So clause form can provide "true nots." But there is an associated danger: when the Prolog rule itself has a not, we must make sure that we can interpret it as provably false in the real world. Otherwise, the clause form only covers part of its meaning.

14.3 EXTENDING PROLOG RULES

Using the preceding clause-form conversion for Prolog rules lets us give meaning to new kinds of rules, rules not legal in Prolog, what we'll call "pseudo-Prolog." Rules with "and"s, "or"s, and not's on their left sides are one example. For instance this:

    (a; b) :- c.

which means that either of a or b is true whenever c is true, becomes in clause form

    a; b; not(c).

And this pseudo-Prolog

    not(a) :- b.

which means a is false whenever b is true, becomes (if that's a "true not")

    not(a); not(b).

Notice that the first clause-form formula has two unnegated expressions, and the second has no unnegated expressions. In general, any Prolog fact or rule without "or"s and nots becomes a clause form having one and only one unnegated expression, what's called a *Horn clause*.

Clause form for a rule can require more than one clause ("or"ed formula). As a more complicated example, consider this pseudo-Prolog

    (a; (b, c)) :- d, not(e).

---

[1] Don't confuse the backward reasoning of the contrapositive with backward chaining. Backward chaining reasons about the left side of some rule, whereas contrapositive reasoning reasons about the *opposite* of the left side.

which has the logical equivalent (assuming that's a "true not")

> a; (b, c); not(d); e.

To get rid of the "and," we can use the distributive law for "or" over "and." This gives two separate statements "and"ed together, which is equivalent to two separate clauses:

> a; b; not(d); e.
> a; c; not(d); e.

And that's the clause form for the original rule.

Rewriting rules in clause form answers some puzzling questions of why rules sometimes seem "and"ed together and other times "or"ed together. Suppose we have two rules

> a :- b.
> a :- c.

A logical equivalent form is

> (a; not(b)), (a; not(c)).

or:

> a; (not(b), not(c)).

using the distributive law of "or" over "and." This can be rewritten as a single rule

> a :- (b;c).

using DeMorgan's Law. So an "and" in the one sense—the "and" of the logical truth of separate rules—is an "or" in another—the "or" of the right sides of rules with the same left side.

14.4 MORE ABOUT CLAUSE FORM _____

So a clause is an "or" of a bunch of things, each of which is either a single predicate expression or the not of one. As usual, expressions can have arguments. For instance, this "santa clause":

> santa(joe); santa(tom); not(santa(bill)).

Any statement we can express in first-order logic has a logical equivalent in a set of clauses. Why is this important? Because there's a simple yet powerful inference

method that can be applied to clauses, *resolution.* It can be proved that *any* inference that logically follows from a set of statements can be found by using resolution
on the clause forms of those statements. So resolution is more powerful than
Prolog-style backward chaining.

But to use resolution, everything must be in clause form. We've already illus-
trated a procedure for translating "pseudo-Prolog" with "or"s, "not"s, and arbitrarily complex formulas on the left sides of rules: just rewrite in *conjunctive normal form* as an "and" of "or"s, using the laws of logic. That covers the first two
limitations of Prolog cited in Section 14.1. But what about existential quantifiers?
They can get complicated.

The simplest case for existential quantifiers is when we want to assert there
exists some variable value such that a predicate expression mentioning that variable
is true. Then we can substitute a constant for the variable, provided that constant
can't be confused with an actual value of the variable, like a constant that is a nonsense word. For instance, if we want to say that there exists an X such that p(X) is
true, then we can could assert fact p(zzxxy) provided that zzxxy is not a symbol for
any of the possible values for X. We can then use this fact p(zzxxy) in chains of
reasoning, just remembering that this value doesn't really mean anything.

But now suppose we want to say that for every Y there exists X such that
p(X,Y) holds. Now we can't just substitute a constant for X because X may depend
on Y: that is, X is a function of Y. This function is a *Skolem function.* We need
one whenever we are trying to represent in clause form a statement containing both
existential and universal quantification. Standard techniques exist for situations
needing Skolem functions, but they are too complicated to discuss here. See books
on "theorem proving" if you're interested.

14.5 RESOLUTION

Resolution is an inference technique that takes two clauses as input, and produces a
clause as output. The output clause, the *resolvent,* represents a true statement consistent with the input clauses, the result of *resolving* them. In other words, the
resolvent is one conclusion we can draw, and not necessarily the only one. If the
resolvent is a fact, then we've proved a fact. If the resolvent consists of no expressions, the *null clause,* we've proved a contradiction. Resolution is particularly
efficient for proof by contradiction: we assume the opposite of some statement we
wish to prove, and see if we can prove the null clause from it.

Resolution requires pairs of opposites within the two input clauses. That is,
one input clause must contain a predicate expression—call it P—for which not(Q)
occurs in the other input clause and where P can match Q, binding variables as
necessary. (Formally, P matches Q if the expression P = Q can succeed.) Then the
resolvent of the two input clauses is the "or" of everything besides P and not(Q) in
the two clauses, eliminating any duplicate or redundant expressions. We say that
the P and the not(Q) "cancel." For instance, if the input clauses are

    a; b; not(c); d.
    e; not(b); a; f.

then a resolvent (output) clause is

a; not(c); d; e; f.

where we eliminated the opposites b and not(b) and a duplicate a fact.

Inference by resolution becomes most useful when we do several resolutions in succession. Here's an example. Let's use Horn clauses (clauses with one and only one unnegated expression), because we already know how Prolog interpreters handle them, and let's avoid variables. Suppose we have these rules and facts:

a :- b, c.
c :- d.
b.
d.

Rewriting in clause form, we get these Horn clauses:

a; not(b); not(c).
c; not(d).
b.
d.

(Prolog facts are identical in clause form.) Now suppose we want to prove a (see Figure 14-2):

1. To do proof by contradiction, we add not(a) to the other four clauses in our database of true statements.

2. Resolving not(a) with the first of the four original statements, the a and not(a) expressions cancel, and the resolvent is not(b); not(c). We can add that new clause to the others.

3. Resolving this new clause with the third of the original clauses, the b and not(b) cancel, and the resolvent is just not(c).

4. Resolving this in turn with a second of the original four clauses, we cancel the c and not(c), giving as resolvent not(d).

5. Finally we resolve this with the last of the original four clauses, and d and not(d) cancel, leaving us with a null clause.

6. Therefore we can prove anything if we assume that a is false. So a must be true. (This assumes that the original set of rules and facts was not self-contradictory, something we could verify by first doing all possible resolutions among them.)

There is a one-to-one correspondence of the steps in the previous *resolution proof* and the steps that Prolog interpreters follow in backward chaining. It's as if they take queries as rules without left sides, entering them as clauses into their databases. To prove a, they would:

1. Take **a** as the goal (query).
2. Find a rule for **a**: the first rule. This says to prove **b**, then **c**.
3. But **b** is a fact (the first fact).
4. To prove **c**, use the second rule, which says to prove **d**.
5. But **d** is a fact (the second fact).
6. Therefore **c** is true and **a** is true.

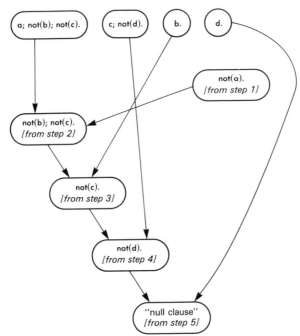

Figure 14-2. Summary of the resolution example.

In general, resolution can do anything backward chaining can do, but not the other way around. Resolution is a more general and flexible form of inference, because it can resolve clauses in many different orders; backward chaining is more rigid. And new resolvent clauses can be used in new resolutions, so resolution possibilities keep increasing—it's a *monotonic* search process.

14.6 RESOLUTION WITH VARIABLES

When predicates have variable arguments, Prolog-style binding of the variables can be done to make the canceling expressions "match" in a resolution. As with Prolog, bindings made to variables apply to all occurrences of the variables within their clauses, so if a **p(X)** in the first input clause matches a **p(4)** in the second input clause, any other **X** in the first clause is bound to 4. Variables can also be bound to other variables. Important note: it's essential that each input clause have different variable names before resolving.

Here's an example of resolution with variables. Suppose the two clauses are

a(3); b(Y); not(c(Z,Y)).
not(a(W)); b(dog); c(W,cat).

The a expressions can cancel with W bound to 3, giving

b(Y); not(c(Z,Y)); b(dog); c(3,cat).

The b(dog) is redundant with b(Y), so we can improve this clause to

b(Y); not(c(Z,Y)); c(3,cat).

But we could resolve the original two clauses another way. The c expressions could cancel, with Z being bound to W and with Y being bound to cat, giving

a(3); b(cat); not(a(W)); b(dog).

This is a completely different resolvent, representing a different conclusion possible from the two input clauses. Notice that we can't eliminate anything here; b(cat) and b(dog) aren't redundant, nor are a(3) and not(a(W)).

Note that bindings are transitive: if A is bound to 9, and B is bound to A, then B is bound to 9 too. So several reasoning steps may be necessary to determine a variable binding.

14.7 THREE IMPORTANT APPLICATIONS OF RESOLUTION

Resolution is a powerful inference technique that can supplant other inference techniques. Three important special cases of resolution are summarized in Figure 14-3: backward chaining, forward chaining, and rule collapsing. To use resolution for backward chaining as in Section 14.5, one starting clause is always the negation (opposite) of something to be proved. To use resolution for forward chaining, one input clause for every resolution is always a fact. Rule collapsing is a way to make rules more efficient, not a control structure itself: it takes two rules, one whose left side can match something on the other's right side, and combines them into a single new rule; this is equivalent to resolving the rules' clauses. Procedure collapsing is important to compilers for programming languages.

14.8 RESOLUTION SEARCH STRATEGIES

Reasoning by resolution means performing a series of resolution operations. This often means more branches to choose among than conflict resolution in rule-based systems, because you must pick pairs of clauses to resolve, and usually there are many pairs. Facts are clauses too, as are the resolvents (results) from past resolutions. So resolution-based reasoning is a search with a high branching factor. This means a breadth-first resolution strategy (resolving every pair of original clauses,

In rule form	*In clause form*
BACKWARD CHAINING:	
QUERY: ?- a.	ASSUMPTION: not(a).
a :- b, c, d.	a; not(b); not(c); not(d).
RESULTS IN:	RESOLVES TO:
?-b, c, d.	not(b); not(c); not(d).
FORWARD CHAINING:	
a :- b, c.	a; not(b); not(c).
c.	c.
RESULTS IN:	RESOLVES TO:
a :- b.	a; not(b).
RULE COLLAPSING:	
a :- b, c, d.	a; not(b); not(c); not(d).
c :- e, f.	c; not(e); not(f).
RESULTS IN:	RESOLVES TO:
a :- b, e, f, d.	a; not(b); not(e); not(f); not(d).

Figure 14-3. Three special cases of resolution.

then every new clause with either an original clause or a new clause, and so on) is very slow. In principle, a breadth-first resolution control structure can prove anything that is a logical consequence of particular facts and rules; but that's no good if it takes a hundred years to do so.

Often we know what we want to prove. Then we can use a *set-of-support* strategy, which we used without saying so in the example of Section 14.5. The idea is to assume the opposite of what we want to prove, and resolve it repeatedly with other clauses until we reach the null clause. That is, we use each resolvent as an input to the next resolution. If no possible resolutions remain at some point (when no other clause has an opposite that can "cancel" an expression in the last resolvent), back up to the last previous resulting clause for which there were alternative resolutions, and take an alternative. This is basically a depth-first resolution strategy starting from the negation of the proof objective.

If we don't have any one thing in particular we want to prove, but we prefer to prove facts, then a *unit-preference* resolution strategy may be good. The idea is to do first all resolutions involving facts and their negatives. If there aren't any more, then perhaps prefer resolutions involving two-expression clauses, and so on. This strategy tends to keep resolvent clauses short, which often means we discover new facts fast.

If our clauses all represent rules, we may want to do the rule collapsing mentioned in the last section. A breadth-first resolution strategy could work for this, since there's no designated objective or facts to work from. For efficiency, we might try instead best-first search with the evaluation function the total number of expressions in the input clauses, which tends to discourage less useful resolutions. In any event, we should arbitrarily stop the search at some point, since there can be an enormous number of possible resolutions, and we don't want to try them all.

Domain-dependent heuristics can help considerably when reasoning with resolution. Heuristics can enhance any of the search strategies mentioned.

14.9 IMPLEMENTING RESOLUTION WITHOUT VARIABLES* _____

Resolution without variables is simple to implement in Prolog. Represent the clauses as list arguments to **clause** facts, so for instance

> a; not(b); not(c); d.

is represented as

> clause([a,not(b),not(c),d]).

Notice lists require commas, so the comma here actually means "or." Then query the predicate **go**. Everything new proved will be printed out. Here's the program:

```
/* Resolution without variables */
go :- resolution(C1,C2,Cnew), !, write(Cnew), nl,
   not(Cnew =[]), go.

resolution(C1,C2,Cnew) :- clause(C1), clause(C2), not(C1 = C2),
   matched_items(C1,C2,C1item,C2item), delete(C1item,C1,C1d),
   delete(C2item,C2,C2d), union(C1d,C2d,Cnew), not(clause(Cnew)),
   not(tautology(Cnew)), not(some_superset(Cnew)),
   asserta(clause(Cnew)).

matched_items(C1,C2,C1item,not(C1item)) :- member(C1item,C1),
   member(not(C1item),C2).
matched_items(C1,C2,not(C2item),C2item) :-
   member(not(C2item),C1), member(C2item,C2).

some_superset(C) :- clause(C2), subset(C2,C).

tautology(C) :- member(X,C), member(not(X),C).
```

Notice that we check new clauses to make sure they're neither previously found, nor tautologies (always-true statements), nor immediately derivable from other clauses by removal of items; only then do we assert a new clause. The assertion uses **asserta**, so a depth-first strategy much like set-of-support will be used.

This requires the **member, delete,** and **subset** predicate definitions from Sections 5.5, 5.6, and 5.7, respectively, plus the **union** predicate from Section 11.4 (which is closely related to the **append** of Section 5.6). Using **union** instead of **append** prevents duplicate expressions in the resolvent.

```
/* Utility functions for resolution */
member(X,[X|L]).
member(X,[Y|L]) :- member(X,L).
```

```
union([],L,L).
union([X|L],L2,L3) :- member(X,L2), !, union(L,L2,L3).
union([X|L],L2,[X|L3]) :- union(L,L2,L3).

delete(X,[],[]).
delete(X,[X|L],M) :- !, delete(X,L,M).
delete(X,[Y|L],[Y|M]) :- delete(X,L,M).

subset([],L).
subset([X|L1],L2) :- member(X,L2), subset(L1,L2).
```

For a demonstration, suppose we have these clauses:

```
clause([a,not(b),not(c)]).
clause([b]).
clause([d,not(a)]).
clause([c,e,f]).
```

Here's what happens when we run the program:

```
?- go.
[a,not(c)]
[not(c),d]
[d,e,f]
[a,e,f]

no
```

Unfortunately, implementing resolution with variables in Prolog is very tricky. The problem is in handling redundancies, the **tautology** and **subset** predicates of the program, for which Prolog's normal variable binding must be subverted. Full resolution-inferencers can be written more easily in more flexible programming languages like Lisp.

KEYWORDS

logic programming
disjunctive fact
negative fact
existential quantifier
second-order logic
clause form
Horn clause
Skolem function
resolution
breadth-first resolution strategy
set-of-support resolution strategy
unit-preference resolution strategy

EXERCISES

14-1. (A) Resolve all possible ways and list bindings:

> state(3,A,X); possible(X,X,A).
> not(possible(5,Y,Z)); state(3,6,Y).

14-2. (R,A) Suppose you are working for a research organization. Suppose you can get travel money if your department chairman approves and your sponsor approves. Alternatively, you can get travel money if your department chairman approves, the boss over him or her approves, and there are discretionary department funds available.

(a) Represent the preceding as two Prolog rules. (Hint: Use one-letter predicate names because you'll have to write them many times in this problem.)

(b) Represent the two rules in clause form.

(c) Suppose that these are the only two ways that you can get travel money. Therefore if you do get travel money, certain things must have been true. Write this implication in "pseudo-Prolog" as a rule with the symbol :-, but with "and"s and "or"s on its left side. Your rule must cover *all* the implications of having travel money.

(d) Convert this pseudo-Prolog rule to clause form. (Hint: Clause form here is three clauses.)

(e) Suppose you can get travel money. What new clauses logically follow from this? (Make sure there are no unnecessary extra expressions in the clauses.)

(f) Suppose you can't get travel money. What new clauses logically follow from this? (Make sure there are no unnecessary extra expressions in the clauses.)

14-3. **(a)** Represent the following in clause form:
> C1: Block A is on the table.
> C2: Block B is on block A.
> C3: Block C is on block A.
> C4: Block D is on block C.
> C5: Block A is blue.
> C6: Block B is blue.
> C7: Block C is red.
> C8: Block D is green.
> C9: A block is above another block X if it is on that block or else if it is on a block which is above X.

(b) Prove by resolution that block D is above a blue block. Give the numbers of statements you resolve, and label your resolvents.

14-4. Suppose we're told to resolve the clauses

> a; b.
> not(a); not(b).

Can we simultaneously cancel out both matched pairs, getting the null clause as resolvent? Why or why not?

14-5. (R,A) By the definition of resolution given in this chapter, if we resolve the clauses

> a; b.
> not(a); c.

we get

> b; c.

But this doesn't seem to make sense if we show what's happening in a Venn diagram (See Figure 14-4). Here the region marked with lines running from southwest to northeast represents the first clause, and the region marked with lines running southeast to northwest represents the second clause. Any pair of clauses that are each individually true can be considered to be "and"ed together. But the region that has both markings (the cross-hatched region) does not correspond to the preceding resolvent clause. What's wrong?

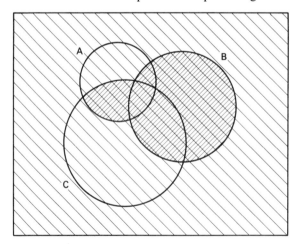

Figure 14-4. Picture for Exercise 14-5.

14-6. (E) Suppose we have these Prolog rules:

> a :- b, c.
> a :- not(b), d.

Suppose that **not** can also be interpreted as a "real" not, one that insists that negative evidence is present.

(a) Write the two rules in clause form.

(b) Now resolve the two clauses from part (a), and write a new Prolog rule without **nots** equivalent to the resolvent clause.

(c) Explain how the idea of the preceding could be generalized to a useful trick to improve rule-based expert systems, one that applies to rules of any length. Explain (i) how you pick appropriate (good) pairs of rules, (ii) how you can avoid converting to clause form, and (iii) under what circumstances you can delete the original rules.

14-7. Prolog interpreters are Horn-clause theorem-proving systems. But consider the following fallacy.

(a) Represent in clause form this pseudo-Prolog:

$$(\text{weekend}(T); \text{holiday}(T)) :\text{-} \text{empty}(\text{spanagel421},T).$$

which means that if Spanagel 421 is empty, it must either be a weekend or a holiday.

(b) Convert this into an equivalent Prolog rule with only one expression, holiday(T), on its left side.

(c) Show that the original rule and the rule for part (b) have equivalent truth value by showing their truth tables.

(d) Part (b) is a legal Prolog rule because it has only one predicate expression on its left side. So it seems we can always implement a non-Horn clause in Prolog. What's wrong with this argument?

14-8. (E) Suppose we wish Prolog interpreters to use mathematical induction proof techniques automatically. Discuss what is wrong with just adding an induction rule to all Prolog programs, saying in essence

"p X is true if p 1 is true
and if for N an integer and $N > 1$,
p N implies $p(N+1)$."

14-9. (A) Consider proving things by resolution as a search problem with one operator: resolve two clauses to get a new clause. Each state can be described as a set of clauses given or proved. Suppose you have N clauses to begin.

(a) What is an upper bound on the initial branching factor?

(b) What is an upper bound on the branching factor after K resolutions have been done?

14-10. (P) The resolution program can be made more efficient.

(a) Improve it so it doesn't examine every pair of clauses, but only pairs in which the first clause precedes the second in the database.

(b) Improve it to remove any clause C that *becomes* redundant, when the expressions of the last clause discovered are a subset of the expressions of C.

15

TESTING & DEBUGGING OF ARTIFICIAL-INTELLIGENCE PROGRAMS

Artificial-intelligence programs tend to be big, complicated programs. (If not in this book, in practical applications.) So careful and extensive testing and debugging is essential. Standard software engineering techniques for managing large programs (modularity, top-down decomposition, good naming, separate testing of components, and so on) help, but certain other less common techniques are particularly important to artificial intelligence. These are summarized in Figure 15-1.

15.1 THE GOLD STANDARD

Artificial-intelligence programs try to show intelligent behavior. But as we said in Chapter 1, "intelligence" is a vague word. So it's often hard to see whether an artificial-intelligence program is working properly. Of course, there are obvious mistakes, like a car repair program that concludes your engine is destroyed when the problem is a flat tire. But the less obvious mistakes can cause more serious problems.

What is usually done is to define an ideal or *gold* standard of behavior against which an artificial-intelligence program can be measured. Often (as for expert systems) a program tries to automate things done by certain humans, so we can just ask these humans whether the program is doing things right. For instance, for auto repair, there are master mechanics; for medical diagnosis, there are doctors that are authorities in their subfield; for scheduling, there are people that must schedule all the time, like some secretaries; for finding routes in a city, there are experienced taxi drivers; for solving puzzles, there are expert puzzlers; and for mellowing out, there are California residents. Sometimes there is no single human expert, but different people are expert on different pieces of a problem and we can pool their expertise, as often is the case with knowledge of how to best accomplish things in a bureaucracy.

Unfortunately humans often hate computers, particularly when they are being replaced by computers without compensating rewards, so we must be extremely careful to make the comparison of computer with human behavior a fair one. It's important to give the humans and the computers the same problems to work on (perhaps not telling the humans that they will be compared to computers and not telling the computers that they will be compared to humans, though computers tend be more broad-minded). Then we can compare results and mark any discrepancy as wrong. If our graders don't know themselves which results were by computers and which by humans, and only some supervisors know, then we have a *double-blind* test, a good form of testing often used in medical research.

1. Methods requiring a gold standard
  (a) Traces
  (b) Confusion matrices
  (c) Comparison of a near miss and example
      (i) No numbers involved
      (ii) Composite results
      (iii) Numbers involved
  (d) Comparison of two examples
      (i) No numbers involved
      (ii) Composite results
      (iii) Numbers involved

2. Methods not requiring a gold standard
  (a) Schema for rules and facts
  (b) User-initiated debugging questions
  (c) Cooperativeness evaluation
  (d) A priori suitability for artificial-intelligence techniques

Figure 15-1. Tools for testing and debugging.

15.2 CASES

Once a gold standard is established, it is important to test an artificial-intelligence system many ways, or against many situations. These situations are called *cases* or *test cases*; a set of cases used for testing is called a *corpus*. The more complicated the program, the more cases we should run. It is important to test a representative spectrum of cases. It is desirable to have at least one test case for each major program behavior, for each significant combination of inputs, and for each significant kind of output. Since this isn't always possible, judgment is required to reach a compromise. Then for each test case we must be able to identify a clear outcome.

15.3 FOCUSING ON BUGS

Testing performance on a set of cases creates two categories: cases for which the standard and the program agree, and cases for which they disagree. The second category is the more interesting one. We can examine these program "failures" and try to identify characteristics that distinguish them from "successes." This helps debug our program.

Several tools can help. A very important one is trace information, the record of reasoning done about a case. Rules that appear often in failure cases are suspect. Search problems provide partial traces in their state-sequence or operator-sequence output. But expert systems usually just give a single answer, and can be considerably enhanced with a trace of what rules were used in reaching the answer. Nearly all Prolog dialects have built-in tracing facilities.

Other useful information is provided by a confusion matrix, something especially helpful with rule-based systems. It summarizes not only when the program went wrong, but how it went wrong. An example for a car-repair expert system is given in Figure 15-2. Program results were grouped into categories and cross-tabulated with the gold standard. Rows represent gold-standard categories and columns represent program-result categories. The entry in row i and column j is the number of times the program gave an answer in category j when the standard gave an answer in category i. (In the example, assume that one of these diagnoses is a default, so the program always concludes one of them.) So a confusion matrix shows which categories tend to be confused with which other categories, and suggests where rule improvements are needed. For instance according to Figure 15-2, the "electrical short" problem is the most frequently misdiagnosed (only 29 out of 55 cases were correctly recognized), suggesting that more rules for electrical shorts or rules with less restrictive conditions are needed. On the other hand, "fuel blockage" is the diagnosis most frequently misapplied (only 25 out of 45 fuel blockage diagnoses were correct), suggesting that more and stronger conditions in its rules are necessary to filter out mistakes.

Guessed cause→ / Actual cause ↓	Battery dead	Electrical short	Fuel blockage	Engine problem
Battery dead	42	1	4	0
Electrical short	15	29	8	3
Fuel blockage	0	2	25	1
Engine problem	1	0	8	12

Figure 15-2. Confusion matrix for an expert system diagnosing situations in which a car won't start.

15.4 EXPLOITING PAIRS OF SIMILAR CASES_____

Pairs of very similar cases are helpful in testing and debugging of artificial-intelligence programs. They can localize problems and provide generalizations.

A particularly interesting case pair is when the standard and the program disagree on one case, but agree on a very similar case. In other words, whenever failing cases are *near misses* to success. Then the reason for the failure must lie in the small difference in characteristics of the two cases, which helps locate the source of the bug. For example, suppose we have in a rule-based system

```
a :- b, c.
```

Now suppose we test (among others) two cases: case X in which facts b and c are true, and case Y in which b, c, and d are true. Suppose X is a near miss for conclusion a, in that the program (or specifically, this rule) concludes that a is true while the gold standard says that a is false. The program will also conclude that a holds in case Y, and assume furthermore that the standard agrees. Since facts b and c are present in both X and Y, we can guess that the d fact makes the difference. There are other explanations, but that seems the simplest. So to get a better rule-based system, we should rewrite the rule as

```
a :- b, c, d.
```

In other words, we figured the original rule was too general, so we fixed it to apply to only one of the two original cases.

Pairs of similar cases can also suggest rule generalizations, a kind of *learning*. Suppose we have in a rule-based system

```
a :- b, c, d.
```

Suppose case Y is as before, with b, c, and d true. Suppose in case Z that b and d are true but c is false. Suppose the gold standard says that Y and Z are both correct cases for conclusion a. Then we can guess that the c doesn't matter, suggesting the rule

```
a :- b, d.
```

This is a riskier change than the previous "near-miss" one, because we are generalizing a rule to apply to more cases. But it's often reasonable.

When the preceding generalization is too strong, we can make weaker changes too. For the appliance application of Chapter 7, we might have written a rule

```
diagnosis('Short in cord') :- askif(device_dead), askif(cord_frayed).
```

Suppose we are now told that when there is a frayed cord and the lights just went out, a "short in cord" diagnosis should also be made. This might suggest

diagnosis('Short in cord') :- askif(cord_frayed).

But that's not a smart idea, because a frayed cord is only a weak symptom and can also suggest a break in the cord (that is, a nonconducting cord). Instead, we should use a concept covering both dead devices and the lights going out: a fuse being blown. That suggests

diagnosis('Short in cord') :- diagnosis('Fuse blown'), askif(cord_frayed).

Figure 15-3 tabulates some inferences of this sort. Current research is extending these ideas to build rule-based systems automatically from examples and nonexamples (that is, descriptions of situations that are definitely not examples of particular concepts) defining appropriate behavior. This is part of the subfield of *automatic programming* within artificial intelligence. The issues are hard—just think how hard it is for you yourself to write a program.

Given the rule a :- b, c.
Assume a, b, c, d, e, f, and g are predicate expressions.

Nature of the new case	Predicate expressions that are true in the new case (those not mentioned are false)	Suggested new rule
example	a and b and c	no change needed
example	a and b	a :- b.
example	a and b and c and d	no change needed
example	a and b and d	a :- b, e. where e is implied by both c and d (if no such e, try a:- b.)
example	f and b and c	g :- b, c. where g is implied by both a and f (if no such g, create a new rule f :- b, c.)
near miss	a and b and c	remove rule entirely
near miss	a and b	no change needed
near miss	a and b and c and d	a :- b, c, not(d).
near miss	a and b and d	no change needed
near miss	f and b and c	no change needed

Figure 15-3. Suggested rule modifications given a new case.

15.5 COMPOSITE RESULTS

If running an artificial-intelligence program gives a result with components, then evaluating the difference between the program and the gold standard is a little more complicated. If the pieces of the result are independent, then the program and standard can be compared separately for each piece, as for a relaxation application in which the result is separate possibility lists for variables. If pieces of the result are linked in a data structure, then structures must be matched to establish corresponding components before comparison, as for a search application in which we must match the list of program operators with the list of gold standard operators in corresponding order. In either case, only the pieces that do not match need be studied further.

Here's an example. Suppose for some search problem the gold standard finds the operator sequence

[a,b,c,d,e,f,g,h]

while the program result is

[a,b,r,s,d,c,e,f,h]

Three things seem to be different in the program result: additional operators r and s have been inserted after action b, operators c and d have been interchanged, and operator g has been omitted. We can thus focus our attention on the parts of the search program that affect those things. So we should check the conditions controlling selection of r and s to see why they were erroneously fulfilled, and check the conditions on g to see why it was erroneously omitted; the switch of c and d suggests a mistake in the priority of those two operators.

15.6 NUMBERS IN COMPARISONS

Numbers—probabilities, evaluation functions, and cost functions—complicate comparisons of a program and a gold standard. There are three ways to handle them. First, we can use the numbers to pick a "best" program result, and compare this to the gold standard. For a diagnosis expert system that assigns probabilities to diagnoses, we can take the diagnosis with the highest probability; for a search program that finds paths to a goal, we can take the lowest-cost path. Second, we can treat the numbered items as a composite structure as discussed in the last section. For an expert system that concludes that diagnoses a, b, c, and d are probable with probabilities 0.9, 0.7, 0.6, and 0.3, respectively, while a gold standard rates them 0.8, 0.5, 0.6, and 0.2, respectively, we can focus the debugging on b and c because their numbers are out of order. Third, we can do statistical analyses; for instance, we can take the sum of the squares of the deviations of the program-result numbers from the gold-standard numbers to measure closeness of the program and the standard. We can then quantify any proposed program improvement by this criterion, so it can be used as an evaluation function in a "search" for a better program.

15.7 PREVENTIVE MEASURES

By current estimates an ounce of prevention is worth 1.07 pounds of fixes, so it's important that an artificial-intelligence programming environment provide software tools to help programmers avoid mistakes in the first place. One big help is predefined expectations about the format of code, as forms or frames in the style of Chapter 12. For rule-based expert systems we can use rule frames or scripts, to capture the frequently strong structural similarities between different rules. For instance, rules in a car-repair diagnosis system usually go like this:

1. localize the problem in a part of the car;
2. ask about easily observable symptoms;
3. if necessary, ask about symptoms that take a little work to establish (like opening up an object);
4. if necessary, ask about experimental actions that need to be done to confirm the diagnosis.

For example,

```
diagnosis('Dead battery') :-
    electrical_problem, lights_dead, not(battery_corroded),
    battery_voltage_low.
```

A programmer writing a new car-diagnosis rule can be provided with this list of four things as a guide, or warned when departing from this format. Or to be more ambitious, a system could automatically find analogous rules to a new rule a programmer wants to write. Inheritance on a hierarchy of rule-class frames is helpful for this.

15.8 SUPPORTING INTUITIVE DEBUGGING BY EXPLANATIONS

A gold standard of performance for an artificial-intelligence program can be hard to get and costly to use. Early in debugging, a more intuitive approach to performance analysis using *explanation* facilities is better, and this is common in artificial-intelligence development software like expert systems *packages* and *shells*. After running a program, these facilities can report on what your program did, how it reached a particular conclusion, or why it considered a particular line of reasoning and not another. Such explanations can be helpful even when the system is fully debugged; they help people understand the system better, use it more effectively, and have more confidence in its results.

The commonest explanation capabilities are for:

- "How" questions: questions as to how the program reached a particular final or intermediate conclusion. When the reasoning is simple, a printout of every step will suffice—just the trace information mentioned in Section 15.3. It can

be printed out like a depth-first search tree. But when reasoning is complicated, this is too much information. For instance, Prolog trace utilities (see
Appendix D.11) generally print out information not only on calling a rule and
succeeding with it, but on failing it and on backtracking to it. (Try tracing
the appliance diagnosis program in Section 7.6 or the flashlight diagnosis
problem in Section 11.5, if you have tracing facilities in your Prolog dialect,
to see the hundreds of reasoning steps done.) So partial summary of trace
information is usually provided in artificial-intelligence environments and
packages. For instance, a "how" explanation can list just the "top-level"
predicates used to reach a conclusion, and then provide the programmer additional details on demand.

- "How not" questions: questions as to why something was *not* concluded.
  These arise when expectations are violated, and there are two very different
  situations. First, reasoning found the conclusion false; then the trace information answers the question. Second, no try was made to prove the conclusion; then the program control structure must be studied to determine why
  different lines of reasoning were pursued instead. For instance, the only rules
  that could have established the conclusion may occur beyond the point where
  processing went in a sequence of rules.

- "Why ask" questions: questions as to what purpose a question to the user
  serves. These are only appropriate in programs that question a user to get
  data, like the appliance repair program in Chapter 7 with its askif predicate.
  Instead of answering a question, a user might reply "Why ask that?" and get
  a deeper justification of the rule being used, or description of a higher-level
  issue the question will help resolve. As with "how" questions, summarization
  helps. That is, a user doesn't usually want just the issue (rule left side)
  immediately responsible for the question but the higher-level issues too.

- "Why better" questions: questions as to why one alternative was judged
  better than another, when alternatives are ranked by numbers (probabilities,
  evaluation functions, or cost functions). These are hard to answer because
  they depend on mathematical formulas as well as logical reasoning. One
  approach is to take the trace record ("how" information) from the two alternatives, eliminate everything identical, and try to find one-to-one correspond-
  ences between the remaining subconclusions. Explanation can focus on the
  relative desirability of corresponding subconclusions.

The hope in providing such information to programmers and users is to permit
them to use their own intuitions on cases, comparing their reasoning with what the
program did. Often artificial-intelligence programs try to formalize human intui-
tion, especially expert systems, so an error by a program can "leap out" at the
human studying its results.

15.9 EVALUATING COOPERATIVENESS

Right answers are not the only criterion we have for evaluating an artificial-
intelligence program. We may also care how friendly or cooperative it is, especially

if it requires a lot of human interaction. Tools such as questionnaires for measuring this are common in organizations that do considerable software development. Some issues to consider:

- Is the output comprehensible?
- Does the program use specialized jargon?
- Can the program paraphrase its questions to the user?
- Can the program explain its reasoning well?
- Does the program catch obvious user mistakes?
- Does the program guess well what the user meant in a mistake?
- Does the program take what the user says too literally?

15.10 ON PROBLEMS UNSUITABLE FOR ARTIFICIAL INTELLIGENCE

The performance of a program may still be unsatisfactory after a long period of testing and debugging. Despite all the clever things that artificial-intelligence techniques can do, they can't solve everything. Sometimes it is hard to know in advance whether a problem is suitable. But some guidelines can be given.

First, a problem suitable for artificial-intelligence techniques must be sufficiently well defined to have clear criteria for success and failure, just as for any other technical method. Otherwise, you can't tell when it's working, and you can't easily test and debug it. For instance, an expert system could create works of art, but it would be hard to evaluate—there's a lot of disagreement between art "experts."

Second, the desired program behavior must be sufficiently stable to permit cost-effective testing and debugging. For instance, an expert system to recommend stock-market investments would be hard to build because investment opportunities are constantly changing ("buy low, sell high" is too general to be useful).

Third, it must be possible to use the program routinely. This is obvious but often overlooked. For instance, most military "battle management" systems are a bad idea because it is too hard to keep them correctly and quickly informed of everything that is happening in a battle (especially with communications equipment itself under attack), though prototype implementations for artificially constructed scenarios might seem to work well.

Fourth, an artificial-intelligence system must not be reductionist in a dangerous way. As we mentioned in Chapter 1, reductionism is the extent to which an artificial-intelligence program fails to capture subtleties of human behavior it is trying to imitate. A highly reductionist program may be safe when its users thoroughly understand its limitations, but can be very dangerous otherwise. For instance, a significantly reductionist battle management system could order troops to fire on themselves or be vulnerable to sabotage in surprising ways.

Fifth, artificial-intelligence techniques should generally not be used when processing time, storage space, or calculation accuracy is critical. The techniques and programs are complicated and often probabilistic or heuristic. A working artificial-intelligence program can often be optimized or compiled to run faster, take up less space, or make more accurate conclusions, but the main idea of artificial intelligence is to provide "intelligence" in computers first, efficiency later. So for instance a "robot warplane," an autonomous military aircraft controlled by real-time artificial-intelligence software, is not likely to work fast enough because things happen too fast in a battle, a large computer imposes a weight penalty on the aircraft, and high accuracy in maneuvers is essential.

Sixth, an artificial-intelligence program must be sufficiently complicated, but not too complicated, so that artificial-intelligence techniques do better than competing approaches. For instance, in spite of Chapter 11, it's a poor idea to write a search program to fix flashlights because people can figure it out themselves. But an expert system to replace all doctors isn't reasonable, because there are millions of diseases and millions of symptoms, and just the rule management and indexing problem for such a huge expert system would be mammoth. And, in the United States anyway, a flawed system could be sued for malpractice.

You must study carefully these criteria before writing an artificial-intelligence program. The criteria are on the borderline between the technical and the non-technical. Should this discourage a programmer from worrying about them? No, not at all. Too often technical people ignore such issues when technical insights about them could be invaluable. Insights about artificial intelligence are particularly important today because so few people understand the field—it's hard to learn, as we said in Chapter 1. But as a new area of research compared to other fields of engineering, artificial intelligence has exciting promises for the future, promises generating considerable enthusiasm. Now that you have read this book you can help fulfill them. Use your knowledge wisely.

KEYWORDS

> *case*
> *gold standard*
> *trace information*
> *confusion matrix*
> *near miss*
> *automatic programming*
> *composite results*
> *explanation facilities*

EXERCISES

15-1. (A) Give a better gold standard for auto repair than an opinion of an expert mechanic.

15-2. Suppose we have a backward-chaining rule-based diagnosis system written as Prolog rules. How could we modify the rules to automatically provide a trace of rules used along with every diagnosis?

15-3. (A) Suppose we have a rule-based system like the appliance diagnosis program in Chapter 7 for which the order of the rules makes a considerable difference in what conclusion is reached first. Suppose for some diagnosis rule-based system, we have the diagnosis rules for two diagnoses in the wrong order. How could a confusion matrix clue us that this is the case?

15-4. Suppose you wanted to construct a rule-based system automatically from examples and nonexamples of its desired behavior, using the ideas of Figure 15-3. The criteria in the figure only refer to rules. How would you get an initial set of rules to work on?

15-5. Rule R1 is redundant with respect to rule R2 if any conclusion proved by R1 can also be proved by R2 in the same circumstances.

    (a) Explain how R1 can have a different left side than R2 even when it is redundant with respect to R2.

    (b) Give a criterion for the redundancy of R1 with respect to R2 that does not require execution of the rules.

15-6. (R,A,E) Discuss the overall suitability of artificial-intelligence techniques as the *major* component in the following.

    (a) An automatic car that will accelerate and steer on highways without human assistance.

    (b) A generator of new cooking recipes.

    (c) A "seduction advisor" expert system that advises you how to succeed with members of the opposite sex.

    (d) A system to coordinate defense from nuclear missiles.

15-7. (H,P,G) Write a program to automatically build ("learn") a rule-based system from examples and near misses (nonexamples) of left-side predicates. Consider only predicate expressions without variables. Use Figure 15-3 as a guide, and break your problem into the following components:

    1. A "comparer" that takes two inputs, a set of rules (a list of lists) and a description of some situation that is either an example or a near miss (a list of facts). It must compute the differences between the situation and the closest rule, the rule that matches the most facts of the situation. For that rule, it should list differences of four kinds: (a) additions (things that must be added to the rule to match a fact of the situation), (b) deletions (things that must be removed from the rule because they have no counterpart in the situation), (c) bindings (variables in a rule that can be matched to a constant argument of the same-named predicate in the situation), and (d) substitutions (constant arguments in a rule that can be matched to a different constant argument of the same-named predicate in the situation).

    2. An "example handler" that takes the same two inputs as the comparer. It hands these two arguments immediately to the comparer, obtaining the list of differences of the situation from one particular rule. It then modifies the rule appropriately, or creates a new rule, to cover the situation. This done, the new generalized rule may cover anything handled by

another rule, and the other rule can be eliminated. The example handler then returns the new set of rules as its result, together with a "gripe amount" indicating how happy it was with the rule modifications it made. If more than one modified set of rules seems equally reasonable, the example handler should permit backtracking into it.

3. A "near miss handler" analogous to the example handler. It should call the comparer, get back a set of differences between a near miss situation and a rule, and modify (specialize) the rule appropriately so it won't apply to the situation. It should check that its changes don't cause contradictions among the rules. Like the example handler, it should return a new set of rules with a "gripe amount," and should give further answers (if any seem good) on backtracking.

4. A "top-level searcher" that supplies examples and near misses to the rest of the system, searching over all possible permutations in the order of supplying them. There's a good cost function in the "gripe amounts" returned by the example and near miss handlers, and there's a good evaluation function in the number of rules plus the number of constants in rules. (Fewer rules means better generalization, and fewer constants mean more generality in rule application). This should use the A* program of Chapter 10, defining the successor function to call the example handler or near miss handler depending on whether the next situation chosen is marked as an example or a near miss.

Try learning rules for some simple diagnosis expert system.

MISCELLANEOUS EXERCISES COVERING THE ENTIRE BOOK

M-1. (A) Backtracking is important in some very different areas of artificial intelligence. For each of the following, say "yes" or "no" as to whether backtracking is usually necessary to implement them. (All these might use backtracking in Prolog implementations, but which need backtracking no matter what language they are implemented in?) By "backtracking" we mean returning to a processing state from which the current processing state is reachable.

(a) Backward chaining

(b) Forward chaining

(c) Best-first search

(d) Answering long queries efficiently by exploiting dependencies

(e) Slot inheritance by querying standard Prolog inheritance rules

(f) Resolution among members of a set of clauses without variables

M-2. Lattices (directed graphs without cycles) are important in many different ways in artificial intelligence. They're important not only as a data structure inside the computer, but as a way of explaining what the computer is doing. Explain what they are useful for in each of the following areas.

(a) Search

(b) Frames

(c) Compiled rule-based systems, in a way different from uncompiled rule-based systems

(d) Resolution

M-3. (R,A) Give the letter for the best match to each item in the first list from the choices in the second list. Each item should be matched to one and only one item. (Hint: Double-check your answers by re-solving from bottom to top, and then by matching the second list to the first list.)

Horn clause
generate-and-test
constraint
forward chaining
default
depth-first control structure
intension
difference table
near miss
Skolem function
caching
dependency
multiple inheritance
decision lattice
Bayes's rule
heuristic
hierarchical reasoning
agenda

(a) a way of reusing results

(b) a weak general-purpose rule or fact

(c) contradictory reasoning is a danger

(d) a theorem

(e) example: prefer investigating further the last thing discovered

(f) "or" with "not" in front of every expression but one

(g) a fast implementation of rule-based systems

(h) recommends an operator

(i) example: the Prolog query ?- $a(X)$, $b(X)$, $c(X)$.

(j) used for existential quantifiers

(k) lists candidates

(l) a description of means-ends analysis

(m) a predicate expression

(n) valuable in debugging all artificial-intelligence systems

(o) reasoning about implications of facts

(p) the abstract meaning of something

(q) requires a stack

(r) when two predicate expressions have some of the same variables

M-4. (R,A) Consider an expert system built to advise Americans which income tax forms and schedules to fill out. There are different ways of satisfying the laws, and some are better for the taxpayer than others. (It matters how much a taxpayer earns and how much of their income is of a certain type. The taxpayer wants the possibility that costs the least money.) Using answers to some simple questions, an expert system could make recommendations without having to ask for a complete financial history. But its conclusions will be necessarily imperfect without such complete information.

(a) Which of the following techniques is most appropriate for this problem? Explain why.

    1. And-or-not lattice

    2. Dependency-based backtracking

    3. Confusion-matrix conflict resolution

    4. Breadth-first resolution strategy

(b) Which of the following techniques is *least* useful for this problem? Explain why not.

    1. Virtual facts

    2. Inference

    3. Depth-first control structure

    4. Concurrency

(c) Which of the following Prolog features is *least* useful in implementing an expert system in Prolog for this problem? Explain.

    1. `asserta` or `assertz`

    2. `repeat`

    3. `write`

    4. `>` [greater-than sign]

M-5. (A) Consider the problem of foot placement for a 6-legged robot. Suppose the robot has a vision system that studies the ground in terms of squares one square meter in area. For each such square the vision system (which you don't need to consider) decides whether that square is a good one to place a leg on. Suppose only 20% of the squares are suitable on the average, and suppose the robot can only extend its legs a certain distance forward. Suppose the vision system only examines squares within a rectangle centered in front of the robot, extending from the front of the robot to ten meters ahead, and ten meters off to the left, and ten meters off to the right. Consider the problem of how to use that information to plan a good sequence of foot placements to the centers of squares, keeping the robot moving ahead in an approximately straight line. The robot is not in a hurry but it doesn't want to ever back up.

(a) Explain which of these search strategies is best for this problem and why.

    1. Best-first search

    2. Weight-first search

    3. Breadth-first search

    4. Branch-and-bound search

(b) Which of the following are also helpful in step planning? Explain why.

    1. Means-ends analysis

    2. Caching

    3. Both means-ends analysis and caching

(c) Which of the following Prolog features is *least* useful for implementing this step-planning (not the vision system) in Prolog? Explain why.

    1. is

    2. assertz (as opposed to asserta)

    3. cut (!)

    4. repeat

M-6. Many artificial-intelligence applications require representation of causation. Suppose we use the Prolog predicate causes(X,Y), where X and Y are names of events such that event X causes event Y to happen. X is assumed to be sufficient for Y to happen (so that any time X happens Y must necessarily happen too), but X is not necessary for Y to happen (Y may have other causes).

(a) Is causes transitive? Explain.

(b) Does causes inherit with respect to part_of? If so, in which direction? Explain.

(c) Consider an alternative representation of causation in Prolog as a rule with the :- symbol. For example

            event(lights_come_on) :- event(turn_wall_switch_to_on).

or better yet

            event(lights_come_on) :- event(turn_wall_switch_to_on),
            not(bulbs_burned_out), not(wiring_defective), not(switch_broken).

But give a major disadvantage of representing causation this way as a rule instead of with causes(X,Y) facts. (Give a "deep" problem; don't consider efficiency.)

M-7. (E) The conjunctions "and" and "or" are very important in artificial intelligence. Consider the conjunction "but."

(a) Suppose we let experts building an expert system use the word "but" in writing rules. How should we translate it into something a programming language like Prolog can handle? Be sure your answer covers most of the usual meaning of "but."

(b) Vocabulary variety makes computer output more comfortable for humans. Discuss when a computer could use "but" in natural language output from a program. In particular, consider a query-answering program. Compare with your answer to part (a).

(c) Would a "but" feature, in addition to "and" and "or," be useful in a logic programming language like Prolog?

M-8. (E) Discuss the possible application of artificial-intelligence techniques to the following two problems:

(a) You are in a submarine and have various sensors. You want to guess the identity of all moving objects up to the limits of your sensor range.

(b) You are positioning army units for a possible battle. You have various kinds of personnel, and various kinds of weapons. You want to position units and equipment in a way that gives you the most tactical advantage.

For each problem, discuss which of the following specific techniques apply: automatic backtracking, generate-and-test, inheritance, defaults, rule-based systems, backward chaining, forward chaining, fixed-order conflict resolution, focus-of-attention conflict resolution, probabilities, depth-first search, breadth-first search, best-first search, A* search, means-ends analysis, frames, relaxation, dependency-based backtracking, resolution

M-9. (H,E) Consider the problem of building an automatic "commercial censor" system that will determine when a television is receiving a commercial, and will turn off the audio and video until the commercial is finished. (This would be nice when videotaping.) An accuracy of 95% within two seconds after a commercial starts or ends is desired. In addition to the frequency analyzer and the low-level vision processor mentioned, assume you have a fast computer with 1 million bytes of random-access memory and 10 million bytes of disk storage. Conduct experiments (involving observation of at least 200 commercials) with a real television to help answer the following questions. An adequate answer to this problem will be 2000 words total.

(a) Categorize clues available from processing of the audio signal. Assume frequency-spectrum calculation hardware (technically, a discrete Fourier transform processor) is available.

(b) Categorize clues available from processing of the video signal. Assume a low-level vision processor (that groups homogeneous two-dimensional regions of a single picture, and calculates their average brightness and color, but slowly).

(c) Categorize clues available from correlation of the results of parts (a) and (b) with an accurate clock connected to the system.

(d) Describe a good control structure (or control structures) for an artificial intelligence system to do this job. Be sure to include whether backward, forward, or hybrid chaining is desirable, and whether depth-first, breadth-first, best-first, or A* searching is desirable.

(e) Suggest good uncertainty combination methods for such an artificial intelligence system. Are numbers a good idea? In particular, suppose each clue from parts (a), (b), and (c) is summarized by a single probability: how would you combine these three?

(f) Where might learning techniques help to automatically improve system performance with time? In particular, discuss how learning from examples can be done. Describe exactly what is learned: how it would be represented in the computer, how it would be modified upon new data, and so on. Remember, artificial-intelligence methods are mostly nonnumeric, so your learning must be mostly nonnumeric.

(g) Describe how you would fairly validate the 95% accuracy claim. When would you run the system, how long, and how many times? Run some simple (not necessarily thorough) tests on a real television of some of the ideas you've developed previously. Explain how you could also use these testing procedures in debugging.

Some hints: Often students are too superficial in their answers to essay questions like these, so err on the side of writing too much rather than writing too little. Don't give definitions of terms and other things that are easy to look up.

BASICS
OF LOGIC

Logic is the study of things that are either true or false and never anything in between. Such things are called *propositions* or *statements*. Propositions can be combined to form more complex propositions using "and," "or," and "not." The "and" of some propositions is true if each is true; the "or" of some propositions is true if one or more are true; and the "not" of a proposition is true if the proposition is false. Otherwise, the result is false. Figure A-1 summarizes these three operations for simple cases; together they define the *propositional calculus*.

A	B	A AND B	A OR B	NOT A
true	true	true	true	false
true	false	false	true	false
false	true	false	true	true
false	false	false	false	true

Figure A-1. Summary of AND, OR, and NOT.

Other operations can be built from these three. For instance, logical implication: A implies B if whenever A is true, B is true too. It's usually interpreted to mean (see discussion in Section 14.2) that this can only be false when A is true and B is false, so an equivalent proposition is "B or not A."

The "and," "or," and "not" operations obey some of the same laws as arithmetic operations. Order in an "and" or "or" doesn't matter, and you can do the operations in pieces, so "and" and "or" are commutative and associative. "And" is distributive with respect to "or," and vice versa:

(A and (B or C)) equals ((A and B) or (A and C))
(A or (B and C)) equals ((A or B) and (A or C))

This means that we can "factor out" repeated propositions, or "factor in" a single proposition, and have an equivalent form. You can do this more than once for complex proposition, as for instance

((A and B) or (C and D)) equals ((A and B) or C) and ((A and B) or D)

equals ((A or C) and (B or C) and (A or D) and (B or D))

A *literal* is either a simple proposition (no "and"s, "or"s, or "not"s in its description) or the "not" of a single simple proposition. By repeated application of a distributive law, you can always convert any complex proposition to an "or," each item of which is an "and" of literals; this is *disjunctive normal form*, and it looks like this:

(A and B and...) or (C and D and ...) or (E and F and ...) or ...

By repeated application of distributivity in just the opposite way, you can always get an "and," each item of which is an "or" of literals. This is *conjunctive normal form*, and it looks like this:

(A or B or ...) and (C or D or ...) and (E or F or ...) and ...

where A, B, C, etc. are literals. Conjunctive normal form is easier to use in Prolog, and is especially important for the resolution methods in Chapter 14 of this book. In putting expressions into normal form, these simplifications help:

(A and A) equals A
(A or A) equals A
(A and (not A)) equals false
(A or (not A)) equals true
(A and true) equals A
(A and false) equals false
(A or true) equals true
(A or false) equals A
(not true) equals false
(not false) equals true

Here are four important examples:

(A and (not(A) or B)) equals ((A and not(A)) or (A and B)) equals (A and B)

(A and (A or B)) equals ((A or false) and (A or B)) equals (A or (false and B)) equals A

(A or (not(A) and B)) equals ((A or not(A)) and (A or B)) equals (A or B)

(A or (A and B)) equals ((A and true) or (A and B)) equals (A and (true or B)) equals A

Distributivity does not hold for "not"s with respect to "and"s and "or"s. But two related formulas hold (DeMorgan's laws):

not(A and B) equals ((not A) or (not B))
not(A or B) equals ((not A) and (not B))

And

not(not(A)) equals A

Hence two important relationships between "and" and "or" are

not(not A and not B) equals (not(not A) or not(not B)) equals A or B
not(not A or not B) equals (not(not A) and not(not B)) equals A and B

"And"s, "or"s, and "not"s can be represented graphically with the standard gate symbols used in hardware design (see Figure A-2). Such a *logic gate* display can help you see patterns you wouldn't see otherwise. The left sides of the gates in the figure represent inputs (operands), and the right sides outputs (operation results). In such displays, it is usually assumed that lines crossing do not connect unless there is a dot at the crossing. Venn diagrams are another useful graphic representation; see Section 8.3.

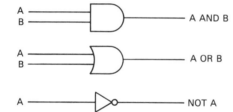

Figure A-2. Standard logic-gate symbols for AND, OR, and NOT.

So far we have only *propositional logic* or the *propositional calculus*. If we let propositions have variables, we get a more powerful kind of logic called *predicate logic* or the *predicate calculus*. We extensively illustrate predicate logic by example in this book, so we won't say much here, but it is important to explain the key feature of *quantification*. If some predicate expression is true for any value of an included variable X, then that the expression is *universally quantified* with respect to X. Another way of saying it is that the expression holds for every X. If an expression is true for some (but not necessarily all) values of an included variable X, then it is *existentially quantified* with respect to X. Alternatively we can say that there exists an X such that the expression is true.

Universal quantification has more practical applications than existential quantification, so we refer to it more. Some additional laws of logic cover universal and existential quantification, but only two are particularly important in this book:

1. The "not" of a proposition existentially quantified is equivalent to the universal quantification of the negation of that proposition.
2. The "not" of a proposition universally quantified is equivalent to the existential quantification of the negation of that proposition.

As an example, suppose an appliance works properly. Then you can say that there does not exist a component X of the appliance such that X is faulty. But that is equivalent to saying that for every component X of the appliance, that component is not faulty.

BASICS
OF RECURSION

Recursion is a valuable computer programming technique. It's a way to get a computer to do something over and over again. Recursion is tricky to understand at first, but once you get comfortable with it, it's easier and safer to program with recursion than with iterative techniques. We especially emphasize recursion in this book because Prolog has a natural affinity for it.

Recursion is a named piece of a program referring to itself. Why do this? Typically, to describe a task or job in the simplest possible way. A good way to explain a complicated job is to break it into components, and that's simplest when those components are the same sort of job. For this to work, we need to guarantee two things: first, that the new jobs are simpler than the old (for otherwise we wouldn't progress); and second, that by decomposition we'll eventually reach "easy" jobs that we can solve quickly without further decomposition. The easy jobs are called the *basis* of a recursion, and the decomposition into similar subjobs is called the *induction* of a recursion. (Recursion is closely related to a mathematical proof technique called *mathematical induction*, and that's where the terms come from.) Any variables involved are usually local to each subjob.

Here's an example (see Figure B-1). Suppose we have employee salaries in our computer, and we want to add 1000 to every one of them. Consider the easiest possible case (basis case) first. That's when there's only one salary, so we just add 1000 to it and store it. But suppose we have 732 salaries. One way to decompose the job (shown in the top diagram in Figure B-1) would be to add 1000 to the first salary, then establish a new job to add 1000 to the other 731 numbers. That new job isn't much simpler, but 731 *is* less than 732 so it is simpler. There are other ways to decompose the job too. For instance (as shown in the bottom diagram in Figure B-1), we can divide the job into equal halves: subjobs of adding 1000 to the first 366 items and adding 1000 to the last 366 items. Each subjob is the same sort of job as the original. Note that successful recursion requires that the new jobs be smaller than the original job; it doesn't matter how many new jobs there are.

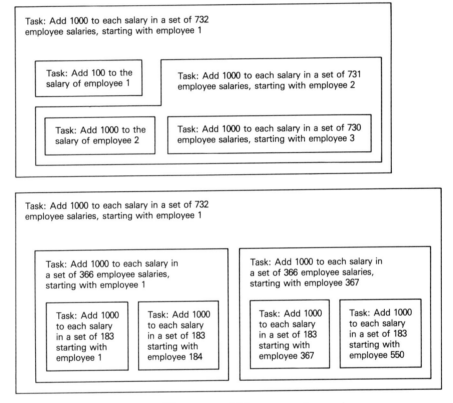

Figure B-1. Two different ways of doing an example recursion.

A recursion can have more than one basis step. For the previous example, a second basis step could handle two-salary jobs, so we wouldn't have to always decompose jobs to single-salary jobs eventually. In Prolog, basis conditions can be either facts (see Chapter 2) or rules (see Chapter 4), but induction conditions are always rules. Note that the first of the two decomposition methods in the last paragraph (binary decomposition in which one part is size 1) is the most common kind of recursive decomposition, because it's *easy to implement* despite the apparent inefficiency of its extreme unevenness of decomposition.

If you are having trouble understanding recursion, you should study some simple recursive programs and try to apply their form to new situations. The simplest form of recursion is *tail recursion*, in which there is only one induction (recursion) case, an extreme uneven decomposition, and its recursive call occurs last in the program. The first of the two ways to update 732 salaries is tail recursion.

Tail recursion is the commonest form of recursion, and has the advantage that it is easy to convert to iteration: the recursive call is like a branch or "goto" at the end of a loop. Recursive programs tend to be a little slower than their equivalent iterative counterparts, so that is one reason to convert them (though the recursive versions tend to be easier to understand). However, any recursion with more than one recursive (self-) reference is hard to convert to iteration, like the second (even-split) way of updating 732 salaries, or the means-ends analysis program in Chapter 11.

Recursion can define functions (in the mathematical sense) as well as subroutines. For instance, suppose the job is to compute the sum of 732 employee salaries (see Figure B-2). The basis case is when there is only one salary, and the sum is then that number. The induction case is when there are N numbers, $N > 1$; let's use tail recursion for it. That means we recursively decompose this problem into a job to find the sum of all but the first one of the numbers, and add to the first number this total. So each level of recursion returns a value to the next highest level.

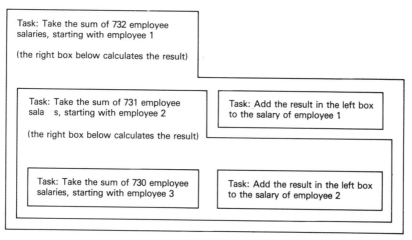

Figure B-2. Example of recursion of a function.

Chapters 4 and 5 introduce recursive programs in Prolog. One word of advice: students often have trouble with recursion when they worry too much about what the program does during execution. You can usually follow the first recursive call, and maybe the second, but after that it gets confusing because it's hard to see where to "go back to" when one recursive call concludes. Human brains just aren't as well equipped as computers for this sort of reasoning. So stick to the *declarative* or *decompositional* description of recursion used in this appendix. Then if your recursive program doesn't work right, use the following checklist:

1. Do the cases meant to be handled by basis conditions work right?
2. Do the basis conditions cover *all* the easy cases that might occur through recursive decomposition?
3. Does the recursive decomposition really decompose the problem into *simpler* subproblems? (How many doesn't matter.)

4. If the recursive program has arguments, are the arguments in the recursive calls correctly different from the arguments at the top of the program?

5. Are all arguments bound or constants at the top of the program also bound or constants in the recursive calls?

6. Are all arguments unbound at the top of the program also initially unbound unbound in the recursive calls?

7. Does every unbound variable eventually get bound?

Usually one of these things will be at fault if a recursive program is not working.

BASICS
OF DATA STRUCTURES

Data structures are ways of storing things inside a computer. The efficiency of an artificial-intelligence program can be affected a good deal by the choices made for its data structures. We summarize the main kinds in Figure C-1. The many books on this subject provide further information.

Basic data structures are ways of storing small single items of data. Programming languages typically provide as basic data structures (or *data types*) integers, real numbers (in floating-point notation), characters (alphanumeric), and bits (things that can be either true or false). Some programming languages also have *pointers* (actual memory addresses).

The simplest of composite data structures is the *array*. It's just a group of data items stored in successive locations in computer memory. The data items can be any of the aforementioned basic types. So we can speak of an *integer array*, a *real array*, or a *character array*; the last is usually called a *character string*. To find the data item in the *K*th position in a plain (*one-dimensional*) array, you give the *index K*. For a *two-dimensional* array, you give two numbers, a *row* and *column* for a data item. Use of an array requires knowing the start of the array and the length of each dimension.

But arrays are a poor data structure when you must frequently add and remove items of data. Then *linked lists*, often called just *lists*, are better. Linked lists store sequences of data items like arrays do, but the items do not have to be in successive locations in computer memory; each is paired with a pointer giving the memory location of the next data item in sequence, with the last data item in the list having a special pointer called *nil*. So a list can be scattered around in computer memory, provided you keep item-pointer pairs together and you know the location of the first data item. Linked lists need more space to store data items than an array would, but allow more flexibility in the use of computer memory. Lists are more common in artificial-intelligence programming than arrays, and in fact the programming language Lisp is built almost entirely around lists: lists even represent programs in Lisp.

Several common data structures are special cases of arrays and lists. If you only insert and delete items at the very end of an array or list, then you have a *stack* data structure. Stacks are essential for managing procedure calls and recursion in programming languages, though their operation is usually hidden from the user; such stacks contain pointers to memory locations of program pieces. If you only delete items at the very front of an array or list, and only insert items at the very end, then you have a *queue* data structure. Queues are used when you want to be "fair" to data items and want the data item that has been in the array or list the longest to be the first removed. So queues are first in, first out. Analogously stacks are last in, first out.

Arrays and lists order their items. An unordered set can be stored as an array or list in some random order, but there is an alternative. If data items can take on one of N data values—as for instance, data items for ages of employees in years, which must be positive integers less than 100—then we can represent sets as an N-element *bit array* (an array whose data items are bits) where a "true" in location K of the array means that the Kth possible is present in the set. Bit arrays can make set operations like intersection run very fast, and many computers have bit-handling instructions to speed things even more.

Data structures can arrange data in more complicated ways too. For instance, consider as data items the names of procedures, and suppose we want to represent how those procedures call one another in a nonrecursive program in which every procedure is called only once (e.g., Figure 7-3). A procedure can call several others, and each of those can call several others, and so on. This sort of branching data structure is called a *tree*. *Binary trees* are those for which every data item has one branch entering and either two or zero branches leaving; they're the most common kind of tree. A tree is usually stored in computer memory as an array of subarrays, each subarray holding a data value and pointers to subarrays of other data items that are linked from it. Trees are useful whenever there are hierarchies or taxonomies in the data. Trees can also be built as an index to sequential data, when you want to be able to find things fast (*search trees*). Trees can be implemented in a list-processing language like Lisp by embedding lists within lists; the same thing can be done in Prolog.

If the paths in a tree can split then join together, then technically you don't have a tree but a *lattice* or *directed acyclic graph*. Lattices and trees can be implemented the same way, and they are often confused. Lattices occur often in computer science. For instance, if the same procedure is used in several different places in a program, the hierarchy of procedures can be represented as a lattice. In general, lattices arise whenever you have partial information about ordering of things, but not complete ordering information.

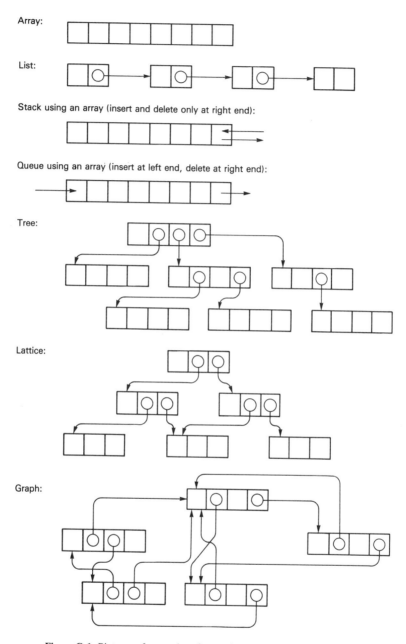

Array:

List:

Stack using an array (insert and delete only at right end):

Queue using an array (insert at left end, delete at right end):

Tree:

Lattice:

Graph:

Figure C-1. Pictures of examples of some famous data structures.

If your data structure has loops so that you can return to some data item by following a sequence of pointers from it, then technically you have a *directed graph*, often just called a *graph*. Graphs are good at modeling arbitrary connections between things. You can implement graphs like trees, as arrays of subarrays containing pointers to other records. Another way is to extend a bit array to a *bit matrix*: for N possible data items, create an N by N array of bits so that the entry in row I and column J of this array is true if and only if there is a connection from data item I to data item J in the graph. Some graphs require that you store data for each connection, not just for each data item, and for these graphs you can use an array but store data other than bits in it. Matrix graph implementations are good whenever there are many connections between relatively few data items.

Still more complex data structures can be made by combining the aforementioned ones in various ways. Data items can themselves be data structures; for instance, data items representing English words can be character arrays. Lists can be items of lists themselves, and such *embedded lists* are used extensively in the language Lisp. If you want to represent a graph in Lisp, you can use a list of lists where each sublist contains a data item value followed by a list of pointers. And all the standard list processing of Lisp can be done analogously in Prolog. (But a word of warning: Lisp uses parentheses to denote lists while Prolog uses brackets.)

Recursion (see Appendix B) is useful for manipulating all these data structures. Lists and arrays suggest tail recursion in the form of a single basis case followed by a single induction case, where the basis case concerns a single item of an array or list, and the induction case decomposes the problem by eliminating from further consideration that single item. Trees, lattices, graphs, and embedded data structures require more complicated forms of recursion involving either multiple induction cases or multiple recursive procedures. Data structures books provide classic recursive algorithms for all these things and they should be consulted for most simple needs instead of your trying to write programs yourself.

SUMMARY OF THE PROLOG DIALECT USED IN THIS BOOK

The Prolog examples in this book use a subset of the "core Prolog" or "standard Prolog" originally developed in several implementations at Edinburgh University and covered in W. F. Clocksin and C. S. Mellish, *Programming in Prolog*, second edition, Springer-Verlag, 1984. Substantially similar dialects are provided for many computers, and include Quintus Prolog, Logicware MPROLOG, Automata Design Associates VMI-Prolog, Arity/Prolog, ASTEC Prolog-KABA, Chalcedony Prolog/i and Prolog/m, Expert Systems International Prolog-1, IF/Prolog, Programming Logic Systems MAC-Prolog and Sigmaprolog, Solution Systems Prolog-86, DEC-10 Prolog, and C-Prolog (companies mentioned hold trademarks). (Programs in this book were tested in Edinburgh C-Prolog.) Borland International Turbo Prolog is close to this standard, but doesn't easily support multiway use, treating rules as data (Section D.8), and has other important differences. Micro-Prolog has major differences; see Appendix E. For compatibility with many of these dialects and better comprehension by the reader, the Prolog subset of this book omits many common and useful features, including other arithmetic operations, input and output, embedded structures (as opposed to embedded lists), functors, modules, graphics, and many debugging tools; see the Prolog books in Appendix F for information about these. This appendix is summarized in Figure D-1.

D.1 MANAGING FACTS AND RULES

We assume Prolog programs (consisting of rules and facts) are written outside the Prolog interpreter. You use your favorite editor to create a text file containing

Built-in predicate	Arguments	Can it succeed on backtracking?	Description
consult	a filename	no	loads a file
listing	a predicate name	no	prints database items with that predicate name
asserta	a fact	no	adds a fact to the front of the database
assertz	a fact	no	adds a fact to the rear of the database
retract	a fact	no	removes a fact
abolish	a predicate name and its number of arguments	no	removes all facts with some predicate name
> [infix]	two numbers	no	greater than
< [infix]	two numbers	no	less than
= [infix]	two numbers	no	equals
is [infix]	variable and a numeric expression	no	arithmetic assignment
number	a variable	no	succeeds if argument is bound to a number
write	a word, variable, or character string	no	prints on the terminal
read	a variable	no	reads a word typed by the user
nl	none	no	issues carriage return to the terminal
not	a predicate expression	no	succeeds if querying its argument fails
fail	none	no	always fails
!	none	no	[see text]
var	a variable	no	succeeds if argument is not bound to anything
call	a predicate expression	yes	queries the predicate
clause	a rule left side and rule right side	yes	binds text of a rule to any variables
= .. [infix]	a query and a list	yes	converts a query to a list or vice versa

Figure D-1. Summary of built-in Prolog predicates assumed in this book.

them. Then you start up the Prolog interpreter (how to do this is implementation-dependent) and load in the files you want by querying **consult**, whose one argument is the name of the editor-created file you want to load. If you have several files to load, do **consult** several times. But be careful not to load definitions twice.

To list all the facts and rules in the Prolog database, query **listing** with no arguments. To list only the facts and rules with a particular predicate name, query with that name as argument.

To add a fact (a single predicate expression without a **not**) to the Prolog database from within the interpreter, query **asserta** or **assertz**. Built-in predicate

asserta adds the new fact at the front of the database, and **assertz** adds it to the end. To remove a fact from the Prolog database, query **retract** with that fact an argument. To remove all the facts and rules with a particular predicate name, query **abolish**, whose first argument is the predicate name and whose second is the number of arguments the first-argument predicate has. All four of these predicates fail on backtracking, so the only way to undo a single **asserta** or **assertz** is a **retract**.

D.2 THE FORMAT OF FACTS, RULES, AND QUERIES

Facts, rules, and queries are all built of the same thing: predicate expressions. A predicate expression consists of a predicate name (starting with a lower-case letter) optionally followed by one or more arguments separated by commas and enclosed in parentheses. Arguments that are constants must be numbers or start with a lower-case letter, and arguments that are variables must start with a capital letter. Facts are just predicate expressions followed by a period (.).

Queries are things you type after the Prolog interpreter types ?- on your terminal; query mode is the interpreter's normal mode. A query is a single predicate expression, or several expressions linked with commas or semicolons, concluded by a period and carriage return. Commas mean "and" and semicolons mean "or." (In some dialects you can equivalently use the words "and" and "or.") You can also specify that the opposite of something be true with the **not** predicate of one argument; its argument is the predicate expression you want to fail.[1]

If you type a semicolon after the interpreter types an answer to a query, the interpreter will go back to work and try to find another answer to the query. You can keep typing semicolons as long as there are more answers. If the interpreter can't find an answer, it will type **no**.

Rules consist of a predicate expression followed by a space, the symbol :- (or in some dialects, the word "if"), another space, a query, and a period. The stuff before the :- is the *left side* and the stuff after is the *right side*. Rules can be read as "if the right side is true then the left side is true."

D.3 PROGRAM LAYOUT

Spaces and carriage returns can be inserted at many places in Prolog programs without changing the meaning. However, it's conventional not to put them in normal predicate expressions (except within strings). A space is generally put after every "and"-comma and "or"-semicolon in a query or rule, as well as before and after the rule symbol :- and the arithmetic-assignment **is**.

Another convention of Prolog programming is to leave blank lines in programs between rules and facts beginning with different predicate names; this makes it easier to see which lines go together.

---

[1] The **not** is denoted with prefix /+ in Quintus Prolog, and it won't work with inside unbound variables in Turbo Prolog. Other dialects don't handle it, strictly speaking, as a predicate.

Comments are preceded with a /* and followed by a */ in most dialects.

D.4 LISTS

Arguments to predicate expressions can be lists. Lists are indicated by the brackets, [and]; commas (not to be confused with the commas between predicate arguments) separate the list items. The list of no items, [], is called the empty list. Lists of any length can be represented by variables, or they can be referred to by the notation [<front_items>|<sublist>]. Here <front_items> represents an item, or several items separated by commas, at the front (left end) of a list, and <sublist> is a variable representing the arbitrarily-long rest of the list. Some or all the items within a list can be variables too.

D.5 NUMBERS

Arguments to predicate expressions can be numbers. (Some dialects accept only integers, and some others only accept decimals with digits before and after the decimal point.) Prolog handles numbers with infix notation to make things easier to read. (Predicate expressions are prefix notation; that is, the predicate name comes first.) The infix comparison predicates are = (equals), > (greater than), < (less than), =< (less than or equal to), and >= (greater than or equal to). Any variables used in these comparisons must be bound to values. (Warning: Some dialects don't allow a space between the symbols in the last two predicates.)

Arithmetic assignment is handled by the is infix symbol.[2] To the left of the is and separated by a space must be the name of a variable; to the right and separated by a space must be an arithmetic expression of constants and/or bound variables. The arithmetic expression is evaluated, and its value bound to the left-side variable. The arithmetic expression must be in infix form, using the standard infix arithmetic symbols +, -, *, and /; parentheses can group terms.

D.6 OUTPUT AND INPUT

To have Prolog write something on the terminal screen, use the write predicate of one argument. The argument can be a word, list, number, string, bound variable (for which it prints the current binding), or even unbound variable (for which it prints the internal code of the variable name). To get a carriage return on the terminal, query the nl (that stands for "new line") predicate of no arguments. The predicate read of one argument, a variable, reads in what the user types on the terminal keyboard and binds the variable to it. What the user types must end with a period, just like everything else in Prolog.

---

[2] Not available in Turbo Prolog: = is dual-purpose.

D.7 STRINGS

Character strings are denoted by single-quotation marks or apostrophes (') around some characters and punctuation marks. Strings can contain capital letters, commas, periods, and other punctuation marks in any order, so they're less restricted than predicate names, variable names, and constants.

D.8 TREATING RULES AND FACTS AS DATA[3]

The predicate **clause** matches its first argument to the left side and its second argument to the right side of a rule or fact in the database (if a fact, its second argument is set to the empty query which always succeeds, "true").[4] The infix "univ" operation represented by the symbol =.. converts queries into lists, and vice versa; the left side of this symbol is the query, and the right side the list. If the left side is bound it is converted into its equivalent list, and if the right side is bound it is converted into its equivalent query. Related to this, the **call** predicate of one argument takes a query and executes it as if it were typed on the terminal.

D.9 MISCELLANEOUS PREDICATES

The **fail** predicate of no arguments provides a predicate expression that always fails, forcing backtracking. The **true** predicate always succeeds. The cut predicate (symbolized by !) of no arguments forces throwing away of certain backtracking information; see Section 10.7 for a detailed discussion. The **var** predicate of one argument succeeds if its argument is unbound. The **number** predicate of one argument succeeds if its argument is a number. The **halt** predicate of no arguments stops the Prolog interpreter and returns you to the operating system; it's the recommended way to finish a session.

D.10 DEFINABLE PREDICATES

Besides the preceding built-in predicates, some predicates defined in this book in terms of others are built-in in many Prolog dialects. The **forall** predicate of two arguments (Section 7.12) checks whether universal quantification holds for some predicate expression; specifically, it checks whether every set of variable bindings that satisfies its first-argument predicate expression also satisfies its second-argument predicate expression. The **doall** predicate of one argument (Section 7.12) repeatedly calls its argument predicate expression until that expression fails. The **repeat** predicate (Section 10.8) of no arguments always succeeds, and always

---

[3] Not supported in Turbo Prolog.

[4] Some Prolog dialects won't accept a **clause** expression unless the left-side predicate name is filled in. But you can get the same effect by iterating over the list of all predicate names, trying each one for the left side.

succeeds afresh on backtracking. The **bagof** predicate[5] of three arguments (Section 10.6) collects into a list all values to which a variable can be bound to satisfy a predicate expression. The first argument is the variable, the second is the expression (somewhere inside which must be the variable), and the third argument is the list of all possible values, the output.

D.11 DEBUGGING

Since the activities of Prolog interpreters can be complicated, good debugging facilities are essential. These facilities differ considerably between dialects. But *trace*, **spy**, and **leash** features are common. These are built-in Prolog predicates that are queried to cause certain side effects. Predicate **trace** is a predicate of no arguments that makes the Prolog interpreter print a running account of everything it is doing; **notrace** undoes it. Predicate **spy** is a predicate of one argument, a predicate name, that makes the Prolog interpreter print everything happening with that predicate; **nospy** with that same argument undoes it. To spy on several predicates, do several **spy** commands. The **trace** and **spy** printouts report calls, successes, failures, and backtracks involving predicate expressions with a given predicate name. The **leash(on)** predicate expression tells the interpreter to stop and pause after every printout line generated by a **trace** or **spy**; **leash(off)** undoes it.

---

[5] Called **findall** in some dialects.

USING THIS BOOK
WITH MICRO-PROLOG

Micro-Prolog is a dialect of Prolog designed to run in a small amount of memory on small computers. It looks different, but its execution (semantics) is very similar. Micro-Prolog is designed primarily for nonprogrammers, people who aren't computer experts. So it is less elegant than standard Prolog, and doesn't have some of the advanced features, but it's easier to learn to use.

In Micro-Prolog, querying is not the default mode, so you must indicate a query by a "?" on the front of the line. You must use parentheses to group things, a lot like the language Lisp. You must surround the query with parentheses. The predicate name goes inside the parentheses used in standard Prolog to group arguments, and spaces are used instead of commas to separate the arguments and the predicate name from the first argument. So the standard Prolog query

   ?- a, b(X), c(X,Y).

becomes in Micro-Prolog

   ? ((a) (b X) (c X Y))

Note a period is not used.

The symbol table is limited in Micro-Prolog, so variable names can only be X, Y, Z, X1, Y1, Z1, X2, Y2, Z2, and so on. Micro-Prolog will not print out variable bindings unless you force it with the equivalent of the standard-Prolog **write**, the "P" predicate. So to print out X and Y for the preceding query you must say

? ((a) (b X) (c X Y) (P X) (P Y))

Predicate names in Micro-Prolog can be capitalized or uncapitalized, just as long as they aren't a possible variable name. (Built-in predicates are usually all capitals.)

Rules in Micro-Prolog look just like queries without the question mark. But the first predicate is interpreted as the left side ("then" part), and the other predicates as the right side ("if" part). So the standard-Prolog rule

Standard Prolog feature	Micro-Prolog feature
consult(<filename>)	LOAD <filename>
listing(<predicatename>)	LIST <predicatename>
asserta(F)	(ADDCL F 0)
assertz(F)	(ADDCL F <number-of-F-facts-and-rules>)
retract(F)	(DELCL F)
abolish(F,2)	KILL F
?-	&.
:-	[see discussion]
,	[see discussion]
p(X); q(X)	(OR ((p X)) ((q X)))
not(p(X))	(NOT p X)
X<Y	(LESS X Y)
X>Y	(LESS Y X)
X = 3	(EQ X 3)
X is 3	(EQ X 3)
X is Y + Z	(SUM Y Z X)
X is Y-Z	(SUM X Z Y)
X is Y*Z	(TIMES Y Z X)
X is Y/Z	(TIMES X Z Y)
[a,b,X]	(a b X)
[X|Y]	(X | Y)
'Character string'	(Character string)
write(X)	(P X)
write(X),nl	(PP X)
read(X)	(R X)
clause(p(X),Y)	((p X) | Y)
P = ..L	[unnecessary--queries are lists]
call(p(X))	(? ((p X)))
fail	(FAIL)
!	!
number(X)	(NUM X)
var(X)	(VAR X)
/* comment */	/* comment
bagof(X,p(X),X2)	(ISALL X2 X (p X))

Figure E-1. Approximate equivalents between the Prolog assumed in this book and Micro-Prolog.

a(X) :- b(X), c(X,3), d(Y,X).

becomes in Micro-Prolog

((a X) (b X) (c X 3) (d Y X))

Figure E-1 gives a table of approximate equivalents between standard Prolog and Micro-Prolog. Micro-Prolog manuals provide further information.

FURTHER READING

We list a few books and articles recommended for additional reading on the topics of this book. We've grouped related entries together.

GENERAL ARTIFICIAL INTELLIGENCE

WINSTON, P. H., *Artificial Intelligence*. 2nd ed. Reading, Mass.: Addison-Wesley, 1984. Useful for basic understanding of artificial intelligence.

CHARNIAK, E. and D. MCDERMOTT, *Introduction to Artificial Intelligence*. Reading, Mass.: Addison-Wesley, 1985. A well-balanced, reasonably detailed treatment of the field at a more advanced level than ours. Also a good source for further information. Uses examples in Lisp.

GEVARTER, W. B., *Intelligent Machines: An Introductory Perspective of Artificial Intelligence and Robotics*. Englewood Cliffs, N. J.: Prentice-Hall, Inc., 1985. A short summary of the key ideas in artificial intelligence.

REITMAN, W. (ed.), *Artificial Intelligence Applications for Business*. Norwood, N. J.: Ablex, 1984. An interesting collection of articles surveying the major commercial applications of artificial intelligence.

FEIGENBAUM, E., and P. MCCORDUCK, *The Fifth Generation: Artificial Intelligence and Japan's Computer Challenge to the World*. Reading, Mass.: Addison-Wesley, 1983. A nontechnical, general-audience book arguing for the critical importance of artificial intelligence in the world's future. Controversial but interesting reading.

402

THE LANGUAGE PROLOG _____

CLOCKSIN, W. and C. MELLISH, *Programming in Prolog*, 2nd ed. Berlin, B.R.D.: Springer-Verlag, 1984. A well-written introduction to Prolog as a programming language, including features not covered in our book. Uses a dialect containing ours.

STERLING, L. and E. SHAPIRO, *The Art of Prolog*. Cambridge, Mass.: MIT Press, 1986. A more detailed introduction to Prolog.

BRATKO, I., *Prolog Programming for Artificial Intelligence*. Reading, Mass.: Addison-Wesley, 1986. Despite its title, mostly a programming language textbook in the manner of Clocksin and Mellish. But it has additional chapters on implementing search in Prolog (Chapters 11, 12, 13, and 15) corresponding to some of our Chapters 9 and 10, a chapter (Chapter 14) on expert systems covering parts of our Chapters 7 and 8, and some material on resolution (Section 16.3) corresponding to the program in our Chapter 14.

WALKER, A. (ed.), *Knowledge Systems and Prolog*. Reading, Mass.: Addison-Wesley, 1987. Again despite its title, mostly a programming-language textbook. Its coverage of artificial intelligence is unbalanced, but it presents many interesting ideas on natural language and expert systems.

ENNALS, R., *Artificial Intelligence: Applications to Logical Reasoning and Historical Research*. New York: Wiley, 1985. A good nonthreatening introduction to Prolog for students without strong computer science backgrounds. Helpful for people finding the early chapters of our book tough going.

CLARK, K., and F. MCCABE, *Micro-Prolog: Programming in Logic*. Englewood Cliffs, N. J.: Prentice-Hall, 1984. An introduction to the Micro-Prolog dialect.

COHEN, J., "Describing Prolog by Its Interpretation and Compilation," *Communications of the ACM, 28*, 12 (December 1985), 1311–1324. A good survey of Prolog from a programmer's point of view.

MARCELLUS, D. H., *Programming Expert Systems in Turbo Prolog*. Englewood Cliffs, N.J.: Prentice-Hall, 1988. Despite its title, it covers other artificial-intelligence programs besides expert systems.

SUBAREAS OF ARTIFICIAL INTELLIGENCE _____

WATERMAN, D., *A Guide to Expert Systems*. Reading, Mass.: Addison-Wesley, 1986. A good introduction to expert systems, though not very technical. Extensive bibliography.

HAYES-ROTH, F., D. LENAT, and D. WATERMAN, (eds.), *Building Expert Systems*. Reading, Mass.: Addison-Wesley, 1983. A more detailed consideration of issues in building expert systems.

WINOGRAD, T., *Language As a Cognitive Process, Volume I: Syntax*. Reading, Mass.: Addison-Wesley, 1983. Overview of the grammar (syntax) side of the natural language subarea.

SCHANK, R. and R. ABELSON, *Scripts, Plans, Goals, and Understanding*. Hillsdale, N.J.: Lawrence Erlbaum, 1977. An integrated discussion of natural-language semantics, frames, and planning. Quite readable.

Special section on Architectures for Knowledge-Based Systems, *Communications of the ACM, 28,* 9 (September 1985), 902–941. Contains three good overview articles on frames, rule-based systems, and logic programming.

BALLARD, D. and C. BROWN, *Computer Vision.* Englewood Cliffs, N.J.: Prentice-Hall, 1982. An overview of the vision subarea of artificial intelligence.

WOS, L., and others, *Automated Reasoning: Introduction and Applications.* Englewood Cliffs, N.J., Prentice-Hall, 1984. Discusses use of a general-purpose theorem prover (based on extensions of resolution) for making inferences for interesting problems. A friendly book with lots of interesting examples, but its theorem-prover is more powerful than Prolog and so programming it is different.

MAIER, D., "Databases in the Fifth Generation Project: Is Prolog a Database Language?," in *New Directions for Database Systems*, G. Ariav, and J. Clifford, eds. Norwood, N.J.: Ablex, 1986, 18–34. Good survey of the considerations necessary to make Prolog efficient with large databases of facts and rules.

FISHMAN, D., "The DBMS—Expert-System Connection," in *New Directions for Database Systems*, G. Ariav, and J. Clifford, eds. Norwood, N.J.: Ablex, 1986, 87–101. Explains how database design considerations are important for expert systems.

MICHALSKI, R., J. CARBONELL, and T. MITCHELL, eds., *Machine Learning: An Artificial Intelligence Approach.* Palo Alto, Calif.: Tioga, 1983. Collection of articles summarizing the learning subarea.

GOLDBERG A., and D. ROBSON, *Smalltalk-80: The Language and Its Implementation.* Reading, Mass.: Addison-Wesley, 1983. An overview of the object-oriented programming language Smalltalk.

WINSTON, P., and B. HORN, *Lisp,* 2nd ed. Reading, Mass.: Addison-Wesley, 1984. A sequel to Winston's *Artificial Intelligence* which shows how to write some interesting artificial-intelligence programs in Lisp. It illustrates well how Lisp programming is different from Prolog programming.

Special issue on hardware design for artificial intelligence, *Computer, 20,* 1 (January 1987). Good survey.

GENERAL BACKGROUND

MENDELSON, E., *Introduction to Mathematical Logic.* New York: Van Nostrand Reinhold, 1964. Just one of many good textbooks on logic from a mathematical perspective.

TENENBAUM, A., and M. AUGENSTEIN, *Data Structures Using Pascal.* Englewood Cliffs, N.J.: Prentice-Hall, 1981. Good coverage of the basics of data structures and recursion.

ZWASS, V., *Introduction to Computer Science.* New York: Barnes and Noble, 1981. Basic survey of the fundamentals of computer science necessary for understanding artificial intelligence.

WULF, W., and others, *Fundamental Structures of Computer Science.* Reading, Mass.: Addison-Wesley, 1981. A more advanced presentation than the preceding. Good coverage of data structures, recursion, and implementation of traditional programming languages.

KOLMAN, B. and R. BUSBY, *Introductory Discrete Structures with Applications.* Englewood Cliffs, N.J.: Prentice-Hall, 1987. Survey of the mathematical fundamentals necessary for artificial intelligence.

LONGLEY-COOK, L., *Statistical Problems and How To Solve Them.* New York: Barnes and Noble, 1970. Just one of many good introductions to statistics and probability. This one is quite friendly.

LINDSAY, P. and D. NORMAN, *Human Information Processing.* New York: Academic Press, 1972. Well-written introduction to the tie-ins between artificial intelligence and research in human cognitive psychology.

ANSWERS TO
SELECTED EXERCISES

(Exercises with answers were marked with an A in the text.)

2-1. The color fact is better, because colors are less based on judgment and context than sizes are. We can define colors by approximate frequency ranges of light waves, but there are no absolute standards of size: a "big" ship is a lot bigger than a "big" molecule. So if you want to refer to sizes in an artificial-intelligence program, you probably should use something more precise.

2-2. Answer (ii). For format (i) the predicate names are just as general as the argument names, meaning many separate predicate names are necessary. And there's no internal indication with format (i) that these are supposed to be memo facts. But format (iii) is too general—any fact can be written this way—and the predicate name isn't informative. Also, (ii) is typical of the predicates used in the chapter.

2-5. The speaker is forgetting that arithmetic operations are functions, and the function result must be an explicit argument in predicate expressions. So one-argument operations become two-argument predicate expressions, and two-argument operations become three-argument expressions. Other than that, the speaker's argument is pretty much correct: logic is part of mathematics, and Prolog is closely related to logic.

2-6. Write each ship fact as five two-argument facts, each with first argument the original first argument of the ship fact. (That is, use the ship name as a *key*.) The second argument will be:

- ship location for predicate name location;
- time at location for predicate name time;
- date at location for predicate name date;
- ship color for predicate name color;
- ship commander for predicate name commander.

So for instance

> ship(enterprise,15n35e,1200,16feb85,gray,j_kirk).

becomes

> location(enterprise,15n35e).
> time(enterprise,1200).
> date(enterprise,16feb85).
> color(enterprise,gray).
> commander(enterprise,j_kirk).

2-7. You might want to reason about a hypothetical situation, a situation not currently true. Advance reasoning might help you plan what to do if the situation occurs, saving you time then and letting you figure the best thing to do. Reasoning about hypothetical situations is also useful for debugging programs. For such reasoning to work, the set of hypothetical facts must be consistent: they can't be false in the sense of being self-contradictory.

3-1. (a) Use DeMorgan's law:

> ?- not(a), not(b).

(b) Use DeMorgan's law and rearrange:

> ?- (a;b), (not(a);not(b)).

3-2. (a)

- What job bosses the boss of a CS professor?
- What person is Rowe's boss?
- Who is the incumbent dean of either IP or IPS? (querier probably doesn't know which is the proper abbreviation)
- What person either has the provost or the IPS dean as a boss?
- What job other than Shrady's is bossed by the superintendent?

(b) First answers found, in order:

$X = $ cschairman
$Y = $ dean_ips

$X = $ csprofessor
$Y = $ cschairman
$Z = $ lum

$X = $ marshall

$J = $ cschairman
$P = $ lum

$P = $ director_milops

3-5. (a) NM (every possible pair, or the *Cartesian product*).
    (b) N (N-1 for each new choice of X, and then one for the final query failure).
    (c) NM (the two parts of the query are independent).
    (d) The minimum of M and N.
    (e) N—it's just like part (b).
    (f) 0. The arguments to p facts may be totally different from the arguments to q facts.

3-6. (a) "Joe" is a constant in the queries, and "someone" is a variable. Every time a new Prolog query is asked, the variable bindings from the previous query are thrown away, and so this only affects the "someone" query. The mistake or *fallacy* is in assuming such bindings persist.
    (b) Assuming that a student gets a single grade on a single test:

$?- $ grade(P,1,G), not(grade(P,1,a)).

    (c) No, this isn't correct. Different people may have taken the two tests: some students may have dropped the course and others may have added the course in between. So the meaning of "class" may have changed.

3-9. (a) $X = $ a, $Y = $ d, $Z = $ e. The first three r facts all eventually fail when used to match X and Y in the first predicate expression in the query. $X = $ a with $Y = $ b fails in the third query expression, $X = $ a with $Y = $ c fails in the fourth query expression, and $X = $ b with $Y = $ a fails in the second query expression.
    (b) Four times: for $Y = $ b and $Z = $ c, $Y = $ b and $Z = $ d, $Y = $ c and $Z = $ d, and $Y = $ c and $Z = $ c. Notice that even though the matching for the second predicate expression can't affect the success of the third expression, the

Prolog interpreter will always backtrack there from the third because it's the immediately previous expression—that is, the interpreter always backtracks *chronologically*.

4-2. (a) Make the left side a fact.

4-5. (b) Delete the rule entirely—it never does any good.

No, not if a is queried with an unbound argument and there is some c fact in the database, say c(3). Then the one-rule form binds X to 3 in a, but the two-rule form can't. But when a is queried with a bound argument, the two forms give the same answers.

4-6. (a) Two different meanings of the word "mayor" are being confused: the job description and the person currently occupying that office. These meanings can't be equated. We'll discuss this distinction more in Chapter 12.

(b) The phrase "a movie star" acts like a noun, whereas "a little stupid" acts like an adjective. So "Clint is a movie star" must be represented by an a_kind_of relationship predicate, whereas "John is a little stupid" must be represented by a property predicate.

4-7. (a) A definition with two things "and"ed together on the right side.

(b) Two different facts about a department chairman (notice they do not define "chairman," just give properties of one).

(c) Here the "and" is more like an "or." So you could write two rules with the same left side (representing "a way to put out a fire") and different right sides for the different methods. Alternatively but less directly, you could write two facts asserting two different "fire methods."

(d) Two a_kind_of facts.

(e) This is an unusual situation in English, an *idiom* in which the words don't mean what they literally say. Here Tom and Dick are not only friends, but implied friends of one another. So two interrelated facts are being asserted, or just a disguised relationship-predicate fact.

4-10. (a) Upward only. If some of Set have Property, then those same items will be present in a set including Set.

(b) No basis conditions are needed because facts will provide them. The induction step looks like this:

some(Set,Property) :- contains(Set,Set2), some(Set2,Property).

(c) Downward only. If all of Set have Property, then all the items of any subset of Set have the same property.

(d) Neither way. "Most" is a statistical generalization about a set, and there's never any guarantee that a statistical generalization about one set applies to a related set. (A subset might just happen to contain atypical items.)

4-11. (a) Yes, something inside something else inside a third thing is inside the third thing.

(b) Yes, it inherits downward in one sense. If A is in front of B, and B contains C, then A is in front of C. However, downward inheritance doesn't work the other way: if A is in front of B and B is inside C, then A is not necessarily in front of C because C could contain A too: let A=battery, B=motor, and C=entire car.

(c) To better talk to people (as when giving them advice) because people understand nonnumeric descriptions better. And if people were given coordinates to locate things, they would need to do a lot of measurements from reference points, which is bothersome. Furthermore, it's tricky to compute object relationships from Cartesian coordinates describing object shapes; a lot of mathematics is necessary, especially when it won't do to just store the center of irregularly shaped objects. So it would be awkward for the computer to store coordinates internally and convert them to physical relationships to talk to people.

On the other hand, Cartesian coordinates are more precise descriptors than relationship predicates: you can compute more accurate spatial relationships, ways to reach parts, etc. Cartesian coordinates might take less memory space than relationship information since you wouldn't have to represent information about an object more than once; for N objects in a car there are $N*(N-1)$ relationships between any two, though inheritance could cut that down. And there are lots of ways to compress numbers to make storing them even more efficient, like keeping relative coordinates of parts. It's not true that relationship predicates are more car-independent (that is, the same description could apply to many different cars) than Cartesian coordinates, since coordinates could have associated tolerance intervals to make them more fuzzy. But "user-friendliness" is the chief disadvantage of Cartesian coordinates.

4-13. (a) The point of this part of the problem is to note the varied forms the same predicate can take. Only two predicates are needed: the **part_of** of Section 2.6, and a **contains** predicate that says that some of an object is a particular material (if you wanted to be fancy, you could have an additional predicate indicating that *all* of an object is of a certain material, but that's not necessary for the questions in part (d)). Note the statements refer to an Acme hotplate, so somehow you should indicate this.

```
part_of(acme_hotplate_cord,acme_hotplate).
part_of(acme_hotplate_body,acme_hotplate).
part_of(acme_hotplate_heating_element,acme_hotplate_body).
part_of(acme_hotplate_cover,acme_hotplate_body).
```

```
part_of(acme_hotplate_knob,acme_hotplate_cover).
part_of(acme_hotplate_wire,acme_hotplate_cord).
part_of(acme_hotplate_insulator,acme_hotplate_cord).

contains(acme_hotplate_heating_element,metal).
contains(acme_hotplate_knob,plastic).
contains(acme_hotplate_wire,metal).
contains(acme_hotplate_insulator,fiber).
```

(b)

```
?- contains(X,metal).
X = acme_hotplate_heating_element;
X = acme_hotplate_wire;
no.
?- part_of(X,acme_hotplate_body).
X = acme_hotplate_heating_element;
X = acme_hotplate_cover;
no.
```

(c)

```
part(X,Y) :- part_of(X,Y).
part(X,Y) :- part_of(X,Z), part(Z,Y).

contains(X,M) :- part_of(Y,X), contains(Y,M).
```

If you use a predicate for things entirely composed of a particular material—call it all_contains—then you need one more rule:

```
contains(X,M) :- all_contains(X,M).
```

(d) The difficulty in the second question is that any **not** must refer to a bound variable. The apparent context is parts of the Acme hotplate. So first define

```
thing(X) :- part_of(X,Y).
thing(X) :- not(part_of(X,Y)), part_of(Y,X).
```

That is, a "thing" is anything mentioned in **part_of** facts. Here are the results for all three questions:

```
?- contains(X,plastic).
X = acme_hotplate_knob;
X = acme_hotplate;
X = acme_hotplate_body;
X = acme_hotplate_cover;
no.
```

?- thing(X), not(contains(X,fiber)).
X = acme_hotplate_body;
X = acme_hotplate_heating_element;
X = acme_hotplate_cover;
X = acme_hotplate_knob;
X = acme_hotplate_wire;
no.

?- contains(X,metal), contains(X,fiber).
X = acme_hotplate;
X = acme_hotplate;
X = acme_hotplate_cord;
no.

5-1. Note no is or = is needed.

max(X,Y,Z,X) :- not(Y>X), not(Z>X).
max(X,Y,Z,Y) :- not(X>Y), not(Z>Y).
max(X,Y,Z,Z) :- not(X>Z), not(Y>Z).

5-2. Write as facts instead of variables. Easy fact representation is a big advantage of Prolog over languages like Pascal.

translate(1,integer_overflow).
translate(2,division_by_zero).
translate(3,unknown_identifier).

In general, is and = should rarely be used for anything other than arithmetic and an occasional local variable. Instead, use the automatic facilities of Prolog for checking and binding values.

5-8. (a) With rules for inferring both starts and ends from the other, we must be careful to avoid infinite loops. We can do this by defining new predicates inferred_end and inferred_start.

inferred_end(E,T) :- end(E,T).
inferred_end(E,T) :- start(E,Tstart), duration(E,Dur),
    T is Tstart + Dur.

inferred_start(E,T) :- start(E,T).
inferred_start(E,T) :- end(E,Tend), duration(E,Dur), T is Tend - Dur.

(b) The second event must be completely over before the first event starts or else after is not a proper term to use in English.

after(E1,E2) :- inferred_end(E2,E2end), inferred_start(E1,E1start),
  E1start > E2end.

(c) The usual English meaning of during is that an event occurred entirely inside the duration of the other.

during(E1,E2) :- inferred_start(E1,E1start), inferred_start(E2,E2start),
  inferred_end(E1,E1end), inferred_end(E2,E2end),
  E1start > E2start, E1end < E2end.

(d) The rules should come after all the facts, so facts will always be preferred to answer queries. The order of the rules among themselves doesn't matter except for the two inferred_start and inferred_end rules, because order of rules having the same predicate name is the only thing the Prolog interpreter considers—it indexes facts and rules with the same predicate name.

5-9. (a) speed(<gear_number>, <speed_in_rpm>). Positive speeds can be clockwise, negative counterclockwise.

(b)

speed(G,S) :- same_shaft(G,G2), speed(G2,S).

(c)

speed(G,S) :- meshed(G,G2), teeth(G,TG), teeth(G2,TG2),
  speed(G2,S2), S is 0 - (S2 * TG2 / TG).

(d) Use the following database:

speed(g1,5000).

same_shaft(g2,g1).

meshed(g3,g2).
meshed(g4,g2).

teeth(g1,100).
teeth(g2,30).
teeth(g3,60).
teeth(g4,90).

speed(G,S) :- same_shaft(G,G2), speed(G2,S).
speed(G,S) :- meshed(G,G2), teeth(G,TG), teeth(G2,TG2),
  speed(G2,S2), S is 0 - (S2 * TG2 / TG).

and issue this query:

?- speed(g4,S).

The one **speed** fact doesn't apply, so the first **speed** rule is tried. But there is no **same_shaft** fact with **g4** as first argument, so the rule fails. Now the second **speed** rule is tried. Gear **g2** can be matched to **G2**, with TG = 90 and TG2 = 30. Then we must find the speed of G2 = g2. No fact applies, but we can use the first **speed** rule: **g2** is the first argument to a **same_shaft** fact having **g1** as second argument, so its speed is the speed of **g1**. And a fact says the speed of **g1** is 5000. So the speed of **g2** is 5000, and we can do the calculation in the second "speed" rule as

S = 0 - (5000 * 30 / 90) = -1667 rpm

and the variable S in the original query is bound to that number.

(e) You could get infinite loops if you had extra redundant facts, like if you had both meshed(g2,g1) and meshed(g1,g2). You could also get infinite loops if you had more than one inference rule of either of the previous types, as for instance if you had

speed(G,S) :- same_shaft(G,G2), speed(G2,S).
speed(G,S) :- same_shaft(G2,G), speed(G2,S).

Generally speaking, gears are intended to transmit power in one particular direction, so you only need one of the above rules. You can encode that direction in the **meshed** facts.

(f) The gears wouldn't turn or would self-destruct; such a contradiction of rotation speeds is an impossibility.

5-14. (a)

member(X,L) :- append(L2,[X|L3],L).

(b)

last(X,L) :- append(L2,[X],L).

(c)

deleteone(I,L,DL) :- append(L1,[I|L2],L), append(L1,L2,DL).

(d)

before(X,Y,L) :- append(L2,[X|L3],L), append(L4,[Y|L5],L3).

5-17. (a) It replaces every other word in the first-argument list with the word "censored," binding the result to the second argument. The rule (third line) just says if you can find an X and Y at the front of your list first argument, change the Y to the word "censored" after recursively doing the same on the rest of the list.

That's a declarative analysis. A procedural understanding comes from figuring out what happens with simple example lists:

> ?- mystery([ ],Z).
> Z = []
> ?- mystery([a],Z).
> Z = [a]
> ?- mystery([a,b],Z).
> Z = [a,censored]

For the last example, the third rule applies for the first time. So X is matched to a, Y is matched to b, and L is matched to [], the empty list. The rule involves a recursive call with first argument L, but L is the empty list, it's the same situation as the first example preceding, and M is bound to the empty list too. So the rule says to take M and X and the word "censored" and assemble them into the result, the list whose first two items are X and "censored" and whose remainder is M. But M is empty, so the result is [a,censored].

Now consider the next hardest case, an example list with three items:

> ?- mystery([a,b,c],Z).

The third rule must be again used. It matches X to a, Y to b, and L to [c], the list containing only c. The rule says to do a recursion with [c] the first argument. But to solve that the second rule will do, so M is bound to [c]. So the answer is assembled from X, the word "censored," and that M, and the result for Z is [a,censored,c].

Now consider an example list with four items:

> ?- mystery([a,b,c,d],L).

In the third rule, X is matched to a, Y is matched to b, and [c,d] is matched to L. The recursion applies mystery to the two-item list [c,d], which by analogy to the preceding two-item example gives [c,censored]. So we assemble the answer from X, the word "censored," and the list [c,censored], and the result for Z is [a,censored,c,censored]. So it looks like the program changes every alternate word in a list to the word "censored."

(b) One for even-length lists, one for odd-length. The rule lops off two items from the list on each recursion, so you can get into two different final situations.

5-19. (a) *N* times, once for every item in the list but not for the empty list; all these invocations will fail.

  (b) $(N - 1)/2$. There are 0 calls if the item is first in the list, one call if the item is second in the list, two calls if the item is third in the list, and so on. These terms form an arithmetic series. The average value of an arithmetic series is the average of the first and last numbers, in this case 0 and $N - 1$.

5-22. Use a list to keep arguments previously used, and just check to make sure a new value found is not in the list. At every recursion, add the new argument to the list. So

  a3(X,Y) :- a2(X,Y,[ ]).

  a2(X,Y,L) :- a(X,Y).
  a2(X,Y,L) :- not(member(X,L),L), a(X,Z), a2(Z,Y,[X|L]).

  member(X,[X|L]).
  member(X,[Y|L]) :- not(X = Y), member(X,L).

Then you query a3 to compute relationships by transitivity. For instance, suppose you have the database

  a(r,s).
  a(s,t).
  a(t,r).

(For instance, predicate a might mean "equals" or "is near.") Then the query

  ?- a3(r,t).

will succeed as it should, as will

  ?- a3(r,r).

But the query

  ?- a3(r,u).

will fail as it should.

6-1. (a) Forward chaining means reasoning from facts to goals. The first fact is c, and it is mentioned in rules R5 and R8, so expressions in those rules are matched in that order. The right side of R8 is eliminated, so b(X) is made a new fact. (X isn't bound, but that's OK.) The b(X) goes at the front of the facts, so we now can match expressions in rules R1 and R3, but neither of those rules is eliminated yet.

So we pick the next fact I. This matches the right side in R7, and g(X) is made a new fact at the front of the fact list. This in turn matches an expression in R2. We next pick fact e(a) and this matches an expression in the simplified version of R5 only. So since c was already matched, the fact d is asserted. But d is a goal, so we stop.

(b) Now we reason from goals to facts. The f(X) is the first goal (hypothesis), invoking R2, and we must prove a(X). This in turn invokes R3, which invokes R8. R8 succeeds because c is a fact. But i is not a fact (nor are there any rules for it), so R3 fails. R3 is the only rule for proving a(X), so R2 fails too.

So we try the next goal, d. R4 is the first applicable rule, and as before, i is not a fact nor provable, so R4 fails. We thus invoke R5 to prove d. The fact e(a) matches e(X), and c is a fact, so d is proved.

(c) Yes, because if c and j(b) come before e(a) in the initial facts, the alternative goal k(b) will be proved first instead.

(d) No, fact order doesn't affect backward chaining unless there are facts with the same predicate name, which isn't true here. (If some of the facts had the same predicate name, different variables might be bound in the final goal, a problem that doesn't arise unless goals have variables.)

6-5. (a) u, b, m(12), a. Steps in order:

1. Fact r creates new rules t :- s. and u :- v.
2. Fact v creates the new rule a :- t., and proves the fact u.
3. Fact u creates the new rule a :- b, not(t).
4. Fact c proves the fact b.
5. Fact b creates the new rules a :- not(t). and m(X) :- n(X).
6. Fact n(12) proves m(12).
7. Fact m(12) proves nothing.
8. No facts remain unexplored, so we examine the rule with the **not**. Since t is not a fact, the **not** succeeds, and this proves a.
9. Fact a proves nothing.

(b) b, u, m(12), a. Fact order doesn't matter here since all facts have different predicate names. Steps in order:

1. The first three rules fail because all mention at least one thing that doesn't match a fact.
2. The fourth rule succeeds since c is a fact, so the new fact b is asserted. The rule is deleted.
3. The fifth rule fails.
4. The sixth and last rule succeeds because v and r are both facts. So

new fact u is asserted. The rule is deleted.

5. The first two rules again fail.

6. The third rule succeeds because n(12) and b are now facts. New fact m(12) is asserted. This rule is not deleted because it contains a variable on its left side.

7. No further rules succeed.

8. Now the nots are considered. In the second rule, t is not a fact, so not(t) succeeds, as well as b and u. So fact a is asserted.

9. No further rules succeed.

(c) Index the predicate names on right sides of rules, and index nots. Then you need only check rules that contain predicate names of facts proved on the last cycle, and you can find nots fast. You can also delete rules that succeed whose left sides do not contain variables.

6-7. The minimum of L and S. Each cycle must prove something to keep things going. There are only L different things provable, so L is an upper bound. But each cycle must match also at least one new predicate name on a rule right side so that a new rule can succeed. So if there are S right-side names, S is an upper bound too.

6-8. (a) Backward chaining means reasoning from hypotheses to facts. Here the hypotheses are actions the robot may take, which we must consider in the order given. Hence the first hypothesis we examine is "turn around," and the rule order is:

> R1 fails, turn-around hypothesis fails, try stop-and-wait hypothesis, R3, R4, R16, R8 fails (no moving branches visible), R9 succeeds (so second object is an animal), R16 fails (four branches not present), R17 succeeds (so second object is a person), R4 succeeds, R3 fails (because robot isn't "beneath" anything), R5 succeeds (the only other way to achieve the stop-and-wait hypothesis, and it succeeds because we've already proved the second object is an animal).

You could also put R10 and R11 before first invocation of R16, if you interpreted "person or vehicle" in rule R4 as a single concept.

(b) Now we take the facts, in order, and reason about what other facts they imply:

- Fact F1 matches expressions in rules R13, R14, and R16.
- Fact F2 matches an expression in rule R13.
- Fact F3 matches an expression in rule R12.
- Fact F4 matches an expression in rule R12, and that rule is completely satisfied. Hence the first object is an obstacle, and call that fact F4.1.
- Fact F4.1 matches expressions in rules R6, R13, R14, and R15. Now R13 is completely satisfied. Hence the object to the right is a

bush, and call this fact F4.2.

- Fact F4.2 matches expressions in rules R2 and R3.
- Fact F5 matches expressions in rules R4 and R5.
- Fact F6 matches expressions in rules R9 and R17, and R9 is satisfied. Hence the second object is an animal, and call that fact F6.1.
- Fact F6.1 matches expressions in R16 and R17, and R17 is completely satisfied. Hence the second object is a person, and call that fact F6.2.
- Fact F6.2 matches an expression in rule R4, and that rule is completely satisfied. Hence we must hide, and call that fact F6.3.
- Fact F6.3 matches an expression in rule R2, and that rule is completely satisfied. Hence we turn toward the bush and move a short distance.

(c) The backwards chaining used a fixed-rule priority conflict resolution, and forward chaining used a fixed-fact-priority (with focus-of-attention) in addition to fixed-rule priority. An alternative for forward chaining would be to add new facts at the end of the list of facts, while we still fetch from the front as with a queue. This would be good when we want to infer everything possible from a set of facts. An alternative for backward chaining would be a "biggest-rule-first" strategy in which the rule with the most conditions in its "if" part is tried first. Concurrency and partitioning ideas could work for both forward and backward control structures. We could also use a "most-related-rule" criterion, if we define "relatedness" for any rule pair.

6-9. (a) No, since a conclusion may depend on the absence of some fact. That fact may no longer be absent when a file is loaded in later.

(b) Yes, because caching just makes things already found easier to verify. Provability of conclusions is not affected, just efficiency.

(c) No, since new facts could be asserted that are unreachable by backward chaining. So a conclusion that depends on the absence of something might suddenly go from being true to being false.

6-12. (a) Forward chaining sounds better, since the system only need reason about sensor readings that changed from its last analysis (assuming we cache the conclusions from the last analysis), and changes to sensor readings will be relatively rare. And probably a lot of different goals (conclusions) can be reached.

(b) It's true that forward chaining caches automatically, so extra caching would seem unnecessary. But the best way to use this rule-based system is to run it repeatedly, once every second or so. Then conclusions learned during the last second could be useful in reasoning during this second—especially conclusions based on things that don't change often—so caching the previous conclusions could be useful. Also, caching could mean storing (in the rule-based system database) facts about the condition of sensors instead of directing the computer to look at its input/output ports to find those values. This also will be good because many sensors will infrequently change with time.

(c) Virtual facts don't make sense with forward chaining. If you suggested backward chaining in part (a), virtual facts might make sense if you interpret them as "queries" to sensor input/output ports. If you interpret them as queries to the user, they don't make sense because that would be a big imposition on the user.

(d) Yes, since there are clear categories of rules that don't interact much. For instance, the rules for handling burglars might not be in the database all the time, but only loaded when there is good evidence that a burglar is present. Rules for fires and other emergencies are similar. However, the rules for *recognizing* potential burglar and fire situations, rules which decide to load the detail-analyzing code, must be kept in main memory at all times.

(e) This is a closer judgment than the other parts of this question, but decision lattices are probably not a good idea. In the first place, you don't want to use them in a way so that you actually ask a human questions—that would be an imposition. But the decision lattice could "ask" questions of the sensors to get their readings. The main difficulty is in building the decision lattice in the first place. There will be many different situations to handle, and it's hard to figure out what questions distinguish situations well, especially when houses are all different and you don't know what situations you'll get into; and it's the very rare emergency situations that are most critical to program properly. Furthermore, decision lattices are hard to modify and hard to partition into modules. So for the advantages of a decision lattice, it would seem better to go with an and-or-not lattice, for which the translation from rules to lattice is much easier.

(f) Yes. Improved speed in inferencing is an obvious advantage over non-compiled forms. And-or-not lattices have the advantage of being easy to partition if the original rule-based system was easy to partition, like this one; partitioning a decision lattice is much harder, and since this application can easily be complex, inability to partition into modules is a serious disadvantage. And-or-not lattices are easier to modify than decision lattices, since they correspond closely to rules. And-or-not lattices could also standardize certain commonly made inferences, so these could be mass produced and a smaller, more house-specific computer could handle the rest of the reasoning. For instance, the conditions for suspecting a burglar and loading burglar-analysis rules are pretty much standard for all houses and with all burglars: check for unusual noises and for windows and doors being forced open, especially at night and when the house is not occupied. As another example, equipment requiring complicated continuous monitoring like an aquarium could be monitored according to a special and-or-not lattice supplied by the aquarium manufacturer, and only reports of major problems passed on to the central processor. It's true that and-or-not lattices have trouble handling variables, but this rule-based system doesn't much need them: use no-argument predicates to represent sensor values and value ranges.

7-1. Here's one way:

```
diagnosis('Fuse blown') :- power_problem, askif(lights_out).
diagnosis('Fuse blown') :- power_problem, askif(hear(pop)).
diagnosis('Break in cord') :- power_problem, askif(cord_frayed).
diagnosis('Short in cord') :- diagnosis('fuse blown'),
   askif(cord_frayed).
diagnosis('Device not turned on') :- power_problem, klutz_user,
   askif(has('an on-off switch or control')), askifnot(device_on).
diagnosis('Cord not in socket properly') :- power_problem,
   klutz_user, askif(just_plugged), askifnot(in_socket).
diagnosis('Internal break in the wiring') :-
   power_problem, jarring.
diagnosis('Foreign matter caught on heating element') :-
   heating_element, not(power_problem), askif(smell_smoke).
diagnosis('Appliance wet—dry it out and try again') :-
   power_problem, klutz_user, askif(liquids).
diagnosis('Controls adjusted improperly') :- klutz_user,
   askif(has('knobs or switches')).
diagnosis('Motor burned out') :- askif(smell_smoke),
   mechanical_problem.
diagnosis('Something blocking the mechanical operation') :-
   mechanical_problem.
diagnosis('Kick it, then try it again') :- mechanical_problem.
diagnosis('Throw it out and get a new one').

power_problem :- askif(device_dead).
power_problem :- askif(has('knobs or switches')),
   askifnot(knobs_do_something).
power_problem :- askif(smell_smoke), not(heating_element).

klutz_user :- askifnot(handyperson).
klutz_user :- askifnot(familiar_appliance).

mechanical_problem :- askif(hear('weird noise')),
   askif(has('moving parts')).

heating_element :- askif(heats).
heating_element :- askif(powerful).

jarring :- askif(dropped).
jarring :- askif(jarred).
```

```
questioncode(device_dead,'Does the device refuse to do anything').
questioncode(knobs_do_something,'Does changing the switch
  positions or turning the knobs change anything').
questioncode(lights_out,
  'Do all the lights in the house seem to be off').
questioncode(code_frayed,
  'Does the outer covering of the cord appear to be coming apart').
questioncode(handyperson,'Are you good at fixing things').
questioncode(familiar_appliance,
  'Are you familiar with how this appliance works').
questioncode(device_on,'Is the ON/OFF switch set to ON').
questioncode(just_plugged,'Did you just plug the appliance in').
questioncode(in_socket,'Is the cord firmly plugged into the socket').
questioncode(smell_smoke,'Do you smell smoke').
questioncode(liquids,
  'Have any liquids spilled on the appliance just now').
questioncode(heats,'Does the appliance heat things').
questioncode(powerful,'Does the appliance require a lot of power').
questioncode(has(X),X) :- write('Does the appliance have ').
questioncode(hear(X),X) :- write('Did you hear a ').
questioncode(dropped,'Has the appliance been dropped recently').
questioncode(jarred,'Has the appliance been violently jarred recently').
```

7-2. Use the same idea of **coded_diagnosis** at the end of Section 7.4. Query instead of **diagnosis**:

$$\text{better\_diagnosis}(D) :- \text{diagnosis}(D), \text{not}(\text{found}(D)), \text{asserta}(\text{found}(D)).$$

Now if the user types a semicolon after a diagnosis, the program will backtrack through the **asserta** and **found** to try to find another, but if **D** gets rebound to any previous value, the **not** will fail and the interpreter returns to **diagnosis**. This also works for any order of diagnosis rules; rules for the same diagnosis need not be together.

7-5. (a) One unit of time is needed if the first cached item matches the query, two units of time if the second matches the query, three units of time if the third, and so on. Since we were told the probabilities are mutually exclusive, the probability that no item in the cache matches the query is $1 - KP$. Then the condition for the problem is

$$P + 2P + 3P + \cdots + KP + (1 - KP)(R + K) < R$$

The left side of the inequality is (excluding the last term) an arithmetic series, so we can substitute its formula and get

$$PK(K + 1)/2 + (1 - KP)K < KPR$$

or

$$(K + 1)/2 + (1/P) - K < R$$

$$(2 + P - PK)/2P < R$$

Since $KP < 0.1$, it's also true that $P < 0.1$, so we can approximate the inequality by just

$$PR > 1$$

(b) Analysis is similar, but the sum over the cache items has a different formula:

$$P + (2*P/2) + (3*P/3) + \cdots (K*P/K) = KP$$

so the criterion becomes

$$KP + (R + K)(1 - P\log_2(K + 1)) < R$$

or

$$K(P + 1) < P(R + K)\log_2(K + 1)$$

If $PK < 0.1$ then, because $P < PK$, we know P is negligible compared to 1, so we can approximate this by

$$1 < P((R/K) + 1)\log_2(K + 1)$$

7-11. (a)

```
or(P,Q) :- call(P).
or(P,Q) :- call(Q).
```

(b)

```
if(P,Q,R) :- call(P), call(Q).
if(P,Q,R) :- not(call(P)), call(R).
```

(c)

```
case(P,N,L) :- call(P), item(N,L,I), call(I).

item(1,[X|L],X).
item(N,[X|L],I) :- N>1, N2 is N-1, item(N2,L,I).
```

8-3. (a) So <prob1> is $200/500 = 0.4$, and <prob2> is $800/1600 = 0.5$. The

1200 flat tires are irrelevant.

(b) The ratio 70/101 is approximately 0.69, and this is closest to 0.7, the independence-assumption combination (obtained from 1 - (1 - 0.4)(1 - 0.5)). The conservative assumption gives $maxfunction(0.4,0.5) = 0.5$, and the liberal gives $0.4 + 0.5 = 0.9$.

8-4. (a) Conservative, since the function is the maximum of the two arguments.

(b) Liberal. It can't be conservative since the values in this table are better than the previous table. It can't be independence-assumption because the combination of two "probably"s is a "definitely," something impossible with the independence formula (that is, the independence formula can't give a 1.0 unless one of its inputs is 1.0). The arithmetic (see part (c)) is consistent with liberal combination too.

(c) Let x be the probability of "probably not," y the probability of "probably." Then the table and the liberal-combination formula say that $x + x = y$ and $minfunction(x + y,1.0) = 1.0$. So $2x = y$ and $minfunction(3x,1.0) = 1.0$. Hence $x > 0.3333$ from the last equation. But y must be less than 1.0 ("probably" should be less certain than "definitely") so $2x < 1.0$ and $x < 0.5$. So x can be anything between 0.3333 and 0.5, and y must be correspondingly between 0.6667 and 1.0. (Notice that an infinity of possible answers doesn't mean *any* answer is right.)

8-5. No. There is no problem with either backward chaining, forward chaining, or any hybrid. Facts must always have probability values filled in (or else be certain, implying a probability of 1.0), so any rules combining those probabilities will work no matter how they're used.

8-6. (a) You must be careful to count separately the length of the list and the number of probabilities greater than 0.5. One way to do it:

```
new_orcombine(PL,P) :- numbigprobs(PL,Nb), length(PL,N), P is Nb / N.

numbigprobs([],0).
numbigprobs([P|PL],N) :- numbigprobs(PL,N), P < 0.5.
numbigprobs([P|PL],N) :- numbigprobs(PL,N2), P > = 0.5, N is N2 + 1

length([],0).
length([X|L],N) :- length(L,N2), N is N2 + 1.
```

Another way is to define a **censor** predicate that removes probabilities from a list that are less than 0.5:

```
new_orcombine(PL,P) :- length(PL,N), censor(PL,CPL), length(CPL,Nbig),
P is Nbig / N.
```

```
length([ ],0).
length([X|L],N) :- length(L,N2), N is N2 + 1.

censor([ ],[ ]).
censor([P|PL],[P|PL2]) :- censor(PL,PL2), P > = 0.5.
censor([P|PL],PL2) :- censor(PL,PL2), P < 0.5.
```

(b) Some answers:

- There are abrupt changes in the total probability when probabilities vary slightly from 0.5. It doesn't seem reasonable that any evidence combination method have such abrupt "jumps" as probabilities vary slightly.
- The number 0.5 is arbitrary—there's no good reason for it.
- The total probability with this method can be less than the "conservative" combination value; for example, [0.4,0.4] has 0 total with the method, 0.4 with the "conservative" method. But the conservative method gives the smallest logically reasonable value, so this method isn't always reasonable.
- This method is inaccurate when few probabilities are combined. If there's only one probability in the list presented for combination, then the cumulative probability is either 0 or 1, totally ignoring the probability of that one item.
- This method can't handle "cascades" very easily. That is, if the result of this method is an input to a combination in another rule, we've lost the important information about the number of probabilities contributing to the first result, which should greatly affect how much it should be counted for in the second combination.

8-9. (a) Newspapers and television report unusual and striking events, so you don't hear about the many more people that spent their money on the lottery and didn't win anything.

(b) In this example, successes in the lottery are broadcast much more strongly than failures, causing overestimation of the probability of success. This "biased sampling" problem is a chief difficulty in building rule-based systems from data: you must be careful there aren't reasons why certain data are overreported or underreported. For instance, embarassment might make people underestimate the frequency with which they forget to plug appliances in.

9-2. For inheritance, the goal state is some other target object that has a value for the property you want, and has an inheriting link, like a_kind_of, or a series of such links to the given object. Looking for such a target object is a search starting from the given object. There can be several inheriting links for each object, each representing an alternative direction to explore, and these represent branches. And one choice affects later choices.

9-10. Just subtract K from the values of the old evaluation function to get a new evaluation function which is guaranteed to be a lower bound. Then you can use A* search with the optimality guarantee.

9-11. (a) See Figure G-1.

   (b) Choose the state (among those so far discovered at some point in the problem) that has lowest evaluation function value. State sequence: a, d, c, b, f, e, g, h.

   (c) Add the cost to reach a state to the evaluation function. Costs to states: a: 0, b: 2, c: 5, d: 9, e: 7, f: 11, g: 7, h: 14. Sum of cost and evaluation function: a: 10, b: 10, c: 12, d: 14, e: 13, f: 15, g: 16, h: 25. State sequence: a, b, c, e, d, f, g, h.

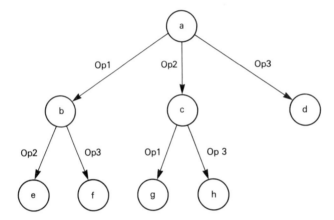

Figure G-1. Answer to Exercise 9-11(a).

9-13. (a) All [<left-bank>,<right-bank>], where <left-bank> and <right-bank> are lists together containing the symbols man, lion, fox, goose, corn, and boat. And <left-bank> is things on the left side of the river, <right-bank> things on the right.

   (b) The start is [[man,lion,fox,goose,corn,boat],[]] and the goal is [[],[man,lion, fox,goose,corn,boat]].

   (c) Man and boat; man, lion, and boat; man, fox, and boat; man, goose, and boat; man, corn, and boat; man, fox, corn, and boat; or man, goose, corn, and boat move from one side of the river to the other. Or maybe there's just one operator: travel across the river.

   (d) The starting state has only one successor, [[lion,goose], [man,fox,corn,boat]], which has three successors of its own (besides the starting state):

   [[man,lion,goose,boat],[fox,corn]].
   [[man,lion,fox,goose,boat],[corn]].
   [[man,lion,goose,corn,boat],[fox]].

(e) $(1 + 3)/2 = 2$

(f) Each thing can be in one of two places, and there are five things (the man must always be with the boat), hence $2^5 = 32$.

(g) No, subparts interact.

9-15. (a) The set of all possible coating patterns.

(b) No, there are many different states (coating patterns) that satisfy the goal conditions, and no easy way to find them. (If you knew any of them, you wouldn't need to search.) So backward search isn't possible, and hence bidirectional search isn't either. (Notice that despite similarities, this problem is quite different from city-route planning: the goal is a configuration of coatings, not a location.)

(c) It always decreases. Every branch involves coating a grid cell, thus removing it from the pool of coatable cells. As you proceed, previously coatable cells may become uncoatable because they would connect coated regions that shouldn't be connected, so the branching factor may decrease by more than one per level, but it will always decrease.

(d) Many heuristics are possible, including:

• Prefer to coat cells adjacent to the last cell you coated (a "focus of attention" heuristic).

• Prefer to coat cells that lie on a straight line between points you want to connect.

• As soon as a desired connection is made between two points, prefer not to coat any cells within five cells of either of those points.

• Prefer to coat cells that continue a straight line (e.g., coat [X,Y] if [X-1,Y] and [X-2,Y] are both coated).

10-1. (a) Define a new predicate

```
depthsearch2(Start,Ans) :- depthsearch(Start,[Start],Ans),
    print_reverse(Ans).
```

and include the definition

```
print_reverse([]) :- !.
print_reverse([X|L]) :- print_reverse(L), write(X), nl.
```

(b) Add to the front of all state lists the name of the last operator used to reach that state (or "none" for the starting state). (This assumes that states are represented by lists, as in most applications.) Then modify all **successor, goalreached, eval,** and **cost** predicate definitions to ignore the first term of the input state description, and modify all **successor** predicate definitions to set the first item of the output successor state to an operator name appropriate to the purpose of each such rule or fact.

(c) Replace the member in not(member(Newstate,Statelist)) by permuted-member, defined as

permutedmember(L1,[L2|LL]) :- subset(L1,L2), subset(L2,L1), !.
permutedmember(L1,[L2|LL]) :- permutedmember(L1,LL).
subset([],L) :- !.
subset([X|L1],L2) :- member(X,L2), !, subset(L1,L2).

where **member** is defined as before.

10-5. Refer to states as a pair of numbers representing fluid quantities in the size 5 and size 7 glasses respectively. So [3, 4] means 3 units in the size 5 glass and 4 units in the size 7 glass.

(a) The states form a circle (excluding [5, 7] which is only reachable when the goal amount is 5 or 7). Two solutions are always found for goal amounts 1, 2, 3, 4, and 6, one from going around the circle clockwise and one counterclockwise, both stopping at the first state satisfying the goal condition. (To see this behavior, it's important to avoid duplicating the same state at different places in the search graph.)

(b) The breadth-first state graph is augmented by extra links to the states [5, 0], [0, 7], and [5, 7]. Links to the first occur from states [5, X] and [X, 0] for certain X, to the second from [X, 7] and [0, X] for certain other X, and to the third from [X, 7] and [5, X] for certain other X. On such transitions, the search "starts over" in the opposite direction around the circle (so if movement was clockwise before the transition, afterward it is counterclockwise). Only one such transition can occur in a solution path, except when the goal amount is 5 or 7.

(c) The eight rules make four pairs, for which the first rule of each pair refers principally to the first glass, the second rule to the second glass. The first pair empties one glass into another, the second pair fills one glass from another, the third pair fills a glass from the faucet, and the fourth pair empties a glass into the drain.

(d) Delete the second **goal_reached** fact.

10-7. Branch-and-bound search is just an A* search in which the evaluation function is always zero. So just use the definition

eval(S,0).

with the A* program. That will work fine if the problem-independent file is always loaded before the problem-dependent file. But if you can't be sure, you can remove the **eval** expression and subsequent sum from the **add_state** predicate definition, and replace D by Cnew.

10-10. (a) Represent states as a list of pairs, where the first element of each pair is the name of a chemical and the second element is its amount in moles. Define **increase** and **remove** predicates that change the amount of a chemical in a state list. (Write remove to fail when it can't find the specified chemical in the state, so you don't need a member predicate.)

go(Ans) :- search([[cl2,2],[mno2,1],[caco3,1],[h2o2,2]],Ans).

goalreached(S) :- member([cacl2,N],S), N > = 1.

successor(S,[[C,Nsum]|S3]) :- remove(C,N1,S,S2),
  remove(C,N2,S2,S3), Nsum is N1 + N2.
successor(S,S6) :- remove(cl2,Ncl2,S,S2), remove(h2o,Nh2o,S2,S3),
  N is Ncl2 - Nh2o, N > = 0, increase(cl2,N,S3,S4),
  increase(hclo,Nh2o,S4,S5), increase(hcl,Nh2o,S5,S6).
successor(S,S6) :- remove(cl2,Ncl2,S,S2),
  remove(h2o,Nh2o,S2,S3), N is Nh2o - Ncl2, N > = 0,
  increase(h2o,N,S3,S4), increase(hclo,Ncl2,S4,S5),
  increase(hcl,Ncl2,S5,S6).
successor(S,S4) :- remove(h2o2,N,S,S2), member([mno2,X],S2),
  HalfN is N / 2, increase(h2o,N,S2,S3),
  increase(o2,HalfN,S3,S4).
successor(S,S6) :- remove(caco3,Ncaco3,S,S2),
  remove(hcl,Nhcl,S2,S3), HalfNhcl is Nhcl/2, Ncaco3 > = HalfNhcl,
  increase(cacl2,HalfNhcl,S3,S4), increase(co2,HalfNhcl,S4,S5),
  increase(h2o,HalfNhcl,S5,S6).
successor(S,S6) :- remove(caco3,Ncaco3,S,S2),
  remove(hcl,Nhcl,S2,S3), HalfNhcl is Nhcl/2, Ncaco3 < HalfNhcl,
  increase(cacl2,Ncaco3,S3,S4), increase(co2,Ncaco3,S4,S5),
  increase(h2o,Ncaco3,S5,S6).
successor(S,S5) :- remove(h2,Nh2,S,S2), remove(cl2,Ncl2,S2,S3),
  Nh2 > = Ncl2, N is Nh2-Ncl2, increase(h2,N,S3,S4),
  TwiceNcl2 is 2*Ncl2, increase(hcl,TwiceNcl2,S4,S5).
successor(S,S5) :- remove(h2,Nh2,S,S2), remove(cl2,Ncl2,S2,S3),
  Nh2 < Ncl2, N is Ncl2-Nh2, increase(cl2,N,S3,S4),
  TwiceNh2 is 2*Nh2, increase(hcl,TwiceNh2,S4,S5).
successor(S,S7) :- remove(hcl,Nhcl,S,S2),
  remove(mno2,Nmno2,S2,S3), QuarterNhcl is Nhcl/4,
  QuarterNhcl > = Nmno2, N is QuarterNhcl - Nmno2,
  increase(hcl,N,S3,S4), TwiceNmno2 is 2*Nmno2,
  increase(mncl2,Nmno2,S4,S5), increase(h2o,TwiceNmno2,S5,S6),
  increase(cl2,Nmno2,S6,S7).
successor(S,S7) :- remove(hcl,Nhcl,S,S2),
  remove(mno2,Nmno2,S2,S3), QuarterNhcl is Nhcl/4,
  QuarterNhcl < Nmno2, N is Nmno2 - QuarterNhcl,
  increase(mno2,N,S3,S4), HalfNhcl is Nhcl/2,
  increase(mncl2,QuarterNhcl,S4,S5),
  increase(h2o,HalfNhcl,S5,S6), increase(cl2,Nmno2,S6,S7).

increase(Chemical,Amount,S,[[Chemical,Newamount]|NewS]) :-
    failing_delete([Chemical,Oldamount],S,NewS),
    Newamount is Oldamount + Amount, !.
increase(Chemical,Amount,S,[[Chemical,Amount]|S]).

remove(Chemical,Amount,S,NewS) :-
    failing_delete([Chemical,Amount],S,NewS).

failing_delete(X,[X|L],L) :- !.
failing_delete(X,[Y|L],[Y|L2]) :- failing_delete(X,L,L2).

(b)

?- go(Answer).

Answer = [[[h2o,1],[co2,1],[cacl2,1],[hclo,2],[cl2,0],[o2,1],[mno2,1]],
    [[hcl,2],[hclo,2],[cl2,0],[o2,1],[mno2,1],[caco3,1]],
    [[o2,1],[h2o,2],[cl2,2],[mno2,1],[caco3,1]],
    [[cl2,2],[mno2,1],[caco3,1],[h2o2,2]]]

(c) Cost could be the monetary cost of the chemicals needed for all the
reactions so far, and the evaluation function could be the average cost of
a chemical times the number of chemicals not yet in the reaction vessel
but desired in the goal state. Or cost could be the danger of doing a
sequence of reactions, and the evaluation function an estimate of the
remaining danger based on the goal state.

(d) In the real world, all possible chemical reactions occur simultaneously.
To model this for our rules, all that apply should work in parallel
somehow. A little of each reaction could be done, time-sharing between
reactions. (To be more precise, reactions should proceed at different
speeds determined by *equilibrium constants* for each reaction, which can
be modeled by "biased" time-sharing.)

10-12. (a) 16 states, if the goal state is on the final (leaf) level.

(b) 16 as well. With best-first search, the agenda can contain states at many
levels. But if it does contain states at levels other than level 4 (the leaf
level), then we could substitute in the successors of those states to get a
bigger possible agenda. Therefore the largest agenda must contain only
level 4 (leaf states), and there are 16 of those.

10-15. This is what the **foriterate** predicate definition does, so just query:

call(P,K) :- foriterate(call(P),K).

So just use the two-argument version of **call** instead of the usual one-
argument form. If for instance you wanted to print out the third value of X to
which the expression a(X) can be matched, you would query:

> ?- call(a(X),3), write(X).

11-1. These correspond to the **recommended** definitions. And rules for such household hints should go in front of default **recommended** rules for the same situations.

11-4. You need new predicates to describe the condition of the plate—let's say **on** and **off** with argument "plate." A starting state for the testing can be

> [closed(case),closed(top),inside(batteries),defective(batteries),
>   defective(light),unbroken(case),on(plate)]

with the goal

> [ok(batteries),ok(light),closed(case),closed(top)]

Define new operators **remove_plate** and **replace_plate** this way:

> recommended([off(plate)],remove_plate).
> recommended([on(plate)],replace_plate).
>
> precondition(remove_plate,[open(top),on(plate)]).
> precondition(replace_plate,[open(top),off(plate)]).
>
> deletepostcondition(remove_plate,[on(plate)]).
> deletepostcondition(replace_plate,[off(plate)]).
>
> addpostcondition(remove_plate,[off(plate)]).
> addpostcondition(replace_plate,[on(plate)]).

To relate the new predicates and operators to the code written before, modify the preconditions of **replace_light** and **assemble_top**:

> precondition(replace_light,[off(plate),open(top)]).
> precondition(assemble_top,[on(plate),open(top)]).

11-6. Means-ends analysis is recursive, and recursion requires a stack when implemented in a computer. Laying out the parts in the order you remove them from the car is like keeping a stack, so you can "pop" them—that is, put them back into the car—in the reverse of the order they came out. It's not fair to say the parts are preconditions to operators, however; they're just props used in achieving preconditions, and the real preconditions are abstract notions.

11-7. Just write two different **precondition** facts, one for each set of preconditions. Put the set you think more likely to succeed first. If it can't be satisfied, backtracking will take the second set of preconditions. Nothing we've said requires a unique **precondition** rule for each operator.

12-3. (a) A value inherited must be for a slot that's filled in for the "purchase order" frame. Unfortunately, the frame is quite abstract, so most of the slots that you could imagine for it wouldn't have values (though those slots themselves will inherit downward via slot inheritance). One answer would be a **purpose** slot in a purchase order, always filled in with the value "purchasing_something." Another answer would be a **where_obtained** slot always filled with value "stockroom," meaning you can get blank purchase orders from the stockroom.

(b) It inherits from P2 too. (That doesn't necessarily mean that P2 has its units slot filled in—P2 could be inheriting that value itself. But that's still "inheritance from P2.")

12-4. Use frames to represent slots themselves. Have the name of each possible slot be the name of a slot-defining frame, in which we have a special slot named **value** to hold the value. Each slot-defining frame can have a slot for each qualifying slot of the original slot, with values filled in as appropriate. Every time you refer to the slot name, you can just inherit qualifying information from its slot-defining frame.

12-5. (a) The value "Floodge Manufacturing Inc." in the manufacturer's name slot, since it must be filled in similarly in any subtype of computer made by Floodge.

(b) The slot **ID-number**, since every computer must have an ID number, but each computer has a different value for it.

(c) Every Floodge computer has a CPU. So every personal computer made by Floodge also has a CPU. The CPU of a personal computer made by Floodge is an example of a part-kind inheritance, inference of a new frame. This new frame is different from the CPU frame for all Floodge computers, because for instance personal computers have slower CPUs.

12-9. The relationship of the Navy to military organizations is **a_kind_of**, whereas the relationship of NPS to the Navy is more like **part_of**. Or you could say the Navy and military organizations are intensions, while NPS is more like an extension.

12-13. The problem of multiple inheritance for qualifying slots should be simpler than the original multiple inheritance problem, since they usually have few value conflicts. So you can just assign priorities of inheritance direction as suggested for the user models example. In other words, any "qualifying-qualifying" slot for inheritance method will be filled with the same value, this direction-priority method.

13-1. We have two orderings to deal with: the order of the three rules, and the order of the two terms in the first rule. The second order involves an "and" and these should be ordered with the thing most likely to fail first. So $c(X)$ should come before $b(X)$ since 0.7 is less than 0.8. Since we're told that all the probabilities are independent, the probability of that first rule succeeding is just the independence-assumption "andcombine" of 0.7 and 0.8, or 0.56.

This 0.56 is greater than 0.1, but less than 0.6. So since we should put the rules with greatest probability of success first, we should put the **e** rule first, then the rule with **b** and **c**, and then the rule with **d**.

13-4. (a) There's a mistake or bug somewhere, because the existence of the picture implies there must be some possible interpretation of it. Maybe our constraints are unreasonable, or maybe the characteristics of the regions of the picture were described incorrectly.

(b) This suggests an optical illusion, a situation for which the human eye could see two possible interpretations. Optical illusions can arise at random, particularly with pictures of geometrical figures and pictures in which objects have lined up in unusual ways.

(c) This suggests not enough constraints or too-weak constraints to solve the problem. That's not necessarily the programmer's fault; many real-world pictures can give this behavior, like those with few sharp boundaries.

13-6. We must first create possibility lists, using the three meal types given and any single-variable constraints. The first constraint is the only single-variable one. So we have the following possibilities (using "m1" for meal 1, "B1" for breakfast on day one, "L2" for lunch on day two, etc.)

> **B1**: [m1]
> **L1**: [m1,m2,m3]
> **D1**: [m1,m2,m3]
> **B2**: [m1,m2,m3]
> **L2**: [m1,m2,m3]
> **D2**: [m1,m2,m3]

Now we do the multivariable part of relaxation starting with the B2 variable. (The instructions also suggest that we start with B2 in the first step, but that doesn't make the difference to the result that it does for this step.) We retrieve the possible values of a variable, and check which of them satisfy constraints C2, C3, and C4. Here is one way:

1. Pick variable B2. Possibility m1 is impossible by constraint 4.

2. Pick variable L2 by the focus-of-attention heuristic. Then m1 is impossible by constraint 4.

3. Pick L1 by the same heuristic. It cannot be m1 by constraint 2. And it can't be m3 be constraint 4. So it must be m2. Possibility lists are now

> **B1**: [m1]
> **L1**: [m2]
> **D1**: [m1,m2,m3]
> **B2**: [m2,m3]
> **L2**: [m2,m3]
> **D2**: [m1,m2,m3]

4. Pick variable L2. Then m2 can be eliminated by constraint 4, so the only remaining possibility is m3.
5. Pick B2. It cannot be m3 by constraint 3, so it must be m2.
6. Pick D1. It cannot be m2 by constraint 2, and it cannot be m3 by constraint 3, so it must be m1.
7. Pick D2. It cannot be m3 by constraint 3, and it cannot be m1 by constraint 1, so it must be m2.

The final possibilities have been reduced to one for each variable, as follows:
B1 = m1, L1 = m2, D1 = m1, B2 = m2, L2 = m3, D2 = m2.

13-13. (a) 162 times, to get the answer X = 4, Y = 3, Z = 5:

1. Three backtracks from n(Y) to n(X), since four X values must be tried.
2. Seventeen backtracks from n(Z) to n(Y), (3*5) + 3 − 1. (The five values for Y must be cycled through three times, then the third value succeeds.)
3. Eighty-nine backtracks from X>Y to n(Z), (17*5) + 5 − 1. (Similar reasoning to the preceding.)
4. Twenty-nine backtracks from the last predicate expression g(X,Y,Z) to not(f(X,X)), (6*5) − 1. (Six (X, Y) pairs are tried: (2, 1), (3, 1), (3, 2), (4, 1), (4, 2), and (4, 3).)
5. Twenty-four backtracks from not(f(X,X)) to X>Y, 29 − 5. (The same as the previous answer except for the X = 2 and Y = 1 case ruled out.)

(b) The g predicate is the hardest to satisfy, and the > comparison is next hardest, so write the query as

?- g(X,Y,Z), X>Y, not(f(X,X)), n(X), n(Y), n(Z).

This will backtrack a mere three times: all three from the X>Y to g(X,Y,Z). The same answer is found.

(c) Thirty-nine times. First figure out where to backtrack to. For predicate expression P, backtrack to the last predicate expression previous to P that binds a variable in P, or the immediately previous expression if no expression binds a variable in P.

n(Y) should backtrack to n(X)
n(Z) should backtrack to n(Y)
X>Y should backtrack to n(Y)
not(f(X,X)) should backtrack to n(X)
g(X,Y,Z) should backtrack to n(Z)

Let's now simulate dependency-based backtracking:

1. We match X = 1, Y = 1, and Z = 1.
2. X>Y fails; we go back to n(Y). (1 backtrack)
3. We pick Y = 2, then return to X>Y, which fails again. Back to n(Y). (1 backtrack)

4. We pick Y = 3, then return to X>Y, which fails again. Back to n(Y). (1 backtrack)

5. This repeats until Y = 5, whereon we fail n(Y). We return to n(X) and pick X = 2. (3 backtracks)

6. We now pick Y = 1, and X>Y succeeds.

7. But f(X,X) succeeds, so not(f(X,X)) fails, so we backtrack to n(X). (1 backtrack)

8. We now take X = 3. We skip n(Y) and n(Z) since they could not have caused the last failure.

9. X>Y holds, as does not(f(X,X)). But g(X,Y,Z) fails, so we backtrack to n(Z). (1 backtrack)

10. Z = 2 is chosen, we return to g(X,Y,Z), but that doesn't work either. We return to n(Z). (1 backtrack)

11. We alternate repeatedly between n(Z) and g(X,Y,Z) until n(Z) fails, whereupon we return to n(Y). (4 backtracks)

12. We pick Y = 2, Z = 1. X>Y succeeds, but g(X,Y,Z) fails. Return to n(Z). (1 backtrack)

13. None of the other values for Z will make g(X,Y,Z) succeed. Fail n(Z). (5 backtracks)

14. We pick Y = 3. X>Y fails. Similarly for Y = 4 and Y = 5. So n(Y) fails. (4 backtracks)

15. We pick X = 4, Y = 1, Z = 1. X>Y and not(f(X,X)) succeed, but g(X,Y,Z) fails. (1 backtrack)

16. Z = 2 is tried and fails g(X,Y,Z), followed by Z = 3, Z = 4, Z = 5. So n(Z) fails. (5 backtracks)

17. Y = 2 is tried and fails g(X,Y,Z) after all Z are tried. (6 backtracks)

18. Y = 3 is tried. Z = 1, Z = 2, Z = 3, and Z = 4 are tried and fail; Z = 5 succeeds. (4 backtracks)

(d) First create possibility lists for X, Y, and Z, using the n and f predicate expressions:

X: [1,3,4,5]
Y: [1,2,3,4,5]
Z: [1,2,3,4,5]

The only multivariable constraints are X>Y and g(X,Y,Z).

1. Pick variable X first since it has the fewest possibilities. X = 1 is not possible with X>Y. And X = 5 is not possible with g(X,Y,Z). So X = 3 or X = 4 only. (Note it's not fair to say that X cannot be 3 now because that could only be shown by considering the two constraints together, X>Y and g(X,Y,Z). Pure relaxation throws away bindings from one constraint when considering another constraint.)

2. Pick variable Y. Y = 3 is the only way to satisfy constraint g(X,Y,Z).

3. Return to variable X. Now by X > Y, X cannot be 3, so it must be 4.

4. Go to variable Z, the only remaining variable with multiple possibilities. It must be 5 by g(X,Y,Z).

13-14. (a) Whenever a unique value is chosen for a variable the unique_values predicate can exploit that new value. So unique_values becomes harder to satisfy, and it must do more backtracking. This slows the program down. When we start with two values for E, things aren't slowed down until O is found to be 0, at which point there are fewer other unassigned variables to worry about, so the slowdown is less dramatic.

(b) Delete the definition of unique_values, and delete its call from the definition of the satisfiable predicate. It isn't necessary for the single-relaxation example in the text.

(c) The predicate duplication catches most of the bad assignments of variables to values, but unique_values catches a few cases that duplication misses. For instance, if each of variables A, B, and C have possibilities of 4 or 5, and each variable must have a different value, there's no way that the conditions can be met; unique_values will catch this.

13-18. (a) A state is any set of possibility lists for the variables, where possibility lists are subsets of the original possibility lists in the starting state, plus a list of which variables are "active." It can be represented as a list of lists.

(b) Depth-first search. It keeps moving ahead, never returning to a previous state. There's no point in returning to a previous state because you keep learning useful things as you proceed, things that can potentially help in future study.

(c) No, because you can't predict what intermediate states you'll get into.

(d) The branching factor always stays the same or decreases by 1. A state transition means either elimination of a single possibility for a variable or no elimination.

(e) If the sum of the number of possibilities on all initial possibility lists is N, then there are 2^N possibility-list configurations obtainable by crossing out 0 to N possibilities. But we haven't included the active variables. There are 2^V configurations of these for each possibility-list configuration, so the total number of states is the product of these two numbers, or 2^{N+V}. (Some of those states have zero possibilities for some variables, but such states are possible when the input has errors.)

14-1. X binds to 5, and Y binds to X, so Y is bound to 5 too. So the possibles cancel, giving as resolvent

state(3,A,5); state(3,6,5).

But the second predicate expression is covered by the first, so we can rewrite this as

state(3,A,5).

That is the only resolution possible.

14-2. (a) Suppose:

t represents your having travel money;
d represents your department chairman approval;
s represents sponsor approval;
b represents the boss of your department chairman approving;
f represents discretionary funds being available.

Then we can write the initial rules as

t :- d, s.
t :- d, b, f.

(b)

t; not(d); not(s).
t; not(d); not(b); not(f).

(c)

(d,s);(d,b,f) :- t.

or equivalently

d,(s;(b,f)) :- t.

(d) The second preceding can be translated to

(d, (s;(b,f))); not(t).

Using the distributive law of "or" over "and"

(d; not(t)), (s; (b,f); not(t)).

d; not(t).
s; (b,f); not(t).

The first of those two is a clause, but we still need to use the distributive law of "or" over "and" on the second. Finally, we have these three clauses:

d; not(t).
s; b; not(t).
s; f; not(t).

(e) Just resolve the fact t with the clauses in part (d), giving

d.
s; b.
s; f.

Since we did all possible resolutions involving all given information, those are all the clauses derivable.

(f) Just resolve the clause not(t) with the clauses in part (b), giving

not(d); not(s).
not(d); not(b); not(f).

14-5. Resolvent clauses are only guaranteed to *include* the truth, not give a precise specification of the truth as the "and" of the two resolvents would. The statement "b or c" does include all the cross-hatched region in the figure, the "and" of the input clauses, which is all that is required.

14-9. (a) The number of possible pairs of clauses or $N(N-1)/2$. (Note that resolution is a commutative operation, hence the division by 2.)

(b) Each successful resolution increases by one the number of clauses, so after K resolutions there will $N + K$ clauses and $(N + K)(N + K - 1)/2$ pairs. K of these pairs will have already been used, so an upper bound on the branching factor is $((N + K)(N + K - 1)/2) - K$.

15-1. The real test is not the opinion of any human being, but whether the car works correctly when the supposed problem is fixed. So the gold standard is the minimum change necessary to get the car working right again. (It's the "minimum" because you can always get any faulty car working again by simply replacing every part with a nonfaulty part.)

15-3. In the confusion matrix, examine the cell pairs symmetric about the diagonal running northwest-southeast (but not including the cells of the diagonal itself.) Look for any pair where (1) one number is much larger than the other, and (2) the cell with the larger number is in a row corresponding to diagnosis rules that precede the rules that correspond to the row for the other diagnosis; such a pair suggests the order of the rows should be reversed. This clue is further strengthened if the other cells in the same two rows and two columns are small, except for the diagonal terms.

15-6. (a) Not a good idea by the third and fourth overall criteria of Section 15.10.

(b) Not a good idea by the first, second, and sixth criteria.

(c) Not a good idea by the second and third criteria.

(d) Not a good idea by the third, fourth, and fifth criteria.

M-1. (a) Yes, backtracking on failure is the whole point.

(b) No, the whole point of forward chaining is to keep moving forward from facts to new conclusions. Choosing new facts and new rules is better done by iteration, not backtracking.

(c) No, since you store things on an agenda and just pick the best thing on the agenda at each point, a form of iteration. The agenda item selected might be something in a far away and/or deeper part of the search lattice than the last agenda item, so you're not necessarily "going back" to anything.

(d) Yes, dependency-based backtracking is included in this.

(e) Yes, because you might have several directions (links) you could follow to find a value for some slot. If one path doesn't pan out, you should backtrack and try another.

(f) No, because it's just an example of forward chaining.

M-3. Horn Clause: f. (the definition)

generate-and-test: i. (variable X is generated, then tested)

constraint: m. (equivalent terminology)

forward chaining: o. (that's the whole idea)

default: b. (the definition)

depth-first control structure: q. (essential even for those depth-first activities that aren't searches)

intension: p. (the definition)

difference table: h. (the main purpose)

near miss: n.

Skolem function: j.

caching: a. (the definition)

dependency: r. (the definition for predicate expressions in the same query)

multiple inheritance: c. (the chief difficulty)

decision lattice: g.

Bayes's rule: d. (it can be proved from probability theory)

heuristic: e. (a famous example)

hierarchical reasoning: l. (hierarchy is in the levels of recursion)

agenda: k. (the definition)

M-4. (a) 1, and-or-not lattice. This sounds like a pretty straightforward application for expert systems; few variables will be needed. So the lattice will be feasible, and will be a simple (and reasonably efficient) implementation method. You could build the lattice with logic gates on a VLSI chip that could be put into a small hand-held device. Dependency-based backtracking is probably too fancy a technique for this problem; you must wait for the user to answer questions, so the extra speed of dependency-based backtracking will usually be wasted. You shouldn't need to backtrack anyway since this sounds good for forward chaining; there are few facts (the problem mentions "simple questions") and probably low "fanout" from facts (multiple references to the same fact in different rules should be rare). A breadth-first resolution strategy is a very slow method of reasoning only appropriate when you want to be sure to reach every valid conclusion, including conclusions with "or"s; here we only want a single conclusion about which tax form to use. Finally, there's no such thing as "confusion-matrix conflict resolution"; conflict resolution is how you decide what to do next in a rule-based system, and confusion matrices are statistical summaries useful in analyzing experiments with system performance.

(b) 4, concurrency. You can only ask questions one at a time, and there's probably low fanout of facts to rules, so there isn't much opportunity for concurrency. (Things are quite different for expert systems with real-time inputs, like the "smart house" in Exercise 6-12.) Virtual facts would be essential if you used backward chaining—you don't want to ask the same question twice. Inference is a general term for all reasoning, and this system must reason. A depth-first control structure is good for many expert systems including this one, regardless of whether they do backward, forward, or hybrid chaining, because it's easy to implement.

(c) 2, repeat. There's not much reason to repeat anything here; after all, an and-or-not lattice sounds good, and that can't accommodate iteration very well. The **asserta** or **assertz** would be necessary for virtual facts. The **write** would be necessary to ask questions of the user. The > could be used in making the needed monetary-amount comparisons.

M-5. (a) 1, best-first search. Deviation from a straight line is a good (and necessary) evaluation function; we clearly don't want to lurch a lot, or we couldn't walk very fast. But there's no obvious cost function; speed is not important, according to the problem statement. And there's no such thing as "weight-first search."

(b) 2, caching only. Caching is helpful for reexamining the same ground as the robot moves forward. Means-ends analysis isn't helpful because there's only one operator, foot placement. So all the tricks that means-ends analysis uses to select operators based on logical conditions don't have anything to work with. Furthermore, the problem is quantitative: it depends on numeric things like the coordinates of a square, the positions of the other legs, the center of gravity of the robot, the direction of motion of the robot, and so on. Means-ends analysis is intended for non-quantitative problems.

(c) 2, **assertz**. No reason to use queues here, about the only reason to ever use an **assertz**. The **is** is always useful with numeric calculations, and the cut and **repeat** predicates could help make search efficient, just as they did for the best-first program in Section 10.9.

INDEX

DATE DUE

BRODART, INC

Cat. No. 23-221